Pittsburgh Series in Bibliography

Pittsburgh Series in Bibliography

HART CRANE: A DESCRIPTIVE BIBLIOGRAPHY
Joseph Schwartz and Robert C. Schweik

F. SCOTT FITZGERALD: A DESCRIPTIVE BIBLIOGRAPHY
Matthew J. Bruccoli

WALLACE STEVENS: A DESCRIPTIVE BIBLIOGRAPHY
J. M. Edelstein

Wallace Stevens

A DESCRIPTIVE BIBLIOGRAPHY

J. M. Edelstein

UNIVERSITY OF
PITTSBURGH PRESS
1973

Grateful acknowledgment is made to the following for permission to quote material that appears in this book:

Alfred A. Knopf, Inc., and Holly Stevens, for letters from *Letters of Wallace Stevens*. Copyright © 1966 by Holly Stevens.

Holly Stevens, for Wallace Stevens' previously unpublished letters and pages from *Epitaphiana* and *Stevens Family Portraits*.

Alfred A. Knopf, Inc., and William A. Koshland, for letters from Alfred A. Knopf, Herbert Weinstock, and Mr. Koshland.

Pierre Berès, Harry Duncan, James Laughlin, and John L. Sweeney, for their letters.

Mrs. Louis Henry Cohn, House of Books Ltd., and Henry W. Wenning, Modern Rare Books, for quotations from their catalogues.

Library of Congress Cataloging in Publication Data

Edelstein, Jerome Melvin, date
Wallace Stevens: a descriptive bibliography.

(Pittsburgh series in bibliography)
1. Stevens, Wallace, 1879–1955 – Bibliography.
I. Title. II. Series.
Z8842.7.E35   016.811'5'2   · 72–91106
ISBN 0-8229-3268-7

for Eleanor

Contents

Acknowledgments

T H E long list of acknowledgments which follows is no mere formulary. Without the help of the many friends, librarians, collectors, booksellers, and publishers whose names appear here I could not have completed this bibliography of Wallace Stevens. It is with gratitude and pleasure that I record their assistance.

I am grateful, above all, to Holly Stevens, the poet's daughter, for her generosity, encouragement, and hospitality over the years. I could not have undertaken this book without her invaluable cooperation; she gave me free access to her files and collection of her father's work as well as liberal amounts of her own time. I thank her for all this and for her permission to quote at length from *The Letters of Wallace Stevens* and from several previously unpublished Stevens letters and to reproduce pages from *Epitaphiana* and *Stevens Family Portraits*.

My indebtedness to Samuel French Morse, Jackson R. Bryer, and Joseph N. Riddel, authors of the *Wallace Stevens Checklist and Bibliography of Stevens Criticism* (Denver: Alan Swallow, 1963), will be immediately obvious. My work is based on the solid foundation of that book and the organization of the Stevens canon in the earlier *Wallace Stevens: A Preliminary Checklist of His Writings: 1898–1954* by Samuel French Morse (New Haven: Yale University Library, 1954). I am grateful to these men, and particularly to Professor

Morse, for their continued help and their willing-
ness to answer, often in great detail, my many
questions.

The Wallace Stevens Newsletter has been indispensable to me. Not only in the pages of the
Newsletter but in person and by mail and telephone, its editor, William T. Ford, has been one of
my greatest sources of information concerning
the bibliography of Stevens. I am grateful to him
for his constant and interested cooperation and for
his frequent generosity.

Alfred A. Knopf, Inc., publishers of Wallace
Stevens, has given me help in large measure as
well as permission to quote from correspondence.
I am grateful to William A. Koshland, Sidney
Jacobs, and the late Herbert Weinstock for the
many facts and figures they supplied which would
have been otherwise inaccessible.

I am indebted and grateful to all of the following:
Jean Aroeste, for her help at the reference desk at
the UCLA library; Herbert S. Bailey, Jr., Director
of the Princeton University Press; John P. Baker,
of the New York Public Library; Edna Beilenson,
of the Peter Pauper Press; Pierre Berès, for his
help with the Dufy pamphlet and permission to
quote from his letter to me; Ruth B. Berry, for
help at the reference desk of the UCLA library;
Nancy Bieber, for a copy of Stevens' letter to
Harvey Breit; Jacob Blanck, for checking the
Houghton Library's copy of the Fortune Press
edition of *Selected Poems;* Fon W. Boardman, Jr.,
Vice President of the Oxford University Press;
Hilda Bohem, for her help in the Department of
Special Collections of the UCLA library; Florence
Bonnell, for information on Conrad Aiken and
Wallace Stevens; Professor Fredson Bowers, of
the University of Virginia, for reading the man-
uscript; Dorothy W. Bridgewater, of the Yale Uni-

versity library, for sending me copies of that library's catalog cards on Stevens; Louisa Browne, of Faber and Faber Ltd, for her answers to my many questions concerning English editions of Stevens; Matthew J. Bruccoli, General Editor of the Pittsburgh Series in Bibliography, for his great help in matters of style and procedure; William R. Cagle, of the Lilly Library, Indiana University, for his careful and thorough reading of the manuscript and his many solid suggestions; Richard W. Centing, of the Ohio State University libraries, for information on Wallace Stevens and Anais Nin; Austin Clarke, for information on the Fortune Press edition of *Selected Poems;* Pat Cody, of Cody's Books, Berkeley, California, for information about the broadside printing of "Cy Est Pourtraicte, Madame Ste Ursule, et Les Unze Mille Vierges"; Helen Cohan, of Appleton-Century-Crofts; Mrs. Louis Henry Cohn, of House of Books Ltd., New York, for permission to quote from her catalogs; Robert Collison, former Head of the Reference Department, UCLA library, for listening patiently to my many questions and always providing the right answer; Allan Covici, of the University of California library at Berkeley, for giving me much of his time and access to his books; Leah Daniels, of Random House, Inc.; W. Steuart Debenham, of the Yale University library, for information about Stevens' National Book Award speech; Gene DeGruson, of the Porter Library, Kansas State College of Pittsburg, for his continued interest and help; Rodney G. Dennis, of the Houghton Library, Harvard University, for checking Stevens manuscript material there; Jonathan Dodd, of Dodd, Mead & Company; Harry Duncan, of The Cummington Press, for permission to quote from his letter to Wallace Stevens; Mario Einaudi, for information about the publication of *Mattino*

Mille Vierges"; Margaret M. McQuillan, of Harcourt, Brace Jovanovich, Inc.; Charles W. Mann, Pennsylvania State University library, for reading the manuscript; Saul Marks, of the Plantin Press, Los Angeles, California, for his help in identifying typefaces; John Martin, President of Black Sparrow Press, for his practical help on many occasions; William Matheson, Chief of the Rare Book Division, Library of Congress, and his staff; Jackson Mathews, for his information about the Valéry *Dialogues;* Helen Mayer, President of Dell Publishing Co., Inc.; Stephen C. Millett, for his complimentary copy of the commemorative volume of The Saint Nicholas Society of the City of New York; Mabel A. Morse, of Doubleday & Company, Inc; Kenneth Nesheim, for his help in making Stevens material available to me at the Beinecke Library, Yale University; Rosemary Neiswender, of the UCLA library, for her help with translations from the Slavic languages; Rex Dennis Parady, for his help with Stevens material in the Harris Collection in the Brown University library; John Pauker, for information concerning the USIA script of "Connecticut"; Geneva Phillips, of the UCLA English Department, for her help with bibliographical problems; Marshall Rissman, for his many helpful suggestions; Lori Ritchie, of the University of California library at Santa Barbara, for her help in locating Stevens material there; F. W. Roberts, for information about Stevens material at the University of Texas; Robert Rosenthal, Curator of Special Collections at the University of Chicago library, for making available the Stevens material in the Ronald Latimer and Harriet Monroe papers; Judith A. Schiff, for her help in the Yale University library; Mary E. Seltzer, of The Johns Hopkins University Press; Christopher J. H. M. Shaw, President, World Publishing Company; Jane W.

Shepherd, for a copy of her "Wallace Stevens: A Bibliography of Criticism," an unpublished paper written under the direction of Professor Jackson Bryer at the University of Maryland; Ernest Siegel, for his help in making available Stevens material in the Los Angeles Public Library; Bruce Stevenson, for the research he did on my behalf on the Fortune Press edition of *Selected Poems;* Roger Stoddard, of the Houghton Library, Harvard University, for checking and rechecking the Houghton copy of the Fortune Press edition of *Selected Poems;* John L. Sweeney, for permission to quote from his correspondence with Wallace Stevens; Lola Szladits, Curator of the Berg Collection, New York Public Library, for her help with Stevens material there; Ruth Trager, of the UCLA library, for her help with translations from the Slavic languages; Elizabeth R. Usher, Chief Librarian, Metropolitan Museum of Art, New York, for her advice; Charles A. Wagner, Executive Secretary of the Poetry Society of America, for his assistance; Henry W. Wenning, for permission to quote from his catalogs; Brooke Whiting, for his help in the Department of Special Collections, UCLA library; Henry H. Wiggins, Assistant Director of the Columbia University Press; Robert A. Wilson, of the Phoenix Book Shop, New York, for bringing Stevens material to my attention; Walter W. Wright, Chief of Special Collections, Dartmouth College library, for making Stevens material available to me; Marjorie G. Wynne, for her help in the Beinecke Library, Yale University; and Richard Zumwinkle, for his help at the reference desk of the UCLA library.

Very special thanks go to Marian Ellithorpe, Brooke Bower, and Debby Farquhar for doing my typing; to Sharon Jaffe for the index; to Joanna Heffington, Ginny Adams, and Maxine Lipeles for helping me read proof; and to Thomas F. J. McGill for innumerable errands and missions. To my sons, Paul and Nathaniel, I am grateful for their cheerful and enthusiastic help with various jobs of sorting and filing.

It has been my good fortune to have Mrs. Louise Craft, Associate Editor of the University of Pittsburgh Press, as my copy editor. Every page of this bibliography is evidence of her skill.

The gratitude I express to all these people in no way makes them responsible for any errors in this book; they all are mine. As for omissions, mistakes, all the things I forgot, that great bookman and my wise old friend, Jake Zeitlin, observes that these too serve a function; he says, "It's nice to leave something for the next guy." I take comfort from that observation.

Introduction

I T has been said before and often: no bibliography is ever finished. If it were not for deadlines and other pressures, this bibliography, too, could be postponed indefinitely. And every day would bring its quota of new finds and new attributions. As it is, the cutoff date in the section of material about Wallace Stevens is 1971 for periodical publications and 1972 for books.

I have tried to incorporate the best features of other bibliographies of modern literary figures. As the reader will quickly see, my models have been the Soho Series of Rupert Hart–Davis Ltd and the Pittsburgh Series in Bibliography, of which this volume is a part. But no two bibliographies are ever alike, and the style of this one evolved into what I hope is the best way to describe Wallace Stevens' published writings, particularly his books which have certain characteristics requiring a specific type of descriptive bibliography.

FORMAT

Section A lists chronologically all books, pamphlets, and broadsides by Wallace Stevens in their first separate or first collected printings. Any material which was previously unpublished is identified. This section also includes descriptive material on reprints and new editions.

The numbering system in Section A indicates the edition and printing for each entry. Thus for

Parts of a World, A 5.a.1 denotes that the entry is
Stevens' fifth published title (5), the first edition
(a), and the first printing (1). Issues are designated
as such without a numerical designation.

A major feature of this bibliography is the annotation provided wherever possible for each entry.
These annotations, which augment the descriptive
material and are usually in Wallace Stevens' own
words, are for the most part taken from his correspondence. They provide, I believe, an unusual
commentary on the bibliographical and publishing
history of the books and on Stevens' close involve-
ment in every aspect of their production. It was
after studying Emily Mitchell Wallace's *Bibliography of William Carlos Williams* (Middletown,
Conn.: Wesleyan, 1968) that the usefulness and
attractiveness of such a commentary became apparent to me.

Section B lists chronologically all titles in which
work by Wallace Stevens appeared for the first
time in a book. Any material which was previously
unpublished is identified. In this section, as in
Section A, some entries are followed by commentary from Stevens' correspondence.

Section C lists chronologically the first publication in newspapers and magazines of work by
Stevens. Included in this section are interviews
with Stevens. Those entries which are not identified otherwise are poems.

Section D lists chronologically miscellaneous
material by Stevens. It consists primarily of blurbs
by Stevens on the dust jackets of his own and other
authors' books and quotations in booksellers' catalogues from previously unpublished material by
Stevens.

Section E lists, alphabetically by language, translations of Stevens' material into other languages.
For each language, entries are listed chronologi-

cally under the headings "Books," "Anthologies," and "Periodicals."

Section F lists chronologically musical settings of material by Stevens.

Section G lists, chronologically by date of publication, recordings made of Stevens' poetry, including readings by Stevens.

Section H lists, alphabetically by author, dedicatory poems and poems referring to or mentioning Stevens.

Section I lists chronologically books entirely devoted to Wallace Stevens.

Section J lists, alphabetically by author, articles about Stevens in books as well as books in which a significant section or number of pages are devoted to him. Articles in books cited in Section I are also included here.

Section K lists, alphabetically by author, articles about Stevens in magazines and newspapers. Reviews of more than average substance are found here as well as in Section L.

Section L lists reviews of books by Stevens. The books are arranged chronologically by date of publication. The reviews for each book are listed alphabetically by author. In most cases it was the first edition of each book which was reviewed. It is so indicated when reviews are of a later edition. The last entry, L 18, gives reviews of Stevens' plays.

Section M lists, alphabetically by author, dissertations either devoted entirely to Stevens or containing a significant portion about him.

TERMS AND METHODS

Edition. All the copies of a book printed from a single setting of type, including all printings from standing type, from plates, or by offset.

Printing. All the copies of an edition printed at one time. This term includes states and issues.

State. States are created within a single printing by some alteration of the text during the course of printing. States occur within printings and normally result from prepublication changes.

Issue. Issues are created by an alteration affecting the conditions of publication (usually a title-page alteration) to some copies of a given printing. Issues occur within printings and normally result from changes made after initial publication of part of the printing.

Brackets surrounding a date in a Section A or B entry indicate that the date itself does not appear on the title page of that book.

In both captions for title-page reproductions and quasi-facsimile material, all printing is in black unless otherwise designated. When title pages, dust jackets, etc., have been transcribed in quasi facsimile, the type is roman unless indicated otherwise, and a vertical rule cancels out any specified color or type variation.

Paper measurements are supplied under the reproductions of the title pages of Section A entries; if there is no reproduction for a first edition, the page measurements are part of the "Typography and paper" entry. In Section B the measurements refer to the front binding sizes.

For binding cloth designations I have used the system in Jacob Blanck's *Bibliography of American Literature* (New Haven: Yale University Press, 1955–). Unless otherwise stated, the spines of bindings and dust jackets are printed horizontally. The term *perfect binding* refers to a style of binding in which all pages are cut and roughed up at the back or binding edge and held together by adhesive.

The dust jacket descriptions for Section A entries have been given only in sufficient detail for identification.

Los Angeles and Washington, D.C.
1973

Abbreviations

CL	Los Angeles Public Library
CLU	University of California at Los Angeles
CP	*The Collected Poems of Wallace Stevens,* A 23
CtY	Yale University Library
CU	University of California at Berkeley
CU-SB	University of California at Santa Barbara
DA	*Dissertation Abstracts International Retrospective Index*
DLC	Library of Congress
H-1923	*Harmonium,* 1923 edition, A 1.a
H-1931	*Harmonium,* 1931 edition, A 1.b
HS	Holly Stevens
ICI-D	Illinois Institute of Technology, Chicago — Institute of Design
InU	Indiana University
JME	J. M. Edelstein
Letters	*Letters of Wallace Stevens,* A 29
MH	Harvard University Library
NA	*The Necessary Angel,* A 17
NN	New York Public Library
OP	*Opus Posthumous,* A 26
Palm	*The Palm at the End of the Mind,* A 30
Poems	*Poems by Wallace Stevens,* A 27
PSt	Pennsylvania State University Library
RPB	Brown University Library
TxU	University of Texas Library
WS	Wallace Stevens
WSN	*The Wallace Stevens Newsletter*

A. Books and Separate Publications

A 1 HARMONIUM

A 1.a
First edition (1923)

Harmonium
by W a l l a c e   S t e v e n s

New York Alfred · A · Knopf Mcmxxiii

A 1.a: $8\frac{1}{16} \times 5\frac{3}{8}$ inches

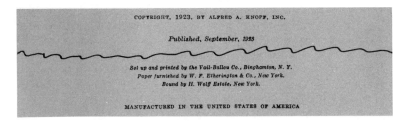

Collation: [1-9]⁸. Pp. [1-8] 9-11 [12-14] 15-44 [45-46] 47-140 [141-144].

Typography and paper: Set in Linotype Caslon. White wove paper.

Pagination: p. 1: half title, 'Harmonium'; p. 2: 'BORZOI POETRY | Fall 1923 | THE PILGRIMAGE OF FESTUS | *Conrad Aiken* | BITTER HERBS | *C. A. Dawson-Scott* | THE PROPHET | *Kahlil Gibran* | *With twelve drawings by the author* | WHIP-PERGINNY | *Robert Graves* | THE TEMPLE AND OTHER POEMS | *Translated from the Chinese* | *by Arthur Waley*'; p. 3: title page; p. 4: copyright page; p. 5: dedication, *'To* | *MY WIFE'*; p. 6: blank; p. 7: acknowledgment, 'The poems in this book, with the exception of | *The Comedian as the Letter C* and a few others, | have been published before in *Others, Secession,* | *Rogue, The Soil, The Modern School, Broom* | *Contact, The New Republic, The Measure, The* | *Little Review, The Dial,* and particularly in | *Poetry: A Magazine of Verse,* of Chicago, | edited by Harriet Monroe.'; p. 8: blank; pp. 9-11: table of contents; p. 12: blank; p. 13: section title, 'Harmonium'; p. 14: blank; pp. 15-44: text; p. 45: section title, 'The Comedian as the Letter C'; p. 46: blank; pp. 47-140: text; pp. 141-144: blank.

Contents: Earthy Anecdote – Invective against Swans – In the Carolinas – The Paltry Nude Starts on a Spring Voyage – The Plot against the Giant – Infanta Marina – Domination of Black – The Snow Man – The Ordinary Women – The Load of Sugar-Cane – Le Monocle de Mon Oncle – Nuances of a Theme by Williams – Metaphors of a Magnifico – Ploughing on Sunday – Cy Est Pourtraicte, Madame Ste Ursule, et Les Unze Mille Vierges – Hibiscus on the Sleeping Shores – Fabliau of Florida – The Doctor of Geneva – Another Weeping Woman – Homunculus et La Belle Etoile – The Comedian as the Letter C (The World without Imagination – Concerning the Thunderstorms of Yucatan – Approaching Carolina – The Idea of a Colony – A Nice Shady Home – And Daughters with Curls) – From the Misery of Don Joost – O Florida, Venereal Soil – Last Looks at the Lilacs – The Worms at Heaven's Gate – The Jack Rabbit – Valley Candle –

Anecdote of Men by the Thousand – The Silver Plough-Boy – The Apostrophe to Vincentine – Floral Decorations for Bananas – Anecdote of Canna – Of the Manner of Addressing Clouds – Of Heaven Considered as a Tomb – Of the Surface of Things – Anecdote of the Prince of Peacocks – A High-Toned Old Christian Woman – The Place of the Solitaires – The Weeping Burgher – The Curtains in the House of the Metaphysician – Banal Sojourn – Depression before Spring – The Emperor of Ice-Cream – The Cuban Doctor – Tea at the Palaz of Hoon – Exposition of the Contents of a Cab – Disillusionment of Ten O'Clock – Sunday Morning – The Virgin Carrying a Lantern – Stars at Tallapoosa – Explanation – Six Significant Landscapes – Bantams in Pine-Woods – Anecdote of the Jar – Palace of the Babies – Frogs Eat Butterflies. Snakes Eat Frogs. Hogs Eat Snakes. Men Eat Hogs – Jasmine's Beautiful Thoughts underneath the Willow – Cortège for Rosenbloom – Tattoo – The Bird with the Coppery, Keen Claws – Life Is Motion – Architecture – The Wind Shifts – Colloquy with a Polish Aunt – Gubbinal – Two Figures in Dense Violet Light – Theory – To the One of Fictive Music – Hymn from a Watermelon Pavilion – Peter Quince at the Clavier – Thirteen Ways of Looking at a Blackbird – Nomad Exquisite – Tea – To the Roaring Wind.

Binding and dust jacket: Three bindings can be identified:

1. The first binding is paper-covered boards in a pattern of blue, red, yellow, and white checks; dark blue cloth spine on which a yellow paper label is pasted at the top; on the label, which sometimes is placed to be read up and sometimes down, is printed in red, within a box of decorative rules and ornaments: '*HARMONIUM | Wallace Stevens*'. Sized white wove endpapers; top edges stained red; fore and bottom edges untrimmed. Yellow dust jacket printed in red; on the front is a biographical sketch of WS; on the back is a list of new Borzoi poetry for fall 1923; on the front and back flaps is the same brief statement in answer to '*What does | BORZOI Mean?*'

The publisher's records show that 500 copies were bound in this checked pattern of "Curwen" paper in August 1923. It is this binding which is on the copyright deposit copy, the receipt date of which is September 18, 1923, and on certain presentation copies, one of which is Carl Van Vechten's, now in the Berg Collection of the New York Public Library.

2. The second binding is paper-covered boards of gray, blue, white, orange, and green stripes in an irregular pattern; dark blue cloth spine on which the same paper label as on no. 1 above has been placed at the top of the spine. Sized white wove end-

papers; top edges stained orange; fore and bottom edges un-trimmed. The dust jacket is the same as no. 1 above.

The publisher's records show that 215 copies of *Harmonium* were bound in this striped pattern of "Roman Pearl #784" paper in November 1924.

3. The third binding is a remainder binding of blue V cloth. The remainder copies were trimmed to $7^{15}/_{16} \times 5^{1}/_{4}$ inches. The same paper label as on nos. 1 and 2 is at the top of the spine. Sized white wove endpapers; all edges trimmed. The dust jacket is the same as nos. 1 and 2 above.

The publisher's records show that the remaining 715 copies of *Harmonium* were "bound for jobbing at a reduced rate" in November 1926.

Published September 7, 1923, at $2.00, in an edition of 1,500 copies.

Reprinting: With the exception of "Silver Plough-Boy," "Exposition of the Contents of a Cab," and "Architecture," which were collected in *OP*, A 26, the entire contents of *H*-1923 were reprinted in *CP*, A 23.

Locations: First binding: DLC (deposit copy stamped "Sept. 18, 1923"), HS, InU, JME, NN; second binding: CtY, CU; third binding: CU, InU.

Annotations: "I was in Charleston when your letter of July 10 reached Hartford, and for that reason have not replied before. No doubt I shall be coming down before long. I feel frightfully uncertain about a book. But we can talk that over, at any rate, among other things." (*Letters*, pp. 227–228: letter to Carl Van Vechten, July 17, 1922)

"Gathering together the things for my book has been so depressing that I wonder at *Poetry*'s friendliness. All my earlier things seem like horrid cocoons from which later abortive insects have sprung. The book will amount to nothing, except that it may teach me something." (*Letters*, p. 231: letter to Harriet Monroe, October 28, 1922)

"My poems are now ready. Shall I leave them at your house some time when I am in New York? I should rather take them down with me than to send them by mail, for it has been an awful job to typewrite them." (*Letters*, p. 232: letter to Carl Van Vechten, November 18, 1922)

"Knopf has my book, the contract is signed and that's done. I have omitted many things, exercising the most fastidious choice, so far as that was possible among my witherlings. To pick a crisp salad from the garbage of the past is no snap . ." (*Letters*, p. 232: letter to Harriet Monroe, December 21, 1922)

"I think that the following:

THE GRAND POEM:
PRELIMINARY MINUTIAE

would be a better title for my book than its present one. It has a good deal more pep to it. If you agree, won't you change the title for me?" (*Letters*, p. 237: letter to Alfred A. Knopf, March 12, 1923)

"USE HARMONIUM
WALLACE STEVENS"
(*Letters*, p. 238: telegram to
Alfred A. Knopf, May 18, 1923)

"I am sending you a copy of Harmonium — since you were its accoucheur. Knopf has done very well by it and I am grateful to both of you." (*Letters*, p. 238: letter to Carl Van Vechten, September 11, 1923)

A 1.b
Second edition (1931)

A 1.b: Borzoi device and border design of lines in magenta, border ornaments and all type in black; $7\frac{1}{2} \times 5\frac{1}{8}$ inches

Collation: [1–8]⁸ [9]⁴ [10–11]⁸. Pp. [*1–2*] [i–viii] ix–xii [1–2]
3–34 [35–36] 37–151 [152–154].

Typography and paper: Set in Linotype Estienne. White laid
paper.

Pagination: pp. *1–2:* blank; p. i: half title, 'HARMONIUM';
p. ii: 'SOME NEW POETRY | on Mr. Knopf's list | by *Humbert
Wolfe* | EARLY POEMS | THE UNCELESTIAL CITY | *by Leo-
nora Speyer* | NAKED HEEL | *by Kahlil Gibran* | THE EARTH
GODS | *by James Laver* | MACROCOSMOS | *by T. S. Eliot* |
POEMS | [Borzoi device in magenta] | *These are Borzoi Books*
[the whole surrounded by a border design of lines in magenta]';
p. iii: title page; p. iv: copyright page; p. v: dedication, 'to | MY
WIFE | AND HOLLY'; p. vi: blank; p. vii: acknowledgment,
same as A 1.a; p. viii: blank; pp. ix–xii: table of contents; p. 1:
section title, 'HARMONIUM'; p. 2: blank; pp. 3–34: text; p. 35:
section title, 'THE COMEDIAN | AS THE LETTER C'; p. 36:
blank; pp. 37–151: text; p. 152: colophon; pp. 153–154: blank.

Contents: The second edition varies from the first in that three
poems from the first edition were dropped and fourteen poems
were included for the first time. The following, in Wallace
Stevens' own words, makes clear the deletions and additions:

> The order of the poems in the original edition of Harmonium
> is satisfactory. In the new edition I should like to omit The
> Silver Plough Boy, on page 78, Exposition of the Contents of
> a [Cab], on page 98, and Architecture, on page 121.
>   The new material is to be inserted after page 138 in the
> following order:
>
> > The Man Whose Pharynx Was Bad
> > The Death Of A Soldier
> > Negation
> > The Surprises Of The Superhuman
> > Sea Surface Full Of Clouds
> > The Revolutionists Stop For Orangeade
> > New England Verses

Lunar Paraphrase
Anatomy Of Monotony
The Public Square
Sonatina To Hans Christian
In The Clear Season Of Grapes
Two At Norfolk
Indian River

After this new material the book is to be closed with the two poems in the original edition, entitled A [*sic*] Tea, on page 139, and To The Roaring Wind, on page 140. (*Letters*, pp. 259–260: letter to Alfred A. Knopf, October 16, 1930)

Note: Two errors occur in the table of contents: at the bottom of p. xi, p. '128' should read p. 127; at the top of p. xii, p. '127' should read p. 128.

Colophon: p. [152]: [six thin, short rules, increasing in length from top to bottom] [Borzoi device] [five thin, short rules, increasing in length from top to bottom] | A NOTE ON THE TYPE IN | WHICH THIS BOOK IS SET | *Estienne is another distinguished book face created by Mr. | George W. Jones, the eminent English printer and the de- | signer of Granjon. Like Granjon it is an exclusive Lino- | type face available in no other form. It was named in | honor of the distinguished sixteenth century printing | family whose work is cherished by posterity. Typog- | raphers and printers will be particularly interested | in the notably new type texture Estienne provides | — a distinctive, wholly charming pattern and | appearance when set in mass form that is unlike | that of any other face. Estienne capitals are | compellingly attractive, possessing a dig- | nity and beauty seldom approached by | present-day book faces. The limpid, | flowing grace and charm of the lower- | case letters with their tall ascenders | and long descenders makes read- | ing easy, even without leading.* | Set up, printed and bound by | The Plimpton Press, Norwood, | Massachusetts. Paper made | by Ticonderoga Pulp and | Paper Co., Ticonderoga, | N.Y.

Binding and dust jacket: Four bindings of the second edition of *Harmonium* can be identified:

1. The first binding is gray paper-covered boards, the gray of the paper designed to simulate wove marks and chain lines; black cloth spine on which a gray, or sometimes an ivory, paper label is pasted to read downward; on the label: '[ornament in magenta] *HARMONIUM:* WALLACE STEVENS [ornament in

magenta]'. White laid endpapers; top edges stained reddish-brown; fore and bottom edges rough trimmed. Gray dust jacket printed in magenta; on the front: '*This new edition contains fourteen poems | never before published in book form.*'; on the back are notices of art and travel books.

The publisher's records show that 500 copies of the second edition of *Harmonium* were bound in June 1931 in "Ravenna Gray" paper with "Hall V275" spine. It is this binding which is on the copyright deposit copy, the receipt date of which is September 26, 1931.

2 and 3. The second and third bindings are of green or blue paper over boards; spines, labels, endpapers, edges, and dust jackets are the same as no. 1 above. The publisher's records show that 100 copies of the sheets were bound in March of 1936, 250 copies were bound in January of 1938, and 252 copies were bound in August of 1942. For the 1936, 1938, and most of the 1942 bindings, the publisher is unable to give specifications of the material used. It can be verified, however, that 75 of the 252 copies bound in August of 1942 were done in blue paper.

4. The fourth binding of the second edition of *Harmonium* is tan V cloth; labels, edges, and dust jacket are the same as nos. 1, 2 and 3; endpapers are white wove unwatermarked sized paper.

The publisher's records show that the remaining 397 copies were bound in tan "Zeppilin 3163" cloth in April of 1944.

Published July 24, 1931, at $2.50, in an edition of 1,500 copies.

Reprinting: The fourteen new poems in this edition were reprinted in *CP*, A 23.

Locations: First binding: DLC (deposit copy stamped "Sept. 26, 1931"), CtY, HS, JME; second and third bindings: HS (green and blue); fourth binding: CLU, CtY, InU.

A I.C.I
Third edition, first printing (1947)

Harmonium

WALLACE STEVENS

ALFRED·A·KNOPF
NEW YORK
1947

A I.C.I: 8³⁄₈ × 5¹⁄₂ inches

Collation: [1–11]⁸ [12]⁴ [13–14]⁸. Pp. [*1–2*] [i–viii] ix–xii [xiii–xiv] [1–2] 3–195 [196–200].

Typography and paper: Set in Linotype Janson. White laid paper, watermarked: 'WARREN'S | OLDE STYLE'.

Pagination: p. *1:* blank; p. *2: 'Also by* | WALLACE STEVENS | [*rule*] | *Ideas of Order* | *The Man with the Blue Guitar* | *Parts of a World* | *Transport to Summer* | 'He is as able a virtuoso, one with as cunning a | rhetoric as we have produced.' | *—Poetry* | *These are* Borzoi Books, *published by* | ALFRED A. KNOPF'; p. i: half title: 'HARMONIUM'; p. ii: blank; p. iii: title page; p. iv: copyright page; p. v: dedication: 'TO MY WIFE | and Holly | [floral ornament]'; p. vi: blank; p. vii: acknowledgment, same as A 1.a and A 1.b; p. viii: blank; p. ix–xiii: table of contents; p. xiv: blank; p. 1: half title, 'HARMONIUM'; p. 2: blank; pp. 3– 196: text; p. 197: blank; p. 198: colophon; pp. 199–200: blank.

Contents: The same as A 1.b.

Colophon: p. [198]: A NOTE ON THE TYPE IN WHICH | THIS BOOK IS SET | *This Book was set on the Linotype in Janson, a recut-* | *ting made direct from the type cast from matrices made* | *by Anton Janson some time between 1660 and 1687.* | *Of Janson's origin nothing is known. He may have* | *been a relative of Justus Janson, a printer of Danish* | *birth who practiced in Leipzig from 1614 to 1635. Some* | *time be- tween 1657 and 1668 Anton Janson, a punch-* | *cutter and type-founder, bought from the Leipzig* | *printer Johann Erich Hahn the type-foundry which* | *had formerly been a part of the printing house of* | *M. Friedrich Lankisch. Janson's types were first shown* | *in a specimen sheet issued at Leipzig about 1675.* | *The book was composed, printed, and bound by The* | *Plimpton Press, Norwood, Massachusetts. Typogra-* | *phy and binding based on original designs by W. A.* | *Dwiggins.*

Binding and dust jacket: Smooth red V cloth over boards; a floral design stamped in blind on front; the Borzoi device stamped in blind on back; on spine, stamped in gold: '[ornament] | *Harmo-* | *nium* | WALLACE | STEVENS | [ornament] | *Knopf'*. Coated white wove endpapers; top edges stained red; fore and bottom edges rough trimmed. Ivory dust jacket printed in blue, with photograph of WS by Sylvia Salmi and eighteen-line biographical note on back; on the front flap is a thirty-three-line blurb containing: 'nearly a quarter-century after its first edition, *Harmonium* appears in its third edition, again completely reset.'; on the back flap is a list of books by WS.

Published June 1947 at $3.00, in a printing of 1,000 copies.

Locations: CtY, DLC, HS, JME, TxU.

Note: For variations in the text of *Harmonium,* cf. William Heyen, "The Text of *Harmonium,*" *Twentieth Century Literature,* XII, no. 3 (October 1966), 3–4, and G. Thomas Tanselle's earlier "The text of Stevens's 'Le Monocle de Mon Oncle,'" *The Library,* 3d series, XIX (1964), 246–248.

A 1.c.2
Third edition, second printing (1950)

This edition has the same specifications as A 1.c.1 except for the following: on title page: '1950'; on page iv: 'PUBLISHED SEPTEMBER 1923 | REVISED EDITION JULY 1931 | RESET AND PRINTED FROM NEW PLATES, APRIL 1947 | REPRINTED AUGUST 1950.'

Published August 1950, in a printing of 1,500 copies.

Locations: CU, CU-SB.

A 1.c.3
Third edition, third printing (1953)

This edition has the same specifications as A 1.c.1 except for the following: on title page: '1953'; on page iv: information added in A 1.c.2, with a final line: 'REPRINTED NOVEMBER 1953'; deeper crimson cloth binding.

Published December 1953, in a printing of 1,250 copies.

Location: CL.

A 2 IDEAS OF ORDER

A 2.a
First edition (1935)

Trade issue

IDEAS OF ORDER

BY
WALLACE STEVENS

NEW YORK
THE ALCESTIS PRESS
551 Fifth Avenue
/// 1935 ///

A 2.a: $9\frac{3}{8} \times 6\frac{1}{4}$ inches

Collation: [1–5]⁸. Pp. [i–vi] [1–4] 5–6 [7–8] 9–63 [64–74].

Typography and paper: Set in Inkunabula; page numbers at the bottom of the page are set off by three vertical slashes on each side of the numeral. White wove "Strathmore Permanent all-rag" paper, watermarked: 'STRATHMORE PERMANENT U.S.A.'

Pagination: pp. i–iv: blank; p. v: half title, '*IDEAS of ORDER*'; p. vi: blank; p. 1: title page; p. 2: copyright page; p. 3: acknowledgment, 'Many of the poems in this book | have been printed before, in | *Alcestis, Direction, Poetry,* | *New Republic, Hound & Horn,* | *The Westminster Magazine,* | *The New Act, Smoke-,* | and *The Harkness Hoot,* | and to the editors of these publications the | author makes his grateful acknowledgment.'; p. 4: blank; pp. 5–6: table of contents; p. 7: half title, '*IDEAS of ORDER*'; p. 8: blank; pp. 9-63: text; p. 64: blank; p. 65: colophon; pp. 66–74: blank.

Contents: Sailing after Lunch – Sad Strains of a Gay Waltz – Dance of the Macabre Mice – Meditation Celestial & Terrestrial – Lions in Sweden – How to Live. What to Do – Some Friends from Pascagoula – Waving Adieu, Adieu, Adieu – The Idea of Order at Key West – The American Sublime – Mozart, 1935 – Snow and Stars – The Sun This March – Botanist on Alp (No. 1) – Botanist on Alp (No. 2) – Evening without Angels – The Brave Man – A Fading of the Sun – Gray Stones and Gray Pigeons – Winter Bells – Academic Discourse at Havana – Nudity at the Capital – Nudity in the Colonies – Re-statement of Romance – The Reader – Mud Master – Anglais Mort à Florence – The Pleasures of Merely Circulating – Like Decorations in a Nigger Cemetery – Autumn Refrain – A Fish-Scale Sunrise – Gallant Chateau – Delightful Evening.

Colophon: p. [65]: THIS FIRST EDITION OF IDEAS OF | ORDER IS STRICTLY LIMITED TO | 165 COPIES, SIGNED BY THE | AUTHOR. TWENTY COPIES, NUM- | BERED I–XX ARE PRINTED ON | DUCA DI MODENA, AN ITALIAN | HANDMADE PAPER, FOR PRESEN- | TATION PURPOSES; 135 COPIES, | NUMBERED 1–135 ON STRATH- | MORE PER- MANENT ALL-RAG | PAPER, ARE FOR SALE, AND 10 | COPIES, MARKED OUT OF SERIES, | ARE FOR REVIEW. PUBLISHED BY | J. RONALD LANE LATIMER & | CHARLES E. HUDEBURG AT THEIR | ALCESTIS PRESS IN JULY, 1935. | THIS COPY IS NUMBER | [number in ink in arabic numerals] |

[WS's signature in ink] | DESIGNED AND PRINTED BY |
LEW NEY WITH INKUNABULA | TYPE SET BY HAND AND
THE | TYPE HAS BEEN DISTRIBUTED

Binding and dust jacket: Heavy ivory paper wrapper folded
over first and last leaves; on the front: 'IDEAS OF ORDER |
WALLACE STEVENS'; on the spine, downward: 'IDEAS *of*
ORDER WALLACE STEVENS.' Top edges trimmed; fore and bottom edges untrimmed. Unprinted glassine dust jacket; some
copies in green cardboard slipcases, others in ivory cardboard
slipcases.

Published August 12, 1935, at $7.50, in an issue of 145 copies
of a total edition of 165 copies.

Reprinting: These poems are reprinted in *CP*, A 23.

Locations: CtY, DLC (deposit copy stamped "August 20,
1935"), HS, JME.

Presentation issue
This issue is the same as A 2.a in all specifications except for the
paper, which is white wove "Duca di Modena," watermarked:
'[heraldic shield] | DUCA DI MODENA', and for the inked
numerals in the colophon, which are roman. The cardboard
slipcases for some copies are green, ivory for others.

Published August 12, 1935, for presentation, in an issue of 20
copies of a total edition of 165 copies.

Locations: CtY, HS, JME, RPB.

Annotation for A 2.a: "The book has just arrived and gives me
the greatest possible pleasure. It must have taken no end of time
and put you and Mr. [Willard] Maas to no end of trouble. But
here it is, and it strikes me, quite regardless of its contents, as
being a very good job. Too bad that I can't read it. Of course if I
were to read any of these things again I should jump out of my
skin.
   "Let me say this: you have been generous in sending me ten
copies, and while that seems to have been our agreement, I had
forgotten it until Mr. Ney [Lew Ney, designer and printer of
Ideas of Order] reminded me of it. The chances are that you
cannot possibly come out whole, even if you sold the whole
edition without difficulty and received the full price for each
copy. If I am right about this, and my guess is that I am, don't
think of sending me any money. The book is a handsome piece
of work, and as it probably will be your first book I should be very

glad to go along with you without any royalties or anything of the sort. In fact, it would jolt me to think of royalties under the circumstances." (*Letters*, pp. 283–284: letter to J. Ronald Lane Latimer, August 10, 1935)

A 2.b
Second edition (1936)

WALLACE STEVENS

IDEAS
OF ORDER

NEW YORK · ALFRED · A · KNOPF · LONDON

1 9 3 6

A 2.b: ornament, Borzoi device, and date in red; $7\frac{1}{2} \times 5$ inches

Collation: [1–3]⁸ [4]⁶ [5]⁸. Pp. [1–4] [i–vi] vii–viii [1–2] 3–61 [62–64].

Typography and paper: Set in Linotype Estienne. White laid paper.

Pagination: pp. *1–3:* blank; p. *4:* 'Also by Wallace Stevens | HARMONIUM | "He is not merely a connoisseur of fine rhythms and the precise | nuances of the lyrical line, but a trained observer who gazes with | an intelligent eye upon the decadence that follows the rapid | acquisition of wealth and power." | — Horace Gregory in New York Herald Tribune Books | PUBLISHED BY ALFRED A. KNOPF'; p. i: half title, 'IDEAS OF ORDER'; p. ii: blank; p. iii: title page; p. iv: copyright page; p. v: acknowledgment, 'Many of the poems in this book have been | printed before, in | ALCESTIS, DIRECTION, POETRY, NEW REPUBLIC | HOUND & HORN, THE WESTMINSTER MAGAZINE, | THE NEW ACT, SMOKE, THE HARKNESS HOOT, | and | CONTEMPORARY POETRY AND PROSE | and to the editors of these publications the author makes | his grateful acknowledgment.'; p. vi: blank; pp. vii–viii: table of contents; p. 1: half title, 'IDEAS OF ORDER'; p. 2: blank; pp. 3–61: text; p. 62: colophon; pp. 63–64: blank.

Contents: In addition to the thirty-three poems of the first edition, there are three new poems: "Farewell to Florida," pp. 3–4; "Ghosts as Cocoons," pp. 5–6; and "A Postcard from the Volcano," pp. 56–57.

Colophon: p. [62]: A NOTE ON THE TYPE | IN WHICH THIS BOOK IS SET | [short rule] | [short rule] | This book is printed in *Estienne*, a linotype face designed | by George W. Jones, the eminent English printer, and | named in honour of the Estienne family. Henri Estienne | (died 1520), a descendant of a Provencal noble family, | came to Paris in 1502 and set up a printing establishment | there. After his death his widow married his foreman, | Simon de Colines, who carried on the business until 1526, | when it passed into the possession of Robert Estienne | (1503–59), Henri's second son, who had been his step- | father's assistant. In 1539 Robert was appointed king's | printer by Francis I. As the result of disputes with the | Faculty of Theology he moved to Geneva in 1551, where | he set up a new printing establishment. His younger | brother, Charles Estienne (c. 1504–64), took over the | Paris establishment in 1551 and was appointed king's | printer. Robert's son Henri Estienne (1531– 98), a | learned scholar, inherited the printing house at Geneva. | Several disputes with the consistory inclined him to | travel extensively in his later years. Later de- | scendants continued the family tradition | for scholarship and fine printing. | [Borzoi device] | THE COMPOSITION, PRINTING, AND BINDING | ARE BY *The Plimpton Press*, NORWOOD, MASS. | THE PAPER IS MADE BY *S. D. Warren Co.*, | BOSTON.

Binding and dust jacket: Three bindings of this edition can be identified:

1. The first binding is vertically striped pink, white, yellow, and gray T cloth; a light gray paper label is pasted to read downward on spine; on the label, printed in brown: '[ornament] *IDEAS OF ORDER:* STEVENS [ornament]'. White laid endpapers of same stock as sheets; top edges stained blue; fore and bottom edges untrimmed. Light gray dust jacket printed in magenta; on the back is a list of 'distinguished poetry on the Borzoi list'; on the front flap, a thirty-two-line blurb consisting for the most part of a three-paragraph statement by WS about the book.

The publisher's records show that 500 copies were bound in "Pekalinen #219" cloth for publication October 19, 1936.

2. The second binding is rose-colored, paper-covered boards. All other details of the binding, including the label, and the dust jacket are the same as no. 1. Endpapers, of the same stock as the sheets, are sized.

The publisher's records show that 250 copies were bound in "Rubicone Red" paper in September 1941.

3. The third binding is yellow paper-covered boards. All other details of the binding, including the label, and the dust jacket are the same as in no. 1. Endpapers, of the same stock as the sheets, are sized.

The publisher's records cannot provide specifications or the date for this binding except for the facts that the paper was "yellow" and that the binding was for "the balance of 250."

Published October 19, 1936, at $2.00, in an edition of 1,000 copies.

Reprinting: All the poems in this edition are reprinted in *CP*, A 23. An excerpt from the dust jacket appears in B 55; the complete dust jacket statement is published for the first time in book form in B 60.

Locations: First binding: CtY, DLC (deposit copy stamped "October 20, 1936"), HS, JME; second binding: CU; third binding: InU.

Annotation: "I have a letter from Mr. Latimer in which he gives up his plan to publish a trade edition of "Ideas of Order". It seems to me that this is a prudent thing for him to do; since it is one thing for him to use his taste in publishing a limited edition, it is quite another thing for him to publish a trade edition with rather vague means of distributing it. [. . .]

"I am grateful to you for your attitude. Of course it must be true that you do not publish poetry with the idea of making any money on it except in an occasionally fortunate instance. My relations with you have always been most agreeable and naturally I am happy to have you ask me to go on with you." (*Letters*, p. 310: letter to Alfred A. Knopf, March 23, 1936)

A 2.c
Third edition (1952)

Published February 27, 1952, at $3.50, together with *The Man with the Blue Guitar*, in an edition of 2,000 copies. See A 4.c, *The Man with the Blue Guitar Including Ideas of Order*, for a description of this book.

A 3 OWL'S CLOVER
[*1936*]

OWL'S CLOVER

WALLACE STEVENS

THE ALCESTIS PRESS. NEW YORK.

A 3: all ornaments in red, rules and type in black; $9^5/_{16} \times 6^1/_4$ inches

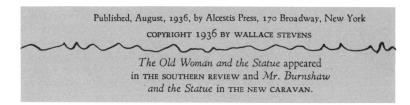

Published, August, 1936, by Alcestis Press, 170 Broadway, New York

COPYRIGHT 1936 BY WALLACE STEVENS

The Old Woman and the Statue appeared
in THE SOUTHERN REVIEW and *Mr. Burnshaw
and the Statue* in THE NEW CARAVAN.

Collation: [1–9]⁴. Pp. [1–10] 11–16 [17–18] 19–28 [29–30] 31–42 [43–44] 45–54 [55–56] 57–65 [66–72].

Typography and paper: Set in Linotype Italian Old Style; Dutch initials, pp. 11, 19, 31, 45, and 57, are in red; section titles, pp. 9, 17, 29, 43, and 55, are in red. White wove "Strathmore Permanent all-rag" paper, watermarked: 'STRATHMORE PERMANENT U.S.A.'

Pagination: pp. 1–2: blank; p. 3: half title, 'OWL'S CLOVER *by Wallace Stevens';* p. 4: *'Other publications of the Alcestis Press* | [nineteen lines]'; p. 5: title page; p. 6: copyright page; p. 7: table of contents; p. 8: blank; p. 9: section title, 'THE OLD WOMAN AND THE STATUE'; p. 10: blank; pp. 11–16: text; p. 17: section title, 'MR. BURNSHAW AND THE STATUE'; p. 18: blank; pp. 19–28: text; p. 29: section title, 'THE GREENEST CONTINENT'; p. 30: blank; pp. 31–42: text; p. 43: section title, 'A DUCK FOR DINNER'; p. 44: blank; pp. 45–54: text; p. 55: section title, 'SOMBRE FIGURATION'; p. 56: blank; pp. 57–65: text; pp. 66–68: blank; p. 69: colophon; pp. 70–72: blank.

Contents: The Old Woman and the Statue – Mr. Burnshaw and the Statue – The Greenest Continent – A Duck for Dinner – Sombre Figuration.

Note: The table of contents calls for "A Duck for Dinner" to begin on 'Page 47'; in fact, the section title, "A Duck for Dinner," is on p. [43] and the text itself begins on p. 45.

Colophon: p. [69]: COLOPHON | This first edition of Wallace Stevens' Owl's Clover is | strictly limited to 105 copies signed by the author. Twenty | copies, numbered i–xx have been printed on Didot hand-made | paper for presentation purposes and 85 copies, numbered 1–85 | have been printed on Strathmore Permanent all-rag paper. | Designed by Vrest Orton to be published by J. Ronald Lane | Latimer at the ALCESTIS PRESS. | [*WS's signature in ink*] | This is number [number in ink in arabic numerals]

Binding: Heavy orange paper wrapper folded over first and last blank leaves; on the front: 'OWL'S CLOVER BY WALLACE

STEVENS | THE ALCESTIS PRESS [ornament] NEW YORK';
on the spine, downward: 'OWL'S CLOVER [ornament] BY
WALLACE STEVENS [ornament] ALCESTIS PRESS'. Top and
bottom edges trimmed; fore edges rough trimmed. Grayish green
cardboard slipcase.

Published November 5, 1936, at $10.00, in an issue of 85 copies
of a total edition of 105 copies.

Reprinting: This version of "Owl's Clover," containing 861
lines, is reprinted in *OP*, A 26. See also A 4.

Locations: CtY, DLC (deposit copy stamped "Oct. 30, 1936"),
HS, RPB (all marked 'out of series').

Presentation issue
This is the same as the trade issue in all specifications but the
paper, which is white wove "Didot hand-made paper," water-
marked: 'DIDOT | MARAIS | FRANCE,' and for the inked nu-
merals in the colophon, which are roman.

Published November 5, 1936, for presentation, in an issue of 20
copies of a total edition of 105 copies.

Locations: HS, JME.

Annotations for A 3: "I am sending you separately the script
of the new book.
    While I am uncertain about it, I think that APHORISMS ON SO-
CIETY is a better title than OWL'S CLOVER. OWL'S CLOVER is a good
title, in the sense that, in spite of the owlishness of the poems,
there is still enough poetry in them to justify the title. On the
other hand, while APHORISMS ON SOCIETY is somewhat preten-
tious, it brings out for the reader the element that is common to
all the poems. After you read the group please let me know which
of these titles you prefer." (*Letters*, p. 311: letter to J. Ronald
Lane Latimer, May 16, 1936)

    "Very well, let's stick to OWL'S CLOVER. I enclose a new title
page with that title. The point of this group in any case is to try
to make poetry out of commonplaces: the day's news; and that
surely is owl's clover." (*Letters*, p. 311: letter to Latimer, May
22, 1936)

    "The book sets a standard. It is easy enough to accept a well-
made book without realizing how much has gone into it. I hope
that the reviewers do you justice.
    "The title is merely a phrase of my own. What I mean by it is
that the reader may at last hope to find here and there the plea-

sure of poetry, if not exactly the pleasure of thought. To combine those two things is one of the jobs that lies ahead." (*Letters*, p. 312: letter to Latimer, October 26, 1936)

A 4 THE MAN WITH THE BLUE GUITAR
AND OTHER POEMS

A 4.a
First edition (1937)

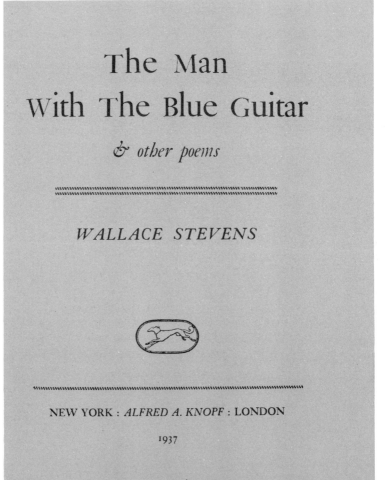

The Man
With The Blue Guitar

& other poems

WALLACE STEVENS

NEW YORK : *ALFRED A. KNOPF* : LONDON

1937

A 4.a: $7^7/_{16} \times 5^1/_{16}$ inches

Collation: [1–6]⁸. Pp. [i–x] [1–2] 3–35 [36–38] 39–72 [73–74] 75–78 [79–80] 81–82 [83–86].

Typography and paper: Set in Linotype Electra and Janson. White laid paper, watermarked with the Borzoi device.

Pagination: p. i: blank; p. ii: '*Also by Wallace Stevens* | HARMONIUM | IDEAS OF ORDER | [nine lines]'; p. iii: half title, 'The Man With The Blue Guitar | *& other poems* | [two ornamental rules]'; p. iv: blank; p. v: title page; p. vi: copyright page; p. vii: acknowledgment, 'Parts of THE MAN WITH THE | BLUE GUITAR appeared in *Poetry:* | *A Magazine of Verse,* and in | *Twentieth Century Verse.* THE | OLD WOMAN AND THE STATUE ap- | peared in *The Southern Review;* | THE STATUE AT THE WORLD'S END, | under a different title, appeared | in *The New Caravan;* A THOUGHT | REVOLVED appeared in *New Direc-* | *tions,* and THE MEN THAT ARE | FALLING appeared in *The Nation.* | [ornamental rule]'; p. viii: blank; p. ix: table of contents; p. x: blank; p. 1: section title, 'The Man With The Blue Guitar'; p. 2: blank; pp. 3–35: text; p. 36: blank; p. 37: section title, 'Owl's Clover'; p. 38: blank; pp. 39–72: text; p. 73: section title, 'A Thought Revolved'; p. 74: blank; pp. 75–78: text; p. 79: section title, 'The Men That Are Falling'; p. 80: blank; pp. 81–82: text; p. 83: blank; p. 84: colophon; pp. 85–86: blank.

Contents: The Man With The Blue Guitar, I–XXXIII – Owl's Clover (I. The Old Woman & the Statue – II. The Statue at the World's End – III. The Greenest Continent – IV. A Duck for Dinner – V. Sombre Figuration) – A Thought Revolved (I. The Mechanical Optimist – II. Mystic Garden & Middling Beast – III. Romanesque Affabulation – IV. The Leader) – The Men That Are Falling.

The version of "Owl's Clover" published here, extensively revised and shortened from the version published in *Owl's Clover,* A 3, contains 607 lines.

Colophon: p. [84]: DESIGNER'S NOTE: This book is printed in | *Electra,* a linotype face designed by William A. | Dwiggins, one of America's leading decorative artists. | A master craftsman and draughtsman, he under- | stands the compulsions, opportunities and limitations | of the machine, and reveals in this type a fusion | of intellectual with mechanic discipline. The title | page, the half title, and the divisional headings are set | in *Janson* type, and the contents page shows a com- | bination of *Janson* with *Electra*. In some of the lines | appear unusual blank spaces and extra-wide spacing of | certain crucial words. By this experimental device the | author wishes to indicate a desirable pause or em- | phasis suggested by the sense. In observing these rests | the reader may feel by so much the closer to the poet's | intention. | [Borzoi device] | Composed, Printed & Bound by H. WOLFF, New York | Paper made by CURTIS & BROTHER, Newark, Del. | Design and Typography by | PAUL STANDARD

Binding and dust jacket: Yellow V cloth, with the Borzoi device stamped in dark blue within a blue circle on the back cover; on the spine, stamped downward in dark blue: '[ornament] The Man With The Blue Guitar: *STEVENS* [ornament]'. Heavy white wove endpapers printed in green and olive with a pattern of the Borzoi device and the words 'BORZOI BOOKS'; top edges trimmed; fore and bottom edges rough trimmed. Yellow dust jacket printed in green. On the front flap of the jacket is a two-paragraph statement by WS about the poems in the book; this statement has not been reprinted elsewhere. There are two printings of the dust jacket: the first has the word "conjunctioning" in the statement by WS on the front flap, line 7 from the bottom; in the second printing of the dust jacket, this line has been reset and the word "conjunctions" substituted for the word "conjunctioning"; see WS's letter of September 16, 1937, to J. R. L. Latimer below.

Published October 4, 1937, at $2.00, in an edition of 1,000 copies.

Locations: Book with first printing of dust jacket: CtY, CU, HS, JME; with second printing of dust jacket: HS, InU, JME; with no dust jacket present: DLC (deposit copy stamped "Oct. 7, 1937").

Annotation: "I am sending a copy of THE MAN WITH THE BLUE GUITAR to you today. It contains no reference to your edition of OWL'S CLOVER. I made a reference to this in a separate paragraph in the acknowledgment, but it was dropped and there was no point to pressing it, since I may want to ask a favor of Mr. Knopf one of these days.

"The only things that I dislike about the book are things that I have had nothing to do with. One is the word *conjunctioning* on the flap of the dust cover. The other is the statement in the designer's note as follows:

In this volume,

which contains Mr. Stevens's most recent work, there are two distinct groups of poems. He writes: "In one group, *Owl's Clover*, while the poems reflect what was then going on in the world, that reflection is merely for the purpose of seizing and stating what makes life intelligible and desirable in the midst of great change and great confusion. The effect of *Owl's Clover* is to emphasize the opposition between things as they are and things imagined; in short, to isolate poetry.

"Since this is of significance, if we are entering a period in which poetry may be of first importance to the spirit, I have been making notes on the subject in the form of short poems during the past winter. These short poems, some thirty of them, form the other group, *The Man with the Blue Guitar*, from which the book takes its title. This group deals with the incessant conjunctionings between things as they are and things imagined. Although the blue guitar is a symbol of the imagination, it is used most often simply as a reference to the individuality of the poet, meaning by the poet any man of imagination."

$2.00
net

In this volume,

which contains Mr. Stevens's most recent work, there are two distinct groups of poems. He writes: "In one group, *Owl's Clover*, while the poems reflect what was then going on in the world, that reflection is merely for the purpose of seizing and stating what makes life intelligible and desirable in the midst of great change and great confusion. The effect of *Owl's Clover* is to emphasize the opposition between things as they are and things imagined; in short, to isolate poetry.

"Since this is of significance, if we are entering a period in which poetry may be of first importance to the spirit, I have been making notes on the subject in the form of short poems during the past winter. These short poems, some thirty of them, form the other group, *The Man with the Blue Guitar*, from which the book takes its title. This group deals with the incessant conjunctionings between things as they are and things imagined. Although the blue guitar is a symbol of the imagination, it is used most often simply as a reference to the individuality of the poet, meaning by the poet any man of imagination."

The Man *with the*
Blue Guitar
& *other poems*

WALLACE STEVENS

ALFRED · A · KNOPF
PUBLISHER NEW YORK

The Man with the Blue Guitar: STEVENS   KNOPF

A 4.a: front and flap of first printing of dust jacket and front flap of second printing. Note line 7 from bottom on the two flaps.

'In some of the lines appear unusual blank spaces *** By this experimental device the author wishes to indicate a desirable pause or emphasis suggested by the sense' etc.

This is pure nonsense. I never said any such thing and have a horror of poetry pretending to be contemporaneous because of typographical queerness. A specimen of this is the poem on page 19. The second and sixth lines of that poem contain their syllables in a relatively few words. For instance, half of the sixth line is in one word. When I read the proofs I said that I thought that the only way of avoiding a very short line was to space between the words. This ordinary solution for an ordinary difficulty becomes 'an experimental device'.

"But it doesn't matter. The printer really did a very good job and his proofs were the best I have ever seen.

"I think the title group would have made a good book for the Alcestis Press, except that the collection was only about half long enough. As it is, all that I care to preserve from what I have done during the last two years is contained in this book." (*Letters*, pp. 325–326: letter to J. Ronald Lane Latimer, September 16, 1937)

A 4.b
Second edition (1945)

The Man
With The Blue Guitar

& other poems

WALLACE STEVENS

NEW YORK: *ALFRED A. KNOPF*

1945

A 4.b: $7^{1}/_{4} \times 4^{13}/_{16}$ inches

Collation: [1–6]⁸. Pp. [i–x] [1–2] 3–35 [36–38] 39–72 [73–74] 75–78 [79–80] 81–82 [83–86].

Typography and paper: Set in Linotype Electra and Janson. White wove paper.

Pagination: The same as A 4.a except for the following: p. ii: 'The Poetry of Wallace Stevens | [fourteen lines]'; p. vi: copyright-page changes as shown in the illustration above.

Contents: The same as A 4.a.

Colophon: p. [84]: The same as A 4.a.

Binding and dust jacket: Smooth maroon V cloth, with the Borzoi device stamped in blind on the back cover; on the spine, stamped downward in gold: '[ornament] The Man With The Blue Guitar: *STEVENS* [ornament]'. Heavy reddish-brown wove endpapers printed in white with a pattern of the Borzoi device and the words 'BORZOI BOOKS'; top edges stained maroon; fore and bottom edges rough trimmed. Ivory dust jacket printed in dark blue; the jacket is the same as the first printing of the A 4.a dust jacket, with the word "conjunctioning" in line 7 from the bottom on the front flap.

Published July 1945, at $2.00, in an edition of 643 copies.

Locations: CU, InU, JME.

A 4.c
Third edition (1952)

The Man

with the Blue Guitar

INCLUDING

Ideas of Order

WALLACE STEVENS

ALFRED · A · KNOPF

NEW YORK

1952

A 4.c: 8³/₈ × 5⁵/₈ inches

Collation: [1]⁸ [2–7]¹⁶. Pp. [*1–4*] [i–vi] vii–ix [x] [*1–2*] 3–47 [48–50] 51–90 [91–92] 93–100 [101–102] 103–105 [106–108] 109–188 [189–194].

Typography and paper: Set in Linotype Janson. White laid paper, watermarked: 'WARREN'S | OLDE STYLE'.

Pagination: pp. *1–3:* blank; p. *4:* 'By | WALLACE STEVENS | [rule] | POEMS | *Harmonium (1923, 1931, 1947)* | *Ideas of Order (1936)* | now included in THE MAN WITH THE BLUE GUITAR | *The Man With the Blue Guitar (1937, 1952)* | includes IDEAS OF ORDER | *Parts of a World (1942, 1951)* | *Transport to Summer* (1947) | *The Auroras of Autumn* (1950) | ESSAYS | *The Necessary Angel:* Essays on Reality | and the Imagination (1951) | THESE ARE BORZOI BOOKS, PUBLISHED BY | *Alfred A. Knopf';* p. i: half title, 'THE MAN WITH THE BLUE GUITAR | [INCLUDING *Ideas of Order*]'; p. ii: blank; p. iii: title page; p. iv: copyright page; p. v: acknowledgment, 'NOTE | Many of the poems in this volume have been printed | before, in *Alcestis, Contemporary Poetry and Prose,* | *Direction, The Harkness Hoot, Hound & Horn, The* | *Nation, The New Act, The New Caravan,* | *New Re-* | *public, Poetry: A Magazine of Verse, Smoke, The* | *Southern Review, Twentieth Century Verse,* and *The* | *Westminster Magazine,* and to the editors of these | publications the author makes his grateful acknowl- | edgments.'; p. vi: blank; pp. vii–ix: table of contents; p. x: blank; p. 1: section title, 'THE MAN WITH THE BLUE GUITAR'; p. 2: blank; pp.

3–47: text; p. 48: blank; p. 49: section title, '[THE MAN WITH THE BLUE GUITAR] | *Owl's Clover';* p. 50: blank; pp. 51–90: text; p. 91: section title, '[THE MAN WITH THE BLUE GUITAR] | *A Thought Revolved';* p. 92: blank; pp. 93–100: text; p. 101: section title, '[THE MAN WITH THE BLUE GUITAR] | *The Men That Are Falling';* p. 102: blank; pp. 103–105: text; p. 106: blank; p. 107: section title, 'IDEAS OF ORDER'; p. 108: blank; pp. 109–188: text; p. 189: blank; p. 190: colophon; pp. 191–194: blank.

Contents: Except for the revised note of acknowledgment, the contents are the same as A 4.a and A 4.b and the 1936 edition of *Ideas of Order* (A 2.b).

Colophon: p. [190]: A NOTE ON THE TYPE IN WHICH | THIS BOOK IS SET | *This book was set on the Linotype in Janson, a recut- | ting made direct from the type cast from matrices made* | by Anton Janson some time between 1660 and 1687. | *Of Janson's origin nothing is known. He may have | been a relative of Justus Janson, a printer of Danish | birth who practiced in Leipzig from 1614 to 1635. Some | time between 1657 and 1668 Anton Janson, a punch- | cutter and type-founder, bought from the Leipzig | printer Johann Erich Hahn the type-foundry which | had formerly been a part of the printing house of | M. Friedrich Lankisch. Janson's types were first shown | in a specimen sheet issued at Leipzig about 1675. | The book was composed, printed and bound by The | Plimpton Press, Norwood, Massachusetts. Typogra- | phy and binding based on original designs by W. A. | Dwiggins.*

Binding and dust jacket: Smooth grayish blue V cloth; floral design stamped in blind on front cover; Borzoi device stamped in blind on back cover; on spine, stamped in gold: '[ornament] | *THE | Man | WITH THE | Blue | Guitar* | INCLUDING | *Ideas of | Order* | WALLACE | STEVENS | [ornament] | *KNOPF.'* White wove endpapers; top edges stained grayish blue; fore and bottom edges rough trimmed. Gray dust jacket printed in maroon, with photograph of WS by John Haley and biographical note on back.

Published February 27, 1952, at $3.50, in an edition of 2,000 copies.

Locations: CLU, CtY, DLC (deposit copy stamped "Jan. 12, 1953"), HS, JME.

Annotation: "Knopf decided to reprint *The Man With The Blue Guitar* and *Ideas of Order* as a single volume to come out next spring. Apparently he is resetting both books. The galley

A 5 PARTS OF A WORLD

A 5.a.1
First printing (1942)

PARTS

OF A WORLD

by

WALLACE STEVENS

ALFRED·A·KNOPF

NEW YORK

1942

A 5.a.1: 8¼ × 5¾ inches

Collation: [1–10]⁸ [11]⁴ [12–13]⁸. Pp. [1–4] [i–vi] vii–ix [x] [1–2] 3–163 [164–166] 167–182 [183–186].

Typography and paper: Set in Linotype Janson. White laid paper.

Pagination: pp. 1–3: blank; p. 4: 'Also by | WALLACE STE- VENS | [rule] | [seven lines]'; p. i: half title, 'PARTS OF A WORLD'; p. ii: blank; p. iii: title page; p. iv: copyright page; p. v: acknowledgment, 'THESE POEMS APPEARED IN | Ac- cent, Compass, Fantasy, Furioso, Harvard Advo- | cate, Hika, Kenyon Review, Nation, New Poetry, | New York Times, Par- tisan Review, Poetry: A | Magazine of Verse, Seven, Southern Review, Twen- | tieth Century Verse.'; p. vi: blank; pp. vii–x: table of contents; p. 1: section title, 'PARTS OF A WORLD'; p. 2: blank; pp. 3–163: text; p. 164: blank; p. 165: section title, 'EXAMINATION OF THE HERO | IN A TIME OF WAR'; p. 166: blank; pp. 167–183: text; p. 184: colophon: pp. 185–186: blank.

Contents: Parochial Theme – Poetry Is a Destructive Force – The Poems of Our Climate – Prelude to Objects – Study of Two Pears – The Glass of Water – Add This to Rhetoric – Dry Loaf – Idiom of the Hero – The Man on the Dump – On the Road Home – The Latest Freed Man – United Dames of America – Country Words – The Dwarf – A Rabbit as King of the Ghosts – Loneliness in Jersey City – Anything Is Beautiful If You Say It Is – A Weak Mind in the Mountains – The Bagatelles the Madrigals – Girl in a Nightgown – Connoisseur of Chaos – The Blue Buildings in the Summer Air – Dezembrum – Poem Written at Morning – Life on a Battleship – The Woman That Had More Babies Than That – Thunder by the Musician – The Common Life – The Sense of the Sleight-Of-Hand Man – The Candle A Saint – A Dish of Peaches in Russia – Arcades of Philadelphia the Past – Of Hart- ford in a Purple Light – Cuisine Bourgeoise – Forces, the Will & the Weather – On an Old Horn – Bouquet of Belle Scavior – Variations on a Summer Day—Yellow Afternoon—Martial Cadenza—Man and Bottle—Of Modern Poetry—Arrival at the Waldorf—Landscape with Boat—On the Adequacy of Landscape—Les Plus Belles Pages—Poem with Rhythms—Woman Looking at a Vase of Flowers—The Well Dressed Man with a Beard—Of Bright & Blue Birds & the Gala Sun—Mrs. Alfred Uruguay—Asides on the Oboe—Extracts from Addresses to the Academy of Fine Ideas—Montrachet-le-Jardin—The News and the Weather—Metamorphosis—Contrary Theses (I)—Phosphor Reading by His Own Light—The Search for Sound Free from Motion—Jumbo—Contrary Theses (II)—The Hand as a Being—Oak Leaves Are Hands—Examination of the Hero in a Time of War—[a prose statement on the relationship of poetry and war, signed 'W.S.']

Colophon: p. [184]: A NOTE ON THE TYPE IN WHICH | THIS BOOK IS SET | *This book was set on the Linotype in Janson, a | recutting made direct from the type cast from | matrices (now in possession of the Stempel | foundry, Frankfurt am Main) made by Anton | Janson some time between 1660 and 1687. | Of Janson's origin nothing is known. He may | have been a relative of Justus Janson, a printer of | Danish birth who practised in Leipzig from 1614 | to 1635. Some time between 1657 and 1668 Anton | Janson, a punch-cutter and type-founder, bought | from the Leipzig printer Johann Erich Hahn the | type-foundry which had formerly been a part of | the printing house of M. Friedrich Lankisch. | Janson's types were first shown in a specimen | sheet issued at Leipzig about 1675. Janson's suc- | cessor, and perhaps his son-in-law, Johann Karl | Edling, issued a specimen sheet of Janson types | in 1689. His heirs sold the Janson matrices in | Holland to Wolffgang Dietrich Erhardt.* | COMPOSED, PRINTED, AND BOUND BY | THE PLIMPTON PRESS, NORWOOD, MASS. | THE BINDING IS AFTER DESIGNS BY | W. A. DWIGGINS

Binding and dust jacket: Smooth blue S cloth; a floral design stamped in blind on front cover; the Borzoi device stamped in blind on back cover; on spine, stamped in gold: '[ornament] | *Parts | of a | World* | WALLACE | STEVENS | [ornament] | *Knopf.*' White laid endpapers; top edges trimmed; fore and bottom edges rough trimmed. Ivory dust jacket, printed in black, on the front, attribute to WS by Gorham Munson; on the back, quotations from reviews of earlier books by WS; on the back flap, information about savings bonds and stamps and an appeal to give the book to a USO library after reading.

Published September 8, 1942, at $2.00, in a printing of 1,000 copies.

A 5.a.2
Second printing (1945)

PARTS

OF A WORLD

by

WALLACE STEVENS

ALFRED·A·KNOPF

NEW YORK

1945

A 5.a.2: $7^{1}/_{4} \times 4^{7}/_{8}$ inches

Except for the date '1945' on the title page, the title page, collation, typography, and paper are the same as A 5.a.1.

Pagination: The same as A 5.a.1 with the following changes:
p. 3: 'TO THE *Purchaser* | of this Book, from its Publisher: − |
ALL PAPER, *including the paper on which books are* | *printed,
as well as the materials which go into the man-* | *ufacture of
paper, is absolutely essential to the prosecu-* | *tion of the war.*
| [double-column list: twenty-three lines in the left column,
twenty-four lines in the right, concerning book-production policy
in time of war] | [facsimile signature of Alfred A. Knopf]'; p. iv:
copyright-page changes as shown in the illustration above.

Binding and dust jacket: Except for S cloth of a much lighter
blue, the binding is the same as A 5.a.1. Except for reduced size
to conform with the book, the dust jacket is the same as A 5.a.1.

Published May 1945, at $2.00, in a printing of 500 copies.

Location: InU, JME.

A 5.a.3
Third printing (1951)

Except for the date '1951' on the title page, the title page, collation, typography, and paper are the same as A 5.a.1.

Pagination: The same as A 5.a.1 with the following change:
p. iv: following the copyright statement, 'PUBLISHED SEP-

TEMBER 8, 1942 | SECOND PRINTING, MAY 1945 | THIRD
PRINTING, JUNE 1951'.

Binding and dust jacket: Except for smooth red cloth and top
edges stained red, the binding is the same as A 5.a.1. White dust
jacket, printed in black; on the front: 'Awarded the Bollingen
Prize in Poetry | of the Yale University Library | for 1949 | Winner
of the 1950 National Book Award | for Poetry.'; on the back,
biographical information of WS by John Haley.

Note: The publisher's binding record shows that only 1,000
copies of this printing were bound in red cloth; it is assumed by
the publisher that the remainder of the sheets were destroyed.

Published June 1951, at $3.00, in a printing of 1,500 copies.

Locations: CL, RPB.

A 6.a: on left-hand page, circle in yellow, rules in gray; on right-hand page, circle in yellow, rule in gray; $8^{5}/_{8} \times 5^{3}/_{4}$ inches

A 6 NOTES TOWARD A SUPREME FICTION

A 6.a
First edition (1942)

Unsigned issue (1 to 190)

Collation: [1–6]⁴. Pp. [i–ii] [1–6] 7 [8–9] 10–19 [20–21] 22–31 [32–33] 34–43 [44] 45 [46].

Typography and paper: Set in Centaur. White laid "Dutch Charcoal" paper.

Pagination: pp. i–ii: blank; p. 1: half title, 'Notes | toward a Supreme Fiction'; pp. 2–3: double title page; p. 4: copyright page; p. 5: dedication, 'To | Henry Church'; p. 6: blank; p. 7: opening stanza, 'AND FOR what, except for you, do I feel love?'; p. 8 '[open circle in yellow] | [thin slanted rule, in gray]'; p. 9: section title, 'It must be abstract | [thin slanted rule, in gray, continued from p. 8]'; pp. 10–19: text; p. 20: '[open circle, in yellow] | [thick rule, in gray]'; p. 21: section title, '[three rules in gray] | It must change | [solid circle in yellow] | [rule in gray] | [solid circle in yellow]'; pp. 22–31: text; p. 32: '[two rules, one thick, one thin, in gray] | [open circle in yellow] | [very thick rule in gray]'; p. 33: section title, 'It must give pleasure' | [two thin rules in gray] | [solid circle in yellow] | [thick rule in gray]'; pp. 34–43: text; p. 44: blank; p. 45: closing stanza, 'SOLDIER, there is a war between the mind'; p. 46: colophon.

Contents: [Opening stanza] AND FOR what, except for you, do I feel love? – It must be abstract – It must change – It must give pleasure. [Closing stanza] SOLDIER, there is a war between the mind.

Colophon: p. [46]: Notes toward a Supreme Fiction | has been hand-set in Centaur types & printed for the first time | by hand on dampened all-rag papers: 190 copies numbered 1 to 190 on Dutch Charcoal, 80 copies numbered I to LXXX | signed by the author on Worthy Hand & Arrows, & 3 copies | lettered A to C on Highclere, an English hand-made paper. | The title-pages are from designs by Alessandro Giampietro. | Completed at Cummington, Massachusetts, September, 1942. | This is copy number [arabic numerals in ink] | [abstract design within a circle by Herman Maril]

Binding and dust jacket: Smooth white V cloth; stamped in black on front cover: 'Notes | toward a Supreme Fiction | Wallace Stevens'; on the back cover, stamped in gray around the four edges of the cover, the first two lines and the last two lines of the closing stanza of the book; on the spine, stamped upward in black: 'Wallace Stevens Notes toward a Supreme Fiction.' Heavy gray laid endpapers, watermarked: 'Hamilton's Victorian'; top edges trimmed; fore and bottom edges untrimmed. Unprinted glassine dust jacket.

Published October 13, 1942, at $3.00, in an issue of 190 copies of a total edition of 273 copies.

Reprinting: Reprinted in A 11; A 19; *CP*, A 23; and *Palm*, A 30.

Locations: CtY, DLC (deposit copy stamped "Oct. 20, 1942"), HS, JME.

Signed issue (I to LXXX)
This issue varies from the unsigned one in the following particulars: the paper is white laid "Worthy Hand & Arrows," watermarked: '[a hand clutching four arrows] | WORTHY.' The colophon is identical except the numerals are written in roman and signed by WS between the numerals and the design.

Published October 13, 1942, at $4.50, in an issue of 80 copies of a total edition of 273 copies.

Locations: CtY, HS, JME.

Signed issue (A to C)
This issue varies from the other two only in one line of the colophon: 'This is copy [printed letter] | [WS's signature in ink],' and in the paper, which is handmade "Highclere" and "English" and is unwatermarked.

Published October 13, 1942, for presentation, in an issue of 3 copies of a total edition of 273 copies.

Note: Although it has been reported that copies A to C were for presentation, copy B, in the possession of Mr. William T. Ford, bears no presentation inscription.

Correspondence between The Cummington Press and WS indicates that there was a special copy for Henry Church, to whom the book was dedicated; whether this was copy A or a copy out of series is not known.

Location: William T. Ford.

Annotations for A 6.a: "I am sending off the manuscript of NOTES, etc., under separate cover. Since I am sending this off almost immediately after it has been typed, it is possible that as I go over it I may want to change a word or two. But if I do, any inconvenience that that may cause ought to be more than balanced by the convenience of having the whole thing on which to start work whenever you like. [. . .]

"You will observe that I have not included an introductory note. I don't like explanations; the chances are that poems are very much better off in the long run without explanations. You will also observe that I have not included an index of first lines. This seems to me to be undesirable.

"A word about the appearance of the book. This again is something about which you have everything to say, and I don't want to do more than suggest that, instead of a book dark in appearance like Blackmur's book, with its dark binding and blue initials, I like things that are light: for instance, a light tan linen or buckram cover. If there are to be colored initials, then I very much prefer red and green to blue. I think this will give you the idea. Let me say that I have been thinking that it might be nice to have on the back outside cover of the book a border consisting of a line or two of the poem beginning 'Soldier, there is a war' etc: enough to state the idea. This is to be entirely as you wish; if you don't like the idea, don't give it a second thought. If you do like it, but don't like the expense, let me know how much it will cost and I shall no doubt be glad to pay it myself. In short, I am sufficiently interested in this as a book to contribute, if necessary, a little something in addition to the poems themselves. This remark is to apply not only to the suggestion that I have just made, but if you don't like that suggestion and have another one to make, then it is to apply to your own suggestion.

"When the book has been printed, I should like to have an unbound copy for myself, to be bound specially." (*Letters*, p. 408: letter to Katharine Frazier, June 1, 1942)

"The text for the border is satisfactory. So is the idea of binding the book in white, provided it is not a white that picks up every thumbprint and fly leg and mosquito head." (Unpublished letter from WS to Katharine Frazier, August 11, 1942)

"The book is a delight. I think that I prefer the copy on Dutch Charcoal, as you do, and I have sent that copy to Gerhard Gerlach in New York to bind. He was a pupil of Wiemüller and is as good a binder as I know of. Besides, he has a small stock of decent leather, which is more than one might say for every binder. [. . .]

"As I understand it, the copy that I am sending to Mr. Gerlach is to be a gift from the PRESS, and I can only say *thanks*. All the other copies, including the special copy to Mr. Church and the five copies to be sent to him directly and fifteen more copies to be sent to me, are to be paid for. I haven't the slightest idea whether there is any difference in the prices." (*Letters*, p. 419: letter to Katharine Frazier, September 17, 1942)

"I ought to have written to thank you for your wire, but put off doing so because I expected to be able to be a little more definite about the appearance of the NOTES, etc. It looks as if this ought to be published this week. It has been at the binders where there was the delay which seems to be indigenous in all binderies.

"I am going to send you a copy on specially good paper (if all goes well) for the living room and then a few other copies for bedroom, bath and kitchen. In any event, I should like one of the extra copies to go to Allen Tate, if you can find it convenient to send it to him. He sent me one of his own books some time ago and I shall be pleased to have him receive a copy of NOTES, etc. This is merely a sort of advance notice, because the books may come at a time when it is not convenient to write. Everything seems to turn up here on Saturdays, when the office is closed." (*Letters*, p. 420: letter to Henry Church, September 28, 1942)

A 6.b
Second edition [1943]

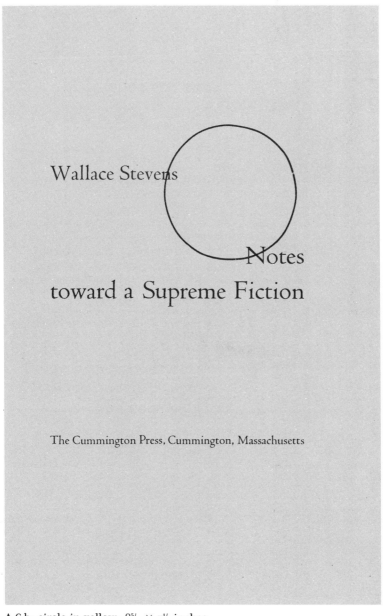

Wallace Stevens

Notes

toward a Supreme Fiction

The Cummington Press, Cummington, Massachusetts

A 6.b: circle in yellow; 8⁵/₁₆ × 5¹/₂ inches

Copyright 1942 by Wallace Stevens

This second edition of Notes toward a Supreme Fiction
is limited to three-hundred-thirty copies set up by hand in
Centaur types and printed at Cummington, Massachusetts
during August and September, 1943.

Collation: [1–4]⁶. Pp. [i–ii] [1–6] 7 [8–9] 10–19 [20–21] 22–31 [32–33] 34–43 [44] 45 [46].

Typography and paper: Set in Centaur. White wove paper, watermarked: 'ANDRIA'.

Pagination: pp. i–ii: blank; p. 1: half title, 'Notes | toward a Supreme Fiction'; p. 2: blank; p. 3: title page; p. 4: copyright page; p. 5: dedication, 'To | Henry Church'; p. 6: blank; p. 7: opening stanza, 'AND FOR what, except for you, do I feel love?'; p. 8: blank; p. 9: section title, in black, preceded by a solid circle, in yellow, 'It must be abstract'; pp. 10–19: text; p. 20: blank; p. 21: section title, in black, preceded by a solid circle, in yellow, 'It must change'; pp. 22–31: text; p. 32: blank; p. 33: section title, in black, preceded by a solid circle, in yellow, 'It must give pleasure'; pp. 34–43: text; p. 44: blank; p. 45: closing stanza, 'SOLDIER, there is a war between the mind'; p. 46: blank.

Contents: The same as A 6.a with the substitution of 'This was . . .' for 'There was . . .' in line 7, p. 37.

Colophon: p. [4]: This second edition of Notes toward a Supreme Fiction | is limited to three-hundred-thirty copies set up by hand in | Centaur types and printed at Cummington, Massachusetts | during August and September, 1943.

Binding and dust jacket: Gray paper-covered boards; yellow V cloth spine, stamped upward in black: 'Wallace Stevens Notes toward a Supreme Fiction'. White wove endpapers; top edges trimmed; fore edges untrimmed; bottom edges rough trimmed. Tissue dust jacket.

Published November 1943, at $2.00, in an edition of 330 copies.

Locations: CtY, HS, JME.

Annotations: "The mood to make changes in the NOTES has gone by, and I am now thinking about other things. There is one mistake that ought to be corrected: Line 7 on page 37 begins: 'there was'; this should be changed to 'This was'. Somewhere else in the text there is an error in punctuation, as I remember

it, but I couldn't find this last evening and I may be wrong."
(Unpublished letter from WS to Katharine Frazier, May 20, 1943)

"Next Wednesday or Thursday we'll begin printing the second
edition of Notes toward a Supreme Fiction. Did you ever re-
discover that other typographical error? Or are there any changes
you'd like to make in the poem?

"The new edition will try to sell for a little less than did the
other, and will not be printed by hand on damp paper. I hope,
however, that the binding at least will be an improvement, for
we've at last found a paper that is exactly the shade of yellow
we'd wanted before. We'd like to incorporate any change, whether
in text or design, that you'd like to see." (Unpublished letter
from Harry Duncan to WS, August 6, 1943)

"Thank you for your increased order for the new edition of
Notes toward a Supreme Fiction. Our binder is having trouble,
with materials and labor, so that the book has been held up quite
long. Also the paper, which was exactly the yellow for the cover,
is no longer made, and although we tried long and desperately to
match it, we could not. Therefore the binding is one of exigency,
for the most part." (Unpublished letter from Harry Duncan to
WS, October 4, 1943)

"The books have come. I think they are very trim, even though
rather prim, and I like the job, if I may call it that, immensely.
Thanks for the pains you have taken." (Unpublished letter from
WS to Harry Duncan, October 28, 1943)

A 7 EPITAPHIANA
[1943]

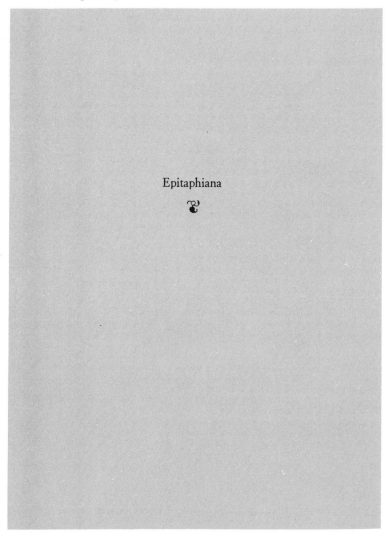

Epitaphiana

A 7: cover title; ornament in red; 7½ × 5½ inches

Collation: Single fold. Pp. [1–4].

Typography and paper: Set in Centaur. White wove paper.

Pagination: p. 1: cover title; p. 2: blank; p. 3: text; p. 4: blank.

Contents: Three paragraphs of prose by WS concerning family history and genealogy, written to accompany a portfolio of photographs of Pennsylvania landscapes taken by Sylvia Salmi.

Text: Because of the rarity of *Epitaphiana*, the complete text is given here, with the permission of Holly Stevens:

> For almost two hundred years the Stevens family was associated with the North and Southampton Reformed Church at Churchville, in Bucks County, Pennsylvania. The first few photographs are photographs of the exterior and interior of the present building of that church and of the cemetery adjoining it. The church was organized in 1710. Its first ministers were sent out from Holland and preached in Dutch to what were essentially Dutch congregations. Its early records were in Dutch.
>
> The first Stevens in Bucks County, Abraham, was active in the church. His son John (recorded as Johannes) married Saartje Stoothof there in 1763. Their grandson, Benjamin Stevens, was superintendent of its Sunday School for forty years. Benjamin Stevens' grandson, also Benjamin Stevens, had the gold-headed cane that was presented to his grandfather when he gave up his work in the Sunday School, and this is now in the possession of his daughter. The church was a vital center for all of them. Benjamin Stevens and his wife, Elizabeth Barcalow, and her parents, Garret Barcalow and his wife, Eleanor Hogeland, and many of their relatives and friends, are buried in this cemetery. A history of the church was printed in a pamphlet issued in 1935. The original Dutch burial ground was not at Churchville but at Feasterville. Here some of the Kroesens and John Stevens and his wife, Saartje Stoothof, are buried. At least one picture of this ancient burial ground is included here. References to these cemeteries in the genealogy of the Stevens family are, of course, based on actual visits by the genealogist.
>
> The photographs were made in October, 1943, by Sylvia Salmi, of New York, who spent several days in Bucks County for that purpose. The landscapes are not pictures of Stevens farms, but merely show the kind of country in which the members of the family spent their lives.
>
> WALLACE STEVENS

Printed November 1943; not for sale; about ten copies. The text has not been published elsewhere.

Locations: HS (pamphlet and portfolio), JME (pamphlet only).

Annotations: "Last week a woman from New York went down to Churchville and made some photographs for me and now, with these and with the copies of the daguerreotypes, and, finally, with your work, I shall have everything." (Unpublished letter from WS to Mrs. Lila James Roney, a professional genealogist employed by WS, October 21, 1943)

"I have a half dozen photographs, or shall have shortly, for which I want to find some kind of container that will keep them clean, preserve them and keep them in shape. [. . .] These are photographs of places in Bucks County, Pa. I have only spoken of having one set, but, as a matter of fact, I shall have three or four sets. [. . .] The container must be something fastidious; the mere fact that it is fastidious is what will interest people in taking care of it to take care of its contents." (Unpublished letter from WS to Harry Duncan at The Cummington Press, October 30, 1943)

A 8 STEVENS FAMILY PORTRAITS
[*1943*]

STEVENS FAMILY
PORTRAITS
———

A 8: cover title; rule in brown; $13^7/_8 \times 11^1/_2$ inches

Collation: Two single leaves, printed on rectos only in black with brown vertical flared rules on either side of the text on each leaf.

Typography and paper: Set in Centaur. White wove paper.

Pagination: Recto of leaf 1: text; verso of leaf 1: blank; recto of leaf 2: text; verso of leaf 2: blank.

Contents: On recto of leaf 1 is a numbered list of eighteen members of the Stevens family whose portraits are included in the portfolio of photographs accompanying this text; on recto of leaf 2 is a two-paragraph commentary by WS on the portraits.

Text: Because of the rarity of *Stevens Family Portraits,* the list of family members and the commentary by WS are given here, with the permission of Holly Stevens:

1. JAN STRYKER

2. GARRET BARCALOW

3. ELEANOR HOGELAND BARCALOW
(wife of Garret Barcalow)

4. ELEANOR HOGELAND BARCALOW

5. BENJAMIN STEVENS
(seated)

6. BENJAMIN STEVENS

7. ELIZABETH STEVENS
(wife of Benjamin Stevens)

8. ELIZABETH STEVENS

9. ELSIE ROADS
(sister of Benjamin Stevens)

10. ELEANOR B. FINNEY
(sister of Elizabeth Stevens)

11. JOHN BARCALOW
(brother of Elizabeth Stevens)

12. GARRET BARCALOW STEVENS
(as a young man)

13. GARRET BARCALOW STEVENS

14. MARGARETHA CATHERINE STEVENS
(wife of Garret Barcalow Stevens)

15. JAMES VAN SANT STEVENS
(brother of Garret Barcalow Stevens)

16. ISAAC BENNET

17. MARIA STEVENS
(as a girl, wife of Isaac Bennet)

18. MRS. JANE BERGEN

The portrait of *Jan Stryker* is from a painting by his brother in the National Gallery at Washington. The portrait of *Mrs. Barcalow* with a book, the one of *Elizabeth Stevens* with headdress, and that of *Elsie Roads* are from daguerreotypes and ambrotypes in the possession of Emma Jobbins of New Brunswick, who has a large number of these. The other photographs have been copied from originals in three albums, one of which belonged to Elizabeth Stevens, the wife of Benjamin Stevens, the second to her daughter, Maria Bennet, the wife of Isaac Bennet, and the third to Mrs. Bennet's daughter Emma. Of these three albums the first two are now owned by Mrs. Jobbins and the third by Jane Stone, of Philadelphia. These albums contain many photographs of members of the family and their friends. The portrait of *Mrs. Barcalow* is the earliest Hogeland portrait available; that of her husband is the earliest Barcalow portrait available. The portrait of *Mrs. Roads*, taken with that of *Benjamin Stevens*, her brother, are the two earliest Stevens portraits available. The portrait of *Mrs. Bergen* has been included as that of one of the friends of Benjamin and Elizabeth Stevens. It is from a photograph in the album that belonged to Elizabeth Stevens.

Comments respecting the subjects of these photographs will be found in the genealogy of the Stevens family, except in the case of Mrs. Bergen, and nothing, therefore, is included here. Mrs. Bergen was Jane Wyckoff, the wife of Garret Bergen of Brooklyn. One of her sons was Teunis G. Bergen. His work on the Bergen family contains portraits of people and pictures of houses that were no doubt familiar to Benjamin and Elizabeth Stevens. Mrs. Bergen's children were the grandchildren of Johanna Stoothof, and Benjamin Stevens and his generation were grandchildren of Johanna's sister, Saartje Stoothof.

Binding: The two leaves are in a folder of heavy tan wove paper; cover title.

Printed late November or early December 1943; not for sale; six copies.

Locations: HS (portfolio and folder); JME (folder only).

Annotations: "I have had copies made of a number of portraits of members of my family. There are 18 of these; they are all mounted on mats. [. . .] Here, again, I want to have these preserved, but in this case I have had drop boxes made with which I am perfectly satisfied because these pictures are mounted. [. . .] There ought to be in each one of these boxes [. . .] a list of the names of the subjects of the portraits with about a page of comment. Instead of typing this, I wonder whether it wouldn't be possible to have it set up and printed, even though there would be only three or four copies. [. . .] There would be 18 names on one page and, in addition, there would be a page or less of comment on the origin of the portraits. [. . .] These two sheets, one containing the names and the other containing the comments, should be enclosed in another folded sheet. [. . .] Is this something you could do? Of course, large pages would require larger than ordinary type. What would it be likely to cost?" (Unpublished letter from WS to Harry Duncan at The Cummington Press, October 30, 1943)

"Inclosed are proofs of the sheets for the collection of portraits. On the outside cover, in caps a little larger, will be STEVENS FAMILY | PORTRAITS. I note you'd like Charing and the tan cover paper. Decorations, I think, will be simply long swelling dashes, and on either side of the two text pages, and smaller ones below and above the legend on the cover. I've taken some liberties with your copy, namely in the use of italics – this was exigent, for I had not enough roman sorts. And also I've added the parentheses, thinking they give more movement to the page, and so perhaps more vitality. The colors will be black for the letters and brown for the decorations. This will require two runs, and since you've given me some lee-way, I'm going to make them; but they'll make the cost fifteen dollars. Is that satisfactory?" (Unpublished letter from Harry Duncan to WS, November 20, 1943)

"The proofs are everything that I could have hoped for. There are no corrections. I think I asked for only three or four of these; we had better make it half a dozen. The list of names seems to me to be extremely well done. The cost is quite all right; don't give it a thought if that is all that it is going to cost." (Unpublished letter from WS to Harry Duncan, November 20, 1943)

"Today the 'Stevens Family Portraits' folder with sheets is being sent you, six copies via parcel post. I could have sent them before, but since they've been completed I've been assailed by considerable doubts. Finally deciding, though, that you should be the final judge, I send them with a request: that if they should be in any way unsatisfactory you'll give me the chance to do it again better. I think $15 is quite a lot for these, but we have ·really put that much into them." (Unpublished letter from Harry Duncan to WS, December 7, 1943)

"Have I told you that the list of portraits, etc. reached me safely? There was a long delay, but it turned up." (Unpublished letter from WS to Harry Duncan, December 22, 1943)

A 9 DESCRIPTION WITHOUT PLACE
(1945)

Description Without Place

BY

WALLACE STEVENS

[Read by the author as the Phi Beta Kappa poem
at Harvard University in June, 1945]

Reprinted from the October Number of

The Sewanee Review

1945

A 9: cover title; 9¼ × 6⅛ inches

Collation: [1]⁴. Pp. [1–8].

Typography and paper: Set in Linotype Caslon. White wove paper, watermarked: 'SUEDE | D [within a diamond] | FINISH'.

Pagination: pp. 1–7: text; p. 8: blank.

Contents: The poem "Description Without Place" as first published in *The Sewanee Review,* C 158.

Binding: Semistiff buff paper wrapper; printed in black on wrapper front. Stapled; all edges trimmed.

Distributed as an offprint from *The Sewanee Review* for October 1945 (see C 158); not for sale; number of copies unknown.

Locations: CtY, HS, JME.

A 10 ESTHÉTIQUE DU MAL
(1945)

Unsigned issue (1 to 300)

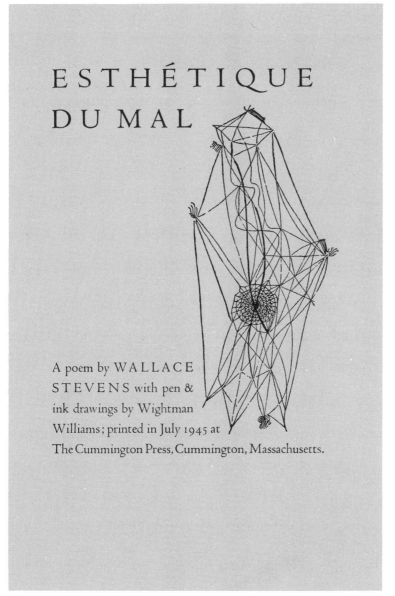

ESTHÉTIQUE
DU MAL

A poem by WALLACE
STEVENS with pen &
ink drawings by Wightman
Williams; printed in July 1945 at
The Cummington Press, Cummington, Massachusetts.

A 10: drawing in brown; $9^9/_{16} \times 6^5/_{16}$ inches

Collation: [1–6]². Pp. [1–24].

Typography and paper: Set in Centaur. Illustrated with sixteen drawings, including one on title page, printed in brown. White laid "Pace paper," watermarked: 'P [with flower above] | Pace'.

Pagination: pp 1–2: blank; p. 3: half title, 'Esthétique | du Mal', with capital *E* printed in brown; p. 4: blank; p. 5: title page; p. 6: copyright page; pp. 7–21: text, with accompanying drawings, printed in brown; p. 22: acknowledgment, *'Acknowledgment | is tendered The Kenyon Review.'*; p. 23: colophon; p. 24: blank.

Contents: The poem "Esthétique du Mal" as first published in *The Kenyon Review*, C 152.

Colophon: p. [23]: *Of this book | three hundred forty copies | have been printed from Centaur types, | those numbered 1 to 300 on Pace paper from Italy | & the others, i to xl, signed by author & artist | with the drawings colored by hand, | on Van Gelder wove paper | from the Netherlands. | This copy is* [arabic numerals in ink]

Binding and dust jacket: Two bindings of the unsigned issue can be identified:

1. The majority of the copies are in green "Natsume" straw-paper-covered boards; stamped in gold on front: 'ESTHÉ- | TIQUE | DU | MAL', with black morocco spine. White laid endpapers of the same stock as sheets; top edges rough trimmed; fore and bottom edges untrimmed. Unprinted glassine dust jacket.

2. A few copies, including one which was WS's own, are in rose "Natsume" straw-paper-covered boards; all other particulars of the binding and dust jacket are the same as no. 1; see Harry Duncan's letter of November 17, 1945, to WS below.

Published November 6, 1945, at $5.00, in an issue of 300 copies of a total edition of 340 copies.

Locations: First binding: CtY, DLC (deposit copy stamped "Dec. 11, 1945"), HS, InU, JME; second binding: HS.

Signed issue (i to xl)
The title page is the same as the unsigned issue except for the

drawings, which are printed in black and hand colored in pink, green, and yellow.

Collation: The same as the unsigned issue.

Typography and paper: The typography is the same as the unsigned issue except that the sixteen drawings, including the one on the title page, are printed in black and hand colored in pink, green, and yellow. White "Van Gelder wove paper," watermarked: 'VAN GELDER ZONEN | HOLLAND'.

Pagination: The same as the unsigned issue, except for the following: p. 3: half title, 'Esthétique | du Mal', with the capital *E* decorated by hand in pink; pp. 7–21: text, with a drawing printed in black and hand colored in pink, green, and yellow on each of these pages and the initial capital letter hand decorated in pink, green, or yellow on each page.

Colophon: p. [23]: The same as that in the unsigned issue, except that the inked numerals are printed in roman and following them are the signatures of, first, WS and, second, Wightman Williams.

Binding and dust jacket: White paper-covered boards, hand colored in vertical yellow and green stripes; stamped in gold on front: 'ESTHE- | TIQUE | DU | MAL', with black morocco spine. Pink laid endpapers; top edges rough trimmed; fore and bottom edges untrimmed. Unprinted glassine dust jacket.

Published November 6, 1945, at $12.50, in an issue of 40 copies of a total edition of 340 copies.

Locations: HS, JME.

Annotations for A 10: "So far as I am concerned, I shall be glad to have you go ahead [with *Esthétique du Mal*]; to be explicit about it, I waive any royalty. This assumes that the edition is to be a limited edition. If you expect to make any money on the book, put it into the book itself, to the cost of which I should even be glad to contribute a little, if that would make the difference between what you would like to do and what it might otherwise be necessary to do.

"The KENYON REVIEW text is correct; if there is anything wrong, I shall pick it up on the proofs, but the KENYON REVIEW proofs were very well done and I think that everything in the text is as it ought to be." (Unpublished letter from WS to Harry Duncan at The Cummington Press, March 2, 1945)

"Finally, a little bit of gossip in which you may be interested is that the Cummington people are going to publish ESTHETIQUE DU MAL, with drawings by Paul [Wightman] Williams. I don't know Mr. Williams but I have seen the drawings, which remind me of an advertisement over the entrance of one of the movie places here which is showing The Picture of Dorian Gray. The advertisement is 'Wilde and Weird'." (*Letters*, p. 498: letter to Allen Tate, May 2, 1945)

"If I were you, I should charge $5 for unsigned copies and $10 for signed copies. People expect to pay more for books now-a-days. [. . .] After all, a collector would be disappointed not to have to pay a little bit out of the ordinary. Personally, I should like to see the book well bound, and my agreement to pay for the cost of the binding, if necessary, is of course good. Yet I think you ought to have a chance to get your cost back with a profit. If you net $3.50 on 260 copies, or $910, and if, in addition, you sell 30 copies at $10, you will take in $1210.00 against an estimated cost of $793.37, which will be more before it is less. I must say that that seems to me to be very little.

"I don't like the idea of green or purple ink in the text: in fact, I cannot even imagine purple. Green is possible, but why not black, with colored initials? I cannot think of a decent book that I have in which the text is printed in colored ink, and I am strongly against it. *However, I leave the make-up of the book to you.* I have at home a book in French which contains a great variety of different colored papers, with the text in different colored inks, which I shall be glad to let you have a look at, if you think it would help you to make up your mind. Books in colored inks are trivial and undignified, or so it seems to me. After all, we are trying to produce a living book and not a *bijou*. I hope you won't mind my saying these things." (*Letters*, p. 503: letter to Harry Duncan, June 11, 1945)

"The unsigned copies of Esthetique du Mal have been at the binder's for some time. We were able, after a long search, to find some black sheepskin, quite satisfactory for the backs. The copies to be signed are still here, however, because it is taking Mr. Williams an unpredictably long time to color the drawings. Since these copies are half-sold already at the advance of $8.00, it would seem advisable to make the price after publication more than we'd originally reckoned; only so can Mr. Williams be paid for these additional labors. Would $12.50 be all right with you? They are very likely to sell at that, for Mr. Williams is also decorating the cover-papers by hand, making the gayest exterior we've put on a book." (Unpublished letter from Harry Duncan to WS, August 24, 1945)

"Esthétique du Mal" has just come back from the bindery, and we are sending you today, by parcel post, some of the books. These include those you ordered and paid for, packaged by themselves, and twenty copies to sign and return. Except for your five, the signed ones aren't completely colored. Mr. Williams is retaining fifteen of these here to work on while the others are away, and these will be sent for your signature later.

"No book, I think, that we printed before has given us continuously so much pleasure all along the line. The binder's delay did cause some anxiety, that's all. I hope that even a little of our appreciation is shown in the book itself." (Unpublished letter from Harry Duncan to WS, November 6, 1945)

"The books are marvelous. I cannot tell you how pleased I am by them. I had made a list of people to whom I wanted to send copies. Now that I have the books, I think I shall have to throw the list away. At least, I am going to keep all of them for a while, until I am quite sure that they go to people who are good enough for them.

"It was very easy to make a fuss over Mr. Williams' part of the job, but I showed No. 1 and also one of the ordinary copies to one of the men here who has a great deal to do with that sort of thing and he was just as much pleased by the other parts of it.

"For my own part, I have nothing to say but that I am grateful to both of you. At the present time, when everything is in such a funk, this book has done more for my own reconversion than anything else that I can think of." (*Letters*, pp. 515–516: letter to Harry Duncan, November 8, 1945)

"Five others [copies of *Esthétique du Mal*] will be mailed to you on Monday. One of these is covered with rose paper, not with the green. [. . .] Only a few copies have it, all the available green paper not quite being enough for the entire edition. [. . .] I should have mentioned above that the name of the paper covering the unsigned copies is called Natsume." (Unpublished letter from Harry Duncan to WS, November 17, 1945)

"I am sending off a copy of the book I spoke of in my last letter today. The back of it is bound in sheep, as you will see at a glance, because there was nothing else available. This is one of the plain copies. There is another edition in which the drawings have been colored. I think that if you have any interest in the book at all you will be interested in one of the plain copies. For an American book, this might be called a cheerful job. I think the title page is nice and I think that the drawings have been placed well. Nevertheless, I shall be interested to know what you, yourself, think not about the poetry, but about the book. What you say would be of value, of course, only if you said what you meant; that is to say, if you do not really like the thing, what would be interesting would be why." (*Letters*, pp. 518–519: letter to James Guthrie, November 23, 1945)

"Although the official announcement to the public hasn't been made and so secrecy is supposed to be kept, I think you should know that Esthétique du Mal has been chosen by The American Institute of Graphic Arts as one of the Fifty Books of 1946. They profess to judge the books for their printing, binding, and illustrations alone, without considering the text except as it presents special problems to these. This method seems to me nonsense: I can't see how printing can be judged apart from its interpretation of the text, and sometimes it may be the text, precisely, on which a printer relies. We so relied on your poem. We could not have printed any other poem in the same way, any more than Mr. Williams could have made the illustrations he did for another text; and it is patent that whatever of our inspiration as printers happened to be good was called up by the text—although I must admit that, in a lesser way, the paper was inspiring too, but then the text inspired the choice of paper. You are, therefore, directly or indirectly, responsible for this recognition; and we are grateful to you." (Unpublished letter from Harry Duncan to WS, February 15, 1946)

"Your letter of February 15th contains lots of bright and cheerful news and a bit of nonsense about the inspiration of the text, etc. I am delighted to hear of the recognition of the job done by yourself and Mr. Williams. The text is at least a change from the SONNETS FROM THE PORTUGESE, but what interests the American Institute is the book itself. No one can say this sort of thing more sincerely than I, because The Cummington Press is very much my dish: it is because I like your work so much that the two books printed by you have come about. As a matter of fact, I thought that the first edition of the NOTES was a superior thing as a book. Perhaps it was too conformist. The ESTHETIQUE contains much more of the individual printer and individual artist and, for that reason, it hangs on.

"Moreover, in the case of the second book, while the special copies are a delight, there is not the difference between the special copies and the bulk of the edition, nor the let-down between the two that one finds so often. The ordinary copies are just as attractive in their way as the special copies. Perhaps a part of the story is that each of us has enjoyed his part of the job." (*Letters*, p. 523: letter to Harry Duncan, February 19, 1946)

A 11 TRANSPORT TO SUMMER

A 11.a.1
First printing (1947)

TRANSPORT

TO SUMMER

Wallace Stevens

1947 : ALFRED A. KNOPF : NEW YORK

A 11.a.1: $7^7/_{16} \times 5^1/_8$ inches

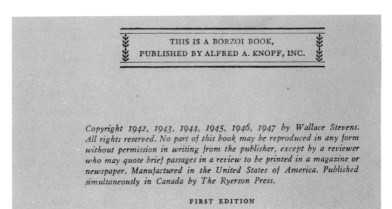

Collation: [1–10]⁸. Pp. [*1–2*] [i–iv] v–vii [viii] [*1–2*] 3–114 [115–116] 117–147 [148–150].

Typography and paper: Set in Linotype Granjon. White wove paper.

Pagination: p. *1*: blank; p. *2*: 'ALSO BY WALLACE STEVENS | *Harmonium (1923, 1931)* | *Ideas of Order (1936)* | *The Man With the Blue Guitar (1937)* | *Parts of a World (1942)* | THESE ARE BORZOI BOOKS | PUBLISHED IN NEW YORK | BY ALFRED A. KNOPF'; p. i: half title, 'TRANSPORT TO SUMMER'; p. ii: blank; p. iii: title page; p. iv: copyright page; pp. v–vii: table of contents; p. viii: acknowledgment, 'NOTE | "Notes toward a Supreme Fiction" is the earliest of the | poems contained in this book. Otherwise the poems are | arranged in the order in which they were written. Some of | them have not been published before. Others have appeared | in: *Accent; American Prefaces; Arizona Quarterly; Briarcliff* | *Quarterly; Chimera; Contemporary Poetry; Furioso; Har-* | *per's Bazaar; Harvard Wake; Horizon; Kenyon Review;* | *Maryland Quarterly; New Poems 1943; New Republic;* | *Origenes; Pacific; Poetry: A Magazine of Verse; Quarterly* | *Review of Literature; Sewanee Review; View; viVa; Voices;* | *Yale Poetry Review.* The author offers his grateful acknow- | edgments to these publications.'; p. *1*: section title, 'TRANSPORT TO SUMMER'; p. *2*: blank; pp. 3–114: text; p. 115: section title, '*To Henry Church* | NOTES TOWARD A SUPREME FICTION'; p. 116: opening stanza; pp. 117–147: text; p. 148: closing stanzas; p. 149: blank; p. 150: colophon.

Contents: God Is Good. It Is a Beautiful Night—Certain Phenomena of Sound—The Motive for Metaphor—Gigantomachia—Dutch Graves in Bucks County—No Possum, No Sop, No Taters—So-and-So Reclining on Her Couch—Chocorua to Its Neighbor—Poésie Abrutie—The Lack of Repose—Somnambulisma—Crude Foyer—Repetitions of a Young Captain—The Creations of Sound—Holiday in Reality—Esthétique du Mal—The Bed of Old John Zeller—Less and Less Human, O Savage Spirit—Wild Ducks, People and Distances—The Pure Good of Theory (All the Preludes to Felicity—Description of a Platonic Person—Fire Monsters in the Milky Brain—Dry Birds Are Fluttering in Blue Leaves)—A Word with José Rodriguez-Feo—Paisant Chronicle—Sketch of the Ultimate Politician—Flyer's Fall—Jouga—Debris of Life and Mind—Description without Place—Two Tales of Liadoff—Analysis of a Theme—Late Hymn from the Myrrh-Mountain—Man Carrying Thing—Pieces—A Completely New Set of Objects—Adult Epigram—Two Versions of the Same Poem—Men Made Out of Words—Thinking of a Relation between the Images of Metaphors—Chaos in Motion and Not in Motion—The House Was Quiet and the World Was Calm—Continual Conversation with a Silent Man—A Woman Sings a Song for a Soldier Come Home—The Pediment of Appearance—Burghers of Petty Death—Human Arrangement—The Good Man Has No Shape—The Red Fern—From the Packet of Anacharsis—The Dove in the Belly—Mountains Covered with Cats—The Prejudice against the Past—Extraordinary References—Attempt to Discover Life—A Lot of People Bathing in a Stream—Credences of Summer—A Pastoral Nun—The Pastor Caballero—Notes toward a Supreme Fiction (It Must Be Abstract—It Must Change—It Must Give Pleasure).

Colophon: p. [150]: A NOTE ON THE TYPE IN WHICH | THIS BOOK IS SET | *This book is set in Granjon, a type named in compliment to | Robert Granjon, type-cutter and printer— Antwerp, Lyon, | Rome, Paris—active from 1523 to 1590. The boldest and most | original designer of his time, he was one of the first to prac-| tise the trade of type-founder apart from that of printer. | This type face was designed by George W. Jones, who | based his drawings upon a type used by Claude Garamond | (1510–61) in his beautiful French books, and more closely | resembles Garamond's own than do any of the various mod-|ern types that bear his name. | The book was composed, printed, and bound by H. Wolff, | New York.*

Binding and dust jacket: Green paper-covered boards, with Borzoi device stamped in blind on back cover; black S cloth spine; light tan or, in some cases, bluish green paper label pasted to read downward on spine; on the label, printed in black: '[ornament] *Transport to Summer:* WALLACE STEVENS [ornament]'. Sized white wove endpapers; top edges stained orange; fore edges untrimmed; bottom edges rough trimmed. Light green dust jacket printed in dark green, with photograph of WS by Sylvia Salmi and seventeen-line biographical note on back.

Published March 20, 1947, at $2.50, in a printing of 1,750 copies.

Locations: CtY, DLC (deposit copy stamped "March 1, 1947"), HS, InU, JME.

Annotations: "The proofs of *Transport to Summer* are being returned by registered mail today. The printer has done a particularly good job. Very few changes are necessary. The following numbers relate to the numbers in your letter of November 7th.

"1. I gather from the proofs that where a poem ends in, say, the middle of the page the next following poem will begin immediately after on the same page and not at the beginning of the next page. To make any change in that respect would, no doubt, spoil the present design. There are, however, several of the poems that I should have preferred to see a little detached from what precedes them as, for example, the *Esthetique, Credences of Summer* and *Notes*. I shall speak about the last poem in a moment. It seems that the designer has tried to avoid putting sequence titles in separate pages by themselves. Perhaps the suggestion that I have just made will serve the same purpose and yet go along with what the designer is trying to do. If he likes this idea, he might use it in connection with some of the longer poems as, for example, *Chocorua, Description without Place*.

"2. The sub-title *THAT WHICH CANNOT BE FIXED* is the title of both sections. In short, it is the title of the poem, each of the sub-sections being a version of it.

"3. The use of numbers is entirely acceptable.

"4. I should prefer to have the title to *Notes* on a separate page with the inscription to Mr. Church just above it to the right in italics. The first introductory eight lines could then be printed on the reverse of that page. The first note *(IT MUST BE ABSTRACT)* could then begin at the top of the next following page. I have no objection to the use of italic letters for *It must be abstract*, etc.; in fact, I prefer italics to the type that has been used in the galleys. If the designer just can't see this, please explain to him that the first eight lines have nothing to do with Mr. Church: they are by way of an introduction to the poem. The truth is that my stenographer and I wrestled with this problem before I sent in the manuscript. The question is how to use the eight lines but at the same time dissociate them from Mr. Church. In the manuscript I put the inscription and the title of the poem on a separate page purposely. If the designer does not like my suggestion, I should think it would be simpler to scrap the eight lines, which I should not want to do. Mr. Church's name should not follow the title because it will then come next to these lines. It should be in italics above the title. Moreover, as this poem is the most important thing in the book, I think that a separate page in this single instance would help to signify that." (*Letters*, pp. 537–538: letter to Herbert Weinstock at Alfred A. Knopf, Inc., November 12, 1946)

"The new book that Knopf is to publish for me is probably at the binder's now or on its way there. This will contain everything written since *Parts Of A World*, including *Notes Toward A Supreme Fiction*. The title will be *Transport To Summer*. Since it is a commercial edition, it will have none of the graces of the Cummington Press books—and yet Knopf has been taking a lot of trouble with it." (*Letters*, p. 542: letter to Henry Church, December 11, 1946)

"Gentlemen:

"The copies of *Transport to Summer* came today. I should like both Mr. Knopf and Mr. Weinstock to know that I think that the book, as a book, is a lollapalooza. That is easier to say than to spell. I like it very much and hope that it brings good luck to all of us. I think I shall have to have about eighteen additional copies now. Please send these to me with a bill. During the last few years a good many people have sent me copies of their own books and of course I want to reciprocate." (*Letters*, p. 547: letter to Alfred A. Knopf, Inc., February 28, 1947)

Canadian publication
The copyright page of the first Knopf printing states that the book was published simultaneously by The Ryerson Press, Toronto. This statement is a copyright formality, and no Toronto imprint has been located.

A 11.a.2
Second printing (1951)

TRANSPORT

TO SUMMER

G.

Wallace Stevens

ALFRED A. KNOPF : NEW YORK

1951

A 11.a.2: 8³⁄₈ × 5¹⁄₂ inches

THIS IS A BORZOI BOOK,
PUBLISHED BY ALFRED A. KNOPF, INC.

PUBLISHED MARCH 20, 1947
SECOND PRINTING, JANUARY 1951

Collation: [1–5]¹⁶. Pp. [1–2] [i–iv] v–vii [viii] [1–2] 3–114 [115–116] 117–147 [148–150].

Typography and paper: Set in Linotype Granjon. White laid paper, watermarked: 'WARREN'S | OLDE STYLE'.

Pagination: The same as A 11.a.1 except for p. iv: copyright-page changes as shown in the illustration above.

Contents: The same as A 11.a.1.

Colophon: p. [150]: The same as A 11.a.1 except for the last sentence, which reads: *'This book was composed by H. Wolff, New York, and | printed and bound by The Plimpton Press, Norwood, Mas- | sachusetts.'*

Binding and dust jacket: Smooth black V cloth; a floral design stamped in blind on front cover; the Borzoi device stamped in blind on back cover; on spine, stamped in gold: '[ornament] | *Trans- | port | TO | Sum- | mer* | WALLACE | STEVENS | [ornament] | *Knopf'*. Sized white wove endpapers; top edges stained orange; fore and bottom edges untrimmed. Buff-colored dust jacket, printed in red; on the front: 'Transport to Summer | [ornament] | *Wallace Stevens* | Awarded the Bollingen Prize in Poetry | of the Yale University Library | for 1949'; on the back: photograph of WS by Sylvia Salmi and a sixteen-line biographical note.

Published January 1951, at $3.00, in a printing of 1,500 copies.

Locations: CL, JME.

Canadian publication
The copyright page of the second Knopf printing states that the book was published simultaneously by McClelland and Stewart, Toronto. This statement is a copyright formality, and no Toronto imprint has been located.

A 12 THREE ACADEMIC PIECES
(1947)

Unsigned issue (1 to 102)

Wallace Stevens

THREE ACADEMIC PIECES

The Realm of Resemblance
Someone Puts a Pineapple Together
Of Ideal Time and Choice

m.cm.xl.vij.
THE CUMMINGTON PRESS

A 12: 7⅜ × 5 inches

Copyright 1947 Wallace Stevens

Collation: [1–7]⁴. Pp. [i–viii] [1–7] 8–37 [38–48].

Typography and paper: Set by hand in Blado and Poliphilus. Initial letters, p. 9, in magenta, p. 27, in green, and, p. 35, in orange, cut by hand in wood. White laid "Worthy Dacian paper," watermarked: 'Dacian'.

Pagination: p. i: blank, pasted down to inside of front cover; pp. ii–viii: blank; p. 1: *'Made at Cummington School of the Arts, | Cummington, Massachusetts in U.S.A.';* p. 2: blank; p. 3: title page; p. 4: copyright page; p. 5: acknowledgment, *'These pieces were read, in February 1947, | at Harvard University under the auspices | of the Morris Gray Fund; they were first | printed in Partisan Review for May 1947, | & appear in the present edition by arrange- | ment with Alfred A. Knopf, Inc., pub- | lisher of Mr. Stevens' Harmonium, Ideas | of Order, The Man with the Blue Guitar, | Parts of a World, & Transport to Sum- mer.';* p. 6: blank; p. 7: half title, *'Three Academic Pieces';* p. 8: section title, 'THE REALM OF RESEMBLANCE'; pp. 9–25: text; p. 26: section title, 'SOMEONE PUTS | A PINEAPPLE TOGETHER'; pp. 27–33: text; p. 34: section title, 'OF IDEAL TIME | AND CHOICE'; pp. 35–37: text; p. 38: blank; p. 39: colophon; pp. 40–47: blank; p. 48: blank, pasted down to inside of back cover.

Contents: The Realm of Resemblance – Someone Puts a Pineapple Together – Of Ideal Time and Choice.

Colophon: p. [39]: *Of an edition limited to two hundred forty- | six copies, printed from Blado & Poliphilus | types and from initial letters cut in wood | by Wightman Williams, this copy is . . . . .* [over the printed periods are arabic numerals] *| of those numbered 1 through 102 on Worthy | Dacian paper.* H. D. & W. W. *finx. & fec.*

Binding and dust jacket: Green paper-covered boards; on the front cover a fleuronlike design, printed vertically in magenta; on the spine, printed upward in magenta: 'WALLACE STE-VENS: THREE ACADEMIC PIECES'. Endpapers of same stock as sheets; top and bottom edges rough trimmed; fore edges untrimmed. Binding by Arno Werner. Plain white wove paper dust jacket.

Published December 8, 1947, at $5.00, in an issue of 102 copies of a total edition of 246 copies.

Reprinting: All three pieces are reprinted in *The Necessary Angel*, A 17; only the two poems are reprinted in *Poems*, A 27, and *Palm*, A 30.

Locations: DLC (deposit copy stamped "Dec. 22, 1947"), InU, JME.

Unsigned issue (i to xcii)
The title page is the same as in the unsigned issue numbered 1 to 102.

Collation: The same as the unsigned issue numbered 1 to 102.

Typography and paper: Initial letters, pp. 9, 27, and 35, printed in black and hand-colored in yellow. "Beauvais Arches paper," watermarked: 'ARCHES (FRANCE)'.

Pagination: The same as the unsigned issue numbered 1 to 102.

Colophon: p. [39]: *Of an edition limited to two hundred forty-* | *six copies, printed from Blado & Poliphilus* | *types and from initial letters cut in wood* | *by Wightman Williams, this copy is* . . . . . [over the printed periods are roman numerals] | *of those numbered i through xcii on Beauvais* | *Arches paper.* H. D. & W. W. *finx. & fec.*

Binding and dust jacket: Light blue paper-covered boards; on the front cover a fleuronlike design, printed vertically in black and hand colored in yellow; on the spine, printed upward in black: 'WALLACE STEVENS: THREE ACADEMIC PIECES'. Endpapers simulated by yellow tissue pasted to pp. ii, iii, 46, and 47; top and bottom edges rough trimmed; fore edges untrimmed. Binding by Arno Werner. Plain white paper dust jacket.

Published December 8, 1947, at $5.00, in an issue of 92 copies of a total edition of 246 copies.

Locations: CLU, CtY, HS, InU, RPB.

Signed issue (I to LII)
Title page is the same as in the unsigned issues.

Collation: The same as the unsigned issues.

Typography and paper: Initial letters, pp. 9, 27, and 35, cut by hand in wood, printed in black and hand-colored in blue and yellow. White laid "Crown & Sceptre paper," watermarked with a crown and scepter on a book and with a heraldic shield.

Pagination: The same as the unsigned issues.

Colophon: p. [39]: *Of an edition limited to two hundred forty- | six copies, printed from Blado & Poliphilus | types and from initial letters cut in wood | by Wightman Williams, this copy is* . . . . . [over the printed periods are roman numerals] | *of those numbered I through LII, signed by | the author and hand-colored, on Crown & | Sceptre paper. H. D. & W. W. finx. & fec.* | [signed in ink by WS]

Binding and dust jacket: Light tan paper-covered boards, hand colored in blue and yellow vertical stripes; tan T cloth spine, stamped upward in blue: 'THREE ACADEMIC PIECES BY WALLACE STEVENS'; vellum corners and inlays at head and tail. White wove endpapers; top and bottom edges rough trimmed; fore edges untrimmed. Binding by Peter Franck. Plain white paper dust jacket. Grayish tan cardboard slipcase.

Published December 8, 1947, at $12.50, in an issue of 52 copies of a total edition of 246 copies.

Locations: HS, JME.

Annotations for A 12: "Mr. Knopf is satisfied that you should do the Three Academic Pieces. Assuming that you have seen the Partisan Review and that it is agreeable, you now have a green light. [. . .]

"As usual, I have only one suggestion to make and that is that the book shall be an agreeable thing in itself: light and bright and cheerful." (*Letters*, p. 551: letter to Harry Duncan, March 21, 1947)

"There appears to be nothing to change in the proofs of the poem and I return the mss. enclosed. If I like the other initials as much as I like the O, I shall be hard to hold down.

"This is the first time I have read this poem since I sent it to you and certainly it says exactly what I intended it to say:

> . . . 'the total artifice reveals itself
> As the total reality.'

"Is this book going to be bound by Gerlach? If it is, it might be a good idea to make him give you his left leg as a hostage or a pledge. I sent him a copy of *Transport to Summer* the first week in March. Not long ago I asked him about it and he then promised to go ahead with it right after Labor Day. So that I shall probably have it for next Easter." (*Letters*, pp. 567–568: letter to Harry Duncan, September 10, 1947)

"Today Three Academic Pieces are at last published. Five of the signed copies went off to you by insured mail yesterday, and three of the unsigned. The latter, you will note, we got bound into boards after all.

"Perhaps you'll be disappointed because the signed copies have no leather on them, excepting that is the vellum corners and inlays at head and tail which are invisible. In our opinion, however, this is the best binding any book of ours has had — any edition, that is. Peter Franck made it, and his meticulous and loving craftsmanship is something for which even the most sumptuous materials cannot substitute. And I should add too that his binding was twice as expensive as any we've had before. Arno Werner bound the other copies. [. . .]

"The making of this book has been another period of great pleasure to us, for the poetry continues fresh and joyful. I wish that our printing were as fecund and elegant as that." (Unpublished letter from Harry Duncan to WS, December 8, 1947)

A 13 A PRIMITIVE LIKE AN ORB
(1948)

A Primitive like an Orb

a poem by Wallace Stevens

with drawings

by Kurt Seligmann

a Prospero pamphlet

printed for THE GOTHAM BOOK MART

at THE BANYAN PRESS

in March 1948

A 13: 10 × 6⁷/₁₆ inches

> Printed in the United States of America
>
> Copyright 1948 by
>
> Wallace Stevens

Collation: [1]⁸. Pp. [1–16]. Illustrations inserted around center fold of text paper, with drawings facing pp. 7 and 10.

Typography and paper: Set by hand in Garamond. The illustrations are reproductions of drawings by Kurt Seligmann, printed in brown on two conjugate leaves of Zuba grass paper. White laid "ETRURIA" paper, watermarked: 'ETRURIA | ITALY | [device]'. Page size, 10 × 6⁷⁄₁₆ inches; wrapper size, 10⅛ × 7 inches.

Pagination: pp. 1–2: blank; p. 3: title page; p. 4: copyright page; pp. 5–11: text; p. 12: blank; p. 13: colophon; pp. 14–16: blank.

Contents: The poem "A Primitive like an Orb."

Colophon: p. [17]: PROSPERO *pamphlets are edited by* | *Frank A. Hale, John Myers & Dmitri Petrov.* | *This pamphlet, published by* THE GOTHAM BOOK MART, | *was designed & printed* | *by* THE BANYAN PRESS *in March* 1948. | *The poem was set by hand in* GARAMOND *faces* | *& printed on* ETRURIA *paper,* | *with drawings on* ZEBU *paper.* | *There are five hundred copies for sale.*

Binding: Semistiff wove paper wrapper, watermarked: 'LOMBARDIA | [heraldic shield] | MADE IN ITALY | [device]'. Three variations in the color of the wrappers can be identified: bright green, olive green, and orange, all of the same stock. Mr. Claude Fredericks of The Banyan Press has told the compiler that there was no priority in the use of these colors, that whichever was at hand was used, and that there seems to have been less of the bright green paper than of the other two. On the front, printed in brown: '*A Primitive like an Orb* | *a poem by Wallace Stevens* | *with drawings* | *by Kurt Seligmann*'. Sewn with brown thread; all edges untrimmed.

Published June 17, 1948, at $1.25, in an edition of 500 copies.

Reprinting: Reprinted in *The Auroras of Autumn*, A 14; *CP*, A 23; *Poems*, A 27; and *Palm*, A 30.

Locations: Olive green: CtY, DLC (deposit copy stamped "June 23, 1948"), HS, InU, JME; orange: HS, JME; bright green: CtY.

Annotation: "The proofs of *A Primitive Like An Orb* seem to require no changes except a misspelling indicated on the first page which escaped me in the script. I am not returning them by special delivery because I don't know what would happen to a letter that was sent special delivery to a post office box.

"On March 18th I am going to give the Bergen Lecture at Yale. This has not yet been announced and accordingly I am telling you about it between us. After the lecture I shall probably have time to read a poem or two. It would be nice to be able to read the present poem, or at least to feel free to read it. Would this be all right with you and Mr. Myers? You can probably reach him by telephone a good deal more quickly than I can by writing. I should merely say that I was reading from a manuscript poem without making any mention of subsequent publication. If this is all right with both of you, I shall be glad to have you send word. On the other hand, I want you to feel free to express your preference if it is otherwise. This is only an afterthought on my part.

"If everything else about this particular pamphlet is as good as your printing, it will be worth while." (*Letters*, p. 581: letter to Claude Fredericks, March 2, 1948)

A 14 THE AURORAS OF AUTUMN

A 14.a.1
First printing (1950)

THE

Auroras

OF

Autumn

WALLACE STEVENS

ALFRED · A · KNOPF

NEW YORK

1950

A 14.a.1: 8⅜ × 5½ inches

Collation: [1–5]^{16} [6]^8 [7]^{16}. Pp. [*1–2*] [i–vi] vii [viii] [1] 2–193 [194–198].

Typography and paper: Set in Linotype Janson. White laid paper, watermarked: 'WARREN'S | OLDE STYLE'.

Pagination: p. *1*: blank: p. *2*: '*Also by* | WALLACE STEVENS | [rule] | *Harmonium (1923, 1931)* | *Ideas of Order (1936)* | *The Man with the Blue Guitar (1937)* | *Parts of a World (1942)* | *Transport to Summer (1947)* | *These are* BORZOI BOOKS, *published in New York by* | ALFRED A. KNOPF'; p. i: half title, 'THE AURORAS OF AUTUMN'; p. ii: blank; p. iii: title page; p. iv: copyright page; p. v: acknowledgment, 'NOTE | *Some of these poems have appeared in magazines:* | Accent, American Letters, Botteghe Oscure, Focus, | Halcyon, Harvard Wake, Horizon, Hudson Re- | view, Kenyon Review, Nation, Poetry, PL, *and* | Voices. *Parts of* "An Ordinary Evening in New | Haven" *were read at the celebration of the one hun- | dred and fiftieth anniversary of the formation of* | The Connecticut Academy of Arts and Sciences and | appeared in its* Transactions. *The author pays his* | *grateful acknowledgments to all these.*'; p. vi: blank; pp. vii–viii: table of contents; p. *1*: half title, 'THE AURORAS OF AUTUMN'; pp. 2–193: text; p. 194: blank; p. 195: colophon; pp. 196–198: blank.

Contents: The Auroras of Autumn (I–X) – Page from a Tale – Large Red Man Reading – This Solitude of Cataracts – In the Element of Antagonisms – In a Bad Time – The Beginning – The Countryman – The Ultimate Poem Is Abstract – Bouquet of Roses in Sunlight – The Owl in the Sarcophagus – Saint John and the Back-Ache – Celle Qui Fût Héaulmiette – Imago – A Primitive like an Orb – Metaphor as Degeneration – The Woman in Sunshine – Reply to Papini – The Bouquet – World without Peculiarity – Our Stars Come from Ireland – The Westwardness of Everything – Puella Parvula – The Novel – What We See Is

What We Think—A Golden Woman in a Silver Mirror—The Old Lutheran Bells at Home—Questions Are Remarks—Study of Images (I–II)—An Ordinary Evening in New Haven (I–XXXI) —Things of August (I–X)—Angel Surrounded by Paysans.

Colophon: p. [195]: A NOTE ON THE TYPE IN WHICH | THIS BOOK IS SET | *This book was set on the Linotype in Janson, a recut-* | *ting made direct from the type cast from matrices made* | *by Anton Janson some time between 1660 and 1687.* | *Of Janson's origin nothing is known. He may have* | *been a relative of Justus Janson, a printer of Danish* | *birth who practiced in Leipzig from 1614 to 1635. Some* | *time between 1657 and 1668 Anton Janson, a punch-* | *cutter and type-founder, bought from the Leipzig* | *printer Johann Erich Hahn the type-foundry which* | *had formerly been a part of the printing house of* | *M. Friedrich Lankisch. Janson's types were first shown* | *in a specimen sheet issued at Leipzig about 1675.* | *The book was composed, printed, and bound by The* | *Plimpton Press, Norwood, Massachusetts. Typogra-* | *phy and binding based on original designs by W. A.* | *Dwiggins.*

Binding and dust jacket: Dark blue V cloth; a floral design stamped in blind on front; the Borzoi device stamped in blind on back; on spine, stamped in gold: '[ornament] | THE | *Auroras* | OF | *Autumn* | WALLACE | STEVENS | [ornament] | *Knopf*'. Sized white wove endpapers; top edges stained blue; fore and bottom edges rough trimmed. Pink dust jacket printed in blue-green; on the front: '*Awarded the* | *Bollingen Prize for Poetry,* 1950'; on the back, photograph of WS by Sylvia Salmi and sixteen-line biographical note.

Published September 11, 1950, at $3.00, in a printing of 3,000 copies.

Locations: CtY, DLC (deposit copy stamped "Aug. 28, 1950"), HS, InU, JME.

Annotations: "Will you do one more book for me before we get out a collection? The book I have in mind is one that I have been thinking a good deal about and have been working on. It will be called The Auroras of Autumn. I should be able to send you the manuscript by the end of the year. Thereafter, we could do a collection. There will be things in The Auroras of Autumn that I should want to put in a collection. This might give us two books within the same year. The new book would not be as large as Transport To Summer. I am immensely interested in this and should like to know what you think." (*Letters*, p. 638: letter to Alfred A. Knopf, June 13, 1949)

"The book of which I spoke to you, *The Auroras of Autumn* will be published by Knopf in the autumn. The mss. was sent to him in December and everything is all set. I had not intended to get around to this quite so soon and it hurts the book not to have had more time. Knopf wants to do a collection which will of course eliminate the necessity of reprinting the separate volumes. It seemed desirable therefore to be able to include the contents of *The Auroras* in the collection when he gets round to the collection." (*Letters*, p. 666: letter to Bernard Heringman, February 10, 1950)

"I am returning the proofs of THE AURORAS OF AUTUMN which you were kind enough to send me. I have o.k'd them as to the text. Here and there where I have noticed mistakes on the part of the printer in other respects I have called attention to them, but I am not competent to make corrections in respect to the printer's end of the job. I believe the text as corrected to be absolutely correct now.

"There is one word that I am uncertain about and that is the word fulfilling in folio 21. I have taken out one of the l's. Yet I think that it ought to remain and if you agree with me please eliminate my correction. You will notice that in folio 65 the word fulfillment occurs twice, or, rather, once in the singular and once in the plural. I have taken out one l in both cases. But you can't take it out in one place and leave it in in another. My guess is that there should be two l's in both cases. The reason that I am not able to decide this for myself is that the Oxford Concise Dictionary that I use at home uses one l; here at the office we have an old-fashioned Webster which uses two although it suggests the spelling with one l as an alternative. I very much prefer two l's." (*Letters*, pp. 673–674: letter to Alfred A. Knopf, Inc., to the attention of Harry Ford, April 3, 1950)

"Since writing to you on August 9, I have had a chance to take a real look at the new book. Someone at home said that it is 'as smart as a new hat'. But looked at as a publication of the kind of poetry that I try to write it seems to me to be perfect. It compels the reader to move through it slowly and deliberately and it gives him the sense of being in appropriate surroundings. He is not pulled away from one thing to the next.

"I don't think you could have done a better job and it goes without saying that I am grateful to you and thank you." (*Letters*, p. 686: letter to Herbert Weinstock, August 11, 1950)

"Your letter takes me completely by surprise. I had not the slightest expectation of winning the [National Book] award. Anyhow, whatever else can be said of *The Auroras of Autumn*, it can surely be said that it is the best looking book of poetry published last year. I am delighted and shall most certainly come down." (*Letters*, p. 708: letter to Alfred Knopf, Jr., February 23, 1951)

Canadian publication
The copyright page of the first Knopf printing states that the book was published simultaneously by McClelland and Stewart, Toronto. This statement is a copyright formality, and no Toronto imprint has been located.

A 14.a.2
Second printing (1952)

Varies from A 14.a.1 in the following particulars: on p. 2 the following is added and substituted after '*Transport to Summer (1947)*': '*The Auroras of Autumn (1950)* | PROSE | *The Necessary Angel:* Essays on Reality | and the Imagination *(1951)* | THESE ARE BORZOI BOOKS, PUBLISHED IN NEW YORK BY | *Alfred A. Knopf';* on the title page '1952' is substituted for '1950'; p. iv: in place of 'FIRST EDITION' is substituted: 'PUBLISHED SEPTEMBER 11, 1950 | SECOND PRINTING, NOVEMBER 1952'.

Published November 1952, at $3.00, in a printing of 1,000 copies.

Locations: CL, CLU, CtY.

Canadian publication
The copyright page of the second Knopf printing states that the book was published simultaneously by McClelland and Stewart, Toronto. This statement is a copyright formality, and no Toronto imprint has been located.

A 15 THE RELATIONS BETWEEN POETRY
AND PAINTING
[*1951*]

wallace stevens

the

relations

between

poetry

and

painting

the museum of modern art new york

A 15: cover title; first and last lines in blue; 10 × 7½ inches

Collation: [1]⁶. Pp. [1–2] 3–10 [11–12].

Typography and paper: Cover and running heads set in Linotype Caslon; text set in Linotype Janson. White wove paper, watermarked: 'SUEDE | D [within a diamond] | FINISH'.

Pagination: p. 1: cover title; p. 2: copyright page; pp. 3–10: text; p. 11: 'BOOKS BY WALLACE STEVENS | PUBLISHED BY ALFRED A. KNOPF, NEW YORK | HARMONIUM, 1923 | *IDEAS OF ORDER, 1936 | *OWL'S CLOVER, 1936 | *THE MAN WITH THE BLUE GUITAR, 1937 | *PARTS OF A WORLD, 1942 | TRANSPORT TO SUMMER, 1947 | THE AURORAS OF AUTUMN, 1950 | *out of print | Additional copies of this pamphlet | may be obtained from | The Museum of Modern Art | 11 West 53 Street, New York 19, N.Y. | at 35¢ each.'; p. 12: blank.

Contents: Note on p. 3: 'A LECTURE DELIVERED AT THE MUSEUM OF MODERN ART ON JANUARY 15, 1951'.

Binding: Wrapper of white wove paper, watermarked: 'SATURN | BOOK'. Stapled; all edges trimmed.

Published 1951 [ca. April 20, 1951], at 35¢; number of copies unknown.

Locations: CtY, DLC (deposit copy stamped "May 2, 1951"), HS, InU, JME.

Annotation: "I am sending you the manuscript of the paper that I read a week or so ago. If after you have examined it you still wish to go ahead, I leave the question of format to you.

"Thanks for what you say about later publication. I have no present intention of ever publishing a volume of prose although several people have asked me to do that." (*Letters*, p. 705: letter to Monroe Wheeler, January 23, 1951)

A 16 TWO OR THREE IDEAS
(1951)

Chap Book

Published by the

COLLEGE ENGLISH ASSOCIATION

UNIVERSITY OF MASSACHUSETTS

As a Supplement to THE CEA CRITIC

MAXWELL H. GOLDBERG, Editor

Vol. XIII, No. 7, October, 1951

Copyright, 1951, by Wallace Stevens

Two or Three Ideas

By

WALLACE STEVENS

Hartford, Connecticut

My first proposition is that the style of a poem and the poem itself are one.

One of the better known poems in *Fleurs du Mal* is the one (XII) entitled *La Vie Antérieure* or *Former Life*. It begins with the line:

J'ai longtemps habité sous de vastes portiques

or

A long time I lived beneath tremendous porches.

It continues:

Which the salt-sea suns tinged with a thousand fires

And which great columns, upright and majestic,

At evening, made resemble basalt grottoes.

The poem concerns the life among the images, sounds and colors of those calm, sensual presences

At the center of azure, of waves, of brilliances,

and so on. I have chosen this poem to illustrate my first proposition, because it happens to be a poem in which the poem itself is immediately recognizable without reference to the manner in which it is rendered. If the style and the poem are one, one ought to choose, for the purpose of illustration, a poem that illustrates this as, for example, Yeats' *Lake-Isle of Innisfree*. To choose a French poem which has to be translated is to choose an example in which the style is lost in the paraphrase of translation. On the other hand, Baudelaire's poem is useful because it identifies what is meant by the poem itself. The idea of an earlier life is like the idea of a later life, or like the idea of a different life, part of the classic repertory of poetic ideas. It is part of one's inherited store of poetic subjects. Precisely, then, because it is traditional and because we understand

A 16: first page; $8^{13}/_{16} \times 5^{7}/_{8}$ inches

Collation: [1]⁴. Pp. [1] 2–8.

Typography and paper: Set in Linotype Garamond; the words 'Chap Book' set in Black Letter. White laid paper.

Pagination: pp. 1–8: text.

Colophon: p. 8: (Prepared for the occasion, the foregoing address was delivered at the spring | meeting of the New England College English Association, Mount Holyoke College, | Saturday, April 28, 1951. . . .)

Unbound; stapled; all edges trimmed.

Distributed as a supplement to *The CEA Critic* for October 1951; number of copies unknown.

Locations: CtY, HS, JME.

A 17 THE NECESSARY ANGEL

A 17.a.1
First American printing (1951)

THE
NECESSARY ANGEL

Essays on Reality and the Imagination

B Y

WALLACE STEVENS

New York ALFRED A KNOPF 1951

A 17.a.1: 8⅜ × 5⅝ inches

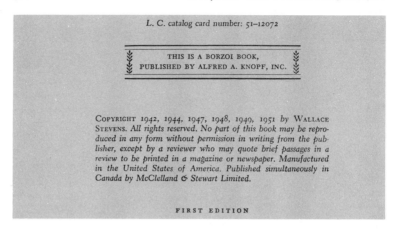

Collation: [1–6]¹⁶. Pp. [1–2] [i–vi] vii–x [xi–xii] [1–2] 3–36 [37–38] 39–67 [68–70] 71–89 [90–92] 93–103 [104–106] 107–130 [131–132] 133–156 [157–158] 159–176 [177–178].

Typography and paper: Set in Linotype Stuyvesant. Running heads, rectos and versos: title and section titles. White laid paper, watermarked: 'WARREN'S | OLDE STYLE'.

Pagination: p 1: blank; p. 2: '[rule] *These are* Borzoi Books | *published by* ALFRED A KNOPF | [rule] | The poetry of WALLACE STEVENS | *Harmonium* (1923, 1931, 1947) | *Ideas of Order* (1936) | *The Man with the Blue Guitar* (1937) | *Parts of a World* (1942, 1951) | *Transport to Summer* (1947) | *The Auroras of Autumn* (1950) | NOTE | *The Man with the Blue Guitar* (1937) includes *Owl's* | *Clover; Transport to Summer* (1947) includes *Es-* | *thétique du Mal* and *Notes toward a Supreme Fiction.* | *The Man with the Blue Guitar* and *Ideas of Order* are | scheduled for republication in 1952 in a single volume | to carry the title *The Man with the Blue Guitar*'; p. i: half title, 'THE | NECESSARY ANGEL'; p. ii: blank; p. iii: title page; p. iv: copyright page; p. v: '. . . *I am the necessary angel of earth,* | *Since,* *in my sight, you see the earth again.* | THE AURORAS OF AUTUMN'; p. vi: blank; pp. vii–viii: 'INTRODUCTION', signed 'WALLACE STEVENS'; pp. ix–x: 'ACKNOWLEDGMENT'; p. xi: table of contents; p. xii: blank; p. 1: section title, 'I | *The Noble Rider* | *and the Sound of Words*'; p. 2: blank; pp. 3–36: text; p. 37: section title, 'II | *The Figure of the Youth* | *as Virile Poet*'; p. 38: blank; pp. 39–67: text; p. 68: blank; p. 69: section title, 'III | *Three Academic Pieces*'; p. 70: blank; pp. 71–89: text; p. 90: blank; p. 91: section title, '*About One of* | *Marianne Moore's Poems*'; p. 92: blank; pp. 93–103: text; p. 104: blank; p. 105: section title, 'Effects of Analogy'; p. 106: blank; pp. 107–

130: text; p. 131: section title, *'Imagination as Value'*; p. 132: blank; pp. 133–156: text; p. 157: section title, *'The Relations* | *between Poetry and Painting'*; p. 158: blank; pp. 159–176: text; p. 177: colophon; p. 178: blank.

Contents: Introduction — Acknowledgment — I. The Noble Rider and the Sound of Words — II. The Figure of the Youth as Virile Poet — III. Three Academic Pieces — IV. About One of Marianne Moore's Poems — V. Effects of Analogy — VI. Imagination as Value — VII. The Relations between Poetry and Painting.

Colophon: p. [177]: TYPE NOTE | *This book is set in an experimental Linotype face* | *called* STUYVESANT. *The roman characters are* | *based on a type face cut by Jacques Francois Rosart* | *(1714–77) at Haarlem about the year 1750. The* | *italic is a new design, drawn in harmony with the* | *Rosart feeling.* | *The book was composed, printed, and bound by* | *The Plimpton Press, Norwood, Massachusetts. The* | *typography and binding are by* W. A. DWIGGINS, | *the designer of Stuyvesant type.* | [device of W. A. Dwiggins]

Binding and dust jacket: Green V cloth; a floral ornamental design stamped in blind on front; the Borzoi device stamped in blind on back; on spine, stamped in gold: '[ornament] | THE | *Neces-* | *sary* | *Angel* | WALLACE | STEVENS | [ornament] *Knopf'*. Sized white wove endpapers; top edges stained green; fore and bottom edges rough trimmed. Orange red and white dust jacket, printed in black and white, with photograph of WS by John Haley and sixteen-line biographical note on back; on the front flap of the jacket: 'TYPOGRAPHY AND BINDING DESIGN: W. A. DWIGGINS | JACKET DESIGN: HARRY FORD'.

Published November 12, 1951, at $3.00, in a printing of 3,000 copies.

Locations: CtY, DLC (deposit copy stamped "Oct. 26, 1951"), HS, InU, JME.

Annotations: "Mr. [Sidney] Jacobs sent me the galleys of *The Necessary Angel* last week and I am returning them to him today. Only a few trivial changes are necessary in the text. However, when these galleys come in, I wish you would ask Mr. Jacobs to let you take a look at them with the following in mind.

"The first paper, *The Noble Rider and the Sound of Words,* galley 1, opens with a quotation from Plato which is set (a) without indenting and (b) in the type of the text. I believe that the point about indenting is unimportant but I call your attention to it so that you can give it a moment's thought from the point of view of following a uniform practice in the setting of the book. If you will then turn to the next paper, *The Figure of the Youth as Virile Poet*, you will find that that paper opens (galley 13) with a series of quotations all of which are indented and all of which are printed in italics and not in the type of the text. This difference leaves me confused as to what the proper procedure is. I realize that when language is quoted within a sentence it is correct to use the type of the text, unless, perhaps, the language is something French or otherwise foreign. Why should the language of Plato be in the type of text and the quoted language in *The Figure of the Youth as Virile Poet* be in italics?

"There are few italics in *The Noble Rider* and those seem to be proper. It seems to me that the use of italics lightens the appearance of the page and increases its interest. In *The Figure of the Youth* there are a great many italics. This suggests that the man who prepared the manuscript for the printer did not follow a uniform practice. I could be quite wrong about this since I don't know what the practice is. I limit myself to calling your attention to it. I have not made any marks whatever with relation to this sort of thing on the face of the galleys except in one or two instances. As to these I felt that, if nothing else was changed, the parts marked by me should be changed.

"Personally, I favor the use of italics with the common exception of internal quotations within a sentence. If this suggestion interests you, it is likely to be a little expensive. I should be glad to pay the cost of making these changes myself if you will bill me for them. But, at the same time, if I am suggesting something unusual or something unnecessary, there is no point to making the changes at all.

"I liked these papers as a book as I read them over the weekend and although they constitute a miscellany, they make a respectable whole.

"About when are you expecting to publish this? I ask because, unless I am mistaken, it was not included in your last list of forthcoming publications. Consequently, I was a little surprised, and very much pleased, when I received the proofs. I expect to be in Hartford all summer and on receipt of page proofs will give them prompt attention." (*Letters*, pp. 723-724: letter to Herbert Weinstock at Alfred A. Knopf, Inc., July 30, 1951)

"You may remember that after you had taken some trouble to bring about the publication of my odds and ends of papers I decided not to publish them. Last spring Mr. Knopf suggested that I gather them together and let him take a look at them. The result is that these papers are going to be published under the title *The Necessary Angel* late in the autumn. The scheduled date of publication is November 12th. At the time when Mr. Knopf took these papers up with me I was having more or less publicity and I suppose that accounts for what has happened. The papers won't do me much good. My hope is that they won't do me any harm. I shall, of course, send you a copy of the book. In the meantime, I want you to know what is going on." (*Letters*, p. 724: letter to William Van O'Connor, August 13, 1951)

Canadian publication
The copyright page of the first Knopf printing states that the book was published simultaneously by McClelland and Stewart, Toronto. This statement is a copyright formality, and no Toronto imprint has been located.

A 17.a.2
First English printing [1960]

THE NECESSARY | ANGEL | *Essays on Reality and* | *the Imagination* | by | WALLACE STEVENS | FABER AND FABER | 24 Russell Square | London

Copyright page: First published in England in mcmlx | by Faber and Faber Limited | 24 Russell Square London W.C. 1 | Printed in Great Britain by | Bradford and Dickens London W.C. 1 | All rights reserved | Copyright 1942, 1944, 1947, 1948, 1951 | by Wallace Stevens

Collation: [A]⁸ B–M⁸. Pp. [*1–2*] [i–iv] v–x [xi–xii] [1–2] 3–36 [37–38] 39–67 [68–70] 71–89 [90–92] 93–103 [104–106] 107–130 [131–132] 133–156 [157–158] 159–176 [177–178].

Typography and paper: Reprinted by offset from the American printing. White wove paper; $8^7/_{16} \times 5^1/_2$ inches.

Pagination and contents: The same as A 17.a.1.

Binding and dust jacket: Blue cloth, stamped downward in gold on spine. White endpapers; all edges trimmed. Yellow dust jacket printed in red and black.

Published January 22, 1960, at 21s., in an issue of 1,500 copies.

Locations: HS.

A 17.a.3
Second English printing [1965]

Binding: White paper wrapper, printed in black, green, and mauve.

Published 1965, at 7s. 6d., by Faber and Faber.

A 17.a.4
Second American printing [1965]

THE | NECESSARY ANGEL | *Essays on Reality and the Imagi-
nation* | BY | WALLACE STEVENS | [device] | VINTAGE
BOOKS | A Division of Random House | New York

Collation: [1–60]¹. In other respects the same as A 17.a.1
except for the absence of pp. [*1–2*] and the addition of pp. [179–
180].

Pagination: The same as A 17.a.1 except for the following:
pp. *1* and 2 not present; p. iv: first line, 'FIRST VINTAGE EDI-
TION, February, 1965'; p. 177: substitution of biographical
note on WS for colophon; pp. 178–180: lists of Vintage books.

Binding: Perfect bound in paper wrapper; front and spine are
purple, printed in red, blue-green, and white; back is white,
printed in red, purple, and blue-green.

Published February 1965, at $1.45, in a printing of 7,500 copies;
Vintage Book V-278.

Locations: CtY, HS, JME.

Canadian publication
The copyright page of the Vintage second printing states that the
book was published simultaneously by Random House of Canada
Ltd., Toronto. This statement is a copyright formality, and no
Toronto imprint has been located.

A17.a.5–A 17.a.9
Third through seventh American printings [*1966–1971*]

There have been seven American printings of this book, six of
which are under the Vintage imprint: third printing, February
1966, 6,000 copies; fourth printing, November 1967, 5,000
copies; fifth printing, October 1969, 3,000 copies; sixth printing,
April 1970, 3,000 copies; seventh printing, June 1971, 3,000
copies.

Note: An unknown number of copies of the Vintage sheets of
one of the later printings, minus the 'FIRST VINTAGE EDI-
TION, February 1965' statement on p. iv, were bound and sewn
in red BF buckram, presumably for library sales; at foot of spine,
stamped in gold: 'BUCKRAM | REINFORCED | V-278'. *Loca-
tions:* CtY, HS, JME.

A 18 SELECTED POEMS
[*1952*]

SELECTED

POEMS

by

WALLACE   STEVENS

Chosen, with a Foreword

by

DENNIS   WILLIAMSON

THE FORTUNE PRESS
LONDON, S.W.1

A 18: $7^7/_{16} \times 5$ inches

Collation: [1–52]¹. Pp. [5–9] 10–107 [108].

Typography and paper: Set in Times Roman. White laid paper, watermarked: 'Croxley Super Brochure'.

Pagination: p. 5: title page; p. 6: blank; pp. 7–9: table of contents; pp. 10–12: 'FOREWORD', signed at end 'D.W.'; pp. 13–107: text, the prose statement on the poetry of war on p. 107 signed 'W.S.'; p. 108: blank.

Contents: Foreword [by Dennis Williamson]—The Plot against the Giant—The Snow Man—Le Monocle de Mon Oncle—Cy Est Pourtraicte, Madame Ste Ursule, et Les Unze Mille Vierges—Hibiscus on the Sleeping Shores—Homunculus et La Belle Etoile—The Comedian as the Letter C (I. The World without Imagination—II. Concerning the Thunderstorms of Yucatan—III. Approaching Carolina—IV. The Idea of a Colony—V. A Nice Shady Home—VI. And Daughters with Curls)—From the Misery of Don Joost—O Florida, Venereal Soil—The Place of the Solitaires—The Emperor of Ice-Cream—Tea at the Palaz of Hoon—Sunday Morning—Stars at Tallapoosa—Palace of the Babies—Cortège for Rosenbloom—The Bird with the Coppery, Keen Claws—To the One of Fictive Music—Hymn from a Watermelon Pavilion—Peter Quince at the Clavier—Nomad Exquisite—The Man Whose Pharynx Was Bad—The Death of a Soldier—Sea Surface Full of Clouds—In the Clear Season of Grapes—Two at Norfolk—Ghosts as Cocoons—Sailing after Lunch—Sad Strains of a Gay Waltz—Meditation Celestial and Terrestrial—Some Friends from Pascagoula—Waving Adieu, Adieu, Adieu—The Idea of Order at Key West—Evening without Angels—A Fading of the Sun—Gray Stones and Gray Pigeons—Academic Discourse at Havana—The Reader—Anglais Mort à Florence—Like Decorations in a Nigger Cemetery—A Postcard from the Volcano—Gallant Chateau—The Poems of Our Climate—Prelude to Objects—The Glass of Water—Dry Loaf—The Latest Freed Man—United Dames of America—A Rabbit as King of the Ghosts—The Bagatelles the Madrigals—Girl in a Nightgown—Poem Written at Morning—Thunder by the Musician—The Sense of the Sleight-of-Hand Man—Forces, the Will and the Weather—Variations on a Summer Day—Yellow Afternoon—Martial Cadenza—Man and Bottle—Of Modern Poetry—Woman Looking at a Vase of Flowers—Mrs. Alfred Uruguay—Contrary Theses (I)—Jumbo—Contrary Theses (II)—Earthy Anecdote—Invective against Swans—The Paltry Nude Starts on a Spring Voyage—Domination of Black—The Doctor of Geneva—Six Significant Landscapes—Jasmine's Beautiful Thoughts underneath the Willow—Farewell to Florida—How to Live. What to Do.—On the

Road Home—Dezembrum—Bouquet of Belle Scavoir—The Hand as a Being—Examination of the Hero in a Time of War—Author's Footnote [prose statement on the poetry of war, signed 'W.S.']

Binding and dust jacket: Perfect bound in black paper-covered boards, grained in imitation of alligator belly; black BF cloth spine, stamped upward in gold: 'SELECTED POEMS—Wallace Stevens'. White wove endpapers; top edges trimmed; fore and bottom edges rough trimmed. White dust jacket, printed in red and black.

Received for deposit in the British Museum, December 31, 1952; to have been published at 12s. 6d.; number of copies unknown. Review copies were distributed, but the book was withdrawn before publication.

Locations: HS, JME, MH, PSt.

Annotations: "I am attaching a letter from the Fortune Press. As you already know, I have never written to these people. You may be interested in getting in touch with them. I think that if anything comes of it the selection should be made by someone in England. Taste in the two countries is quite different. Anyhow, I should not be willing to make the selection." (Unpublished letter from WS to Alfred A. Knopf, November 8, 1946)

"Many thanks for yours of November 8th. I will write the Fortune Press in answer to their letter to you telling them what you say. It might be best if they would abandon the whole enterprise and let us start fresh." (Unpublished letter from Alfred A. Knopf to WS, November 12, 1946)

"I am delighted to tell you that we have at last signed a contract with Faber & Faber for a volume of your SELECTED POEMS. You are now assured of a decent and adequate presentation in England—for a starter at any rate." (Unpublished letter from Alfred A. Knopf to WS, December 4, 1951)

"Apparently there is being published in London a selection from my things chosen by Dennis Williamson. The book is called *Selected Poems* and is published by the Fortune Press. Do you know anything about this? I had not heard of it until someone referred to it in a recent letter to which I paid no attention because I thought it was really a reference to the Faber selection. But a friend of mine sent me a review of both volumes. I have not yet seen either one." (*Letters*, p. 770: letter to Herbert Weinstock at Alfred A. Knopf, Inc., February 24, 1953. The review referred to in the letter above is that of Austin Clarke in the *Irish Times*.)

"This morning I have your letter of February 28th and also a letter from Mr. Knopf. He had made a contract with the Fortune Press which eventually he cancelled. Later he made arrangements with Faber & Faber. [. . .] This makes me all the more eager to have a copy and makes it all the less likely that you will be able to procure one unless there is someone in Dublin willing to ask Austin Clarke for his copy." (*Letters*, p. 770: letter to John L. Sweeney, March 2, 1953. The elision indicated by the ellipsis points following "Faber & Faber" represents a quotation from a previously unpublished letter by Alfred A. Knopf to WS. That letter reads, in part: "To our consternation we later heard that Fortune Press, despite the cancellation of the contract, was proceeding to publish. [. . .] When simple suasion failed, we had a firm of barristers take the matter in hand. [. . .] The barristers had some trouble locating the proprietor. At last, he agreed to withdraw the book and destroy all copies of it except a few that had already gone out to reviewers.")

"Austin Clarke's copy of the Fortune Press edition of your poems reached me today and I shall forward it to you at once. If you have already acquired a copy please return this one to me for the Poetry Room collection [at Harvard University]. In case you should care to write Austin Clarke his address is . . . ." (Unpublished letter from John L. Sweeney to WS, May 25, 1953)

"Your letter of May 25th is a pleasant surprise because I had rather given up hope of being able to pick up a copy of the Fortune Press edition. I have written to Austin Clarke and send you a copy of my letter [see below]. [. . .]

"You know how greatly I thank you for the book and, therefore, I shall let it go at that." (*Letters*, pp. 776–777: letter to John L. Sweeney, May 26, 1953)

"Jack Sweeney of Boston has just written me to say that he has received your copy of the Fortune Press edition of my poems and that he is sending it to me. There can be very few copies of this left because the publisher was required to destroy the whole edition except as copies had been distributed for review. I appreciate your courtesy more than I can tell you." (Unpublished letter from WS to Austin Clarke, May 26, 1953)

A 19 SELECTED POEMS

A 19.a.1
First printing [1953]

SELECTED POEMS

by
WALLACE STEVENS

FABER AND FABER LIMITED
24 Russell Square
London

A 19.a.1: 8 × 5⅛ inches

First published in mcmliii
by Faber and Faber Limited
24 Russell Square London WC1
Printed in Great Britain by
The Shenval Press, London and Hertford
All rights reserved

Collation: [A]⁸ B–I⁸. Pp. [1–4] 5–7 [8] 9–143 [144].

Typography and paper: Set in Monotype Bell; titles in Mono-type Bell italic. White wove paper.

Pagination: p. 1: half title, 'SELECTED POEMS'; p. 2: blank; p. 3: title page; p. 4: copyright page; pp. 5–6: table of contents; p. 7: acknowledgment, '*Acknowledgments* | The poems in this book have been previously published by | Messrs Alfred A. Knopf, New York, in the collections as | follows: *Harmonium, The Man with the Blue Guitar, Ideas of* | *Order, Parts of a World, Transport to Summer* and *The* | *Auroras of Autumn. Final Soliloquy of the Interior Paramour* | is reprinted from *The Hudson Review.* The short version of | *An Ordinary Eve-ning in New Haven* is reprinted from *Trans-* | *actions of the Con-necticut Academy of Arts and Sciences* instead of | the extended version published in *The Auroras of Autumn.*'; p. 8: blank; pp. 9–143: text; p. 144: blank.

Contents: Earthy Anecdote – In the Carolinas – The Paltry Nude Starts on a Spring Voyage – The Plot against the Giant – Infanta Marina – Domination of Black – The Snow Man – Le Monocle de Mon Oncle – Ploughing on Sunday – Cy Est Pour-traicte, Madame Ste Ursule, et Les Unze Mille Vierges – Fabliau of Florida – Another Weeping Woman – From the Misery of Don Joost – The Worms at Heaven's Gate – On the Manner of Address-ing Clouds – Of Heaven Considered as a Tomb – A High-Toned Old Christian Woman – Depression before Spring – The Emperor of Ice-Cream – Tea at the Palaz of Hoon – Disillusionment of Ten O'Clock – Sunday Morning – The Virgin Carrying a Lan-tern – Bantams in Pine-Woods – Anecdote of the Jar – The Bird with the Coppery, Keen Claws – Life Is Motion – To the One of Fictive Music – Hymn from a Watermelon Pavilion – Peter Quince at the Clavier – Thirteen Ways of Looking at a Blackbird – Nomad Exquisite – Sea Surface Full of Clouds – Tea – The Man with the Blue Guitar – The Men That Are Falling – Sad Strains of a Gay Waltz – The Idea of Order at Key West – The Sun This March – Evening without Angels – Dry Loaf – Country Words – A Rabbit as King of the Ghosts – Asides on the Oboe – Metamor-phosis – Flyer's Fall – Late Hymn from the Myrrh-Mountain – A

Completely New Set of Objects – Men Made Out of Words – The House Was Quiet and the World Was Calm – Extraordinary References – Credences of Summer – Notes toward a Supreme Fiction – Large Red Man Reading – This Solitude of Cataracts – An Ordinary Evening in New Haven – Angel Surrounded by Paysans – Final Soliloquy of the Interior Paramour.

Binding and dust jacket: Purple V cloth; on the spine, stamped downward in silver within silver rules: 'SELECTED POEMS OF WALLACE STEVENS'; at foot of spine, stamped horizontally in silver: 'Faber'. White wove endpapers of same stock as sheets; all edges trimmed. Tan dust jacket printed in black and rust; on the back is a list entitled 'Faber Poetry'.

Published February 6, 1953, at 12s. 6d., in a printing of 2,000 copies.

Locations: CtY, DLC, HS, InU, JME, NN.

Annotations: "If Marianne Moore is free to make the selection [for an English edition], I should rather have her do it. On the other hand, if her relations with Macmillan make it impossible for her to lend a hand, or if she is not willing to lend a hand for other reasons, then I shall do it. [. . .]

"The problem of getting the thing copied is a real problem. Only this morning my stenographer went to the hospital where she will be for several weeks. After she comes out of the hospital, there may be a little period of convalescence. I shall be perfectly willing to let Miss Moore have the copy of my own selection. That might save her a lot of work. She and Mr. Eliot are very good friends. Apparently he would like the idea, and I am certain that I would, not only on account of the typing problem but because I am a great admirer of Miss Moore. Moreover, I have considerable doubt whether I should be likely to pick the same things that other people would pick." (*Letters*, pp. 732–733: letter to Herbert Weinstock at Alfred A. Knopf, Inc., November 5, 1951)

"Here is a list of selections which I think is representative. It is based on a different theory than was at the bottom of the selection I made for you some time ago. It is not a list of things that are what 'the author wishes to preserve.' It should not be advertised that way; it is representative." (*Letters*, p. 732: letter to Herbert Weinstock, November 12, 1951)

"The other day I met Marianne Moore in New York. She asked me whether I had included the enclosed poem ['Final Soliloquy of the Interior Paramour'] in the selection for Faber & Faber. I said that I had not but that I had thought of it and wished that I had included it. It is something that you have not yet published, which appeared a while back in the Hudson Review. She seemed to know Mr. [Peter] du Sautoy of Faber and Faber, and I said that, if she would make a copy of the poem and send it to Mr. du Sautoy as the concluding poem in the book, I should be very glad to have her do so. She did this. I hope this is all right with you. As a matter of fact, Marianne Moore definitely played a part in interesting Faber & Faber. In any event, this is an extremely good poem with which to wind up the English book.

"I am afraid I rather lost sight of the right way to have gone about this, because it all occurred during the course of a conversation. Do please let me know that this is satisfactory to you." (*Letters*, pp. 733–734: letter to Herbert Weinstock, November 29, 1951)

See Alfred A. Knopf's letter of December 4, 1951, to WS, quoted under A 18.

"The selections for the Faber book were made by myself. Mr. Weinstock of Knopf's office seemed to think it was a good selection. He has had a lot of experience with just that sort of thing and he ought to know. My own choice would not likely be what others would choose. Nevertheless, I tried to choose what I thought would be representative." (*Letters*, p. 750: letter to Bernard Heringman, May 13, 1952)

"There is going to be a *Selected Poems* published in London shortly. I returned the proofs yesterday. The book seemed rather slight and small to me – and unbelievably irrelevant to our actual world. It may be that all poetry has seemed like that at all times and always will." (*Letters*, p. 760: letter to Barbara Church, September 10, 1952)

A 19.a.2
Second printing [1954]

no

This printing has the same specifications as A 19.a.1 except for p. 4: '*Second impression January mcmliv*'.

Published January 1954, at 15s., in a printing of 1,000 copies.

Locations: HS, JME.

A 19.a.3
Third printing [1965]

no

This "Faber paper covered Editions" printing has the same specifications as A 19.a.1 except for the following: on p. 4: 'First published in this edition mcmlxv'; stiff coated white paper wrapper, printed in black, purple, and green.

Published May 1965, at 7s. 6d., in a printing of 1,000 copies.

Raoul Dufy

A NOTE BY

WALLACE STEVENS

A 20: cover title; printed in dark blue on light blue paper; 9 × 11 inches

A 20 RAOUL DUFY
[*1953*]

Copyright statement: Rubber-stamped in black, at bottom of verso of front cover: Copyright 1953 by Pierre Berès, Inc. New York.

Collation: [1]². Pp. [1–4].

Typography and paper: Set in Linotype Janson; blue initial 'R' at beginning of text and the words "Raoul Dufy" in the title cut by hand; colophon set in Foundry Janson. White wove Arnold paper, watermarked: 'UNBLEACHED ARNOLD'.

Pagination: pp. 1–4: text.

Contents: Essay on Raoul Dufy's *La Fée Electricite.*

Colophon: p. [4]: [abbreviation 'No.' and Arabic numerals, written in ink] | *Copyright 1953 by Pierre Berès, Inc. New York.* | *Printed by the Ram Press in an edition of* 200 *numbered copies on handmade Arnold paper.*

Binding: Semistiff blue laid paper wrapper, watermarked: 'Ticonderoga Text', tied with a silken red cord. Printed on front in blue.

Published 1953 [ca. August 8, 1953], at $2.00, in an edition of 200 copies.

Reprinting: Reprinted on pp. 286–289 of *OP*, A 26, along with the subtitle on p. 286: '(A NOTE ON La Fée Electricité)'.

Locations: CtY, DLC (deposit copy stamped "Aug. 3, 1953"), HS, InU, JME.

Note: This text by WS was never published as the introduction to a volume of Dufy lithographs, as has been reported. In a letter of May 12, 1971, to the compiler, Pierre Berès wrote: "The Note by Wallace Stevens was only a blurb. The Dufy lithographs were published in a large 10-page portfolio in limited number with no covering text." The only text that was published with a reproduction of Dufy's *La Fée Electricité* was Bernard Dorival's *La belle histoire de la fee Electricité de Raoul Dufy* (Paris: Berès, 1953).

A 21 MATTINO DOMENICALE
[*1954*]

WALLACE STEVENS

MATTINO DOMENICALE

ED ALTRE POESIE

A CURA DI RENATO POGGIOLI

GIULIO EINAUDI EDITORE

A 21: $8^{1}/_{2} \times 6^{1}/_{8}$ inches

Collation: [1]⁸ 2-11⁸ 12² 12*⁴. Pp. [1-6] 7 [8-12] 13-18 [19-21] 22-37 [38-39] 40-49 [50-51] 52-117 [118-119] 120-139 [140-141] 142-165 [166-168] 169-185 [186-188].

Typography and paper: Set in Monotype Elzevir. White wove paper.

Pagination: pp. 1-2: blank; p. 3: series note, 'NUOVA COL-LANA DI POETI TRADOTTI | CON TESTO A FRONT | 3.'; p. 4: copyright page; p. 5: title page; p. 6: blank; p. 7: table of contents; p. 8: blank; p. 9: dedication, 'A Harry Levin | R.P.'; p. 10: blank; p. 11: section title, 'INTRODUZIONE'; p. 12: blank; pp. 13-16: text, signed 'RENATO POGGIOLI'; pp. 17-18: 'NOTA BIBLIOGRAFICA'; p. 19: section title, 'POEMETTI'; p. 20: blank; p. 21: section title, 'SUNDAY MORNING | MAT-TINO DOMENICALE'; pp. 22-37: text; p. 38: blank; p. 39: section title, 'PETER QUINCE AT THE CLAVIER | PETER QUINCE ALLA SPINETTA'; pp. 40-49: text; p. 50: blank; p. 51: section title, 'THE MAN WITH THE BLUE GUITAR | UOMO DALLA CHITARR AZURRA'; pp. 52-117: text; p. 118: blank; p. 119: section title, 'CREDENCES OF SUMMER | CREDENZE D'ESTATE'; pp. 120-139: text; p. 140: blank; p. 141: section title, 'LIRICHE'; pp. 142-165: test; p. 166: blank; p. 167: section title, 'POSTILLE'; p. 168: blank; pp. 169-185: text; p. 186: blank; p. 187: colophon; p. 188: blank.

Contents: Introduzione (by Renato Poggioli)—Sunday Morning (Mattino domenicale)—Peter Quince at the Clavier (Peter Quince alla spinetta)—The Man with the Blue Guitar (L'uomo dalla chitarra azzura)—Credences of Summer (Credenze d'estate)—Infanta Marina (Infanta Marina)—Domination of Black (Dominio del nero)—The Snow Man (L'uomo di neve)—Disil-lusionment of Ten O'Clock (Delusione alla dieci)—Thirteen Ways of Looking at a Blackbird (Tredici maniere di guardare un merlo)—The Sun This March (Il sole questo marzo)—The House Was Quiet and the World Was Calm (Era in quiete la casa e il mondo in calma)—The River of Rivers in Connecticut (Il fiume dei fiumi in Connecticut)—Postille.

Note: In addition to the first appearance in print of "The River of Rivers in Connecticut," p. 164 in English, p. 165 in Italian, this book contains extensive commentaries on the poems by WS in English; these explanatory comments had been sent to Renato Poggioli in letters by WS and are reprinted in *Letters*, A 29.

The English and Italian texts of the poems are printed *en face*.

Colophon: p. [187]: Finito di stampare | dalla Stamperia Artistica Nazionale | Torino. il 23 dicembre 1953.

Binding and dust jacket: Stiff white paper wrapper, printed in black on front and on spine; on front: 'NUOVA COLLANA DI POETI TRADOTTI | CON TESTO A FRONTE | WALLACE STEVENS | MATTINO DOMENICALE | ED ALTRE POESIE | A CURA DI RENATO POGGIOLI | [device]'; on spine: 'STEVENS | MATTINO | DOME- | NICALE | EINAUDI'. All edges rough trimmed. Pasted to inside of back wrapper is ticket: 'Wallace Stevens | Mattino domenicale L. 1500 | Giulio Einaudi editore'. Unprinted glassine dust jacket.

Published January 1954, at Lire 1500, in an edition of 3,000 copies.

Locations: CtY, DLC, HS, JME, PSt, TxU.

Annotations: "The copies of *Mattino Domenicale* came a few days ago giving quite a flutter to the colored boy who brought them in to me. He collects stamps. They gave me no less of a flutter when I saw what a handsome book Einaudi has made. The format is fastidious in every respect. I could not be more pleased. It is possible that in Italy poems indifferent to form, or, rather, poems in familiar forms, will be regarded as lacking something, although I hope not. One runs a risk by this indifference. Yet I have never felt that form matters enough to allow myself to be controlled by it.

"It has been a great pleasure to work with you and, now that the job is done and the result is visible, I salute you." (*Letters*, p. 817: letter to Renato Poggioli, February 5, 1954)

"Several of my friends have received copies of *Mattino Domenicale* and have written to praise it in every way. They think the book as a piece of book-making is a handsome job. They like your own work to the extent that they are able to appreciate it and even the Italian language comes in for a bouquet. One friend wrote to say that Italian is, par excellence, a language to read out loud and she said that this book because of the juxtaposition of the poems makes it possible for her to read the Italian and at the same time enjoy it in the face of the original." (*Letters*, p. 824: letter to Renato Poggioli, March 4, 1954)

no

OPCI

7/27

A 22 THIRTEEN WAYS OF LOOKING
AT A BLACKBIRD
[*1954*]

[Double title page, in gray] [left] thirteen ways of | [right] WALLACE STEVENS | looking at a blackbird | with thirteen plates by Michael Train

Collation: [1]¹⁶. Pp. [1–32].

Typography and paper: Set by hand; capitals, including 'WALLACE STEVENS' on the title page, and numerals for each section of the poem in Bulmer; lowercase letters in Garamond Bold; colophon in Times Roman. Heavy white wove paper, except for pp. [1–2] and [31–32] which are heavy black wove paper; $9^{11}/_{16} \times 7^{11}/_{16}$ inches. Illustrations made from wood blocks printed on the text paper.

Pagination: p. 1: blank; p. 2: title page, left; p. 3: title page, right; pp. 4–29: illustrations and text of poem, the thirteen plates each on versos, the text on rectos, with each of the thirteen sections of the poem on a separate page; p. 30: colophon, pp. 31–32: blank.

Contents: Thirteen-section poem.

Note: The gray of the print is the same on both verso and recto of the title page, but seems lighter on the verso because of the black paper.

Colophon: p. [30]: Reprinted from HARMONIUM by Wallace Stevens | by permission of the publisher Alfred A. Knopf, Inc. | Copyright 1923, 1931 by Alfred A. Knopf, Inc. | Designed and printed with thirteen original plates | by Michael Train. Chicago May, 1954 at the | Institute of Design, I.I.T. 100 copies

Binding: Heavy gray wove paper wrapper, printed on front in red: 'thirteen ways of looking at a blackbird'. Stapled; all edges trimmed.

Published May 1954, in an edition of 100 copies; not for sale. First published in *Others*, December 1917 (C 53), and reprinted in *Others An Anthology of the New Verse*, 1917 (B 8), *H-1923* (A 1), and elsewhere, including *CP* (A 23), *Poems* (A 27), and *Palm* (A 30), this was the poem's first separate publication.

Locations: HS, ICI-D, JME.

A 23 COLLECTED POEMS

A 23.a.1
First American printing (1954)

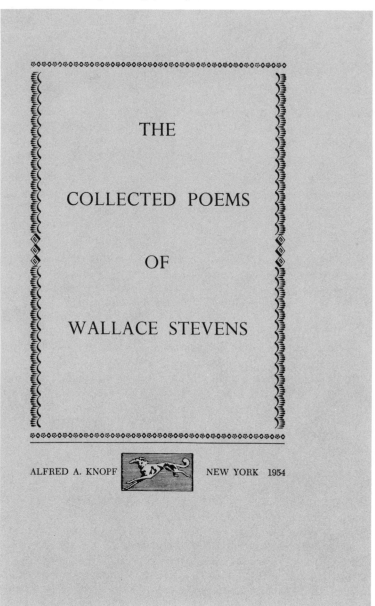

A 23.a.1: 9⅜ × 6³⁄₁₆ inches

Collation: [1–15]¹⁶ [16]⁸ [17–18]¹⁶. Pp. [*1–2*] [i–iv] v–xv [xvi] [1–2] 3–113 [114–116] 117–162 [163–164] 165–188 [189–190] 191–281 [282–284] 285–408 [409–410] 411–497 [498–500] 501–534 i–v [vi–viii]. Frontispiece tipped in facing p. [iii].

Typography and paper: Set in Linotype Electra. White laid paper, watermarked: 'WARREN'S | OLDE STYLE'.

Pagination: p. 1: blank; p. 2: limitation statement; p. i: half title, 'THE COLLECTED POEMS | OF | WALLACE STEVENS'; p. ii: 'BY | *Wallace Stevens* | [thirteen lines]'; tipped in leaf, recto blank, verso frontispiece photograph of WS by Sylvia Salmi; p. iii: title page; p. iv: copyright page; pp. v–xvi: table of contents; p. 1: section title, 'HARMONIUM'; p. 2: blank; pp. 3–113: text; p. 114: blank; p. 115: section title, 'IDEAS OF ORDER'; p. 116: blank; pp. 117–162: text; p. 163: section title, 'THE MAN | WITH THE BLUE GUITAR'; p. 164: blank; pp. 165–188: text; p. 189: section title, 'PARTS OF A WORLD'; p. 190: blank; pp. 191–281: text; p. 282: blank; p. 283: section title, 'TRANSPORT TO SUMMER'; p. 284: blank; pp. 285–408: text; p. 409: section title, 'THE AURORAS OF AUTUMN'; p. 410: blank; pp. 411–497: text; p. 498: blank; p. 499: section title, 'THE ROCK'; p. 500: blank; pp. 501–534: text; pp. i–v: 'INDEX OF TITLES OF POEMS'; p. vi: colophon; pp. vii–viii: blank.

Contents: HARMONIUM – IDEAS OF ORDER – THE MAN WITH THE BLUE GUITAR – PARTS OF A WORLD – TRANSPORT TO SUMMER – THE AURORAS OF AUTUMN – The Rock (An Old Man Asleep – The Irish Cliffs of Moher – The Plain Sense of Things – One of the Inhabitants of the West – Lebensweisheitspielerei – The Hermitage at the Centre – The Green Plant – Madame La Fleurie – To an Old Philosopher in Rome – Vacancy in the Park – The Poem That Took the Place of a Mountain – Two Illustrations That the World Is What You Make of It: The Constant Disquisition of the Wind and The World Is Larger in Summer – Prologues to What Is Possible – Looking across the Fields and Watching the Birds Fly – Song of Fixed Accord – The World as Meditation – Long and Sluggish Lines – A Quiet Normal Life – Final Soliloquy of the Interior Paramour – The Rock: Seventy Years Later; The Poem as Icon; and Forms of the Rock in a Night-Hymn – St. Armorer's Church from the Outside – Note on Moonlight – The Planet on the Table – The River of Rivers in Connecticut – Not Ideas about the Thing but the Thing Itself).

Limitation statement: p. [2]: THE FIRST EDITION OF | *The Collected Poems of Wallace Stevens* | IS LIMITED TO | TWENTY-FIVE HUNDRED NUMBERED COPIES | *This is number* [numerals in ink]

Colophon: p. [vii, at end]: A NOTE ON THE TYPE | *This book is set in Electra, a Linotype face designed by W. A. Dwiggins. This face cannot be classified as either | modern or old-style. It is not based on any historical | model, nor does it echo any particular period or style. | It avoids the extreme contrast between thick and thin | elements that marks most modern faces, and attempts | to give a feeling of fluidity, power, and speed. | The typography and binding were designed by W. A. | Dwiggins. | The book was composed by The Plimpton Press, | Norwood, Mass., and printed and bound by Kingsport | Press, Inc., Kingsport, Tennessee.* | [device of W. A. Dwiggins]

Binding and dust jacket: Maroon V cloth; on the front cover an abstract design stamped in gold with the initials 'WS' above it stamped in silver; on the back cover the Borzoi device stamped in blind; on the spine two designs stamped in gold, the rest stamped in silver: '[design] | THE | COLLECTED | POEMS | OF | WALLACE | STEVENS | [design] | ALFRED · A · KNOPF'. Sized white wove endpapers; top edges stained yellow; fore and bottom edges rough trimmed. Dust jacket, printed in red, white, and black; Sylvia Salmi's photograph of WS on front; sixteen-line biographical note on back; on the front flap: '. . . The present volume is being published to honor him on his seventy-fifth birthday, October 2, 1954.' and in red 'THE FIRST EDITION OF *The Collected Poems of* | *Wallace Stevens* IS LIMITED TO TWENTY-FIVE | HUNDRED NUMBERED COPIES . . .'; on the back flap, a listing of the contents.

Published October 1, 1954, at $7.50, in a printing of 2,500 copies.

Note: *Harmonium* is reprinted from the 1931 edition; its contents, as well as those of all the early books, are reprinted here with the exception of "Owl's Clover," which had been included in *The Man with the Blue Guitar*, and "The Woman That Had More Babies Than That" and "Life on a Battleship," both of which had been in *Parts of a World*. With the exception of six poems ("To an Old Philosopher in Rome," "Two Illustrations that the World Is What You Make It," "Prologues to What Is Possible," "Song of Fixed Accord," "Final Soliloquy of the Interior Paramour," and "The River of Rivers in Connecticut"), the poems in the section "The Rock" appear here for the first time in book form.

Locations: CLU, CtY, DLC (deposit copy stamped "Sept. 20, 1954"), HS, InU, JME, RPB.

Annotations: "Thanks for your note of August 27th. It came on the eve of the holiday and as I wanted to think about your suggestion I put off answering it until now.

"My 75th birthday falls in the autumn of 1954. That may be an appropriate time to publish a selected volume. In any event, I favor a selected volume as against a collected volume.

"Your check came this morning and cheered me up because it made me feel that my books are at least paying their way." (*Letters*, pp. 759–760: letter to Alfred A. Knopf, September 2, 1952)

"I think that I should have difficulty in putting together another volume of poems, as much as I should prefer that to a collection. But I might as well face the fact. If, therefore, you are interested in a collected volume, it is all right with me. It would save a lot of work, assuming that you have a complete set of my books which you could use to work from, if I could send you a list of the things that I don't want to go into a collected edition. Moreover, this would expedite the job. My seventy-fifth birthday falls on October 2, which is only about five months away." (*Letters*, p. 829: letter to Alfred A. Knopf, April 22, 1954)

"Some years ago Knopf and I met in New York to discuss a selection or a collection, as a result of which I sent him AURORAS OF AUTUMN. A collection is very much like sweeping under the rug. As for a selection, I always thought that someone else should make it. But the question has come up again. I had written to him to say that I was content to have a collection published and that is probably what will be published because if anything is to be published at all more or less at the same time as my birthday it ought to be started at once since it takes about six months to manufacture a book.

"I have no particular objection to a selection against a collection. They are different in the sense that people read selected poems but don't buy them. On the other hand, they buy collected poems but don't read them. I am willing to do anything that Knopf wants." (*Letters*, p. 829: letter to Norman Holmes Pearson, April 27, 1954)

"My idea of a volume of collected poems would be to include everything in HARMONIUM, everything in IDEAS OF ORDER, everything in THE MAN WITH THE BLUE GUITAR except *Owl's Clover* of which there are about thirty pages, everything in PARTS OF A WORLD except *Life on a Battleship* and *The Woman That Had More Babies Than That*, everything in TRANSPORT TO SUMMER and everything in AURORAS OF AUTUMN. If this is not what you have in mind, this will give you a chance to express your own idea.

"When PARTS OF A WORLD was printed, the type was set in a way that indicated that I thought that a space between words could be used as a significant element in poetry, which is not true. If the work has to be re-set, it should be done in a perfectly normal way.

"There is attached a sheet on which I have placed a proposed title ['THE WHOLE OF HARMONIUM / COLLECTED POEMS / OF / W.S.'] in an effort to get away from the customary sort of thing. I know that it is a bit early to think about the title.

"I had a letter yesterday from Norman Holmes Pearson of New Haven who has been speaking of a volume of selected poems something like the Faber selection. I purposely omitted from the Faber book a number of things that I like. If you thought that a full sized Collected Poems would be less attractive than a selection, I could add to the Faber collection; let us say, include in a fresh collection everything that is in the Faber selection and other things like *The Comedian as the Letter C*, etc. In any event, there is no reason why if a first selection went well, a second selection could not follow. I shall assume, however, that what you want is a complete collection. I am sending you the present letter with that in mind so that you can get under way. There are some poems that I shall want to add by manuscript which I shall send you after we are all set. It is unnecessary to send these today." (*Letters*, pp. 830–831: letter to Alfred A. Knopf, April 27, 1954)

"I have your two letters of May 5 for both of which I am sincerely grateful. I believe that this takes care of everything except the following. I was not very alert when I approved of the words LATER POEMS for the new section. Last night I thought of a number of other possible titles for this section and still further possibilities may occur. The one that I liked best is AMBER UMBER. These words have identity, which is more than can be said for LATER POEMS." (*Letters*, p. 831: letter to Herbert Weinstock at Alfred A. Knopf, Inc., May 6, 1954)

"We shall not be able to use AMBER UMBER. I liked the words even though they sounded like Hopkins. But, as I have not read Hopkins, that was not a difficulty. It turns out, however, that these exact words have been used by Christopher Fry. I have not read Fry either. But, under the circumstances, I shall have to think of something else. I have a number of other things in mind. However, I shall have to write you later when I have made a choice." (*Letters*, p. 833: letter to Herbert Weinstock, May 12, 1954)

"I suggest that we call the final section THE ROCK. This is the name of one of the poems in that section that I particularly like. If you think well of this title, please go ahead and use it." (*Letters*, p. 833: letter to Herbert Weinstock, May 13, 1954)

"I thought of all the objections which you suggest in your letter of May 24 to the title THE WHOLE OF HARMONIUM and brushed them aside. But with all those wise people you speak of thinking that the thing should be called THE COLLECTED POEMS OF WALLACE STEVENS, a machine-made title if there ever was one, it is all right with me." (*Letters*, p. 834: letter to Alfred A. Knopf, May 25, 1954)

Canadian publication
The copyright page of the first Knopf printing states that the book was published simultaneously by McClelland and Stewart, Toronto. This statement is a copyright formality, and no Toronto imprint has been located.

A 23.a.2–A 23.a.7
Second through seventh American printings (1955–1964)

To date, there have been seven American printings of this book, including the initial one: second printing, February 1955, 2,100 copies; third printing, May 1955, 4,000 copies; fourth printing, December 1957, 3,325 copies; fifth printing, July 1961, 3,125 copies; sixth printing, February 1963, 3,000 copies; and seventh printing, March 1964, 3,000 copies. The later printings vary from the first only in details of the binding and the dust jacket, p. [2] from which the limitation statement has been removed, the date on the title page, and the information on p. [iv]. The later printings are in bindings of blue cloth; their top edges are stained red; green or blue is substituted for red on the dust jackets of the later printings; on the front flap of the later jackets, in place of the limitation statement, is: '1955 WINNER OF THE | PUL-ITZER PRIZE IN POETRY | AND THE NATIONAL BOOK AWARD | IN POETRY'. On p. [iv] a new date is added for each new printing, for example, second printing: 'FIRST COL-LECTED EDITION PUBLISHED OCTOBER 1, 1954 | SECOND PRINTING, FEBRUARY 1955'; third printing: 'FIRST COL-LECTED EDITION PUBLISHED OCTOBER 1, 1954 | SECOND PRINTING, FEBRUARY 1955 | THIRD PRINTING, MAY 1955'.

A 23.a.8
First English printing [1955]

[Within a frame of ornaments] THE | COLLECTED POEMS | OF | WALLACE STEVENS | [below the frame, rule] | FABER AND FABER LIMITED 24 RUSSELL SQUARE | LONDON

Collation: [1]⁸ 2–35⁸. The remainder of the collation is the same as A 23.a.1.

Typography and paper: Reprinted by offset from the first American printing. White wove paper; $8^9/_{16} \times 5^3/_4$ inches.

Pagination: The same as A 23.a.1 except for the absence of the limitation statement on p. [2]; on p. iv, in place of the copy-right statement, is: '*First published in England in mcmlv*'.

Binding and dust jacket: Gray S cloth; on spine, stamped in gold: 'THE | COLLECTED | POEMS | OF | WALLACE | STE-VENS | FABER AND | FABER'. Green dust jacket printed in red and black, with a list of some Faber poetry on back.

Published October 14, 1955, at 42s., in a printing of 2,000 copies.

Locations: DLC, HS.

A 23.a.9 and A 23.a.10
Second and third English printings [1959, 1961]

The same as A 23.a.8.

A 24 NATIONAL BOOK AWARD SPEECH
(*1955*)

[At top of first page and on left side] Address of Wallace Stevens | National Book Award | New York City | January 25, 1955 | [on right side] HOLD FOR RELEASE | 6 P.M. Tuesday, January 25, 1955

No copyright statement appears on this speech.

Collation: Two leaves. Pp. [1–2] 3 [4].

Typography and paper: Mimeographed, rectos only, from typewritten copy. White wove paper; 10 × 8⅛ inches.

Pagination: p. 1: title and text; p. 2: blank; p. 3: text, at bottom '# 330'; p. 4: blank.

Unbound; stapled in upper left-hand corner.

Note: WS received the National Book Award for *The Collected Poems of Wallace Stevens*. This speech by WS, not reprinted in its entirety elsewhere, was delivered by him at the Hotel Commodore in New York City, January 25, 1955. An excerpt from the speech appeared in *Publishers Weekly* for February 5, 1955. See C 217.

Released January 25, 1955; not for sale; number of copies unknown.

Locations: HS, W. Stuart Debenham.

A 25 CONNECTICUT
(1955)

[On upper third of first page] THIS SCRIPT IS THE PROPERTY OF THE USA. | IT MAY NOT BE USED FOR COMMERCIAL | PURPOSES AND IS SUBJECT TO RECALL ON | DEMAND.| CENTRAL PROGRAM SERVICES DIVISION | TALKS AND FEATURES BRANCH | THIS IS AMERICA # 3 | John Pauker August, 1955 | *WALLACE STEVENS ON CONNECTICUT*

No copyright statement appears on this radio script.

Collation: Five leaves. Pp. [1] 2–5.

Typography and paper: Mimeographed, rectos only, from typewritten copy. White wove paper; 11 × 8½ inches.

Pagination: p. 1: title, directional material, and announcer's preliminary remarks, including biographical note on WS; p. 2: blank; p. 3: biographical note continued and beginning of text; p. 4: blank; p. 5: text; p. 6: blank; p. 7: text and announcer's closing remarks; p. 8: blank; p. 9: end of announcer's remarks; p. 10: blank.

Unbound; stapled in upper left-hand corner.

Note: The typescript submitted by WS to the United States Information Agency bears the title 'Connecticut Composed' and was received in the offices of the Agency on April 20, 1955. Before the script was typed and mimeographed as it is here and reprinted in *The Hartford Courant* for July 21, 1955, as 'This is Connecticut', C 223, and in *OP*, A 26, as 'Connecticut', about 335 words were deleted from it by the Agency's editor, John Pauker, who was chief of the Talks and Features Branch.
    This Voice of America broadcast was not delivered by WS himself, but was read by an announcer.

Issued August, 1955; not for sale; number of copies unknown.

Location: JME.

A 26 OPUS POSTHUMOUS

A 26.a.1
First American printing (1957)

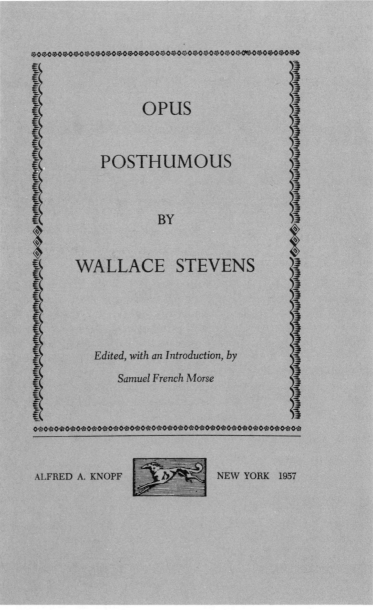

OPUS

POSTHUMOUS

BY

WALLACE STEVENS

Edited, with an Introduction, by

Samuel French Morse

ALFRED A. KNOPF   NEW YORK   1957

A 26.a.1: $9\frac{3}{8} \times 6\frac{1}{4}$ inches

Collation: [1–11]¹⁶. Pp. [1–4] [i–iv] v–vi [vii–viii] ix–xi [xii]
xiii–xxxvii [xxxviii–xl] [1–2] 3–124 [125–126] 127–153 [154–
156] 157–180 [181–182] 183–300 [301–308].

Typography and paper: Set in Linotype Electra. Ornamental
rules are used throughout at the beginning of sections and as
dividers. White laid paper, watermarked: 'WARREN'S | OLDE
STYLE'.

Pagination: pp. *1–3:* blank; p. *4:* 'THE BOOKS OF / *WALLACE
STEVENS* / [twelve lines]'; p. i: half title, 'OPUS / POSTHU-
MOUS'; p. ii: blank; p. iii: title page; p. iv: copyright page; pp.
v–vii: 'Preface'; p. viii: blank; pp. ix–xii: table of contents; pp.
xiii–xxxviii: 'Introduction'; p. xxxix: two quotations on '*Cézanne
at the Lefèvre*'; p. xl: blank; p. 1: section title, 'POEMS'; p. 2:
blank; pp. 3–124: text; p. 125: section title, 'PLAYS'; p. 126:
blank; pp. 127–153: text; p. 154: blank; p. 155: section title,
'ADAGIA'; p. 156: blank; pp. 157–180: text; p. 181: section title,
'PROSE'; p. 182: blank; pp. 183–296: text; pp. 297–301: 'A
NOTE ON THE DATES'; p. 302: blank; p. 303: '*A NOTE ON
THE AUTHOR*'; p. 304: 'A NOTE ON THE TYPE'; pp. 305–308:
blank.

Contents: Preface [signed 'S.F.M.'] – Introduction [by Samuel
French Morse] – Poems from Phases, I–VI – The Silver Plough-
Boy – Bowl – Poems from Primordia, 1–7 – Blanche McCarthy –
Poems from Lettres d'un Soldat, I–IX – Architecture – Stanzas
from Le Monocle de Mon Oncle – Peter Parasol – Exposition of
the Contents of a Cab – Piano Practice at the Academy of the
Holy Angels – The Indigo Glass in the Grass – Romance for a
Demoiselle Lying in the Grass – Anecdote of the Abnormal –
Infernale – This Vast Inelegance – Lulu Gay – Lulu Morose –

Saturday Night at the Chiropodist's — Mandolin and Liqueurs — The Shape of the Coroner — Red Loves Kit — Metropolitan Melancholy — Annual Gaiety — Good Man, Bad Woman — The Woman Who Blamed Life on a Spaniard — Secret Man — The Drum-Majors in the Labor Day Parade — Polo Ponies Practicing — Lytton Strachey, Also, Enters into Heaven — Table Talk — A Room on a Garden — Agenda — Owl's Clover (The Old Woman and the Statue — Mr. Burnshaw and the Statue — The Greenest Continent — A Duck for Dinner — Sombre Figuration) — stanzas from The Man with the Blue Guitar — Five Grotesque Pieces — Life on a Battleship — The Woman That Had More Babies than That — Stanzas for Examination of the Hero in a Time of War — Desire & the Object — Recitation after Dinner — This as Including That — Memorandum — First Warmth — The Sick Man — As at a Theatre — The Desire to Make Love in a Pagoda — Nuns Painting Water-Lilies — The Role of the Idea in Poetry — Americans — The Souls of Women at Night — A Discovery of Thought — The Course of a Particular — How Now, O, Brightener . . . — The Dove in Spring — Farewell without a Guitar — The Sail of Ulysses — Presence of an External Master of Knowledge — A Child Asleep in Its Own Life — Two Letters — Conversation with Three Women of New England — Dinner Bell in the Woods — Reality Is an Activity of the Most August Imagination — Solitaire under the Oaks — Local Objects — Artificial Populations — A Clear Day and No Memories — Banjo Boomer — July Mountain — The Region November — On the Way to the Bus — As You Leave the Room — Of Mere Being — A Mythology Reflects Its Region — Moment of Light — Three Paraphrases from Leon-Paul Fargue — Three Travelers Watch a Sunrise — Carlos among the Candles — A Ceremony — Adagia — A Collect of Philosophy — Two or Three Ideas — The Irrational Element in Poetry — The Whole Man: Perspectives, Horizons — On Poetic Truth — Honors and Acts — A Poet That Matters — Williams — Rubbings of Reality — John Crowe Ransom: Tennessean — The Shaper — A Note on Martha Champion — A Note on Samuel French Morse — Two Prefaces — Raoul Dufy — Marcel Gromaire — Notes on Jean Labasque — A Note on "Les Plus Belles Pages" — Connecticut — A Note on the Dates.

Note: The essay "On Poetic Truth," pp. 235–238, is not by WS; it was included here because it was found in WS's handwriting among his papers. The essay is by H. D. Lewis and was first published in the July 1946 issue of *Philosophy: The Journal of the British Institute of Philosophy*. Identification of this error was made by Joseph N. Riddel in "The Authorship of Wallace Stevens' 'On Poetic Truth'," *Modern Language Notes,*

LXXVI (February 1961), 126–129. The version of "Owl's Clover" reprinted here is the version originally published by The Alcestis Press (A 3). The word *air* appears instead of *ear* in "The Course of a Particular," p. 97, line 14.

Colophon: p. [304]: A NOTE ON THE TYPE | *This book is set in* ELECTRA, *a Linotype face designed by* | W. A. DWIGGINS (1880–1956), *who was responsible for so* | *much that is good in contemporary book design. Although* | *much of his early work was in advertising and he was the* | *author of the standard volume* Layout in Advertising, *Mr.* | *Dwiggins later devoted his prolific talents to book typog-* | *raphy and type design, and worked with great distinction* | *in both fields. In addition to his designs for Electra, he* | *created the Metro, Caledonia, and Eldorado series of type* | *faces, as well as a number of experimental cuttings that* | *have never been issued commercially.* | *Electra cannot be classified as either modern or old-* | *style. It is not based on any historical model, nor does it* | *echo a particular period or style. It avoids the extreme* | *contrast between thick and thin elements which marks* | *most modern faces, and attempts to give a feeling of fluid-* | *ity, power, and speed.* | *This book was composed, printed, and bound by Kings-* | *port Press, Inc., Kingsport, Tenn. The paper was manu-* | *factured by S. D. Warren Co., Boston. The typography* | *and binding are based on designs by W. A. Dwiggins.*

Binding and dust jacket: Reddish brown V cloth; an abstract ornament stamped in gold and the initials 'WS' stamped in silver on the front cover; the Borzoi device stamped in blind on the back cover; on the spine, stamped in silver except for the ornaments, which are stamped in gold: '[ornament] | OPUS | POST- | HUMOUS | Poems, | Plays, | Prose | BY | WALLACE | STEVENS | [ornament] | ALFRED·A·KNOPF'. Sized white wove endpapers; top edges stained purple; fore and bottom edges rough trimmed. White and green dust jacket, printed in green, white, and black; Sylvia Salmi's photograph of WS on front; on the back a twenty-one line biographical note on WS and a six-line biographical note on the editor.

Published August 19, 1957, at $6.75, in a printing of 4,800 copies.

Locations: CLU, CtY, DLC (deposit copy stamped "July 31, 1957"), HS, InU, JME.

Canadian publication
The copyright page of the first Knopf printing states that the book was published simultaneously by McClelland and Stewart,

Toronto. This statement is a copyright formality, and no Toronto imprint has been located.

A 26.a.2–A 26.a.4
Second through fourth American printings (1966, 1969, 1971)

Two thousand copies were published in September 1966; on p. iv of this printing is the notation: 'Second Printing, July 1966'. One thousand copies were published in October 1969; on p. iv of this printing is the notation: 'Third Printing, September 1969'. One thousand copies were published in May 1971; on p. iv of this printing is the notation: 'Fourth Printing, May 1971'.

In these printings the fourteenth line of "The Course of a Particular" reads: 'Then they are in the final finding of the ear, in the thing'.

In the fourth printing of May 1971, the following note by the publisher is added on p. vii: 'After publication of *Opus Posthumous* in 1957, it was learned that the essay included herein (pp. 235–8) as "On Poetic Truth" had not been written by Wallace Stevens but had been copied out by him for future reference from an essay of the same title by H. D. Lewis, first printed in the July 1946 issue of *Philosophy: The Journal of the British Institute of Philosophy*. For further details, see Joseph N. Riddel's article "The Authorship of Wallace Stevens' 'On Poetic Truth'" in *Modern Language Notes*, Vol. LXXVI, February 1961, pp. 126–9.'

A 26.a.5
First English printing [1959]

[rule] | [ornamental rule] | OPUS POSTHUMOUS | [ornamental rule] | WALLACE STEVENS | *Edited, with an Introduction, by* | *Samuel French Morse* | FABER AND FABER LTD | 24 Russell Square | London

Collation: [A]⁸ B–U⁸ V⁸ W⁴; the printer has varied the traditional alphabet, using both U and V, but omitting J. Pp. [i–iv] v–vi [vii–viii] ix–xi [xii] xiii–xxxvii [xxxviii–xl] [1–2] 3–124 [125–126] 127–153 [154–156] 157–180 [181–182] 183–300 [301–304].

Typography and paper: Reprinted by offset from the first American printing, A 26.a.1. White wove paper; $8^{7}/_{16} \times 5^{1}/_{2}$ inches.

Pagination: Substituted for the copyright statement on p. iv of the American printing is a new statement that begins '*First published in mcmlix* | *by Faber and Faber Limited* | . . .'.

Binding and dust jacket: Blue S cloth; stamped on the spine, in gold: 'OPUS POSTHUMOUS *by Wallace Stevens* [all within gold-stamped rules]' and across foot of spine, stamped in gold: 'FABER'. Sized white wove endpapers; all edges trimmed. Pink and gray dust jacket, printed in black; on the back is a list of some Faber poetry; on the back flap are excerpts from some reviews of earlier works by WS.

Published December 18, 1959, at 36s., in a printing of 1,500 copies.

Locations: DLC, HS, InU, JME.

POEMS

BY

WALLACE
STEVENS

SELECTED,

AND WITH AN

INTRODUCTION,

BY

SAMUEL FRENCH MORSE

VINTAGE

BOOKS

■

NEW YORK

1959

A 27.a.1 : 7³/₁₆ × 4¹/₄ inches

A 27 POEMS BY WALLACE STEVENS

A 27.a.1
First printing (1959)

A NOTE OF ACKNOWLEDGMENT

no

OPC1

7/87

FOR permission to use such new material as appears in the
Introduction of this volume I am indebted first of all to
Mrs. Holly Stephenson. I should also like to thank Mr.
Thomas McGreevy of Dublin, Ireland, who made available to me copies of letters written by Wallace Stevens.
The excerpts from letters written to M. Paule Vidal were
first printed in the KENYON REVIEW in an essay entitled
"The Native Element." Thanks are also due to the American Philosophical Society, for assistance in making it possible for me to obtain material I should not otherwise
have been able to use.

S. F. M.

© *Elsie Stevens and Holly Stevens, 1957, 1959;
Samuel French Morse, 1959*

PUBLISHED BY VINTAGE BOOKS, INC.

Reprinted by arrangement with ALFRED A. KNOPF, INC.

FIRST VINTAGE EDITION

Collation: [1–104]¹. Pp. [1–2] [i–iv] v–xxiii [xxiv] [1–2] 3–169
[170] 171–173 [174–182].

Typography and paper: Set in Linotype Janson. White wove
paper.

Pagination: pp. *1–2:* blank; p. i: half title, 'Poems | [solid black square ornament] | WALLACE | STEVENS'; p. ii: title page, left; p. iii: title page, right; p. iv: copyright page with 'A NOTE OF ACKNOWLEDGMENT'; pp. v–xx: 'INTRODUC-TION'; pp. xxi–xxiii: table of contents; p. xxiv: blank; p. 1: half title, 'POEMS' | [solid black square ornament] | WALLACE | STEVENS'; p. 2: blank; pp. 3–169: text; p. 170: blank; pp. 171–173: 'A NOTE ON THE DATES'; p. 174: blank; p. 175: bio-graphical note on WS at top of page, colophon at bottom of page; p. 176: blank; pp. 177–180: a list of Vintage books; pp. 181–182: blank.

Contents: A Note of Acknowledgment [signed 'S.F.M.'] – Introduction | [by Samuel French Morse] – Cy Est Pourtraicte, Madame Ste Ursule, et Les Unze Mille Vierges – Peter Quince at the Clavier – Disillusionment of Ten O'Clock – Sunday Morn-ing – Domination of Black – Thirteen Ways of Looking at a Blackbird – The Death of a Soldier – Metaphors of a Magnifico – Depression before Spring – Le Monocle de Mon Oncle – Plough-ing on Sunday – The Indigo Glass in the Grass – Anecdote of the Jar – The Man Whose Pharynx Was Bad – Gubbinal – The Snow Man – Tea at the Palaz of Hoon – Anecdote of the Prince of Peacocks – Bantams in Pine-Woods – Frogs Eat Butterflies. Snakes Eat Frogs. Hogs Eat Snakes. Men Eat Hogs – A High-Toned Old Christian Woman – O Florida, Venereal Soil – The Emperor of Ice-Cream – To the One of Fictive Music – The Comedian as the Letter C – Floral Decoration for Bananas – Academic Discourse at Havana – Sea Surface Full of Clouds – Autumn Refrain – The Pleasures of Merely Circulating – The Idea of Order at Key West – Lions in Sweden – Table Talk – Evening without Angels – Like Decorations in a Nigger Ceme-tery – Sailing after Lunch – The American Sublime – Some Friends from Pascagoula – Anglais Mort à Florence – Farewell to Florida – A Postcard from the Volcano – The Men That Are Falling – The Man with the Blue Guitar – A Rabbit as King of the Ghosts – Country Words – Loneliness in Jersey City – Poetry Is a Destructive Force – The Poems of Our Climate – Study of Two Pears – The Man on the Dump – Connoisseur of Chaos – The Common Life – The Sense of the Sleight-of-Hand Man – Martial Cadenza – Arrival at the Waldorf – Mrs. Alfred Uru-guay – Asides on the Oboe – The Well Dressed Man with a Beard – The News and Weather – Montrachet-le-Jardin – The Motive for Metaphor – Dutch Graves in Bucks County – No Possum, No Sop, No Taters – So-and-So Reclining on Her Couch – Esthétique du Mal – Less and Less Human, O Savage Spirit –

The House Was Quiet and the World Was Calm—Continual Conversation with a Silent Man—A Woman Sings a Song for a Soldier Come Home—The Good Man Has No Shape—The Red Fern—The Prejudice against the Past—Credences of Summer—Someone Puts a Pineapple Together—Of Ideal Time and Choice—A Primitive like an Orb—Our Stars Come from Ireland (I–II)—Questions Are Remarks—An Ordinary Evening in New Haven (I–XI)—Angel Surrounded by Paysans—The Rock—The Course of a Particular—Final Soliloquy of the Interior Paramour—A Quiet Normal Life—To an Old Philosopher in Rome—Prologues to What Is Possible—The World as Meditation—The River of Rivers in Connecticut—The Irish Cliffs of Moher—Not Ideas about the Thing but the Thing Itself—A Child Asleep in Its Own Life—Reality Is an Activity of the Most August Imagination—A Clear Day and No Memories—As You Leave the Room—Of Mere Being—A Note on the Dates [signed 'S.F.M.']

Colophon: p. [175]: *The text of this book was set on the Linotype in Janson, an | excellent example of the influential and sturdy Dutch types that | prevailed in England prior to the development by William | Caslon of his own designs, which he evolved from these Dutch | faces. Of Janson himself little is known, except that he was a | practising typefounder at Leipzig during the years 1660–1687. | The book was composed, printed, and bound by* THE COLONIAL | PRESS, INC., Clinton, Massachusetts. Paper manufactured by S. D. | WARREN COMPANY, Boston. Cover design by LEO LIONNI.

Binding: Perfect bound in heavy white coated paper wrapper; printed in blue, black, and green; on the back are quotations from Louise Bogan, Delmore Schwartz, and S. F. Morse's 'Introduction'. All edges trimmed.

Published August 21, 1959, at $1.25, in a printing of 12,000 copies; Vintage Book K85.

Locations: DLC (deposit copy stamped "Sept. 28, 1959"), HS, JME.

Canadian publication
The copyright page of the first Vintage printing states that the book was published simultaneously by McClelland and Stewart, Toronto. This is a copyright formality, and no Toronto imprint has been located.

A 28 CY EST POURTRAICTE, MADAME STE
URSULE, ET LES UNZE MILLE VIERGES
(1966)

CY EST POURTRAICTE, MADAME STE URSULE, ET LES
UNZE MILLE VIERGES

Collation: Broadside.

Typography and paper: Set by hand in Optima. Heavy coated
white wove paper; 20½ × 13 inches.

Contents: At the top of the broadside, extending for slightly
more than half the sheet, is a black and white gravure, measur-
ing 11¹¹/₁₆ × 14 inches. It is surrounded at top and sides by half-
inch margins. The poem occupies the lower part of the broadside. The title is between the photograph and the text; the text
of the poem is set in two columns: 'FRAIL AS APRIL SNOW'
ending the first column; 'WALLACE STEVENS' at the bottom
and slightly to the right of the second column. Across the bottom of the broadside appears: 'CODY'S BOOKS INC. SPRING
1966. REPRINTED FROM 'THE COLLECTED POEMS OF
WALLACE STEVENS' BY KIND PERMISSION OF ALFRED A.
KNOPF INC. COPYRIGHT 1951 BY WALLACE STEVENS.
PHOTOGRAPH BY WILLIAM PILTZER.'

Note: The illustration is a rotogravure by Charles R. Wood of
Stecher-Traung Lithograph Corp. of San Francisco from a
photograph of iris leaves by William Piltzer; after the graphic
process was completed, the text of the broadside was printed
by Graham Mackintosh in San Francisco.

Published June 1966, in an edition of 2,000 copies; not for sale.
This is the poem's first separate publication. First published in
Rogue, 1915 (C 44), and reprinted in *Others,* 1917 (B 8), *H-1923*
(A 1), *CP* (A 23), *Palm* (A 30), and elsewhere.

Locations: CtY, CU, CU-SB, JME.

A 29 LETTERS OF WALLACE STEVENS

A 29.a.1
First printing (1966)

LETTERS
of WALLACE
STEVENS

SELECTED AND EDITED BY
HOLLY STEVENS
ALFRED·A·KNOPF·NEW YORK·1966

A 29.a.1: $9^{5}/_{16} \times 6^{1}/_{4}$ inches

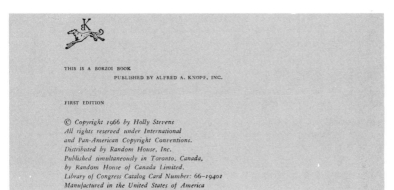

Collation: [1–29]¹⁶ [30]⁸ [31]¹⁶. Pp. *[1–2]* [i–vii] viii–x [xi] xii–xiii [xiv–xv] xvi–xxxviii [xxxix–xl] [1–3] 4–10 [11–13] 14–34 [35–37] 38–53 [54–57] 58–74 [75–77] 78–161 [162–165] 166–186 [187–189] 190–238 [239–241] 242–252 [253–255] 256–394 [395–397] 398–552 [553–555] 556–807 [808–811] 812–890 [891–892] [i] ii–xxxix [xl–xlii].

Typography and paper: Set in Linotype Janson. Running heads, rectos and versos: section titles. Twenty photographic plates tipped in following pp. 22, [54], 86, 118, 182, 214, 310, 342, 854, and 886. White wove paper.

Pagination: p. *1:* blank; p. *2:* 'BY WALLACE STEVENS | [sixteen lines]'; p. i: half title, 'LETTERS OF WALLACE STE-VENS'; p. ii: blank; p. iii: title page; p. iv: copyright page; p. v: dedication, 'FOR PETE'; p. vi: blank; pp. vii–x: 'ACKNOWL-EDGMENTS'; pp. xi–xiii: 'NOTES ON THE EDITING'; p. xiv: blank; pp. xv–xxxviii: 'TABLE OF THE LETTERS'; p. xxxix: 'ILLUSTRATIONS'; p. xl: blank; p. 1: section title, 'I [ornament] 1895–1896 | CUFF-NOTES'; p. 2: blank; pp. 3–10: text; p. 11: section title, 'II [ornament] 1897–1900 | AN ANCHORAGE OF THOUGHT'; p. 12: blank; pp. 13–34: text; p. 35: section title, 'III [ornament] 1900–1901 | A WINDOW IN THE SLUMS'; p. 36: blank; pp. 37–53: text; p. 54: blank; p. 55: section title, 'IV [ornament] 1902–1904 | THINGS AS THEY ARE'; p. 56: blank; pp. 57–74: text; p. 75: section title, 'V [ornament] 1904–1909 | LIGHT AND SHADOW'; p. 76: blank; pp. 77–161: text; p. 162: blank; p. 163: section title, 'VI [ornament] 1910–1915 | VISI-BLE THINGS'; p. 164: blank; pp. 165–186: text; p. 187: section title, 'VII [ornament] 1916–1923 | PRELIMINARY MINU-TIAE'; p. 188: blank; pp. 189–238: text; p. 239: section title, 'VIII [ornament] 1924–1929 | THE EVERYDAY WORLD'; p. 240: blank; pp. 241–252: text; p. 253: section title, 'IX [ornament] 1930–1941 | A FRESHENING OF LIFE'; p. 254: blank; pp. 255–394: text; p. 395: section title, 'X [ornament] 1942– 1947 | THE WORLD ITSELF'; p. 396: blank; pp. 397–552: text; p. 553: section title, 'XI [ornament] 1947–1953 | SPHERES WITHIN SPHERES'; p. 554: blank; pp. 555–807: text; p. 808: blank; p. 809: section title, 'XII [ornament] 1954–1955 | IT MUST BE HUMAN'; p. 810: blank; pp. 811–890: text; p. 891: section title, 'INDEX'; p. 892: blank; pp. i–xxxix: text of index; p. xl: colophon; pp. xli–xlii: blank.

Contents: A collection of 992 letters and journal entries that WS wrote from July 23, 1895, to July 15, 1955.

Colophon: p. [xl, at end]: A NOTE ON THE TYPE | [three asterisks] | *The text of this book was set on the Linotype in Janson, a | recutting made direct from type cast from matrices long | thought to have been made by the Dutchman Anton Janson, | who was a practicing type founder in Leipzig during the years | 1668–87. However, it has been conclusively demonstrated that | these types are actually the work of Nicholas Kis (1650–1702), | a Hungarian, who most probably learned his trade from the | master Dutch type founder Kirk Voskens. The type is an | excellent example of the influential and sturdy Dutch types | that prevailed in England up to the time William Caslon de- | veloped his own incomparable designs from these Dutch faces. | The book was designed by Betty Anderson and was composed, | printed, and bound by The Haddon Craftsmen, Inc., Scranton, | Pennsylvania. The illustrations were printed by Halliday Litho- | graph Corporation, West Hanover, Massachusetts.*

Binding and dust jacket: Gray linen over boards; on the front, stamped in gold on a black rectangle, is a facsimile of WS's signature; on the back the Borzoi device is stamped in blind; on the spine, above and below a large black rectangle, is a band of ornaments stamped in gold; on the black rectangle: 'LETTERS | OF | WALLACE | STEVENS | • | EDITED | BY | HOLLY | STEVENS | • | KNOPF'. Tan and green endpapers, printed in brown, reproducing in facsimile WS's letter of February 2, 1923, to his wife (pp. 233–234 in the text); top edges stained yellow; fore and bottom edges rough trimmed. Dust jacket, black on front, printed in red and white with photograph of WS; white and gray on back, with a quotation from Randall Jarrell's essay "Reflections on Wallace Stevens" printed in red and black; on the front flap of the jacket, printed in red: 'Jacket design by Guy Fleming | Jacket photograph by Sylvia Salmi'; on the back flap a twenty-one-line biographical note on WS.

Published November 10, 1966, at $17.50, in a printing of 6,000 copies; of these, 1,455 copies in sheets were sold to Faber and Faber for the English issue (see below).

Locations: CtY, DLC (deposit copy stamped "Jan. 30, 1967"), HS, InU, JME.

Note: In addition to punctuation and typographical errors of a minor nature, the following list of errors was supplied by Holly Stevens; these will be corrected in a later edition: p. 161, middle, "I look notes" should be "I took notes"; p. 292, line 13, "way" before "MR. BURNSHAW" should be "why"; p. 425, last line, "Everyone feels this when first" should be supplied where it is omitted; p. 438, twelfth line from bottom, "clouds" should be "chords"; p. 445, at end of letter no. 479, the sentence "How he ever became a Canon is the real problem." should be "How he ever became a Canon is the real problem or part of the general problem."; p. 476, middle, "by eyesight" should be "my eyesight"; p. 541, footnote, "Bertraut" should be "VERTRAUT"; p. 596, footnote 2, should be *Mythes et Portraits*, p. 112."

Canadian publication
The copyright page of the first Knopf printing states that the book was published simultaneously by Random House of Canada Ltd., Toronto. This statement is a copyright formality, and no Toronto imprint has been located.

A 29.a.2
First English printing [1967]

LETTERS | *of* WALLACE | STEVENS | [rule of ornaments] | [rule] | SELECTED AND EDITED BY | HOLLY STEVENS | FABER AND FABER · 24 RUSSELL SQUARE · LONDON | [rule] | [rule of ornaments]

Collation, typography, paper, and pagination are the same as in the American edition, A 29.a.1. $9^{3}/_{16} \times 6$ inches. On page iv is a copyright statement that begins '*First published in mcmlxvii | by Faber and Faber Limited | 24 Russell Square London WC 1 | Printed in the U.S.A. | . . .*'

Binding and dust jacket: Rust red S cloth; spine stamped in gold: '[within a single-rule frame on a black panel] LETTERS | OF | WALLACE | STEVENS | [below the framed panel] *edited by* | HOLLY | STEVENS | FABER AND | FABER'. Endpapers same as in A 29.a.1; top edges stained blue; fore and bottom edges trimmed. White dust jacket printed in red and black, with photograph of WS on front.

Note: On p. 425 an erratum slip is inserted on which is printed the words 'Everyone feels this when first' which had been omitted at the bottom of the page (see "Note" under American edition, A 29.a.1).

Published February 9, 1967, at 7 gns., in an edition of 1,455 copies from the American sheets.

Locations: HS, InU, JME.

A 29.a.3
Second American printing (1970)

no
o pc/
7/87

This printing varies from A 29.a.1 only in the change of the date on the title page and the addition of the slug on p. iv: 'SECOND PRINTING, JULY, 1970'.

A 30 THE PALM AT THE END OF THE MIND
(1971)

THE
PALM AT
THE END
OF THE
MIND

Selected Poems and a Play by
WALLACE
STEVENS

Edited by
HOLLY STEVENS

ALFRED A. KNOPF
1971 NEW YORK

A 30: 9⁵/₁₆ × 6¼ inches

This is a Borzoi Book
Published by Alfred A. Knopf, Inc.

Copyright 1967, 1969, 1971 by Holly Stevens
All rights reserved under International and
Pan-American Copyright Conventions.
Published in the United States by Alfred A. Knopf, Inc.,
New York, and simultaneously in Canada by
Random House of Canada Limited, Toronto.
Distributed by Random House, Inc., New York
ISBN: 0-394-46908-9
Library of Congress Catalog Card Number: 75-136350
"Bowl, Cat and Broomstick," a play, was originally
published in the *Quarterly Review of Literature,*
July 30, 1969, Princeton, New Jersey
Manufactured in the United States of America

First Edition

Collation: [1–14]¹⁶. Pp. [1–4] [i–viii] ix–xv [xvi] [1–2] 3–398 [399–400] 401–404 [i–ii] iii–viii [ix–x] xi–xvi [xvii–xxiv].

Typography and paper: Set in Linotype Electra; title page is in Electra and Perpetua Italic; half title, preface title, table of contents title, section titles, and titles of individual poems are in Perpetua Italic. White laid paper.

Pagination: pp. *1–3:* blank; p. *4:* 'OTHER BOOKS BY WALLACE STEVENS | [three lines]'; p. i: half title, *'THE PALM AT THE END | OF THE MIND';* p. ii: blank; p. iii: title page; p. iv: copyright page; p. v: '"The palm at the end of the mind, | Beyond the last thought, rises | In the bronze decor . . ." | *–"Of Mere Being"';* p. vi: blank; p. vii: *'PREFACE';* p. viii: blank; pp. ix–xv: table of contents; p. xvi: blank; p. 1: half title, *'THE PALM AT THE END | OF THE MIND';* p. 2: blank; pp. 3–398: text; p. 399: section title, *'NOTES';* p. 400: blank; pp. 401–404: text of notes; p. i: section title, *'INDEX OF FIRST LINES';* p. ii: blank; pp. iii–viii: text of index of first lines; p. ix: section title, *'INDEX OF TITLES';* p. x: blank; pp. xi–xvi: text of index of titles; p. xvii: 'A NOTE ON THE AUTHOR'; p. xviii: blank; p. xix: 'A NOTE ON THE TYPE'; pp. xx–xxiv: blank.

Contents: Blanche McCarthy – Cy Est Pourtraicte, Madame Ste Ursule, et Les Unze Mille Vierges – Tea – Sunday Morning – Peter Quince at the Clavier – The Silver Plough-Boy – Disillusionment of Ten O'Clock – For an Old Woman in a Wig – Domination of Black – Six Significant Landscapes – Inscription for a Monument – The Worms at Heaven's Gate – In the Carolinas – Indian River – To the Roaring Wind – Valley Candle – Thirteen Ways of Looking at a Blackbird – The Plot against the Giant – Gray Room – Bowl, Cat and Broomstick – The Death of a Soldier – Metaphors of a Magnifico – Depression before Spring

statement on the poetry of war]—Notes Toward a Supreme
Fiction—God Is Good. It Is a Beautiful Night—Certain Phenomena of Sound—Dutch Graves in Bucks County—The Motive
for Metaphor—Chocorua to Its Neighbor—So-And-So Reclining
on Her Couch—No Possum, No Sop, No Taters—The Lack of
Repose—Somnambulisma—The Creations of Sound—Esthétique du Mal—The Bed of Old John Zeller—Less and Less
Human, O Savage Spirit—The Pure Good of Theory—Paisant
Chronicle—Flyer's Fall—Description without Place—Thinking
of a Relation between the Images of Metaphors—Chaos in
Motion and Not in Motion—The House Was Quiet and the World
Was Calm—Late Hymn from the Myrrh-Mountain—Man Carry-
ing Thing—Men Made out of Words—A Woman Sings a Song for
a Soldier Come Home—The Good Man Has No Shape—From the
Packet of Anacharsis—The Dove in the Belly—Mountains
Covered with Cats—The Prejudice Against the Past—Credences
of Summer—A Pastoral Nun—Two Versions of the Same Poem
—Someone Puts a Pineapple Together—Of Ideal Time and
Choice—The Ultimate Poem Is Abstract—The Owl in the Sarco-
phagus—The Auroras of Autumn—A Primitive Like an Orb
—Large Red Man Reading—This Solitude of Cataracts—In a
Bad Time—Metaphor as Degeneration—Our Stars Come from
Ireland—World Without Peculiarity—The Woman in Sunshine
—Imago—Saint John and the Back-Ache—Puella Parvula—An
Ordinary Evening in New Haven—The Old Lutheran Bells at
Home—Questions Are Remarks—Angel Surrounded by Paysans
—Things of August—As at a Theatre—The Rock—A Discovery
of Thought—The Course of a Particular—Final Soliloquy of the
Interior Paramour—Madame La Fleurie—A Quiet Normal Life
—Long and Sluggish Lines—To an Old Philosopher in Rome—
The Poem That Took the Place of a Mountain—Two Illustrations
That the World Is What You Make of It—Prologues to What Is
Possible—Looking Across the Fields and Watching the Birds
Fly—The World as Meditation—An Old Man Asleep—The Plain
Sense of Things—Lebensweisheitspielerei—The Hermitage at
the Centre—The Dove in Spring—The Planet on the Table—The
River of Rivers in Connecticut—Not Ideas about the Thing but
the Thing Itself—The Sail of Ulysses—A Child Asleep in Its
Own Life—On the Way to the Bus—First Warmth—As You Leave
the Room—Reality Is an Activity of the Most August Imagination
—A Clear Day and No Memories—A Mythology Reflects Its
Region—Of Mere Being.

Note: On p. 13 the last word of the first stanza in Section III
of "For an Old Woman in a Wig" is "yellows"; on p. 215 of Robert
Buttel's *Wallace Stevens: The Making of Harmonium* (B 58),

where the poem first appeared in book form, the word is "yellow." The transposition of lines 84 and 86 of "Le Monocle de Mon Oncle," pointed out in G. Thomas Tanselle's "The Text of Stevens's 'Le Monocle de Mon Oncle'," *The Library*, 3rd Ser. XIX (1964), 246–248, was not corrected here. 'NOTES', pp. 401–404, in addition to explanatory material, contains revisions of and additions to the poems which appear in the text.

Colophon: p. [xvii, at end]: A NOTE ON THE TYPE | *This book is set in Electra, a Linotype face de-* | *signed by W. A. Dwiggins. This face cannot be* | *classified as either modern or old-style. It is not* | *based on any historical model, nor does it echo* | *any particular period or style. It avoids the ex-* | *treme contrast between thick and thin elements* | *that marks most modern faces, and attempts to* | *give a feeling of fluidity, power, and speed.* | *The book was composed by The Haddon Crafts-* | *men, Scranton, Pa. and printed and bound by The* | *Haddon Craftsmen, Scranton, Pa.*

Note: A letter of May 3, 1971, from Herbert Weinstock, Editor, Alfred A. Knopf, Inc., to the compiler, states: ". . . most of the type in this book was not freshly set, but was taken from THE COLLECTED POEMS OF WALLACE STEVENS and OPUS POSTHUMOUS. It was all repaged, of course, and new type was set for altered lines, fresh material, notes, and the two indexes."

Binding and dust jacket: Gold cloth; 'WS' stamped in blind on front; Borzoi device stamped in blind on back; on spine, stamped in silver: '[fleuron of rules] | THE | PALM AT | THE END | OF THE | MIND | [fleuron of rules] | WALLACE | STEVENS | [fleuron of rules] | KNOPF | [fleuron of rules]'. White wove unwatermarked endpapers; top edges stained black; fore and bottom edges rough trimmed. Black dust jacket printed in white, gold, and gray; on back is a quotation from Randall Jarrell's essay "Reflections on Wallace Stevens"; on front flap is the notation 'Jacket design by Muriel Nasser'; on back flap is the notation 'Printed in U.S.A. 4/71' and a thirty-one-line biographical note.

Published May 12, 1971, at $10.00, in a printing of 4,000 copies.

Note: The following were published here for the first time in book form: the complete play *Bowl, Cat and Broomstick*, pp. 24–34; lines 10 through 13 of "The Man Whose Pharynx Was Bad," p. 52, as they had appeared originally in *The New Republic* for September 14, 1921 (C 65) (these lines had been omitted from *H-1931*, A 1.b, and from *CP*, A 23); the eighth line of "Autumn Refrain," p. 95, as it had appeared originally in *The Hound and Horn* for Winter 1932 (C 83) (it had been omitted from *Ideas of Order* [1935 and 1936], A 2.a and A 2.b; from *CP*, A 23; and from *Poems*, A 27), the previously unpublished word "things" ending line 9 of Section VII of "The Sail of Ulysses," p. 392; a previously unpublished variant of the third line of the first stanza of "Of Mere Being," p. 398, in which the word "decor" is substituted for the word "distance" as had been printed in *OP*, A 26; the previously unpublished last line "Fruits, forms, flowers, flakes and fountains." of "Nomad Exquisite," p. 401, note; an early, previously unpublished, twelve-line version of "Anecdote of the Prince of Peacocks," p. 402, note; the word "pastiche" in the first line of Section XXVI of "Like Decorations in a Nigger Cemetery," p. 402, note, as previously published in *Poetry* for February 1935 (C 94); three previously unpublished lines found on the reverse of the manuscript "The Old Lutheran Bells at Home," p. 403, note; a six-line previously unpublished variant of the second stanza of "To an Old Philosopher in Rome" and a previously unpublished variant of the first line of the eighth stanza of the same poem, p. 403, note; ten previously unpublished glosses by WS on the carbon typescript of "The Sail of Ulysses," p. 404, note.

Locations: CLU, CtY, DLC (deposit copy stamped "Sept. 2, 1971"), HS, JME.

Canadian publication
The copyright page of the first Knopf printing states that the book was published simultaneously by Random House of Canada Ltd., Toronto. This statement is a copyright formality, and no Toronto imprint has been located.

B. Contributions to Books

B 1 HARVARD LYRICS
(1899)

[in red] HARVARD LYRICS | [in red] *And Other Verses* | [double rule] | BEING SELECTIONS OF THE BEST VERSE | WRITTEN BY HARVARD UNDERGRADU- | ATES WITHIN THE LAST TEN YEARS | SELECTED BY | CHARLES LIVING-STONE STEBBINS | OF THE CLASS OF NINETY-SEVEN | [double rule] | [ornament] | [double rule] | BOSTON | [in red] BROWN AND COMPANY | 144 Purchase Street | M DCCC XCIX [the whole enclosed within a double-rule frame]

1 blank leaf, x, 13–153 pp., 1 blank leaf. Frontispiece drawing of the Johnston Gate in the College Yard, protected by tissue. $7\frac{1}{2} \times 5$ inches. Dark crimson cloth, stamped on front and spine in gold. White endpapers; top edges gilt; fore and bottom edges rough trimmed. No dust jacket seen.

Contains "Vita Mea," p. 28. First published in C 5, this is the poem's only book publication.

Published April 17, 1899, at $1.25.

B 2 ODE
(1900)

HARVARD CLASS | OF '01 | POEM | BY | WILLIAM BOND WHEELWRIGHT | ODE | BY | WALLACE STEVENS | JUNIOR DINNER | May 1, 1900

Cover title. 12 pp. $7\frac{1}{8} \times 5\frac{3}{8}$ inches. Heavy off-white paper, printed in black. Stapled.

Contains "Ode" ('A night in May! | And the whole of us gathered into a room'), pp. 10–12. This is the poem's only publication.

Distributed May 1, 1900, as a keepsake; not for sale.

B 3   CAP AND GOWN
(*1903*)

p PC 1

7/87

[in red] Cap and Gown | (Trade Mark) | Third Series [these first three lines in Black Letter] | [rule] | *Selected by* | *R. L. PAGET* | [rule] | [device] | *BOSTON* | [in red] *L. C. PAGE & COMPANY* | *MDCCCCIII* [the whole enclosed within a single-rule frame]

xiv, 331 pp., 1 blank leaf. Frontispiece portrait, protected by tissue. $7^1/_{16} \times 4^5/_8$ inches. Tan cloth, stamped on front in red, with a vignette of an academic procession stamped in green, black, brown, blue, gray, and the monogram **FR**, thus: 'CAP AND GOWN | R. L. PAGET | [vignette] | THIRD SERIES OF | COLLEGE VERSE'; on spine, stamped in red: 'CAP AND | GOWN | THIRD SERIES OF | COLLEGE VERSE | PAGET | PAGE | [rule] | BOSTON'. White endpapers; top edges gilt; fore and bottom edges rough trimmed. No dust jacket seen.

Note: Two variant bindings have been seen: One is in the same tan cloth, stamped on front in red, with the same vignette, but thus: '[in red] CAP AND GOWN | [in red] R. L. PAGET | [vignette] | [crossed Harvard flags, stamped in red, black, and white] | [in black] HARVARD EDITION'; on spine, stamped in red: 'CAP AND | GOWN | THIRD SERIES OF | COLLEGE VERSE | PAGET | HARVARD | EDITION | PAGE | [rule] | BOSTON'. The second variant binding is for a Yale edition and is identical to the Harvard edition except for the crossed flags which are stamped in blue, black, and white, with a 'Y' instead of an 'H' on each flag; the words 'YALE EDITION' are stamped on the front in black and on the spine in blue. In addition, *The United States Catalog Supplement Books Published 1902– 1905 . . .* records that there were copies bound in "³/₄ levant morocco"; however, a copy so bound has not been located.

The monogram on the front cover is for Amy Rand, the Boston book designer. R. L. Paget is a pseudonym for Frederic Lawrence Knowles, 1869–1905.

Contains "Sonnet" ('There shines the morning star!'), p. 215. First published in C 10, this is the first book publication; reprinted in B 4, B 45, and B 57.

Published 1903, at $1.25 for cloth copies and $2.50 for copies bound in ³/₄ levant morocco.

Variant issue
The same as B 3 in every other respect, a "Cornell edition" has a different binding and at the end, instead of one blank leaf,

three printed leaves containing advertisements and one blank leaf. The binding is tan cloth, stamped on front in red, with a vignette of a woman in academic cap and gown playing a banjo; the initials A.S., which stand for Amy M. Sacker; and a series of banners with the Cornell "C" on them. 'CORNELL EDITION' is stamped in red on the spine. The second page of advertisements announces: 'Cap and Gown. Third Series. | (Trade Mark.) | Selected by R. L. PAGET. | This is a selection of the most recent college verse, | none of which has previously appeared in any similar | compilation, forming a companion volume to "Cap and Gown," first and second series. | Special editions are bound in the colors of the follow- | ing colleges: HARVARD. YALE. PRINCETON. | UNIVERSITY OF PENNSYLVANIA.' There is no mention of the Cornell edition as part of the series.

B 4 VERSES FROM THE HARVARD ADVOCATE
(1906)

[in Black Letter] Dulce est periculum | VERSES | FROM THE | HARVARD ADVOCATE | THIRD SERIES | 1886–1906 | [device] | Thy son, thy servant, dearest Mother mine, | Lays this poor offering on thy holy shrine, – | Would that my tribute worthier were of thee. | Oliver Wendell Holmes, '29 | CAMBRIDGE | THE HARVARD ADVOCATE | 1906 | [in Black Letter] Veritas nihil veretur

1 blank leaf, xiii, 214 pp., 1 leaf, 1 blank leaf. $8^7/_8 \times 6^1/_4$ inches. Crimson cloth, stamped on front and spine in gold. White endpapers; top edges gilt; fore and bottom edges rough trimmed. No dust jacket seen.

Contains "Song" ('She loves me or loves me not,'), p. 74; "Song" ('Ah yes! beyond these barren walls'), p. 74; "Street Songs" ("The Pigeons," "Statuary," "The Minstrel"), pp. 116–117; "Outside the Hospital," p. 118; and "Sonnet" ('There shines the morning star!'), p. 160.

When published originally in The Harvard Advocate, C 26, "Street Songs" included a fourth poem, "The Beggar." Except for "Sonnet" ('There shines the morning star!'), B 3, this is the first publication in book form of these poems; all, including the complete "Street Songs," are reprinted in B 45 and B 57.

Published October 27, 1906, at $2.00.

B 5 ANTHOLOGY OF MAGAZINE VERSE FOR 1915
(1915)

ANTHOLOGY | OF | MAGAZINE VERSE | FOR 1915 | AND
YEAR BOOK OF | AMERICAN POETRY | EDITED BY | WIL-
LIAM STANLEY BRAITHWAITE | [ornament] | NEW YORK
| GOMME & MARSHALL | 1915

xxvii, 1 leaf, 296 pp. $8\frac{5}{8} \times 5\frac{11}{16}$ inches. Tan paper-covered boards
with brown cloth back; white paper labels printed in black on
front and spine. Endpapers; top edges gilt; fore and bottom
edges rough trimmed. Cream dust jacket printed in black.

Contains "Peter Quince at the Clavier," pp. 15–17. Collected
in *CP*, *Poems*, and *Palm*. Reprinted in B 6.

Published November 30, 1915, at $1.75.

B 6 OTHERS
(1916)

OTHERS | AN ANTHOLOGY OF THE NEW VERSE | EDITED
BY | ALFRED KREYMBORG | [device] | [rule] | NEW YORK |
[ornament] ALFRED A KNOPF [ornament] MCMXVI

4 leaves, 152 pp. $8\frac{1}{4} \times 5\frac{1}{4}$ inches. Brown paper-covered boards,
stamped in red (or in gold) on front and spine; Borzoi device
stamped in blind on back. Brown (or white) endpapers; top
edges stained brown in some copies, unstained in others. Orange
dust jacket printed in reddish orange or in black.

Contains "Peter Quince at the Clavier," pp. 122–124; "The Silver
Plough-Boy," p. 125; "Six Significant Landscapes," pp. 125–127;
"The Florist Wears Knee-Breeches," p. 128; "Tattoo," pp. 128–
129; "Song" ('There are great things doing'), p. 129; "Inscription
for a Monument," pp. 129–130; "Bowl," p. 130; and "Domination
of Black," pp. 131–132.

Except for "Peter Quince at the Clavier," the first book publication of which was in B 5, these poems are published here for
the first time in book form. "The Florist Wears Knee-Breeches"
and "Song" ('There are great things doing') were not reprinted
in later compilations of WS's poems. "Peter Quince at the Clavier"
and "Domination of Black" are in *CP*, *Poems*, and *Palm*; "The
Silver Plough-Boy," in *OP*, and *Palm*; "Six Significant Landscapes," in *CP* and *Palm*; "Tattoo," in *CP*; "Inscription For A
Monument," in *Palm*; "Bowl," in *OP*.

Published March 25, 1916, at $1.50. On copyright page: '. . .
Published March, 1916'.

B 7 THE NEW POETRY
(1917)

THE NEW POETRY | AN ANTHOLOGY | EDITED BY | HAR-
RIET MONROE | AND | ALICE CORBIN HENDERSON |
EDITORS OF POETRY | [in Black Letter] New York | THE
MACMILLAN COMPANY | 1917 | *All rights reserved*

xxxi, 1 leaf, 404 pp., 4 leaves, 1 blank leaf. 7¾ × 5¼ inches.
Green cloth, stamped in blind and in gold on front and in gold on
spine. White endpapers; top edges stained brown in some copies,
unstained in others; fore and bottom edges rough trimmed.
Light tan dust jacket printed in brown.

Contains "Peter Quince at the Clavier," "In Battle," and "Sunday
Morning," pp. 320–325.
   "In Battle" appeared originally as "Death's nobility again," the
fourth section of the group called "Phases" in *Poetry*, C 43; first
published in book form here, it was reprinted as part of the
original group in *OP.* "Sunday Morning" is the original five-
stanza version that appeared in *Poetry*, C 47; first published in
book form here and collected in *CP*, *Poems*, and *Palm*.

Published February 28, 1917, at $1.75, in an edition of 4,000
copies. On copyright page: '. . . Set up and electrotyped. Published February, 1917.'

B 8 OTHERS
(1917)

OTHERS | AN ANTHOLOGY OF THE NEW VERSE | (1917) |
EDITED BY ALFRED KREYMBORG | [device] | [rule] | NEW
YORK [ornament] ALFRED A KNOPF [ornament] MCMXVII

120 pp. 7¹³⁄₁₆ × 5¼ inches. Pale orange paper-covered boards,
printed in blue on front and spine. White endpapers; top edges
stained tan; fore and bottom edges rough trimmed. Orange dust
jacket printed in black.

Contains "The Worms at Heaven's Gate," p. 103; "Valley-
Candle," p. 103; "Gray Room," pp. 103–104; "Explanation,"
p. 104; "Theory," p. 105; "Cy Est Pourtraicte, Madame Ste
Ursule, et Les Unze Milles Vierges," pp. 105–106; "Disillusion-
ment of Ten O'Clock," p. 107; "The Plot against the Giant," pp.
107–108; "The Wind Shifts," p. 108; and "Thirteen Ways of
Looking at a Blackbird," pp. 109–111.
   This is the first publication in book form of all these poems;

for "Explanation," "Theory," and "The Plot against the Giant" it is the first publication. "Gray Room" is collected in *Palm*; "Explanation," "Theory," and "The Wind Shifts" are in *CP*; the others are in both *CP* and *Palm*.

Published October 31, 1917, at $1.50. On copyright page: '... Published October, 1917 ...'.

B 9 OTHERS FOR 1919
(1920)

OTHERS FOR 1919 | *An Anthology of the New Verse* | *Edited by Alfred Kreymborg* | NICHOLAS L. BROWN | NEW YORK MCMXX [the whole enclosed within a black single-rule frame]

xiv, 190 pp. 7⅞ × 5⁵/₁₆ inches. Blue paper-covered boards with pale yellow paper labels printed in brown on front cover and spine. White endpapers; fore and bottom edges rough trimmed. Pale yellow dust jacket printed in black.

Contains "Le Monocle de Mon Oncle," pp. 169–174, and eight poems from "Pecksniffiana" ("Fabliau of Florida," "Homunculus et La Belle Etoile," "Exposition of the Contents of a Cab," "Ploughing on Sunday," "Banal Sojourn," "Of the Surface of Things," "The Curtains in the House of the Metaphysician," and "The Paltry Nude Starts on a Spring Voyage"), pp. 175–182.

All published here for the first time in book form. When first published in *Poetry*, C 62, "Pecksniffiana" contained fourteen poems. Except for "Exposition of the Contents of a Cab," which is in *OP*, all of these poems are in *CP*. The poems from "Pecksniffiana" are reprinted in B 14 and B 17.

Published April 24, 1920, at $2.00.

B 10 KORA IN HELL
(1920)

KORA IN HELL: | IMPROVISATIONS | BY | WILLIAM CARLOS WILLIAMS | [device] | BOSTON | THE FOUR SEAS COMPANY | 1920

86 pp., 3 blank leaves. Frontispiece by Stuart Davis tipped in between pp. [2] and [3]. 9⅝ × 6⁵/₁₆ inches. Gray paper-covered boards, stamped in black on front and downward on spine. White endpapers; top edges trimmed; fore and bottom edges rough

trimmed. Orange dust jacket printed in black on some copies; glassine wrapper on others.

Contains a letter on poetry by WS to William Carlos Williams, pp. 17–18. Not reprinted elsewhere.

Published September 1, 1920, at $1.50, in an edition of 1,000 copies.

B 11 FIFTY CONTEMPORARY ONE-ACT PLAYS
[1921]

FIFTY CONTEMPORARY | ONE-ACT PLAYS | SELECTED AND EDITED | BY | FRANK SHAY | AND | PIERRE LOVING | [device] | CINCINNATI | STEWART & KIDD COMPANY | PUBLISHERS

1 blank leaf, viii, 582 pp., 7 leaves, 1 blank leaf. $8^7/_{16} \times 5^7/_8$ inches. Dark blue cloth, stamped in blind and in gold on front and in gold on spine. White endpapers; top edges stained orange; fore and bottom edges trimmed. No dust jacket seen.

Contains *Three Travelers Watch a Sunrise*, pp. 494–500. First published in *Poetry*, C 49, this is the first book publication; reprinted in *OP*.

Published January 1921, at $5.00.

B 12 ANTHOLOGY OF MAGAZINE VERSE FOR 1921
[1921]

ANTHOLOGY | OF | MAGAZINE VERSE | FOR 1921 | AND YEAR BOOK OF | AMERICAN POETRY | EDITED BY | WILLIAM STANLEY BRAITHWAITE | [device] | BOSTON | SMALL, MAYNARD & COMPANY | PUBLISHERS

1 blank leaf, xiii, 6–294 pp. $8^1/_2 \times 5^7/_{16}$ inches. Dark brown paper-covered boards with brown cloth back and white paper labels printed in black on front and spine. White endpapers; top edges trimmed; fore and bottom edges rough trimmed. Cream dust jacket printed in black.

Contains "Cortège for Rosenbloom," pp. 164–165. First published in *The Measure*, C 64, and reprinted in *CP* and *Palm*.

Published November 9, 1921, at $2.25.

B 13 ANTHOLOGY OF MAGAZINE VERSE FOR 1922
[1923]

ANTHOLOGY | OF | MAGAZINE VERSE | FOR 1922 | AND YEARBOOK OF | AMERICAN POETRY | EDITED BY | WILLIAM STANLEY BRAITHWAITE | [device] | BOSTON | SMALL, MAYNARD & COMPANY | PUBLISHERS

xxiv, 387 pp., 1 blank leaf. 8⅝ × 5½ inches. Dark brown paper-covered boards with brown cloth back and white paper labels printed in black on front and spine. White endpapers; top edges trimmed; fore and bottom edges rough trimmed. Cream dust jacket printed in black.

Contains "Of the Manner of Addressing Clouds," p. 199; "A High-Toned Old Christian Woman," p. 200; and "The Bird with the Coppery, Keen Claws," pp. 200–201. All are collected in CP and *Palm*.

Published February 10, 1923, at $2.25.

B 14 THE NEW POETRY NEW AND ENLARGED
(1923)

THE NEW POETRY | AN ANTHOLOGY | OF TWENTIETH-CENTURY VERSE IN | ENGLISH | NEW AND ENLARGED EDITION | EDITED BY | HARRIET MONROE | EDITOR OF *Poetry: A Magazine of Verse* | AND | ALICE CORBIN HEN-DERSON | [in Black Letter] New York | THE MACMILLAN COMPANY | 1923 | *All rights reserved*

lii, 1 leaf, 640 pp., 5 blank leaves. 8⅛ × 5½ inches. Green cloth, stamped in blind on front and in gold on spine. White endpapers; top edges trimmed; fore and bottom edges rough trimmed. Pale yellow dust jacket printed in brown.

Contains "Peter Quince at the Clavier," pp. 492–494; "In Battle," p. 494; "Sunday Morning," pp. 494–496; "Bowl," p. 497; "Tattoo," p. 497; "Death of the Soldier," p. 498; "The Worms at Heaven's Gate," p. 498; "Pecksniffiana" ("Fabliau of Florida," "The Weeping Burgher," "Peter Parasol," "Of the Surface of Things," "The Place of the Solitaires," "The Paltry Nude Starts on a Spring Voyage"), pp. 499–502; "Sur Ma Guzzla Gracile" ("The Snow Man," "Tea at the Palaz of Hoon," "Another Weeping Woman," "The Load of Sugar-Cane," "Hibiscus on the Sleeping Shores"), pp. 502–504; and "Le Monocle de Mon Oncle," pp. 504–508.

"Death of the Soldier," three of the poems from "Pecksniffiana" ("The Weeping Burgher," "Peter Parasol," and "The Place of the Solitaires"), and the five poems from "Sur Ma Guzzla Gracile" are published here for the first time in book form; and, except for "Peter Parasol," which is in *OP*, all are reprinted in *CP*.

Published May 1, 1923, at $3.50. On copyright page: 'Set up and electrotyped. Published February 1917. New and enlarged Edition, April, 1923.'

B 15 ANTHOLOGY OF MAGAZINE VERSE FOR 1923
(*1923*)

Anthology of Magazine Verse | for 1923 | and | Yearbook of American Poetry | Edited by | WILLIAM STANLEY BRAITHWAITE | [vignette containing scroll lettered: 'ANTHOLOGY | of | MAGAZINE | VERSE | WILLIAM STANLEY | BRAITHWAITE'] | BOSTON | B. J. BRIMMER COMPANY | 1923

1 blank leaf, xix, 376 pp. (Part I), 188 pp. (Part II). $8\frac{9}{16} \times 5\frac{5}{8}$ inches. Dark brown paper-covered boards with brown cloth back and white paper labels printed in black pasted on front and spine. White endpapers; top edges trimmed; fore and bottom edges rough trimmed. Cream dust jacket printed in black.

Contains "To the One of Fictive Music," pp. 324–325, and "The Shape of the Coroner," p. 326. "To the One of Fictive Music" is in *CP* and *Palm;* "The Shape of the Coroner," in *OP*.

Note: The Acknowledgments, p. xviii, thank Alfred A. Knopf for "'New England Verses' and 'The Shape of the Coroner' in *Harmonium* by Wallace Stevens." Neither of these poems was published in the first edition of *Harmonium*, and "To the One of Fictive Music" was obviously substituted for "New England Verses" in this anthology.

Published November 26, 1923, at $3.00, in an issue of 3,375 copies of a total edition of 3,650 copies. On copyright page: 'FIRST IMPRESSION, NOVEMBER, 1923'.

Special issue
The title page is the same as in the regular issue.

1 blank leaf, xix, 376 pp. (Part I), 188 pp. (Part II), 2 blank leaves. $9\frac{13}{16} \times 6\frac{1}{2}$ inches. Dark brown paper-covered boards with corners and spine of brown cloth, white paper labels printed in black pasted on front and spine. White endpapers; top edges gilt; fore

and bottom edges rough trimmed. Cream dust jacket printed in black.

Colophon: p. [iv]: This Special Edition of the | ANTHOLOGY OF MAGAZINE VERSE FOR 1923 | AND YEARBOOK OF AMERICAN POETRY | consists of 245 signed and numbered | copies, of which this is | Number . . . . . . | [signed in ink: 'William Stanley Braithwaite']

Published November 26, 1923, at $7.50, in an issue of 245 copies of a total edition of 3,650 copies.

B 16 ANTHOLOGY OF MAGAZINE VERSE FOR 1924
(1924)

Anthology of Magazine Verse | for 1924 | and | Yearbook of American Poetry | Edited by | WILLIAM STANLEY BRAITHWAITE | [vignette containing scroll lettered: 'ANTHOLOGY | of | MAGAZINE | VERSE | WILLIAM STANLEY | BRAITHWAITE'] | BOSTON | B. J. BRIMMER COMPANY | 1924

1 blank leaf, xxii, 298 pp. (Part I), 159 pp. (Part II). $8\frac{3}{8} \times 5\frac{1}{2}$ inches. Dark brown paper-covered boards with brown cloth back and white paper labels printed in black pasted on front and spine. White endpapers; top edges trimmed; fore and bottom edges rough trimmed. Cream dust jacket printed in black.

Contains "Sea Surface Full of Clouds," pp. 243–246. First published in *The Dial*, C 78, and collected in *CP*, *Poems*, and *Palm*.

Published December 24, 1924, at $3.00, in an edition of 1,000 copies.

B 17 PRIZE POEMS ★ 1913 ★ 1929
(1930)

PRIZE POEMS | ★ 1913 ★ 1929 ★ | *EDITED BY* | *CHARLES A WAGNER* | *WITH AN INTRODUCTION BY* | *MARK VAN DOREN* | 19 [vignette by Rockwell Kent] 30 | *Charles Boni* PAPER BOOKS *New York*

1 blank leaf, 247 pp., 1 leaf, 2 blank leaves. $7\frac{5}{8} \times 5\frac{1}{4}$ inches. Natural colored cloth, stamped in black with the enlarged title-page design by Rockwell Kent; black stamping on spine and white paper label printed downward in black on spine. Endpapers printed in blue with design of books and skyscrapers.

Contains "Pecksniffiana" ("Fabliau of Florida," "Homunculus et La Belle Etoile," "The Weeping Burgher," "Peter Parasol," "Exposition of the Contents of a Cab," "Ploughing on Sunday," "Banal Sojourn," "The Indigo Glass in the Grass," "Anecdote of the Jar," "Of the Surface of Things," "The Curtains in the House of the Metaphysician," "The Place of the Solitaires," "The Paltry Nude Starts on a Spring Voyage," "Colloquy with a Polish Aunt"), pp. 55–65.

Only "The Indigo Glass in the Grass" is published here for the first time in book form; it is collected in OP and *Poems*.

Published April 25, 1930, at $1.50. On copyright page: 'PUB-LISHED APRIL, 1930'.

Paper issue
The specifications are the same as for the cloth issue, except for stiff white paper covers, 7⅜ × 5 inches, printed in shades of purple and blue in a design by Rockwell Kent and printed upward in white on spine.

Issued simultaneously April 25, 1930, at 50¢.

B 18 MODERN AMERICAN POETRY
[1930]

MODERN | AMERICAN POETRY | *A CRITICAL ANTHOLOGY* | *Edited by Louis Untermeyer* | [large circular ornament] | FOURTH REVISED EDITION | HARCOURT, BRACE AND COMPANY | NEW YORK

3588
.922
.U

xxxviii, 850 pp. 8⁵⁄₁₆ × 5¼ inches. Gray green or blue cloth, with title-page ornament stamped in blind on front, stamped in gold on spine. White endpapers; top edges stained yellow. Cream dust jacket printed in black and blue.

Contains "Peter Quince at the Clavier," "To the One of Fictive Music," "Sunday Morning," "Domination of Black," "Sea Surface Full of Clouds," and "Annual Gaiety," pp. 380–390. Of these poems only "Annual Gaiety" is published here for the first time in book form; collected in OP.

Note: A biographical sketch of WS is on pp. 379–380.

Published June 14, 1930, at $3.50, in an edition of 6,800 copies. On copyright page: '*Typography by Robert S. Josephy* | PRINTED IN THE UNITED STATES OF AMERICA | BY QUINN & BODEN COMPANY, INC., RAHWAY, N.J.'.

Annotation: "Thanks for this pleasant letter. So far as I am concerned you can use anything of mine that interests you. But Knopf is the legal owner, I believe.

"If you care for the poem below ["Annual Gaiety"] you are welcome to it. It will give you something of mine that has not appeared elsewhere. . . ." (*Letters*, p. 252: letter to Louis Untermeyer, June 11, 1929)

B 19 FIFTY POETS
[1933]

FIFTY POETS | An | AMERICAN | Auto-Anthology | [ornamental design of flowers and hands] | EDITED BY WILLIAM ROSE BENÉT | Duffield and Green | New York City

xii, 153 pp., 1 blank leaf. $8^3/_4 \times 5^9/_{16}$ inches. Green cloth, stamped in gold and black on spine. White endpapers; all edges trimmed. No dust jacket seen.

Contains "The Emperor of Ice-Cream," page 47, and a ten-line statement by WS, p. 46, giving his reasons for selecting this "favorite" poem for inclusion in this anthology. The statement consists of the first paragraph of WS's first letter under "Annotations" below and the last paragraph of his second letter. Not reprinted elsewhere.

Published June 19, 1933, at $2.50, in an edition of 2,127 copies.

Annotations: "I think I should select from my poems as my favorite the Emperor of Ice Cream. This wears a deliberately commonplace costume, and yet seems to me to contain something of the essential gaudiness of poetry; that is the reason why I like it.

"The poem appears in Harmonium, the only volume that I have published. Knopf owns the copyright, and I believe that you will have to apply to him for permission to use the poem and will also have to pay whatever is to be paid to him.

"I shall sign my name a little below the end of this letter, so that you can clip it off and reproduce the signature." (*Letters*, p. 263: letter to William Rose Benét, January 6, 1933)

"Suppose you substitute the following paragraph for the one I sent you some time ago by way of explaining my liking for The Emperor of Ice Cream:

"I do not remember the circumstances under which this poem was written, unless this means the state of mind from which it came. I dislike niggling, and like letting myself go. This poem is an instance of letting myself go. Poems of this sort are the pleasantest on which to look back, because they seem to remain fresher than others. This represented what was in my mind at the moment, with the least possible manipulation." (*Letters*, p. 264: letter to William Rose Benét, January 24, 1933)

B 20 COLLECTED POEMS 1921–1931
WILLIAM CARLOS WILLIAMS
(1934)

WILLIAM CARLOS WILLIAMS | COLLECTED POEMS | 1921–1931 | WITH A PREFACE BY WALLACE STEVENS | THE OBJECTIVIST PRESS | 10 WEST 36 STREET, NEW YORK | 1934

viii, 134 pp., 1 blank leaf. $7^{11}/_{16} \times 5^{1}/_{4}$ inches. Crimson cloth with white paper label printed in black on spine. White endpapers; top edges trimmed; fore and bottom edges rough trimmed. Gray dust jacket printed in crimson.

Contains the preface entitled "Williams," pp. 1–4. Reprinted in *OP.*

Published January 20, 1934, at $2.00, in an edition of 500 copies. On copyright page: 'Printed in the United States of America by | J. J. LITTLE AND IVES COMPANY, NEW YORK'.

B 21 MODERN THINGS
[*1934*]

MODERN | THINGS – | [double rule] | EDITED BY | PARKER TYLER | [device] | NEW YORK | THE GALLEON PRESS

92 pp., 2 blank leaves. $8^{13}/_{16} \times 5^{1}/_{2}$ inches. Lavender cloth, stamped in white on front, with white linen spine. White endpapers; top edges stained red; fore and bottom edges trimmed. Gray dust jacket printed in lavender and black; on front flap of dust jacket: 'This collection of the newer poems (the majority here for the first time published) of first-class modern poets means an indispensable volume is ready for all serious readers of poetry as well as for the large public which is still to be persuaded of the popular virtues of modernist work.'

Contains "Secret Man" and "Snow and Stars," pp. 37–38. "Secret Man" is collected in *OP;* "Snow and Stars," in *CP.*

Published September 1934, at $2.00.

B 22 TRIAL BALANCES
(1935)

3588
.412

[double rule] | [rule] | TRIAL BALANCES | *Edited by* | Ann Winslow | NEW YORK | THE MACMILLAN COMPANY | 1935 | [rule] | [double rule]

(Ann
Winslow
= pseud.
for
GRUBBS,
Verna (Elizabeth)

xvi, 1 leaf, 225 pp., 2 blank leaves. 8¾ × 5⅞ inches. Dark blue cloth, stamped on front and spine in silver. White endpapers; top and bottom edges trimmed; fore edges rough trimmed. Silver dust jacket printed in blue.

Contains a commentary by WS, pp. 155–157, on Martha Champion, whose poems precede his remarks. Reprinted in *OP*.

Published October 8, 1935, at $2.00, in an edition of 2,500 copies. On copyright page: 'Published October, 1935. | PRINTED IN THE UNITED STATES OF AMERICA | BY THE STRATFORD PRESS, INC., NEW YORK'.

B 23 THE NEW CARAVAN
[1936]

3588
.668

also in
Beach
3588
.668
and
Ex
3588
.673

THE NEW | CARAVAN | EDITED BY Alfred Kreymborg | Lewis Mumford, Paul Rosenfeld | W · W · NORTON & COMPANY, INC · | PUBLISHERS · NEW YORK

ix, 1 leaf, 663 pp. 8¾ × 5¾ inches. Natural colored cloth, stamped in crimson on spine. White endpapers; top edges stained crimson; fore and bottom edges trimmed. White dust jacket printed in orange and black.

Contains "Mr. Burnshaw and the Statue," pp. 72–77, and a one-sentence autobiographical note, p. 662, by WS.

  In *OP* and *Palm*. This version of "Mr. Burnshaw and the Statue" appeared as Section II of *Owl's Clover* in The Alcestis Press edition, 1936, A 3. Shortened, revised, and renamed "The Statue at the World's End," the poem was published as Section II of "Owl's Clover" in *The Man with the Blue Guitar & other poems*, 1937, A 4.

Note: On p. 656 of this anthology is the note by Stanley Burnshaw: 'The subject of Wallace Stevens' poem in this New Caravan arose from my review of his book which was printed in *The New Masses*.' This review in *New Masses* of October 1,

1935, pp. 41–42, was reprinted, with a commentary by Burn-shaw, in *The Sewanee Review* of Summer 1961, pp. 355–366; cf. WS's letters of October 9, 1935, and November 5, 1935, to Ronald Lane Latimer in *Letters*, pp. 286–287 and 288–289, for his comment on this review.

Published November 2, 1936, at $3.95, in an edition of 1,350 copies.

B 24 NEW DIRECTIONS IN PROSE AND POETRY
(1936)

NEW DIRECTIONS | in | Prose and Poetry | [rule] | Edited by | James Laughlin IV | NEW DIRECTIONS | NORFOLK, CT. | 1936

[unpaged] 104 leaves. 9¼ × 6¼ inches. Yellow paper-covered boards printed in red and black on front and in black on spine. White endpapers; all edges trimmed. No dust jacket.

Contains "A Thought Revolved" ("I. The Mechanical Optimist," "II. Mystic Garden & Middling Beast," "III. Romanesque Affabulation," "IV. The Leader"), pp. [13–15]. In *CP* and *Palm*.

Published November 16, 1936, at $2.00, in an issue of about 700 copies, of which 234 went to New Books, London.

Paper issue
The specifications are the same as for the cloth issue, except for the paper wrapper, which is made of the same paper used to cover the boards in the hardbound copies, 8¹⁵⁄₁₆ × 6 inches.

Published simultaneously November 16, 1936, in an issue of 507 copies, of which 100 went to New Books, London.

Annotation: "Memory is a bit vague about how I got this from him [Stevens], but probably I just wrote. . . . Many of the contributors in the first Annual were included because Ezra [Pound] had suggested them. But I don't believe there was ever any tie between Ezra and Stevens, so probably I just learned about him from Dudley Fitts, or someone else, and wrote him 'cold,' and he was nice enough to want to contribute." (Unpublished letter from James Laughlin to the compiler, April 13, 1971)

B 25 THE OXFORD ANTHOLOGY OF AMERICAN
LITERATURE
(1938)

3588
.6887

THE | OXFORD ANTHOLOGY | OF | AMERICAN LITERA-
TURE | CHOSEN AND EDITED BY | WILLIAM ROSE BENÉT |
AND | NORMAN HOLMES PEARSON | New York | OXFORD
UNIVERSITY PRESS | 1938

xxx, 1,705 pp. $9^7/_{16} \times 6^5/_8$ inches. Maroon cloth, stamped in gold
on spine. White endpapers; top edges stained gold; fore and bottom edges trimmed. Blue dust jacket printed in red.

Contains "The Worms at Heaven's Gate," "The Emperor of Ice-
Cream," "Sunday Morning," "The Bird with the Coppery, Keen
Claws," "To the One of Fictive Music," "Peter Quince at the
Clavier," "Sea Surface Full of Clouds," "The Idea of Order at
Key West," "A Postcard from the Volcano," "Sombre Figuration"
from "Owl's Clover," "Romanesque Affabulation" from "A
Thought Revolved," pp. 1325-1333, and, on p. 1325, a brief
statement on poetry entitled "A Note on Poetry."
  All the poetry is reprinted from earlier works. This is the only
publication of the statement.

Published October 27, 1938, at $6.00, in an issue of 5,000 copies.
On copyright page: 'First edition'.

College issue
Of the 5,000 copies published on October 27, 1938, an undetermined number were issued in a binding of blue cloth over
boards, as a college edition.

Issued simultaneously October 27, 1938, at $4.50.

3598
.618

also :

Ex

3598
.6148

B 26 NEW POEMS: 1940
(1941)

[six thin rules] | NEW POEMS: | 1940 | An Anthology of British
and American Verse | Edited by Oscar Williams [ornament] A
Living Age Book | The Yardstick Press [ornament] New York
[ornament] 1941 | [six thin rules]

5 leaves, 9-276 pp., 1 blank leaf. Illustrated with thirty photographs of poets, but not WS. $8^1/_4 \times 5^5/_8$ inches. Grayish white cloth,
stamped in red and gold on spine. White endpapers; top edges

stained red; fore and bottom edges rough trimmed. Red dust jacket printed in black and white.

Contains "Extracts from Addresses to the Academy of Fine Ideas," pp. 200–207. In *CP* and *Palm*.

Published April 17, 1941, at $2.50. On copyright page: 'FIRST PRINTING | PRINTED IN THE UNITED STATES OF AMER-ICA | BY J. J. LITTLE & IVES COMPANY, NEW YORK'.

Annotations: "I enclose a poem for your collection. This has not been published. One of the characteristics of the world today is the Lightness with which ideas are asserted, held, abandoned, etc. That is what this poem grows out of." (*Letters*, p. 380: letter to Oscar Williams, November 18, 1940)

"I should like to make this general comment. Often in my manuscript I leave broad spaces in short lines that follow long lines in order that the short lines will not look so short. This is merely something for the eye. The stenographer usually copies these spaces because she thinks that they mean something. But they don't mean a thing except to the eye. Then the printer comes along and repeats these spaces, doing exactly what no printer should do, that is, leaving holes in the lines. I have called your particular attention to one or two instances of this on the proofs. But, take the last section of this poem, Section VIII: there are several instances of what I am speaking that ought not to be there. Perhaps it doesn't matter and certainly I don't want to put you to any expense. What the printer should do is to separate the words or the letters in one or two words. This is simply a part of the normal job of making a page of poetry look decent. I say this because I don't want you to get the idea that I believe in queer punctuation." (*Letters*, p. 387: letter to Oscar Williams, March 4, 1941)

B 27 THE LANGUAGE OF POETRY
[1942]

THE LANGUAGE | OF POETRY | BY | Philip Wheelwright · Cleanth Brooks | I. A. Richards · Wallace Stevens | *Edited by* Allen Tate | [in brown: floral ornament] | Princeton | PRINCE-TON UNIVERSITY PRESS | LONDON: HUMPHREY MIL-FORD | OXFORD UNIVERSITY PRESS

viii, 1 leaf, 125 pp. 8¼ × 5½ inches. Ornamental purplish brown paper-covered boards with tan linen spine, stamped upward in gold. White endpapers; top edges stained brown; fore and bottom edges trimmed. Glassine dust jacket.

Contains the essay "The Noble Rider and the Sound of Words," pp. 91–125. In *NA*.

Note: The preface, pp. vii–viii, states: 'The four essays collected here under the title *The Language of Poetry* were read to audiences at Princeton University in the spring of 1941 under the auspices of the Creative Arts Program. . . . The Creative Arts Program is grateful to the contributors for their cooperation, and to the Mesures Fund for bringing them to Princeton. This Fund, which has been given to the Creative Arts Program by the editor of *Mesures*, the French quarterly now temporarily suspended, provides for four more symposiums on literary problems. To Mr. Henry Church, the donor, we owe our chief gratitude. Allen Tate'.

Published February 6, 1942, at $2.00; the *Mesures* Series in Literary Criticism.

Annotation: "In May I went down to Princeton and read a paper which is going to be published in a small group of papers by the University Press in the autumn. No one would be likely to suppose from that paper what a lot of serious reading it required preceding it, and how much time it took. It was worth doing (for me), although the visit to Princeton gave me a glimpse of a life which I am profoundly glad that I don't share. The people I met were the nicest people in the world, but how they keep alive is more than I can imagine." (*Letters*, p. 392: letter to Hi Simons, July 8, 1941)

B 28 NEW POEMS 1942
[*1942*]

NEW | POEMS | 1942 [these first three lines printed in white on a solid rectangle of orange red, around the edges of which is a single rule in white] | An Anthology of | British and | American Verse | *EDITED BY* | Oscar Williams [the whole, including the orange red rectangle, within a double-rule border] | PETER PAUPER PRESS · MOUNT VERNON · N.Y.

286 pp., 1 leaf. Illustrated with photographs of poets, but not WS. $8\frac{3}{8} \times 6\frac{1}{4}$ inches. Dark blue cloth with orange red paper labels printed in white on front and on spine. White endpapers;

top edges stained red; fore and bottom edges trimmed. Glassine dust jacket.

Contains "Six Discordant Songs" ("I. Metamorphosis," "II. Contrary Theses [I]," "III. Phosphor Reading by His Own Light," "IV. The Search for Sound Free from Motion," "V. Jumbo," "VI. Contrary Theses [II]"), pp. 221–226. All are in *CP*.

Colophon: verso of last leaf: This book has been designed by | Peter Beilenson, set in Electra types, | and printed on Ticonderoga paper | at the Walpole Printing Office, | Mount Vernon

Published April 17, 1942, at $3.00.

Autographed issue
The specifications are the same, except for the following: four pages tipped in containing all the contributors' signatures (WS's signature is the fifth one on the fourth page); $9^7/_{16} \times 6^3/_8$ inches; multicolored French-paper-covered boards with ivory linen spine and corners, a green paper label on spine; dark green board slipcase. Glassine dust jacket.

Published simultaneously April 17, 1942, at $25.00, in an issue of twenty-six copies.

B 29 THE FORTUNE ANTHOLOGY
[1942]

THE FORTUNE | ANTHOLOGY | *Stories, Criticism and Poems* | by | WALLACE STEVENS | OSBERT SITWELL | CONRAD AIKEN | HENRY MILLER | ALFRED PERLÈS | ITHELL COLQUHOUN | LAWRENCE DURRELL | ANNE RIDLER | CHRISTOPHER FRY | J. MACLAREN-ROSS | RUSSELL CLARKE | NICHOLAS MOORE | DEREK STANFORD | DOUGLAS NEWTON | JOHN BAYLISS | THE FORTUNE PRESS | 12 BUCKINGHAM PALACE ROAD | LONDON

79, [1] pp. $7^3/_4 \times 5^1/_8$ inches. Green cloth, stamped upward in gold on spine. White endpapers; top edges trimmed; fore and bottom edges rough trimmed. Yellow dust jacket printed in red.

Note: There are three variant bindings: (1) the bibliography by Samuel F. Morse et al. calls for "glazed black linen"; (2) a copy in the Brown University Library is bound in blue cloth with gray endpapers; and (3) the compiler has a copy bound in blue paper-covered boards with dark blue cloth spine and white endpapers.

Contains "Asides on the Oboe" and "Mrs. Alfred Uruguay," pp. 11–13. Both poems are collected in *CP*, *Poems*, and *Palm*.

Published June 1942, at 6s.

B 30 AN AMERICAN ANTHOLOGY
[1942]

[in blue] AN | [in blue] AMERICAN | [in blue] ANTHOLOGY | *67 poems now in anthology form* | *for the first time* | Edited by | [script] Tom Boggs | *The world is, after all, served only by* | *what is out of the ordinary.* | *GOETHE* | THE PRESS OF JAMES A. DECKER | *Prairie City, Illinois*

ix, 1 leaf, 13–96 pp. 8⅛ × 5⅛ inches. Blue cloth, stamped in gold on front ('AN | AMERICAN | ANTHOLOGY') and downward on spine ('AN AMERICAN ANTHOLOGY BOGGS DECKER'). White endpapers; all edges trimmed. Greenish blue dust jacket printed in rust and black.

Note: Some copies have the following variations: 8¼ × 5¼ inches. Brown cloth, stamped in gold on front ('AN | AMERICAN | ANTHOLOGY'). Greenish blue dust jacket printed in gold and black.

Contains "The Pleasures of Merely Circulating," "Like Decorations in a Nigger Cemetery" (Sections III, VIII, XIII, XVII, XVIII, XIX, XXII, XXV, XXVIII, XXXIII, VL, XLI, L), "Hieroglyphica," "Botanist on Alp (No. 2)," "Anglais Mort a Florence," "Oak Leaves Are Hands," "Mozart 1935," "The Sense of the Sleight-of-Hand Man," "A Duck for Dinner," "The Well Dressed Man with a Beard," and "A Fading of the Sun," pp. 78–89.
    Of these poems, the following are published here for the first time in book form: "Hieroglyphica," in the five-stanza version first published in *Direction*, C 90; "Oak Leaves Are Hands," with a note stating 'Written 1941.'; "The Sense of the Sleight-of-Hand Man"; and "The Well Dressed Man with a Beard." "Hieroglyphica" is in *OP;* the remaining area in *CP* and *Palm.*

Colophon: p. [96]: AN AMERICAN ANTHOLOGY, set in Inter- | type Waverley, was printed in April | and May, 1942, at the Press of James | A. Decker.

Published July 1942, at $2.00.

B 31 THIS IS MY BEST
(*1942*)

America's 93 Greatest Living Authors Present | [script] This Is
My Best | [ornament] OVER 150 SELF-CHOSEN AND | COM-
PLETE MASTERPIECES, TOGETHER WITH | THEIR REA-
SONS FOR THEIR SELECTIONS | [device] *Edited by Whit
Burnett* | Burton C. Hoffman THE DIAL PRESS New York,
1942

xiv, 1,180 pp., 2 blank leaves. 8¾ × 6 inches. Tan cloth, stamped
with device in gold on front and in blue green and gold on spine.
White endpapers; top edges stained blue green; fore and bottom
edges rough trimmed. Tan dust jacket printed in black, white,
and red.

Contains "Domination of Black," pp. 652–653, and the statement, "Why he selected DOMINATION of BLACK," by WS, p.
652. This is the only publication of the statement, which is
dated 'Hartford, Conn. August, 1942'.

Published October 13, 1942, at $3.50, in an edition of 70,000
copies.

B 32 AMERICAN DECADE
[*1943*]

AMERICAN DECADE | 68 Poems for the First Time in an
Anthology | *by* | ELIZABETH BISHOP, R. P. BLACKMUR,
TOM BOGGS, | MYRON H. BROOMELL, JOHN CIARDI,
ROBERT CLAIRMONT, | MALCOLM COWLEY, E. E. CUM-
MINGS, REUEL DENNEY, | THOMAS W. DUNCAN, KEN-
NETH FEARING, THOMAS HORNSBY | FERRIL, LLOYD
FRANKENBERG, ROBERT FROST, CLIFFORD | GESSLER,
W. W. GIBSON, HORACE GREGORY, LANGSTON | HUGHES,
ROBINSON JEFFERS, WELDON KEES, E. L. MAYO, | JOSE-
PHINE MILES, SAMUEL FRENCH MORSE, MURIEL | RU-
KEYSER, CARL SANDBURG, WINFIELD TOWNLEY SCOTT,
KARL JAY SHAPIRO, THEODORE SPENCER, WALLACE
STEVENS, MARK VAN DOREN, EDWARD WEISMILLER,
JOHN WHEELWRIGHT, WILLIAM CARLOS WILLIAMS
[ornament] | *EDITED BY TOM BOGGS* | *And star-dials pointed
to morn.*—POE | [ornament] | THE CUMMINGTON PRESS,
Publishers

93, [3] pp. $9^{11}/_{16} \times 6^3/_8$ inches. Blue cloth, stamped in white downward on spine. White endpapers; top edges trimmed; fore and bottom edges rough trimmed. White dust jacket printed in blue; on the dust jacket: 'The edition is limited to 500 copies, of which 25 are on special rag paper and bound by hand.'

Contains "The Glass of Water," "Loneliness in Jersey City," "The American Sublime," "Dry Loaf," "Connoisseur of Chaos," "Gigantomachia," "One of Those Hibiscuses of Damozels," and "Certain Phenomena of Sound," pp. 74–83.

Of these poems, "Gigantomachia" is published here for the first time; "One of Those Hibiscuses of Damozels" and "Certain Phenomena of Sound" appear here for the first time in book form. "Gigantomachia" is reprinted in *CP;* "One of Those Hibiscuses of Damozels," in *OP;* Certain Phenomena of Sound," in *CP* and *Palm.*

Colophon: p. [96]: AMERICAN DECADE | has been set up in Linotype Baskerville and printed | by The Southworth-Anthoensen Press at Portland, | Maine. Four-hundred-seventy-five copies, of which | fifty are not for sale, are on Andria paper, and twenty- | five, especially bound by hand and numbered 1 to | 25, on Sterling Laid. It has been designed and | published by The Cummington Press, | Cummington, Massachusetts. | [ornament]

Published June 24, 1943, at $3.50, in an issue of 475 copies.

Handbound issue
The specifications are the same, except for blue, white, and black paper-covered boards with natural-colored linen back and white paper label printed downward on spine.

Published simultaneously June 24, 1943, at $7.50, in an issue of twenty-five copies.

B 33 NEW POEMS 1943
[*1943*]

NEW POEMS | 1943 An Anthology of | British and American Verse | *Edited by* OSCAR WILLIAMS | [rule] | HOWELL, SOSKIN, PUBLISHERS

xiv, 13–325 pp. Illustrated with thirty-two photographs of poets, but not WS. $8^3/_{16} \times 5^1/_2$ inches. Gray cloth, stamped downward in black on spine. White endpapers; all edges trimmed. Tan dust jacket printed in black and white.

Published August 17, 1943, at $2.75.

Contains "Chocorua to Its Neighbor," pp. 226–232; "So-and-So Reclining on Her Couch," pp. 232–233; "Dutch Graves in Bucks County," pp. 233–236; "No Possum, No Sop, No Taters," pp. 236–237; and "Return," p. 237.

"Dutch Graves in Bucks County" was first published in *The Sewanee Review,* C 146, and is collected in *CP, Poems,* and *Palm.* All the others appear here in print for the first time. "Chocorua to Its Neighbor" is collected in *CP* and *Palm;* "So-and-So Reclining on Her Couch" and "No Possum, No Sop, No Taters," in *CP, Poems,* and *Palm.* "Return" is reprinted in *Transport to Summer,* and in *CP* under the title "Poésie Abrutie."

B 34 TIME OF YEAR
[*1944*]

Samuel French Morse | [in brown] TIME OF YEAR | a first book of poems introduced by | Wallace Stevens |[in brown: an ornament of the zodiac enclosing the quotation: ' "as the | days of man" | JOB × 5'] | THE CUMMINGTON PRESS, 1943

1 blank leaf, viii, 1 leaf, [11]–52 pp., 1 leaf. 9¼ × 6 inches. Reddish brown paper-covered boards with zodiac design printed on front in yellow and printed upward in yellow on spine. White endpapers; all edges rough trimmed. Glassine dust jacket.

Contains an introduction by WS, pp. vi–viii. Included in *OP.*

Colophon: p. [53]: Just 275 copies of TIME OF YEAR have been printed at Cummington, | Massachusetts, from hand-set Centaur & Arrighi types. The zodiac on | the title was drawn by Eugene Canade from an old device.

Published February 15, 1944, at $2.75, in an edition of 275 copies.

Annotations: "On Sunday I studied a small group of poems by an unfamiliar poet which the Cummington Press intends to publish and to which I am going to write a note of introduction. The poet begins his book with a quotation from Thoreau, which contains all of Thoreau's plain-speaking transcendentalism. One of the best poems in the book is about an abandoned road. [. . .] This young poet writes very awkwardly, but there is a rectitude about him that makes his book precious." (*Letters,* pp. 436–437: letter to Henry Church, January 25, 1943)

"There is another thing that I ought to speak of: The poem that you have inscribed to me is one of the best in the group, and I shall be happy to allow the inscription to stand. However, I don't think that it would do both for me to introduce the book and to have this inscription. Perhaps it would be better to sacrifice the inscription, which might involve a change of title. The significant symbol in that poem is the house, and perhaps you could call it that and drop the inscription." (*Letters*, p. 437: letter to Samuel French Morse, January 26, 1943)

"I received the copy of Time of Year and really liked it very much as I do everything done by The Cummington Press. I am keen for bright colors, even in bindings. These quiet down after one has had them a bit. Dark colors merely grow dull after one has had them a bit." (*Letters*, p. 462: letter to Harry Duncan, March 13, 1944)

B 35 NEW POEMS 1944
[*1944*]

['N' and 'P' in script] NEW POEMS 1944 | AN ANTHOLOGY OF AMERICAN AND | BRITISH VERSE, WITH A SELECTION | OF POEMS FROM THE ARMED FORCES | Edited By OSCAR WILLIAMS [three ornaments] | *New York* | HOWELL, SOSKIN, PUBLISHERS

1 blank leaf, 2 leaves, iii–xiv, 1 leaf, 17–330 pp., 1 blank leaf. Illustrated with thirty-six photographs of poets, but not WS. $7^{11}/_{16} \times 5^{1}/_{4}$ inches. Rust-colored cloth, stamped downward on spine in black. White endpapers; all edges trimmed. Tan, green, and white dust jacket printed in overlapping green, tan, black, and white.

Contains "Repetitions of a Young Captain," pp. 145–149.
    The Acknowledgments, p. 330, state: 'The following poems (from manuscript) are printed here for the first time: . . . "Repetitions of a Young Captain" by Wallace Stevens . . . .' The poem had appeared, however, in the spring 1944 issue of the *Quarterly Review of Literature*, C 149. It should be pointed out that Oscar Williams's Introduction, pp. iii–vi, is dated 'May 14, 1944'. Included in *CP*.

Published August 15, 1944, at $3.00.

B 36 THE WAR POETS
[*1945*]

The War Poets | *An Anthology of the War Poetry* | *of the 20th Century* | *Edited with an Introduction by* | Oscar Williams | The John Day Company · New York

6 leaves, 3–485 pp. Illustrated with seventy-two photographs of poets, but not WS. 7⅝ × 6 inches. Tan cloth, stamped in red and gold on front and on spine. White endpapers; top edges stained light red; fore and bottom edges trimmed. Pink dust jacket printed in black and white.

Contains "How Red the Rose That Is the Soldier's Wound," p. 420. This poem, which is Section VIII of "Esthétique du Mal," is published here for the first time, and as part of the longer work is included in *CP*, *Poems*, and *Palm*. The anthology also reprints WS's statement "Poetry of War" from *Parts of a World*, p. 23, and "Repetitions of a Young Captain," pp. 420–424.

Published June 19, 1945, at $5.00.

B 37 THE SAINT NICHOLAS SOCIETY
(*1945*)

THE SAINT NICHOLAS SOCIETY | OF THE CITY OF NEW YORK | [seal of the Society] | *Organized February 28, 1835* | *Incorporated April 17, 1841* | Containing Chronological Record for the Years 1938–1945 | Genealogical Record 1934–1945. | Constitution and By-laws as of March 1, 1945. | The Saint Nicholas Society Medal of Merit 1937–1945 | List of Officers, Former Officers and Members | and Other Matters of Interest to the | Members of the Saint Nicholas Society | 1945

[viii] 174 pp., 1 blank leaf. Fifteen plates on thirteen leaves. 9½ × 6³⁄₁₆ inches. Smooth orange cloth, the society's seal stamped on front in gold. White endpapers; all edges trimmed. White wove paper, watermarked: 'Warren's Olde Style'. Glassine dust jacket.

Contains "Tradition," pp. 17–19. Reprinted with changes in *OP*, under the title "Recitation After Dinner."

Colophon: p. [i]: Of this Edition there are | printed for The Saint Nicholas | Society of the City of New | York 1,000 volumes of which | this number is . . . . [number in ink]

Published 1945 in an edition of 1,000 copies; not for sale.

Note: Preceding the poem, on p. 17, is the note: '*Among the members of the Society is the distinguished poet, Wallace Stevens. It was suggested that Mr. Stevens be asked to write a poem commemorating the one hundredth Paas Festival, to which suggestion he cheerfully acquiesced by composing the following poem.*'

On p. 134 is WS's "Genealogical Record," which traces his ancestors on both sides to the seventeenth century.

In the Saint Nicholas Society volume the first stanza of the poem reads:

> A poem about tradition could easily be
> A windy thing . . . However, since we are parts
> Of traditino, cousins of the calendar
> If not of kin, suppose we identify
> Its actual appearance, if we can,
> By giving it a form. But the character
> Of tradition does not easily take form.

In *OP*, this stanza reads:

> A poem about tradition could easily be
> A windy thing . . . However, since we are here,
> Cousins of the calendar if not of kin,
> To be a part of tradition, to identify
> Its actual appearance, suppose we begin
> By giving it a form. But the character
> Of tradition does not easily take form.

Three other changes were made in the *OP* version:

stanza 3, l. 4   didstance   [distance
stanza 5, l. 7   A legend scrawled in a script we cannot read?
    [A legend scrawled in script we cannot read?
stanza 7, l. 6   Nicolas Poussin   [Nicholas Poussin

B 38 ACCENT ANTHOLOGY
[*1946*]

Accent | ANTHOLOGY | Selections from *Accent,* | A Quarterly of New | Literature, *1940–1945* | *Edited by* | KERKER QUINN *and* | CHARLES SHATTUCK | HARCOURT, BRACE AND COMPANY, NEW YORK xiv, 687 pp. 8³/₁₆ × 5⁵/₈ inches. Reddish brown cloth, stamped in black and gold on spine. White endpapers; all edges trimmed. Salmon dust jacket printed in black and white.

Contains "Landscape with Boat," pp. 428–429; "The Bed of Old John Zeller," pp. 429–430; and "Less and Less Human, O Savage Spirit," pp. 430–431. "The Bed of Old John Zeller" and "Less and Less Human, O Savage Spirit" are published here for the first time in book form. "Landscape with Boat" had been published in *Parts of a World*, A 5. All are collected in *CP* and *Palm*.

Published August 19, 1946, at $4.00, in an edition of 4,000 copies. On copyright page: 'first edition'.

B 39 THE PARTISAN READER
(1946)

[printed downward] THE | PARTISAN | [printed downward] READER | TEN YEARS OF PARTISAN REVIEW | 1934–1944: AN ANTHOLOGY | EDITED BY | WILLIAM PHILLIPS AND PHILIP RAHV | INTRODUCTION BY | LIONEL TRILLING | THE DIAL PRESS, NEW YORK, 1946

xvi, 688 pp. 8¹/₂ × 5⁵/₈ inches. Yellow cloth, stamped in black on front and downward on spine. White endpapers; all edges trimmed. Gray and white dust jacket printed in yellow, white, and red.

Contains "The Dwarf," p. 220, and "The Woman That Had More Babies Than That," pp. 233–234. "The Dwarf" is in *CP* and *Palm;* "The Woman That Had More Babies Than That," only in *OP*. In addition, the anthology contains the only book appearance of WS's reply, pp. 619–620, to the journal's questionnaire "The Situation in American Writing," reprinted from the summer 1939 issue, C 124.

Published September 9, 1946, at $3.75.

B 40 HOMMAGE A HENRY CHURCH
(1948)

HOMMAGE | A | HENRY CHURCH | MESURES | 15 AVRIL 1948

83 pp. Photographic illustrations tipped in. 9⁵/₁₆ × 7³/₈ inches. Manila paper wrapper printed in black on front and upward on spine.

Contains "Portrait," in French, pp. 12–14, translated by Pierre Leyris from WS's English text. The English text was first published in *Letters*, pp. 570–571, following the letter that is quoted below.

Published April 15, 1948; not for sale. On p. [84] 'Imprimerie F. Paillart | Abbeville | O. 8. L. 31.0832 | (D. 2209) | Dépôt légal: 1er trimestre 1948'.

Annotation: "I am enclosing a copy of the page that I sent to Jean Paulhan. As I told you over the telephone last evening, I have not yet received the 'traduction'—and I may not because his acknowledgment was addressed to Wallace Stevens, Home Office, Hartford, Conn., which he took from our business letterhead. This was almost too much for the post office and since I should really like to see the traduction I expect that the letter containing it will go astray." (*Letters*, p. 570: letter to Barbara Church, November 26, 1947)

B 41 PAUL ROSENFELD
(1948)

3912
.83
.848

PAUL ROSENFELD | *Voyager in the Arts* | *Edited by Jerome Mellquist and Lucie Wiese* | CREATIVE AGE PRESS INC · 1948 · NEW YORK

xxxv, 284 pp. Frontispiece photograph of Paul Rosenfeld tipped in. 9⅛ × 6 inches. Blue green cloth, with dark blue cloth spine stamped in silver. White endpapers; all edges trimmed. Light tan dust jacket printed in red, black, and blue; on back flap: 'Jacket Drawing by John Marin'; folded around dust jacket is a slip, three inches high, with a tribute to Rosenfeld by Van Wyck Brooks.

Contains "The Shaper," pp. 98–100. Included in *OP*.

Published April 16, 1948, at $3.00. On copyright page: '. . . Designed by Stefan Salter. Manufactured in the United States of | America by American Book–Stratford Press, Inc., New York.'

B 42 ENGLISH INSTITUTE ESSAYS 1948
(1949)

3520
.3285

English Institute | Essays [ornament] 1948 | *Edited by* | D. A. Robertson, Jr. | [ornament] | NEW YORK · COLUMBIA UNIVERSITY PRESS · 1949

also

Se
3520
.3285

x, 219 pp., 1 blank leaf. $7\frac{1}{2} \times 5\frac{1}{8}$ inches. Gray cloth, publisher's device stamped in blind on front, stamped in green and gold on spine. White endpapers; top edges stained green; fore and bottom edges trimmed. Green and white dust jacket printed in green.

Contains "Imagination as Value," pp. 3–25. This paper was read by WS at the English Institute of Columbia University on the evening of September 10, 1948. Included in *NA*.

Published December 27, 1949, at $3.00, in an edition of 800 copies.

Annotation: "I am going down to New York on Friday to read a paper on *Imagination As Value.* The other day they sent me a copy of the program. For the next three days professors will by reading papers and then on Friday evening I shall get up before this group, which by that time will be thoroughly flabbergasted by all that they have heard, and try to set them on fire. It sounds like quite a job. Perhaps if I could have that bottle of Jameson of which you spoke, on the reading stand, I could really get somewhere. As it has turned out, this subject grew larger and larger the more I thought about it, but I have done no reading and now that the paper is written I am more curious about the subject than I was before I began to work on it." (*Letters*, pp. 613–614: letter to Barbara Church, September 7, 1948)

B 43 GROMAIRE
(1949)

GROMAIRE | *Exhibition of Paintings* | *December 5–31, 1949* | LOUIS CARRÉ GALLERY | *712 Fifth Avenue, New York*

[Unpaged] 4 leaves. Illustrated with three plates in black and white. 9×6 inches. Heavy coated paper wrapper, with a Gromaire painting reproduced on front in black and white; printed in red on front and back. Stapled.

Contains "Marcel Gromaire," pp. [2–3]. In *OP*.

Distributed December 1949; not for sale.

B 44 MODERN AMERICAN POETRY
[1950]

MODERN AMERICAN POETRY | EDITED BY B. RAJAN | FREDERICK BRANTLEY | DAVID DAICHES | VIVIENNE

KOCH | JAMES LAUGHLIN | ROBERT LOWELL | ARCHI-
BALD MACLEISH | NORMAN MACLEOD | LOUIS L. MARTZ |
MARIANNE MOORE | EZRA POUND | B. RAJAN | THEODORE
SPENCER | WALLACE STEVENS | JOSE GARCIA VILLA |
ROBERT PENN WARREN | WILLIAM CARLOS WILLIAMS |
YVOR WINTERS [names of contributors enclosed in single-
rule box] | [device] | London: Dennis Dobson Ltd

190 pp., 1 leaf. $8^5/_8 \times 5^1/_2$ inches. Green cloth, stamped in blind
on back and in black on spine. White endpapers; top edges
stained green; fore and bottom edges trimmed. Green dust
jacket printed in red and green.

Contains "Credences of Summer," "Imago," "Celle Qui Fût
Héaulmiette," and "St. John and the Back-Ache," pp. 149–157.
In addition, WS's replies to "American and English Poetry,"
pp. 183–184, received their only publication here.
    "Credences of Summer" is reprinted from *Transport to Sum-
mer,* A 11; "Imago," "Celle Qui Fût Héaulmiette," and "St. John
and the Back-Ache" are published here for the first time in book
form; all the poems are included in *CP;* all but "Celle Qui Fût
Héaulmiette" are also in *Palm.*

Published May 1950, at 8s. 6d., in an issue of 1,500 copies. Series
title: p. [1]: FOCUS FIVE.

American issue
The English sheets were used, and the American publisher's
name, Roy Publishers, New York, was substituted.

Published September 30, 1952, at $3.50.

B 45 THE HARVARD ADVOCATE ANTHOLOGY
[1951]

The | HARVARD | [in script] ADVOCATE | Anthology | Edited
by DONALD HALL | [row of ornaments] | *"If one seeks a monu-
ment to the little old paper, | let him look about in the list of
young writers, | and see how many of them became famous."* |
—W. G. Peckham, '67, in *The Harvard Advocate;* | *Fifty Year
Book,* 1916 | [row of ornaments] | TWAYNE PUBLISHERS,
INC. · NEW YORK

327 pp. Four pages of photographs tipped in. $9^1/_8 \times 6$ inches. Red
cloth, stamped in gold on front and on spine. White endpapers;
top edges stained red; fore and bottom edges trimmed. Gray
dust jacket printed in dark gray and red.

Contains "Sonnet" ('There shines the morning star!'), "Quatrain" ('Go not, young cloud, too boldly through the sky,'), "Song" ('Ah yes! beyond these barren walls'), "Outside the Hospital," "Street Songs" ("I. The Pigeons," "II. The Beggar," "III. Statuary," "IV. The Minstrel"), "Night Song," "Sonnet" ('Lo, even as I passed beside the booth'), "Ballade of the Pink Parasol," "Quatrain" ('He sought the music of the distant spheres'), and "Song" ('She loves me or loves me not,'), pp. 60–67.

Of these poems, "Sonnet" ('There shines the morning star!') was included in B 3 and B 4 and is reprinted in B 57; "Quatrain" ('Go not, young cloud, too boldly through the sky,') has its only book publication here; "Song" ('Ah yes! beyond these barren walls') was included in B 3 and B 4 and is reprinted in B 57; "Outside the Hospital" was included in B 4 and is reprinted in B 57; "Street Songs" ("II. The Beggar") has its first book publication here; the complete group is reprinted in B 57; "Night Song" has its first book publication here and is reprinted in B 57; "Sonnet" ('Lo, even as I passed beside the booth') has its first book publication here and is reprinted in B 57; "Ballade of the Pink Parasol" has its only book publication here; "Quatrain" ('He sought the music of the distant spheres') has its first book publication here and is reprinted in B 57; and "Song" ('She loves me or loves me not,') was included in B 4 and is reprinted in B 57.

Published January 22, 1951, at $5.00, in an edition of 4,200 copies.

Annotations: "While I should no doubt be willing to have you use almost anything that you liked, nevertheless, since you will be making copies of anything that you are thinking of using, could you not let me see these before you include them in your manuscript? In short, I should rather give you permission after I know what you have chosen and have had a chance to look at it again. Some of one's early things give one the creeps." (*Letters*, p. 667: letter to Donald Hall, February 16, 1950)

"If you use the things which you enclosed with your letter of June 20th, I shall have to go out and drown myself. This is especially true as to the poems. Have a heart. Of the two prose pieces I remember the first but not the second — yet I suppose that I wrote the second. Definitely: no.

"Why not content yourself with the other things of which you speak? I must have a number of copies of the number of ADVOCATE that was devoted to my things but when I went up to the attic last night to look for one I was not able to find it. You say there are thirteen poems. Assuming that these thirteen are poems that were printed when I was an undergraduate, I don't object to your using them if you think that they are worth while as juvenilia. I remember contributing a number of things to that number which were later published in one of my books and this consent of course has no relation to those poems which are under the control of Mr. Knopf. The things not published later by Mr. Knopf, that is to say, the purely undergraduate poems are subject only to my own consent and, as I say, you can use them if you think it worth while. (Vita Mea seems a particularly horrid mess.)" (*Letters*, pp. 683–684: letter to Donald Hall, June 28, 1950)

B 46 MODERN POETRY
AMERICAN AND BRITISH
[1951]

Modern Poetry | AMERICAN | AND | BRITISH | [ornament] | EDITED BY | KIMON FRIAR | AND | JOHN MALCOLM BRIN-NIN | [device] | *New York* | APPLETON-CENTURY-CROFTS, Inc.

xviii, 1 leaf, 580 pp., 4 blank leaves. $8^{11}/_{16} \times 5^{3}/_{8}$ inches. Blue cloth, stamped in silver on front and in silver and black on spine. White endpapers; all edges trimmed. Pink, brown, and white dust jacket printed in brown and white.

Contains brief notes by WS, pp. 537–538, on the poems included; the poems are: "Notes Toward a Supreme Fiction" (Sections II, V, VII, and XVI), "Mrs. Alfred Uruguay," "The Sense of the Sleight-of-Hand Man," "Connoisseur of Chaos," "The Glass of Water," "The Poems of Our Climate," "Academic Discourse at Havana," "Evening Without Angels," "The Idea of Order in [*sic*] Key West," "Sailing After Lunch," and "The Emperor of Ice-Cream," pp. 75–87.
  This is the only publication of the notes.

Published February 27, 1951, at $4,00, in an issue of 6,850 copies.

Library issue
Of the 6,850 copies published on February 27, 1951, an undetermined number were issued in a binding of red cloth over boards, with the words 'LIBRARY EDITION' stamped in black on the spine, and in the same dust jacket.

Issued simultaneously February 27, 1951, at $4.00.

B 47 AMERICAN SAMPLER
(1951)

AMERICAN | [in red] *Sampler* | A SELECTION OF NEW POETRY | *Edited by* | Francis Coleman Rosenberger | [in red: rule] | *The Prairie Press: Iowa City* | 1951

70 pp., 3 leaves, 2 blank leaves. 10 × 6 inches. Rust-colored cloth, stamped downward in black on spine. White endpapers; fore and bottom edges rough trimmed. White dust jacket printed in blue green and red.

Contains "Memorandum," p. 15. In *OP*.

Colophon: p. [75]: This book has been designed and printed by Carroll | Coleman at his Prairie Press in Iowa City, Iowa. The | type is Bulmer, hand set, and the paper W & A Arak

Published November 1951, at $3.00.

B 48 NEW POEMS BY AMERICAN POETS
(1953)

NEW | POEMS | *By American Poets* | [rule] | Edited by ROLFE HUMPHRIES | BALLANTINE BOOKS · NEW YORK · 1953

10 leaves, 179, [1] pp. 8 × 5¼ inches. Green paper-covered boards, stamped in yellow on front and downward on spine. White endpapers; all edges trimmed. Dust jacket printed in white, blue, yellow, and black.

Contains "Song of Fixed Accord," "Two Illustrations That the World Is What You Make of It," and "Prologues to What Is Possible," pp. 152–156. All are collected in *CP;* "Two Illustrations That the World Is What You Make of It" and "Prologues to What Is Possible" are also in *Palm.*

Published September 21, 1953, at $2.00, in an issue of 3,000 copies.

Paper issue
The paperbound copies have the same title page as the hardbound issue and coated paper covers similar to its dust jacket.

Published simultaneously September 21, 1953, in an issue of 100,000 copies.

B 49 SEVEN ARTS # TWO
[*1954*]

7 ARTS | # Two | Selected and edited by | FERNANDO PUMA |
[reproduction of Marino Marini's drawing *Horse and Rider*]
| PERMABOOKS | a division of | Doubleday & Company, Inc.,
Garden City, N.Y.

196 pp., 2 leaves. Forty-eight pages of reproductions bound in
between pages 80 and 81. 7⅛ × 4¼ inches. Coated yellow paper
wrapper, printed in blue, black, red, and magenta. All edges
stained red.

Contains "The Dove in Spring," p. 59. This appearance of the
poem in book form is its first publication. In *OP* and *Palm*.

Published February 1, 1954, at 50¢ (60¢ in Canada), in an edition
of 102,605 copies; A Perma Special Doubleday P 262 S. On
copyright page: 'DESIGN BY DIANA KLEMIN'.

B 50 THE POCKET BOOK OF MODERN VERSE
[*1954*]

THE POCKET BOOK OF | modern verse | [a line of thirty-two
dots] | ENGLISH AND AMERICAN POETRY OF | THE LAST
HUNDRED YEARS FROM | WALT WHITMAN TO DYLAN
THOMAS | EDITED BY | oscar williams | [device] | POCKET
BOOKS, INC. · NEW YORK

638 pp., 1 leaf. 6⅜ × 4⅛ inches. Coated paper wrapper, printed
in blue, black, gold, white, red, and yellow, with photographs
of poets on front, back, and insides of covers; photograph of WS
on inside of front cover. All edges stained yellow.

Contains "Peter Quince at the Clavier," "Connoisseur of Chaos,"
"The Glass of Water," "The Idea of Order in [*sic*] Key West,"
"Sunday Morning," "The Sense of the Sleight-of-Hand Man,"
"The Poems of Our Climate," "An Extract from Addresses to
the Academy of Fine Ideas" (IV), "A Postcard from the Volcano,"
"Parochial Theme," "The Woman That Had More Babies Than
That," "On an Old Horn," 'The President ordains the bee to
be' [from *Notes Toward a Supreme Fiction*], and "To an Old
Philosopher in Rome," pp. 273–292.
    Of these poems, only "To an Old Philosopher in Rome" is
published here for the first time in book form; collected in *CP*,
Poems, and *Palm*.

Published April 1954, at 50¢; A Cardinal Giant GC-16. On copyright page: 'This original Cardinal Giant anthology, prepared es- | pecially for Pocket Books, Inc., is printed from brand-new | plates made from newly set, clear, easy-to-read type. | [rule] | the pocket book of modern verse | CARDINAL GIANT edition published April, 1954 | 1st printing . . . . February, 1954'.

B 51 NEW WORLD WRITING
[1954]

New | WORLD | WRITING | FIFTH MENTOR SELECTION | PUBLISHED BY [device] | THE NEW AMERICAN LIBRARY

337 pp., 3 leaves. 7⅛ × 4⅛ inches. Coated paper wrapper, printed in blue, black, yellow, orange, and white. All edges stained red.

Contains "Farewell Without a Guitar," p. 76. This appearance of the poem in book form is its first publication; in *OP*.

Published April 1954, at 50¢; Mentor Selection 106. On copyright page: 'Published as a MENTOR SELECTION | First issued, April, 1954'.

B 52 THE NEW POCKET ANTHOLOGY OF
AMERICAN VERSE
[1955]

[ornamental rule] | THE *New* POCKET ANTHOLOGY OF | AMERICAN VERSE | *From Colonial Days to the Present* | Edited by | OSCAR WILLIAMS | [device] | [ornamental rule] | THE POCKET LIBRARY

638 pp., 1 leaf. 6⅜ × 4¼ inches. Red and blue paper wrapper, printed in black and white, with photographs of poets, including WS, on front, back, and insides of covers. All edges stained yellow.

Contains "Of Modern Poetry," "Martial Cadenza," "Dance of the Macabre Mice," "The Emperor of Ice-Cream," "Anecdote of the Jar," "Sunday Morning," "Conversation with Three Women of New England," "The Comedian as the Letter C," "Crude Foyer," "Notes Toward a Supreme Fiction" ('It is the celestial ennui of apartments', 'The lion roars at the enraging desert', 'It feels good as it is without the giant', 'Bethou me, said sparrow, to the crackled blade', 'Soldier, there is a war between

the mind'), "Mrs. Alfred Uruguay," "Presence of an External Master of Knowledge," "Continual Conversation with a Silent Man," and "Holiday in Reality," pp. 464–496.

Of these poems, "Conversation with Three Women of New England" and "Presence of an External Master of Knowledge" are published here for the first time in book form; both are collected in *OP*.

Published August 1955, at 50¢, in an edition of 6,000 copies. On p. [1]: 'This book is published in affiliation with The World Publishing Company which offers a hard cover edition at $3.50.' This hardbound edition has not been seen by the compiler. On copyright page: 'POCKET LIBRARY edition published August, 1955 | 1st printing . . . . June, 1955'.

B 53 PAUL VALERY DIALOGUES
[*1956*]

PAUL VALÉRY | [in light brown] DIALOGUES | *Translated by* | *William McCausland Stewart* | [in light brown: ornament] | *With Two Prefaces by* | *Wallace Stevens* | BOLLINGEN SERIES XLV · 4 | [rule] | PANTHEON BOOKS

xxviii, 195 pp., 1 leaf, 1 blank leaf. 8⅛ × 5 inches. Beige cloth, stamped in gold on front and in brown and gold on spine. White endpapers; top edges stained brown; fore and bottom edges trimmed. Tan and black dust jacket printed in white and black.

Contains two Prefaces, "Gloire du long Désir, Idées," pp. ix–xxi, and "Chose légère, ailée, sacrée," pp. xxii–xxviii, by WS. These two prefaces were written for this volume and are published here for the first time; in *OP*.

Published December 28, 1956, at $3.00, in an edition of 5,000 copies. On copyright page: 'THIS IS VOLUME FOUR OF THE | COLLECTED WORKS OF PAUL VALÉRY | CONSTITUTING NUMBER XLV IN BOLLINGEN SERIES, | SPONSORED BY AND PUBLISHED FOR BOLLINGEN FOUNDATION. | IT IS THE FIRST VOLUME OF THE | COLLECTED WORKS TO APPEAR. . . . | DESIGNED BY ANDOR BRAUN'.

English issue
An additional 1,000 sheets of the American issue were sent to England for distribution by Routledge and Kegan Paul.

Annotation: "I enclose the introductions to *Eupalinos* and

L'Ame et la Danse. These have been prepared as a single paper. If you wish to separate them, the dividing line is obvious (page 18). If they are separated, the title for the introduction to *L'Ame et la Danse* should be:

Chose Légère, Ailée, Sacrée.

You will have to divide the notes too. [. . .]

"I have limited myself to setting the works forth and emphasizing in that way the aspects that interested me. The dialogues raise the question of the value of aesthetics and this is, no doubt, what I ought to have discussed. I thought it better not to do so. For one thing, I shall not be in conflict with anyone else who may have discussed the question in his own introduction. As to what I have said I don't think that I shall be in competition with anyone. [. . .]

"I hope that you find the paper acceptable. It was a great pleasure to be asked to take part in this job and I look forward to the excitement of publication of the whole collection." (*Letters*, pp. 877–878: letter to Jackson Matthews, March 24, 1955)

B 54 THE ACHIEVEMENT OF WALLACE STEVENS [*1962*]

the ACHIEVEMENT of | WALLACE STEVENS | *edited by* ASHLEY BROWN | *and* ROBERT S. HALLER | [device] | J. B. LIPPINCOTT · PHILADELPHIA · NEW YORK

287 pp. 8¼ × 5⁹⁄₁₆ inches. Green cloth, stamped in black on front and on spine. Green endpapers; top edges stained green; fore and bottom edges trimmed. Green and white dust jacket printed in brown.

Contains, pp. 200–201, as part of S. F. Morse's essay "The Native Element" (C 228), excerpts from three letters by WS to Paule Vidal, September 30, 1949, October 5, 1949, and October 31, 1949, published here for the first time in book form and included in *Letters;* p. 207, as part of S. F. Morse's same essay, WS's note of explication on "The Emperor of Ice-Cream," which had appeared in *The Explicator,* C 185, and is published here in its only book form; and p. 235, as part of Michel Benamou's essay "Wallace Stevens: Some Relations Between Poetry and Painting" (C 229), an excerpt from a letter by WS to Paule Vidal, January 30, 1948, published here for the first time in book form and included in *Letters.*

3 944

.23

.603

(also in

Poetry Room)

Note: This book is made up of nineteen essays on WS, with an introduction and bibliography; see I 6 for contents.

Published April 20, 1962, at $5.00, in an edition of 3,500 copies.

B 55 THE CLAIRVOYANT EYE
(1965)

[script] The | [script] Clairvoyant Eye | *The Poetry and Poetics of Wallace Stevens* | JOSEPH N. RIDDEL | Louisiana State University Press | Baton Rouge, 1965

ix, 1 leaf, 308 pp. 9½ × 6¼ inches. Dark blue cloth over boards, stamped in silver on spine. White endpapers; all edges trimmed. Blue dust jacket printed in pink and black.

Contains, p. 61, quotation from an unpublished interpretation of *Carlos among the Candles* sent by WS to Bancel La Farge in 1917 (the manuscript of which is in the Houghton Library of Harvard University); p. 110, quotation from WS's statement on front flap of dust jacket of *Ideas of Order* (1936), A 2.b, published here for the first time in book form and reprinted in full in B 60; pp. 121 and 135, quotations from WS's statement on front flap of dust jacket of *The Man with the Blue Guitar and Other Poems* (1937), A 4.a, their only publication in book form (on p. 135, the word 'conjunctioning' is quoted; see A 4.a); p. 289, note 4, quotation from WS's letter of October 9, 1935, to J. Ronald Lane Latimer, published in *Letters;* and p. 293, note 11, quotation from WS's letter of November 18, 1940, to Oscar Williams, published in *Letters.*

Published January 10, 1965, at $7.50, in an edition of 2,000 copies. On p. viii: 'Stevens' daughter, Holly Stevens . . . is at present working on a collection of her father's letters. . . . The letters used herein are quoted with her permission.'

Second printing
A second printing, bound in both cloth and paper, was issued May 30, 1967.

B 56 THE ACT OF THE MIND
[*1965*]

THE ACT | OF THE MIND | Essays on the Poetry of Wallace Stevens | Edited by | Roy Harvey Pearce and J. Hillis Miller | The Johns Hopkins Press, Baltimore, Maryland xi, 1 leaf, 287 pp., 1 leaf. $9\frac{3}{16} \times 6\frac{1}{4}$ inches. Blue cloth, stamped down in silver on spine. White endpapers; all edges trimmed.

Contains, pp. 58–91, excerpts from eighteen letters by WS in S. F. Morse's essay "Wallace Stevens, Bergson, Pater" and, pp. 92–119, excerpts from two letters by WS in Michel Benamou's essay "Wallace Stevens and the Symbolist Imagination." These letters, all published here for the first time in book form, are listed in C 231.

Note: The book is made up of eight reprinted and four original essays on WS; see I 16 for contents.

Colophon: recto of last leaf: THE ACT OF THE MIND | *Essays on the Poetry of Wallace Stevens* | edited by | ROY HARVEY PEARCE AND J. HILLIS MILLER | *designer:* Edward King | *compositor:* J. H. Furst Co. | *typefaces:* Scotch and Caslon Openface | *printer:* J. H. Furst Co. | *paper:* Perkins and Squier GM | *binder:* Moore & Co. | *cover material:* Columbia Milbank Linen

Published March 26, 1965, at $5.95, in an edition of 3,563 copies.

B 57 HARVARD ADVOCATE CENTENNIAL
ANTHOLOGY
[1966]

HARVARD ADVOCATE | CENTENNIAL | ANTHOLOGY | *edited by* Jonathan D. Culler | SCHENKMAN PUBLISHING CO., INC. | Cambridge, Massachusetts

xxxi, 1 leaf, 460 pp. $9\frac{1}{2} \times 6\frac{5}{8}$ inches. Photograph of WS as a young man, facing p. 47. Crimson cloth, stamped in black and gold on spine. White endpapers; all edges trimmed. White dust jacket printed in red, purple, black, and olive.

Contains, pp. 37–53, reprintings of "Sonnet" ('There shines the morning star!'), "Song" ('Ah yes! beyond these barren walls'), "Outside the Hospital," "Street Songs" ("I. The Pigeons," "II. The Beggar," "III. Statuary," "IV. The Minstrel"), "Night Song," "Sonnet" ('Lo, even as I passed . . .'), "Quatrain" ('He sought the music . . .'), "Song" ('She loves me or loves me not,'), "Of Bright & Blue Birds & The Gala Sun," "Mrs. Alfred Uruguay," "Asides on the Oboe," and "Examination of the Hero in Time of War."
Contributions by WS published here for the first time in book form are, p. xvi, an excerpt from *The Harvard Advocate* editorial on putting a fence around Harvard Yard, C 23; p. xvii, an excerpt from the *Advocate* editorial on the need for a new Harvard cheer,

C 31, reprinted on the back of the dust jacket; and, p. 73, WS's tribute to T. S. Eliot in the *Advocate,* C 121.

Published March 17, 1966, at $11.25, in an edition of 3,000 copies.

B 58 WALLACE STEVENS   THE MAKING OF
HARMONIUM
(1967)

[in script] Wallace Stevens | THE MAKING OF | [in script] Harmonium | BY ROBERT BUTTEL | PRINCETON UNIVER-SITY PRESS | PRINCETON, NEW JERSEY | 1967

xv, 2 leaves, 3–269 pp. 8¾ × 5⅝ inches. Blue cloth, stamped on spine in green and silver. Blue endpapers; all edges trimmed. Blue green dust jacket printed in white.

Contains the following poems previously published but not in book form: "To the Morn," C 19; "Carnet de Voyage" (I. 'An odor from a star', II. 'One More Sunset', III. 'Here the grass grows' ["called 'Concert of Fishes', III in 1909 Little June Book" – Buttel], IV. 'She that winked her sandal fan' ["IX in 1909 Little June Book" – Buttel], V. 'I am weary of the plum and of the cherry' ["XVII in 1909 Little June Book" – Buttel], VI. 'Man from the waste evolved' ["VIII in 1909 Little June Book" – Buttel], VII. "Chinese Rocket" ["untitled, XIX in 1909 Little June Book" – Buttel], VIII. "On an Old Guitar," C 41; "From a Junk" and "Home Again" ["XIX in 1908 June Book of 20 poems" – Buttel], C 42). Except for "To the Morn," which is on p. 13, the page numbers for these poems are given on p. 255 of Buttel.

Contains the following poems, a play, and a miscellaneous manuscript by WS not published before: "Afield"; untitled poem, 'All things imagined are of earth compact'; "Ancient Rendezvous" ["called 'Winter Melody', VIII in 1908 June Book" – Buttel]; "Anecdote of the Prince of Peacocks"; "April" ["called 'In April', XIV in 1909 Little June Book" – Buttel]; "Chiaroscuro"; "Colors"; "Dolls"; "Eight Significant Landscapes" (V. 'Wrestle with morning glories', VI. 'Crenellations of mountains' ["V and VI presumably omitted from 'Six Significant Landscapes'" – Buttel]); "An Exercise for Professor X"; "For an Old Woman in a Wig"; untitled poem, 'Hung up brave tapestries' ["IV in 1908 June Book" – Buttel]; "Headache"; untitled poem, 'He sang and in her heart the sound' ["XVI in 1909 Little June Book" – Buttel];

untitled poem, 'If only birds of sudden white' ["II in 1909 Little June Book"–Buttel]; untitled poem, 'I have lived so long with the rhetoricians'; untitled poem 'I lie dreaming 'neath the moon' ["called 'Pierrot', XX, last poem in 1909 Little June Book"– Buttel]; "L'Essor Saccade"; untitled poem 'Life is long in the desert' ["IV in 1909 Little June Book"–Buttel]; "The Lilac Bush" ["untitled in 1909 Little June Book"–Buttel]; untitled poem, 'The night wind of August'; untitled poem 'Noon, and a wind on the hill' ["called 'New Life', II in 1908 June Book"– Buttel]; "Noon Clearing" ["VII in 1909 Little June Book"– Buttel]; untitled poem 'An odorous bush I seek' ["XVIII in 1909 Little June Book"–Buttel]; "Phases"; "Shower" ["XI in 1909 Little June Book"–Buttel]; "Testamentum"; "Tides" ["VII in 1908 June Book"–Buttel]; "To Madame Alda, Singing a Song, in a White Gown" ["VI above title, evidently part of an unknown series"–Buttel]; excerpts from the play *Bowl, Cat and Broomstick;* and portions from the miscellaneous manuscript "From Pieces of Paper." The page numbers for this material are given on pp. 255–256 of Buttel.

The complete *Bowl, Cat and Broomstick* is in *Palm.*

Published March 17, 1967, at $6.95, in an edition of 2,500 copies.

B 59 THE DOME AND THE ROCK
[*1968*]

[double title page] [left] "The gold dome of things is the perfected spirit." | THE DOME AND | STRUCTURE IN THE POETRY | by James Baird | [right] Wallace Stevens: From the "Adagia" | THE ROCK [ornament] | OF WALLACE STEVENS | The Johns Hopkins Press: Baltimore

xxxi, 1 leaf, 334 pp. 9¼ × 6¼ inches. Blue cloth, stamped in silver on front and in silver and black on spine. Blue endpapers; all edges trimmed. Blue dust jacket printed in black.

Contains a quotation from a previously unpublished letter by WS of April 20, 1955, to Jackson Matthews, p. 3; a quotation from a previously unpublished letter of July 22, 1953, to Paule Vidal, p. 182; and a quotation from a previously unpublished letter of April 7, 1955, to Sister M. Bernetta Quinn, p. 305.

Published October 10, 1968, at $8.95, in an edition of 3,500 copies.

B 60 WALLACE STEVENS   POETRY AS LIFE
[*1970*]

WALLACE STEVENS | POETRY AS LIFE [ornament] | BY
SAMUEL FRENCH MORSE | PEGASUS [device] NEW YORK

xv, [17]-232 pp. 8¼ × 5⁹⁄₁₆ inches. Orange yellow cloth, stamped
in green on spine. White endpapers; all edges trimmed. White
dust jacket printed in green, black, and brown, with photographs
of WS on front and the author on back; title on the front is:
'Wallace Stevens Life as Poetry'; spine carries the same title as
the title page.

Contains, p. 150, the complete dust jacket statement by WS for
Ideas of Order, 1936, A 2.b; pp. 80–82, fragments from *Bowl,
Cat and Broomstick;* and, p. 101, lines 10 through 13 of "The
Man Whose Pharynx Was Bad," printed here as they appeared
in *The New Republic,* C 65 (see *Palm,* p. 401, note). All are pub-
lished here for the first time in book form.

Published July 24, 1970, at $6.95, in an edition of 5,000 copies;
Pegasus Series No. P1229.

C. Contributions to Periodicals

C 1

"Greatest Need of the Age." Reading (Pa.) *Eagle*, December 23, 1896, p. 5, col. 2.

An essay for which WS received a prize given by the *Eagle* of Reading, Pa., and the Alumni Medal for Oration at the Reading, Pa., Boys' High School. A sketch of WS appeared in the *Eagle* the following day.

C 2

"The Thessalians." Reading (Pa.) *Eagle,* June 24, 1897, p. 5, col. 1.

WS's commencement address at the Reading, Pa., Boys' High School.

C 3

"Autumn." *The Red and Black*, I, 3 (January 1898), 1.

The Red and Black was the magazine of the Reading, Pa., Boys' High School.

C 4

"Who Lies Dead?" *The Harvard Advocate*, LXVI, 4 (November 28, 1898), 57.

C 5

"Vita Mea." *The Harvard Advocate*, LXVI, 5 (December 12, 1898), 78.

In B 1.

C 6

"Her First Escapade." *The Harvard Advocate*, LXVI, 7 (January 16, 1899), 104–108.

Prose.

189

C 7
"Sonnet" ('If we are leaves that fall . . .'). *Harvard Monthly*, XXVIII, 1 (March 1899), 31.

C 8
"A Day in February." *The Harvard Advocate*, LXVI, 9 (March 6, 1899), 135–136.

Prose.

C 9
"Song" ('She loves me or loves me not'). *The Harvard Advocate*, LXVI, 10 (March 13, 1899), 150.

In B 4.

C 10
"Sonnet" ('There shines the morning star!'). *The Harvard Advocate*, LXVII, 2 (April 10, 1899), 18.

In B 3.

C 11
"Part of His Education." *The Harvard Advocate*, LXVII, 3 (April 24, 1899), 35–37.

Prose.

C 12
"Sonnet" ('Cathedrals are not built along the sea . . .'). *Harvard Monthly*, XXVIII, 3 (May 1899), 95.

Unsigned.

Annotations: "About Santayana. I never took any of his courses and I don't believe that I ever heard him lecture. But I knew him quite well. [. . .] Once he asked me to come and read some of my things to him. I read one of them in which the first line was 'Cathedrals are not built along the sea.' " (*Letters*, p. 637: letter to Bernard Heringman, May 3, 1949)

"Stevens' sonnet 'Cathedrals are not built along the sea,' was written on March 12, 1899; it is the ninth in a sequence of sonnets written in his Journal between February 22 and April 14, 1899." (*Letters*, p. 482: footnote by HS to WS's letter of January 4, 1945, to José Rodríguez-Feo, in which he refers to the sonnet)

C 13
"The Higher Life." *The Harvard Advocate*, LXVII, 8 (June 12, 1899), 123–124.

Prose.

C 14
"Sonnet" ('I strode along my beaches . . .'). *Harvard Monthly*, XXVIII, 5 (July 1899), 188.

Signed 'John Morris 2nd'.

C 15
"Pursuit." *The Harvard Advocate*, LXVIII, 2 (October 18, 1899), 19–20.

Prose.

C 16
"The Revelation." *The Harvard Advocate*, LXVIII, 4 (November 13, 1899), 54–56.

C 17
"Quatrain" ('Go not, young cloud, . . .'). *The Harvard Advocate*, LXVIII, 4 (November 13, 1899), 63.

In B 45.

C 18
"The Nymph." *The Harvard Advocate*, LXVIII, 6 (December 6, 1899), 86–87.

Prose. Signed 'John Fiske Towne'.

C 19
"To the Morn." *Harvard Monthly*, XXIX, 3 (December 1899), 128.

Signed 'Hillary Harness'. In B 58.

C 20
Untitled editorial. *The Harvard Advocate*, LXIX, 1 (March 10, 1900), 1–2.

Written as president of the *Advocate* in three parts: on the re-tiring boards of the magazine, on keeping a journal of activities as an officer of the university, and on a combination ticket for athletic activities. Unsigned.

C 21

"Song" ('Ah yes! beyond these barren walls'). *The Harvard Advocate*, LXIX, 1 (March 10, 1900), 5.

In B 4.

C 22

"Hawkins of Cold Cape." *The Harvard Advocate*, LXIX, 1 (March 10, 1900), 8–12.

Prose. Signed 'Carrol Moore'.

C 23

Untitled editorial. *The Harvard Advocate*, LXIX, 2 (March 24, 1900), 17–18.

Written as president of the *Advocate* in three parts: on a proposed trip for a choral group, on putting a fence around the Yard, and on the desirability of informed political discussion. Unsigned. An excerpt from the section on the fence is in B 57.

C 24

"Outside the Hospital." *The Harvard Advocate*, LXIX, 2 (March 24, 1900), 18.

Signed 'R. Jerries'. In B 4.

C 25

Untitled editorial. *The Harvard Advocate*, LXIX, 3 (April 3, 1900), 33–34.

Written as president of the *Advocate* on gymnastic decrepitude at Harvard and why it should not be encouraged: 'We have been convinced for a long time that gymnastics are a means, not an end.' Unsigned.

C 26

"Street Songs." *The Harvard Advocate*, LXIX, 3 (April 3, 1900), 42–43.

Contents: I. The Pigeons – II. The Beggar – III. Statuary – IV. The Minstrel.

Nos. I, III, and IV in B 4; all four sections in B 45.

C 27

Untitled editorial. *The Harvard Advocate*, LXIX, 4 (April 13, 1900), 49–50.

Written as president of the *Advocate* in four parts: on the Warren House library, on admittance to courses in music, on the preferability of an iron fence around the Yard, and on the question of smoking in Brooks House. Untitled.

C 28
"Sonnet" ('Come, said the world . . .'). *East & West*, I (May 1900), 201.

C 29
Untitled editorial. *The Harvard Advocate*, LXIX, 5 (May 10, 1900), 65–66.

Written as president of the *Advocate* on the exaggerated use of local color in stories and poems submitted to the magazine. Unsigned.

C 30
"Night Song." *The Harvard Advocate*, LXIX, 5 (May 10, 1900), 66.

Signed 'Kenneth Malone'. In B 45.

C 31
Untitled editorial. *The Harvard Advocate*, LXIX, 6 (May 23, 1900), 81–82.

Written as president of the *Advocate* in two parts: on the need for a more equitable distribution of usherships at games and on the need for a new Harvard cheer. Unsigned. An excerpt from the section on the cheer is in B 57.

C 32
"Ballade of the Pink Parasol." *The Harvard Advocate*, LXIX, 6 (May 23, 1900), 82.

Signed 'Carrol More'. In B 45.

C 33
"In the Dead of Night." *The Harvard Advocate*, LXIX, 6 (May 23, 1900), 83–86.

Prose.

C 34
"Sonnet" ('Lo, even as I passed . . .'). *The Harvard Advocate*, LXIX, 6 (May 23, 1900), 86.

Signed 'R. Jerries'. In B 45.

C 35
Untitled editorial. *The Harvard Advocate*, LXIX, 7 (June 2, 1900), 97–98.

Written as president of the *Advocate* in three parts: on the use of Memorial Hall by summer school students, on the faults of the present Harvard cheer, and on the impropriety of solicitation on campus by agents of Colonial Hall. Unsigned.

C 36
"Quatrain" ('He sought the music . . .'). *The Harvard Advocate*, LXIX, 7 (June 2, 1900), 110.

Signed 'Henry Marshall'. In B 45.

C 37
Untitled editorial. *The Harvard Advocate*, LXIX, 8 (June 16, 1900), 113–114.

Written as president of the *Advocate* in four parts: on the preferability of an iron panel fence for the Yard; on the unsuitability of memorial plaques on the fence; on the seclusion which the fence would provide: 'The seclusion the fence is meant to secure is not a seclusion of aloofness but of distinct whereabouts, of separateness.'; and on the purchase of cups for the interclass debating teams. Unsigned.

C 38
"Four Characters." *The Harvard Advocate*, LXIX, 8 (June 16, 1900), 119–120.

Prose.

C 39
"Funeral of Stephen Crane." *New York Tribune*, June 29, 1900, p. 8, col. 2.

Prose. Unsigned; attributed to WS.

C 40
"In Memoriam of J. L. Kuechler." *The Reading* (Pa.) *Times*, January 7, 1904, p. 2, col. 6.

A prose piece that contains a portion of a letter from WS to his father.

C 41
"Carnet de Voyage." *The Trend*, VII, 6 (September 1914), 743–746.

Contents: I. 'An odor from a star' – II. One More Sunset – III. 'Here the grass grows' – IV. 'She that winked her sandal fan' – V. 'I am weary of the plum . . .' – VI. 'Man from the waste evolved' – VII. Chinese Rocket – VIII. On an Old Guitar.

"On an Old Guitar" in B 58.

C 42
"Two Poems." *The Trend*, VIII, 2 (November 1914), 117.

Contents: From a Junk – Home Again.

In B 58.

C 43
"Phases." *Poetry*, V, 2 (November 1914), 70–71.

Contents: I. 'There's a little square in Paris' – II. 'This was the salty taste of glory' – III. 'But the bugles, in the night' – IV. 'Death's nobility again'.

These four short poems were selected by Harriet Monroe for her "Poems of War" issue of *Poetry* from a larger number submitted by WS. Of these pieces only "Death's nobility again" was reprinted; it appeared in *The New Poetry* (1917) with the title "In Battle" (B 7). From the original manuscript of eleven poems submitted to *Poetry*, two additional poems, "V. Belgian Farm, October, 1914" and "VI. There was heaven," were included with I through IV in *OP*.

C 44
Two poems. *Rogue*, I, 1 (March 15, 1915), 12.

Contents: Cy est Pourtraicte, Madame Ste Ursule, et Les Unze Mille Vierges – Tea.

Both poems in *CP* and *Palm*.

C 45
Two poems. *Others*, I, 2 (August 1915), 31–34.

Contents: Peter Quince at the Clavier – The Silver Plough-Boy.

"Peter Quince . . ." in *CP* and *Palm;* "The Silver Plough-Boy" in *OP* and *Palm*.

C 46
"Disillusionment of Ten O'Clock." *Rogue*, II, 2 (September 15, 1915), 7.

In *CP* and *Palm*.

C 47
"Sunday Morning." *Poetry*, VII, 2 (November 1915), 81–83.

Harriet Monroe printed five of the eight stanzas of the poem
which WS submitted to *Poetry* and which were finally brought
together in *H-1923*. At WS's request the stanzas were printed
in the following order: I, VIII, IV, V, and VII, but numbered
I through V. In addition, *Poetry* substituted the words 'And
plums in ponderous piles.' in the fourteenth line of stanza V in
place of the words 'On disregarded plate.' which were used when
the poem appeared in *H-1923*. In *CP*, *Poems*, and *Palm*.

Annotations: "Provided your selection of the numbers of
Sunday Morning is printed in the following order: I, VIII, IV,
V, I see no objection to cutting down. The order is necessary to
the idea.
    "I was born in Reading, Pennsylvania, am thirty-five years
old, a lawyer, reside in New-York and have published no books."
(*Letters*, p. 183: letter to Harriet Monroe, June 6, 1915)

"No. 7 of *Sunday Morning* is, as you suggest, of a different
tone, but it does not seem to me to be too detached to conclude
with.
    "The words 'On disregarded plate' in No. 5 are, apparently,
obscure. Plate is used in the sense of so-called family plate. Disregarded refers to the disuse into which things fall that have
been possessed for a long time. I mean, therefore, that death
releases and renews. What the old have come to disregard, the
young inherit and make use of. Used in these senses, the words
have a value in the lines which I find it difficult to retain in any
change. Does this explanation help? Or can you make any suggestion? I ask this because your criticism is clearly well-founded.
    "The lines might read,

> She causes boys to bring sweet-smelling pears,
> And plums in ponderous piles. The maidens taste
> And stray etc.

"But such a change is somewhat pointless. I should prefer
to keep the lines unchanged, although, if you like the variation
proposed, for the sake of clearness, I should be satisfied.
    "The order is satisfactory. Thanks for your very friendly
interest." (*Letters*, pp. 183–184: letter to Harriet Monroe, June
23, 1915)

C 48
Seven poems. *Others*, II, 3, (March 1916), 171–177.

Contents: Domination of Black – Tattoo – The Florist Wears Knee-Breeches – Song ('There are great things doing') – Six Significant Landscapes – Inscription for a Monument – Bowl.

"Domination . . ." in *CP, Poems,* and *Palm;* "Tattoo" in *CP;* "The Florist . . ." and "Song" reprinted only in B 6; "Six Significant Landscapes" in *CP* and *Palm;* "Inscription . . ." in *Palm;* "Bowl" in *OP.*

C 49
"Three Travelers Watch a Sunrise." *Poetry,* VIII, 4 (July 1916), 163–179.

A one-act play in verse for which WS received a prize of $100, awarded by the Players' Producing Company. The donor and the staff on *Poetry* were the judges. In *OP.* The play was produced at the Provincetown Playhouse in New York on February 13, 1920; the cast included Remo Bufano, William Dunbar, Harry Winston, James Butler, Charles Ellis, and Kathleen Millay.

Annotations: "Thanks to you and the donor and to Mr. [Max] Michelson. This is a feather in my cap and I make my first bow with it to Chicago. I shall make every effort to get the revised copy in your hands by June 8th. Mr. Michelson's notes seem to be valuable. What I tried to do was to create a poetic atmosphere with a minimum of narration. It was the first thing of the kind I had ever done and I am, of course, delighted with the result. So is Mrs. Stevens. May I ask you to correct the proof of the title? It should be *Travelers.* The printer appears to believe that travelers are full of l, so that he makes it travellers." (*Letters,* pp. 193–194: letter to Harriet Monroe, May 22, 1916)

"I am not proud because I desire to have the play a play and not merely a poem, if possible. With that in mind, I enclose a new copy, which embodies at least some of the suggestions made by you and Mr. Michelson." (*Letters,* p. 194: letter to Harriet Monroe, May 29, 1916. The remainder of this letter, concerning the many changes in the play, is too long to quote here. The fully revised version, based on a comparison of the two manuscripts of the play in the Harriet Monroe Poetry Library of the University of Chicago Library, is that which appears in *OP.*)

C 50
"The Worms at Heaven's Gate." *Others,* III, 1 (July 1916), 6.

In *CP* and *Palm.*

C 51
"Primordia." *Soil.* I, 2 (January 1917), 76–78.

Contents: In the Northwest (1. 'All over Minnesota' – 2. 'The child's hair is of the color of the hay . . .' – 3. 'The blunt ice flows down the Mississippi' – 4. 'The horses gnaw the bark from the trees' – 5. 'The birch trees draw up whiteness from the ground') – In the South (6. 'Unctuous furrows' – 7. 'The lilacs wither in the Carolinas' – 8. 'The black mother of eleven children' – 9. 'The trade wind jingles the rings in the nets . . .') – To the Roaring Wind.

No. 7, 'The lilacs wither in the Carolinas', under the title "In the Carolinas," and "To the Roaring Wind" were published in *H-1923;* no. 9, 'The trade wind jingles the rings in the nets . . .', under the title "Indian River," was published in *H-1931.* The remaining pieces were not reprinted until the appearance of *OP.* "To the Roaring Wind" is also in *CP* and *Palm.*

C 52
"Carlos among the Candles." *Poetry,* XI, 3 (December 1917), 115–123.

A one-act play in prose. In *OP.* Written for the Wisconsin Players, it had one performance, October 20, 1917, at the Neighborhood Playhouse, New York.

Annotation: "I should be glad to have you use Carlos. But perhaps you would like to read the criticisms first. You might change your mind, then. I shall try to post them to-morrow. The play had one performance. I leave the details until some other time." (*Letters,* p. 202: letter to Harriet Monroe, October 30, 1917)

C 53
Five poems. *Others* (special number), [December 1917], pp. 25–28.

Contents: Valley Candle – Thirteen Ways of Looking at a Blackbird – The Wind Shifts – Meditation – Gray Room.

"Valley Candle" in *CP* and *Palm;* "Thirteen Ways . . ." in *CP, Poems,* and *Palm;* "The Wind Shifts" in *CP;* "Meditation" has not been reprinted; "Gray Room" in *Palm.*

On the contents page of this undated special number: 'A number for the mind's eye | Not to be read aloud'.

C 54
"Lettres d'un Soldat." *Poetry,* XII, 2 (May 1918), 59–65.

Contents: I. "The spirit wakes in the night wind – is naked' – II. Anecdotal Revery – III. Morale – IV. Comme Dieu Dispense de Graces – V. The Surprises of the Superhuman – VI. 'There is another mother whom I love' – VII. Negation – VIII. 'John Smith and his son John Smith' – IX. 'Life contracts and death is expected'.

Of these poems three were reprinted in *H-1931:* "V. The Surprises of the Superhuman," "VII. Negation," and IX. 'Life contracts and death is expected'. There they appear without the citations (see WS's letter below) which prefaced all of the poems as they were printed in *Poetry. H-1931* also included "Lunar Paraphrases," which *Poetry* did not print. These four were again reprinted in *CP*, still without the citations. All the poems in *Poetry*, I through IX, were published in *OP*, with the citations and with "Common Soldier" which, although one of the original series submitted by WS to *Poetry*, had never before been printed. (See *OP*, p. xix, for additional comment by S. F. Morse.)

Annotation: "I want to get the enclosed poems started in your direction since we leave this place [Woodstock, N.Y.] in a day or two and shall be nowhere in particular until we return to Hartford in about a week. I send you the book on which the poems are based [Eugène Emmanuel Lemercier, *Lettres d'un soldat (août 1914–avril 1915)* (Paris: Chapelot, 1916)]. A translation of the book has been published by McClurg of Chicago [Eugène Emmanuel Lemercier, *A soldier of France to his mother; letters from the trenches on the western front*, trans., with an introduction, by Theodore Stanton (Chicago: McClurg, 1917)]. If you care for the poems, you might like to refer to the translation, even to extract my citations in a note, although I assume that most of your readers know French sufficiently not to need a translation. But if you use a translation of the citations; please put it away from my text, somewhere in the back of the magazine." (*Letters*, p. 202: letter to Harriet Monroe, September 1, 1917)

C 55
"Poems." *The Little Review*, VI [*sic*, for V], 2 (June 1918), 3–5.

Contents: Anecdote of Men by the Thousand – Metaphors of a Magnifico – Depression before Spring.

"Anecdote . . ." in *CP*; "Metaphors . . ." and "Depression . . ." in *CP*, *Poems*, and *Palm*.

C 56
"Earthy Anecdote." *Modern School,* V, 7 (July 1918), 193.

In *CP* and *Palm.*

C 57
"Moment of Light." *Modern School,* V, 10 (October 1918), 289–291.

Translation of "Instant de Clarté," by Jean Le Roy. In *OP.*

C 58
"The Apostrophe to Vincentine." *Modern School,* V, 12 (December 1918), 353–354.

In *CP* and *Palm.*

C 59
"Poems." *The Little Review,* V, 8 (December 1918), 10–13.

Contents: Architecture for the Adoration of Beauty – Nuances of a Theme by Williams – Anecdote of Canna.

Of these poems "Architecture for the Adoration of Beauty," under the title of "Architecture," appeared in *H-1923;* the remaining two appeared in both *H-1923* and *H-1931.* "Architecture" in *OP;* "Nuances . . ." in *CP* and *Palm;* "Anecdote . . ." in *CP.* The preliminary stanza of "Nuances of a Theme by Williams" is William Carlos Williams's poem "El Hombre."

C 60
"Le Monocle de Mon Oncle." *Others,* V, 1 (December 1918), 9–12.

In *CP, Poems,* and *Palm.*

C 61
Two poems. *Others,* V, 6, (July 1919), 14.

Contents: Life Is Motion – Earthy Anecdote.

"Life . . ." in *CP* and *Palm;* "Earthy Anecdote" reprinted from C 56.

C 62
"Pecksniffiana." *Poetry,* XV, 1 (October 1919), 1–11.

Contents: Fabliau of Florida – Homunculus et La Belle Etoile – The Weeping Burgher – Peter Parasol – Exposition of the Contents of a Cab – Ploughing on Sunday – Banal Sojourn – The Indigo Glass in the Grass – Anecdote of the Jar – Of the Surface of Things – The Curtains in the House of the Metaphysician – The Place of the Solitaires – The Paltry Nude Starts on a Spring Voyage – Colloquy with a Polish Aunt.

All but two of these poems appeared in *H-1923;* all but three, in *H-1931.* "Peter Parasol," until it appeared in *OP*, was reprinted only in anthologies, for the first time in *The New Poetry* (1923), B 14. "The Indigo Glass in the Grass," until it appeared in *OP*, was reprinted only in anthologies, for the first time in *Prize Poems, 1913-1929*, B 17. "Exposition of the Contents of a Cab" was dropped from *H-1931.*

"Fabliau . . ." in *CP* and *Palm;* "Homunculus . . ." and "The Weeping Burgher" in *CP;* "Peter Parasol" and "Exposition . . ." in *OP;* "Ploughing . . ." in *CP, Poems,* and *Palm;* "Banal Sojourn" in *CP* and *Palm;* "The Indigo Glass . . ." in *OP* and *Poems;* "Anecdote . . ." in *CP, Poems,* and *Palm;* "Of the Surface . . ." and "The Curtains . . ." in *CP;* "The Place . . ." and "The Paltry Nude . . ." in *CP* and *Palm;* "Colloquy . . ." in *CP.*

The announcement of the award of the Helen Haire Levinson prize to Wallace Stevens for "Pecksniffiana" appeared in *Poetry,* XVII, 2 (November 1920), 106.

Annotation: "As part of the campaign against the horrors of beauty, I write on this pumpkin-colored paper.

"Briefly, what I want is this: Maintaining the present order of the poems you have, substitute The Weeping Burgher for Aux Taureaux Dieu Cornes Donnes ["Aux Taureaux Dieu Cornes Donnes" is the poem entitled "Peter Parasol" in *OP*], Banal Sojourn for Exposition Of the Contents Of a Cab and Anecdote Of The Jar for Piano Practice At The Academy Of the Holy Angels. ["Piano Practice at the Academy of the Holy Angels" was not published until *OP*.] I enclose the new poems mentioned and also a trifle, The Indigo Glass In The Grass, which might fit after Of the Surface Of Things.

"Not to provoke, but to stifle, discussion, my reasons are that the element of pastiche present in Aux Taureaux will not be apparent and the poem will go off on its substance and not on its style, that I have not yet learned how to do things like the Exposition and that I am uncertain about the Piano Practice – as I recall it, it is cabbage instead of the crisp lettuce intended." (*Letters*, p. 214: letter to Harriet Monroe, August 16?, 1919)

C 63
Two poems. *Contact* (January 1921), p. [4].

Contents: Invective against Swans – Infanta Marina.

"Invective . . ." in *CP;* "Infanta Marina" in *CP* and *Palm.*

C 64
"Cortège for Rosenbloom." *The Measure,* no. 1 (March 1921), 10–11.

In *CP* and *Palm.*

C 65
"The Man Whose Pharynx Was Bad." *The New Republic,* XXVIII, 354 (September 14, 1921), 74.

When reprinted in *H-1931* the poem was revised and shortened. There are five stanzas of four lines each in *The New Republic* version; four stanzas in *H-1931.* The first, second, and last stanzas are the same in both versions. In *The New Republic* the third and fourth stanzas read: 'The malady of the quotidian . . . | Perhaps, if summer ever came to rest | And lengthened, deepened, comforted, caressed | Through days like oceans in obsidian | Horizons full of night's midsummer blaze; | Perhaps, if winter once could penetrate | Through all its purples to the final slate, | Persisting bleakly in an icy haze;'. In *H-1931* and also in *CP,* the third stanza reads: 'The malady of the quotidian. . . . | Perhaps, if winter once could penetrate | Through all its purples to the final slate, | Persisting bleakly in an icy haze,'. Revised and printed in full in *Palm.*

C 66
"Sur Ma Guzzla Gracile." *Poetry,* XIX, 1 (October 1921), 1–9.

Contents: Palace of the Babies – From the Misery of Don Joost – The Doctor of Geneva – Gubbinal – The Snow Man – Tea at the Palaz of Hoon – The Cuban Doctor – Another Weeping Woman – Of the Manner of Addressing Clouds – Of Heaven Considered as a Tomb – The Load of Sugar Cane – Hibiscus on the Sleeping Shores.

"Palace . . . ," "From the Misery . . . ," "The Cuban Doctor," "The Load . . . ," and "Hibiscus . . ." in *CP;* "The Doctor . . . ," "Another Weeping Woman," "Of the Manner . . . ," and "Of Heaven Considered" in *CP* and *Palm;* "Gubbinal," "The Snow Man," and "Tea . . ." in *CP, Poems,* and *Palm.* In both *CP* and *Palm,* "Of the Manner of Addressing Clouds" is entitled "On the Manner of Addressing Clouds."

C 67
"The Bird with the Coppery, Keen Claws." *Broom*, II [*sic*, for I], 2 (December 1921), 173.

In *CP* and *Palm*.

C 68
Two poems. *Contact* (1921), 8.

Contents: Lulu Gay — Lulu Morose.

In *OP*.

C 69
"Hymn from a Watermelon Pavilion." *Broom*, II, 3 (June 1922), 185.

In *CP* and *Palm*.

C 70
"Stars at Tallapoosa." *Broom*, II, 3 (June 1922), 236.

In *CP* and *Palm*.

C 71
"Revue." *The Dial*, LXXIII, 1 (July 1922), 89–93.

Contents: Bantams in Pine-Woods — The Ordinary Women — Frogs Eat Butterflies. Snakes Eat Frogs. Hogs Eat Snakes. Men Eat Hogs — A High-Toned Old Christian Woman — O Florida, Venereal Soil — The Emperor of Ice-Cream.

"Bantams . . . ," "A High-Toned Old Christian Woman," "O Florida . . . ," and "The Emperor . . ." in *CP*, *Poems*, and *Palm;* "The Ordinary Women" in *CP* and *Palm;* "Frogs . . ." in *CP* and *Poems*.

Annotation: ". . . I have no desire to be persnickety about the arrangement of the group, except to make a good beginning and a good end. Accordingly, it does not matter how much you arrange the poems, if you begin with The Bantams and end with The Emperor. Do as you like about the hog poems; that is to say, you can include it as one of the group or publish it separately. Inasmuch as two of the poems returned by you were moonlight poems, I think I shall have to suggest another title. How would *Revue* do?

"Do, please, excuse me from the biographical note. I am a lawyer and live in Hartford. But such facts are neither gay nor instructive." (*Letters*, p. 227: letter to Gilbert Seldes, editor of *The Dial*, May 5, 1922. Holly Stevens' footnote to this letter states: "In a letter to Seldes, April 3, 1922, Stevens had suggested calling the group 'Mostly Moonlight'. No record has been found of the poems returned.")

C 72

"To the One of Fictive Music." *The New Republic*, XXXII, 415 (November 15, 1922), 308.

In *CP*, *Poems*, and *Palm*.

C 73

"Last Looks at the Lilacs." *Secession*, no. 4 (January 1923), 19.

In *CP*.

C 74

Three poems. *The Measure*, no. 26 (April 1923), 3–7.

Contents: New England Verses (sixteen couplets: I. The Whole World Including the Speaker – II. The Whole World Excluding the Speaker – III. Soupe Aux Perles – IV. Soupe Sans Perles – V. Boston with a Note-Book – VI. Boston without a Note-Book – VII. Artist in Tropic – VIII. Artist in Arctic – IX. Statue against a Clear Sky – X. Statue against a Cloudy Sky – XI. Land of Locust – XII. Land of Pine and Marble – XIII. The Male Nude – XIV. The Female Nude – XV. Scène Flétrie – XVI. Scène Feurie) – Floral Decorations for Bananas – How the Constable Carried the Pot across the Public Square.

Of these poems only "Floral Decorations for Bananas" appeared in *H-1923*. "New England Verses," with a revision of "III. Soupe Aux Perles," and "How the Constable Carried the Pot across the Public Square," under the title of "The Public Square," appeared in *H-1931*. In *The Measure*, "Soupe Aux Perles" reads: 'Health-o, when cheese and guava peels bewitch | The vile antithesis of poor and rich.' In *H-1931*, the lines read: 'Health-o, when ginger and fromage bewitch | The vile antithesis of poor and rich.'

"New England Verses" and "How the Constable Carried the Pot . . ." in *CP*; "Floral Decorations . . ." in *CP*, *Poems*, and *Palm*.

C 75

"Mandolin and Liquers." *The Chapbook*, no. 36 (April 1923), 15.

In *OP*. This is WS's first original publication in England. Previous English publications had been reprints: four stanzas from

"Sunday Morning" in *The Chapbook* (May 1920) and a selection of five poems in *Modern American Poets*, selected by Conrad Aiken (London: Martin Secker, 1922).

C 76
"The Shape of the Coroner." *The Measure*, no. 27 (May 1923), 10.

In *OP*.

C 77
"Discourse in a Cantina at Havana." *Broom*, V, 4 (November 1923), 201–203.

Reprinted in *The Hound and Horn*, III, 1 (Fall 1929), 53–56, under the title "Academic Discourse at Havana." In *CP*, *Poems*, and *Palm*.

Annotation: "The fact that the poem to which you refer [. . .] was reprinted is merely a tribute to my poor memory; no one could be more surprised than I was to find that the thing had appeared in BROOM. I have a copy of HOUND AND HORN and also a copy of BROOM, but have not compared the two versions, which are probably identical.

"There was a man running a bookshop in Cambridge 15 years ago or so who planned to issue a collection of poems by various poets. Nothing came of this. DISCOURSE was to have been my contribution to that project. My guess about the reprint is this: When I sent the poem to the man in Cambridge it was considerably longer than it should have been. Later I cut it down very materially and then appear to have sent it to BROOM. Thereafter, when HOUND AND HORN wrote to me for something, after the lapse of a number of years, I had plainly forgotten all about BROOM, although I remembered clearly thinking that the poem was unpublished, probably because, having cut it down, it appeared to me to be something that had not been seen by anyone else. I don't know that this is the right explanation." (*Letters*, pp. 334–335: letter to Hi Simons, September 26, 1938)

C 78
"Sea Surface Full of Clouds." *The Dial*, LXXVII, 1 (July 1924), 51–54.

In *CP*, *Poems*, and *Palm*.

C 79
"Red Loves Kit." *The Measure*, no. 42 (August 1924), 8–9.

In *OP*.

C 80
"The Sun This March." *The New Republic*, LXII, 802 (April 16, 1930), 242.

In *CP* and *Palm*.

C 81
"Cattle Kings of Florida." *The Atlanta* (Ga.) *Journal*, December 14, 1930, p. 11.

A prose piece by WS, the subhead of which reads: 'Florida's Pioneer Cattlemen Frequently Carried Fortunes in Their Saddle Bags, and the Coffee Can or Cooking Pot on a Cabin Shelf Often Held a King's Ransom in Gold. An Unlettered Cowboy Financed the First Free School in Polk County and Provided the Land for Orlando's Famous Parks.'

C 82
"Good Man, Bad Woman." *Poetry*, XLI, 1 (October 1932), 6.

In *OP*.

Annotation: "I am enclosing another scrap, but it is the best I can do. If it is of no use, don't hesitate to say so. Of course, I shall be furious. But what of it? The egotism of poets is disgusting." (*Letters*, p. 262: letter to Harriet Monroe, August 5, 1932)

C 83
"Autumn Refrain." *The Hound and Horn*, V, 2 (Winter 1932), 222.

In *CP*, *Poems*, and *Palm*.

C 84
"The Woman Who Blamed Life on a Spaniard." *Contempo*, III, 3 (December 15, 1932), 1.

In *OP*.

Annotation: "Some time ago *Contempo* wrote to me and I looked round and found a few scraps, which I sent to it. I don't know what would happen if, shortly after telling you that I had not a thing to my name, *Contempo* should come out containing what I sent." (*Letters*, p. 262: letter to Harriet Monroe, August 5, 1932)

C 85
"Snow and Stars." *New Act*, no. 2 (June 1933), 76.

In *CP*.

Annotation: "You will also find two copies of THE NEW ACT which you may like to have, because, as I understand it, there were only two copies published. [. . .]

"As I was gathering these together, I wondered whether you understood how I came to contribute to all these things. I always contributed because somebody asked me to do so, and never by way of sending things round. This is just the opposite of the common experience and is, of course, due to the fact that one is always running round in circles in New York." (*Letters,* pp. 335-336: letter to Hi Simons, October 11, 1938)

C 86
"Two Poems." *Harkness Hoot,* IV, 2 (November 1933), 25.

Contents: The Brave Man—A Fading of the Sun.

Both poems in *CP* and *Palm.*

C 87
"The Pleasures of Merely Circulating." *Smoke,* III, 2 (Spring 1934), [4].

In *CP, Poems,* and *Palm.*

C 88
"Eight Poems." *Alcestis,* I, 1 (October 1934), [2-6].

Contents: The Idea of Order at Key West—Lions in Sweden— Evening without Angels—Nudity at the Capital—Nudity in the Colonies—A Fish-Scale Sunrise—Delightful Evening—What They Call Red Cherry Pie.

"The Idea . . . ," "Lions . . . ," and "Evening without Angels" in *CP, Poems,* and *Palm;* "Nudity at the Capital," "Nudity in the Colonies," "A Fish-Scale Sunrise," and "Delightful Evening" in *CP;* "What They Call . . ." in *OP.*

C 89
Answer to an inquiry. *New Verse,* no. 11 (October 1934), 15.

Six brief replies by WS to a six-part questionnaire on poetry and poets.

C 90
Two poems. *Direction,* I, 1 (Autumn 1934), 12-13.

Contents: Botanist on Alp [I]—Hieroglyphica.

"Botanist . . . [I]" in *CP;* "Hieroglyphica" in *OP.*

C 91
"The Drum-Majors in the Labor Day Parade," *Smoke*, III, 4 (Autumn 1934), [3].

In *OP*.

C 92
"Three Poems." *Westminster Magazine*, XXIII, 3 (Autumn 1934), 186–187.

Contents: Gallant Chateau — Gray Stones and Gray Pigeons — Polo Ponies Practicing.

"Gallant Chateau" and "Gray Stones . . ." in *CP*; "Polo Ponies . . ." in *OP*.

C 93
"The Reader." *The New Republic*, LXXXI, 1052 (January 30, 1935), 332.

In *CP* and *Palm*.

C 94
"Like Decorations in a Nigger Cemetery." *Poetry*, XLV, 5 (February 1935), 239–249.

In *CP*, *Poems*, and *Palm*.

Annotation: "If you do not like these, do not hesitate to say so. It is very difficult for me to find the time to write poetry, and most of these have been written on the way to and from the office.
   "The title refers to the litter that one usually finds in a nigger cemetery and is a phrase used by Judge Powell [Judge Arthur Powell] last winter in Key West." (*Letters*, p. 272: letter to Morton Dauwen Zabel, December 6, 1934)

C 95
"Re-statement of Romance." *The New Republic*, LXXXII, 1057 (March 6, 1935), 100.

In *CP* and *Palm*.

C 96
"How to Live. What to Do." *Direction*, I, 3 (April–June 1935), 136.

In *CP*.

C 97
"Lytton Strachey, Also, Enters into Heaven." *Rocking Horse,*
II, 3 (Spring 1935), 2–3.

In *OP* and *Palm.*

C 98
"Five Poems." *Alcestis,* I, 3 (Spring 1935), [2–6].

Contents: Sailing after Lunch – Meditation Celestial and Terrestrial – Mozart, 1935 – The American Sublime – Waving Adieu,
Adieu, Adieu.

"Sailing . . ." and "The American Sublime" in *CP, Poems,* and
Palm; "Meditation . . ." in *CP;* and "Mozart, 1935" and "Waving
Adieu . . ." in *CP* and *Palm.*

Annotations: "I am sending you with this letter four poems for
ALCESTIS. You might very well like other things of mine and yet
like none of these. If so, the only sensible thing for you to do
would be to say so.
  "They are all things that I have written recently for the book
which you have in mind and, as you see, they are not particularly
warm or high-spirited. At first I liked POETIC AS A FOUNTAIN
[Holly Stevens' footnote at this point in the letter reads: "No
publication of a Stevens poem with this title has been found."]
extremely. But coming back to it after an absence, it seems to
lack the spontaneity and fluidity that I wanted it to have. I shall
therefore be interested to know how it strikes you. If you don't
like it, please substitute for it THE AMERICAN SUBLIME. On the
other hand, if you like it, please return THE AMERICAN SUBLIME,
which I am thinking of using elsewhere.
  "The poems should be printed in the following order:

  1. MEDITATION CELESTIAL & TERRESTRIAL
  2. MOZART, 1935
  3. POETIC AS A FOUNTAIN (or THE AMERICAN SUBLIME)
  4. WAVING ADIEU, ADIEU, ADIEU"
(*Letters,* p. 276: letter to Ronald Lane Latimer, March 5, 1935)

  "I am [. . .] sending you another poem: SAILING AFTER LUNCH.
[. . .] the occasion for sending it to you now is that you might like
to use it in connection with the group that I sent you a few days
ago, putting this at the beginning of the group. [. . .]
  "Naturally, if you don't like it or cannot use it, send it back."
(*Letters,* pp. 276–277: letter to Ronald Lane Latimer, March 12,
1935)

C 99
"Sad Strains of a Gay Waltz." *The New Republic*, LXXXIII,
1068 (May 22, 1935), 45.

In *CP* and *Palm*.

C 100
"Dance of the Macabre Mice." *The New Republic*, LXXXIII,
1070 (June 5, 1935), 98.

In *CP* and *Palm*.

C 101
"Agenda." *Smoke*, IV, 3 (Summer 1935), [3].

In *OP*.

C 102
"The Old Woman and the Statue." *The Southern Review*, I,
1 (Summer 1935), 78–81.

Reprinted as Part I of *Owl's Clover*, A 3, with one change: Section III, line 13 of "The Old Woman and the Statue" as it appears
in *The Southern Review* reads: 'To search for accent all an
afternoon'. The same line in *Owl's Clover* reads: 'To search for
clearness all an afternoon'. In *OP*.

C 103
"A Poet That Matters." *Life and Letters Today*, XIII, 2 (December 1935), 61–65.

A review of Marianne Moore's *Selected Poems* (New York:
Macmillan, 1935). In *OP*.

Annotations: "Thanks for your letter of March 20th. I am,
however, planning to start a piece of work which is likely to
keep me busy for some time to come, and for that reason I do
not think that I can undertake Miss Moore's volume.
    "If, however, you did not want the review until autumn, I
might be able to do it for you: I mean to say for your autumn
number. [. . .]
    "I cannot do anything whatever about it if you want the re-
view before summer, as you probably do." (*Letters*, pp. 278–279:
letter to T. C. Wilson, associate editor of *Westminster Magazine*,
March 25, 1935; Wilson had asked WS for a review of *Selected
Poems.*)

    "I should be very glad to have you let Miss Moore read my
note on her book. After that the two of you can decide whether
or not she wants to send it to LIFE AND LETTERS. [. . .]

"It is curious that, after taking LIFE AND LETTERS from the beginning, I dropped it two or three months ago. It is a very good thing, but cheaply printed. However, I have been fed up on a good many things that I have taken and that was one of the things that I did not renew.

"As far as the discontinuance of the WESTMINSTER REVIEW is concerned, no apology is necessary. Somehow that does not sound quite right. What I mean is that I wrote about Miss Moore because I enjoyed writing about her, and it does not make the slightest difference to me whether what I wrote is published in Atlanta or London or nowhere." (*Letters*, p. 281: letter to T. C. Wilson, July 1, 1935)

"I have re-written the first page of the note on SELECTED POEMS, and I enclose it.

"Some changes should be made elsewhere, as follows:
On page 2, in the third line from the end of the first paragraph, I use the word *syllables;* perhaps it would be better to say *groups of letters.*
On page 5, in the sixth line from the top, change *fastidious* to *sensitive.*
On page 6, in the fourth line of the second paragraph, change *constitute* to *constitutes.*
On page 7, in the sixth line, in the word Prouts', the apostrophe should be before the *s:* Prout's.

"Some of these changes may have been made in the text actually sent to you; it often happens that I do not change my carbon copies. I shall be grateful to you if you will make these changes for me. [. . .]

"People think in batches. The predominating batch today seems to think that the romantic as we know it is the slightest possible aspect of the thing. The English feel as badly about the romantic as they do about the sentimental. It is possible, therefore, that there would be more point to publishing the note in LIFE AND LETTERS than in Georgia." (*Letters*, p. 282: letter to T. C. Wilson, July 12, 1935)

C 104
"A Postcard from the Volcano." *Smoke*, V, 2 (Summer 1936), [2].

In *CP*, *Poems*, and *Palm*.

C 105
"Farewell to Florida." *Contemporary Poetry and Prose*, no. 3 (July 1936), 52–53.

In *CP*, *Poems*, and *Palm*.

C 106
"The Men That Are Falling." *The Nation*, 143, 17 (October 24, 1936), 479.

The Nation Prize Poem for 1936. In *CP*, *Poems*, and *Palm*.

C 107
Four-paragraph tribute in memory of Harriet Monroe. *Poetry*, XLIX, 3 (December 1936), 154–155.

C 108
"Two Poems." *Twentieth Century Verse*, no. 3 (April–May 1937), [3].

Contents: Inaccessible Utopia – The Place of Poetry. Reprinted as Sections V and XXVI of *The Man with the Blue Guitar*, A 4. In *CP*, *Poems*, and *Palm*.

C 109
"The Man with the Blue Guitar." *Poetry*, L, II [*sic*, for 2] (May 1937), 61–69.

These thirteen poems were reprinted as Sections II, IX, XV, XVII, XVIII, XXIV, XXVII, XXVIII, XXIX, XXX, XXXI, and XXXIII of the complete version, A 4. In *CP*, *Poems*, and *Palm*.

C 110
"Insurance and Social Change." *The Hartford Agent*, XXIX, 4 (October 1937), 49–50.

By-line: 'By Wallace Stevens, Vice-President Hartford Accident and Indemnity Company, Hartford, Conn.'

C 111
"A Rabbit as King of the Ghosts." *Poetry*, LI, 6 (October 1937), 1–2.

In *CP*, *Poems*, and *Palm*.

C 112
"United Dames of America." *New York Times*, November 7, 1937, section 4, p. 8E, column 7.

In *CP* and *Palm*.

C 113
"The Dwarf." *Partisan Review*, IV, 1 (December 1937), 12.

. In *CP* and *Palm*.

C 114
"Country Words." *New York Times*, December 19, 1937, section 4, p. 8E, column 6.

In *CP* and *Poems*.

C 115
"The Blue Buildings in the Summer Air." *Seven*, no. 3 (Winter 1938), 2.

In *CP*.

C 116
Two poems. *Partisan Review*, IV, 3 (February 1938), 11–12.

Contents: Loneliness in Jersey City – Anything Is Beautiful If You Say It Is.

"Loneliness . . ." in *CP*, *Poems*, and *Palm;* "Anything Is Beautiful . . ." in *CP* and *Palm*.

C 117
"Force of Illusions." *New York Times*, July 10, 1938, section 4, p. 8E, column 7.

Reprinted in *Parts of a Woria*, A 5, under the title "A Weak Mind in the Mountains." In *CP* and *Palm*.

C 118
"Canonica." *The Southern Review*, IV, 2 (Autumn 1938), 382–395.

Contents: Parochial Theme – Poetry Is a Destructive Force – The Poems of Our Climate – Prelude to Objects – Study of Two Pears – The Glass of Water – Add This to Rhetoric – Dry Loaf – Idiom of the Hero – The Man on The Dump – On the Road Home – The Latest Freed Man.

"Idiom of the Hero" in *CP;* "Parochial Theme," "The Glass of Water," "Add This to Rhetoric," "Dry Loaf," "On the Road Home," and "The Latest Freed Man" in *CP* and *Palm;* "Poetry Is a Destructive Force," "The Poems of Our Climate," "Prelude to Objects," "Study of Two Pears," and "The Man on the Dump" in *CP*, *Poems*, and *Palm*.

C 119
"Connoisseur of Chaos." *Twentieth Century Verse* (American number), no. 12–13 (October 1938), 90.

In *CP*, *Poems*, and *Palm*.

Annotation: "Here is something for your American number, which I hope you will like. The ink on it is hardly dry." (*Letters*, p. 330: letter to Julian Symons, editor of *Twentieth Century Verse*, April 18, 1938)

C 120
Reply to a questionnaire. *Twentieth Century Verse* (American number), no. 12–13 (October 1938), 112

Three short paragraphs in answer to a three-part questionnaire about American poetry.

C 121
Contribution to a symposium in honor of T. S. Eliot. *The Harvard Advocate* (T. S. Eliot issue), CXXXV, 3 (December 1938), 41.

Reprinted in *Harvard Advocate Centennial Anthology*, B 57.

C 122
Two poems. *Partisan Review*, VI, 3 (Spring 1939), 21–25.

Contents: The Woman That Had More Babies Than That — Life on a Battleship.

"The Woman . . ." in *OP*; "Life on a Battleship" reprinted only in *Parts of a World*, A 5.

C 123
"Thunder by the Musician." *Seven*, no. 4 (Summer 1939), 7–8.

In *CP*.

C 124
Reply to questionnaire "The Situation in American Writing: Seven Questions." *Partisan Review*, VI, 4 (Summer 1939), 39–40.

Reprinted in *The Partisan Reader*, B 39.

C 125
"Illustrations of the Poetic as a Sense." *Poetry*, LIV, 4 (July 1939), 177–183.

Contents: The Common Life — The Sense of the Sleight-of-Hand Man — The Candle a Saint — A Dish of Peaches in Russia — Arcades of Philadelphia the Past — Of Hartford in a Purple Light.

"The Common Life" in *CP* and *Poems*; "The Sense . . ." in *CP*

Poems, and *Palm;* "The Candle . . . ," "A Dish . . . ," and "Arcades . . ." in *CP;* "Of Hartford . . ." in *CP* and *Palm.*

C 126
"Cuisine Bourgeoise." *Poetry World,* vol. 10, no. 12, and vol. 11, no. 1 (July–August 1939), 5.

In *CP.*

C 127
"On an Old Horn." *The Nation,* CXLIX, 14 (September 30, 1939), 350.

In *CP.*

C 128
"Bouquet of Belle Scavoir." *Fantasy,* sixth year, no. 3 (1939), 3.

In *CP.*

C 129
"Variations on a Summer Day." *The Kenyon Review,* II, 1 (Winter 1940), 72–75.

In *CP* and *Palm.*

C 130
"Martial Cadenza." *Compass,* II, 2–3, issue 6 (February 1940), 12.

In *CP* and *Poems.*

C 131
"Yellow Afternoon." *Seven,* no. 7 (Spring 1940), 12.

In *CP.*

C 132
"Two Theoretic Poems." *Hika* (guest contributor issue), VI, 7 (May 1940), 6–7.

Contents: Man and Bottle – Of Modern Poetry.

Both poems in *CP* and *Palm.*

C 133
"Materia Poetica." *View,* I, 1 (September 1940), 3.

These aphorisms on poetry and the imagination were published in *OP* under the title "Adagia." (See C 143.) In this issue of *View*

there is also an interview with WS, entitled "Verlaine in Hartford," by Charles Henri Ford.

C 134
Two poems. *Accent*, I, 1 (Autumn, 1940), 12–14.

Contents: Landscape with Boat – On the Adequacy of Landscape.

"Landscape with Boat" in *CP* and *Palm;* "On the Adequacy of
Landscape" in *CP*.

C 135
"Three Poems, 1940." *The Harvard Advocate* (Wallace Stevens
number), CXXVII, 3 (December 1940), 3–4.

Contents: Of Bright & Blue Birds & the Gala Sun – Mrs. Alfred
Uruguay – Asides on the Oboe.

"Of Bright & Blue Birds . . ." in *CP* and *Palm;* "Mrs. Alfred
Uruguay" and "Asides . . ." in *CP*, *Poems*, and *Palm*. Under the
title of "Poems 1899–1901", thirteen of WS's undergraduate
poems, published earlier in *The Harvard Advocate*, are reprinted in this issue. In addition, there are articles and state-
ments by Howard Baker, Cleanth Brooks, John Finch, Harry
Levin, F. O. Matthiessen, Marianne Moore, Delmore Schwartz,
Hi Simons, Theodore Spencer, Allen Tate, Robert Penn Warren,
William Carlos Williams, and Morton Dauwen Zabel.

C 136
"Four Poems." *Furioso*, I, 4 (Summer 1941), 34–36.

Contents: Les Plus Belle Pages – Poem with Rhythms – Woman
Looking at a Vase of Flowers – The Well Dressed Man with a
Beard.

"Les Plus . . ." and "Woman . . ." in *CP;* "Poem with Rhythms"
in *CP* and *Palm;* "The Well Dressed Man . . ." in *CP*, *Poems*,
and *Palm*.

C 137
"The News and the Weather." *Accent*, I, 4 (Summer 1941), 229.

In *CP* and *Poems*.

C 138
"Montrachet-le-Jardin." *Partisan Review*, IX, 1 (January–
February 1942), 34–37.

In *CP*, *Poems*, and *Palm*.

C 139
"Five Grotesque Pieces." *Trend*, I, 3 (March 1942), 12–13.

Contents: I. One of Those Hibiscuses of Damozels – II. Hieroglyphica – III. Communications of Meaning – IV. What They Call
Red Cherry Pie – V. Outside of Wedlock.

"What They Call Red Cherry Pie" and "Hieroglyphica" are reprinted from C 88 and C 90 respectively. All five poems are in
OP.

C 140
"Examination of the Hero in a Time of War." *The Harvard
Advocate* (75th anniversary issue), CXXVIII, 4 (April 1942),
3–5.

In *CP* and *Palm*.

C 141
"Desire & the Object." *Accent*, 2, 4 (Summer 1942), 223.

In *OP*.

C 142
"Certain Phenomena of Sound." *Poetry*, LXI, 1 (October 1942),
358–359.

In *CP* and *Palm*.

C 143
"Materia Poetica." *View*, 2d series, no. 3 (October 1942), 28.

These aphorisms on poetry and the imagination were published
in *OP* under the title "Adagia." (See C 133.)

C 144
"God Is Good. It Is a Beautiful Night." *Harper's Bazaar* (75th
year), 2773 (December 1942), 49.

In *CP* and *Palm*.

C 145
"The Motive for Metaphor." *The Chimera*, I, 3 (Winter 1943), 42.

In *CP*, *Poems*, and *Palm*.

C 146
"Dutch Graves in Bucks County." *The Sewanee Review*, LI, 1
(Winter 1943), 14–16.

In *CP*, *Poems*, and *Palm*.

C 147
"The Lack of Repose." *American Prefaces*, VIII, 4 (Summer 1943), 225.

In *CP* and *Palm*.

C 148
"Somnambulisma." *The New Republic*, CIX, 8, issue 1499 (August 23, 1943), 251.

In *CP* and *Palm*.

C 149
"Repetitions of a Young Captain." *Quarterly Review of Literature*, I, 3 (Spring 1944), 155–158.

In *CP*.

C 150
"The Creations of Sound." *Maryland Quarterly*, no. 2 (Spring 1944), 33–34.

In *CP* and *Palm*.

C 151
"Holiday in Reality." *The Chimera*, II, 4 (Summer 1944), 17–18.

In *CP*.

C 152
"Esthétique du Mal." *The Kenyon Review*, VI, 4 (Autumn 1944), 489–503.

In *CP*, *Poems*, and *Palm*.

Annotation: "Shortly after I wrote to you the last time I started on the poem, and here it is. I hope you will like it. If you use it, you are most welcome to it without any expectation of payment on my part.

"The title is not quite right in the sense that anything of that sort seems to be not quite right now-a-days, but it is better than any substitute that I have been able to think of.

"There are some odds and ends: 'ensolacings' at the end of [section X], for instance, which you may not like. However, I think that there is more to be said for them than there is against them. If you feel strongly otherwise, I shall be glad to suggest something. The last poem ought to end with an interrogation mark, I suppose, but I have punctuated it in such a way as to indicate an abandonment of the question, because I cannot bring myself to end the thing with an interrogation mark." (*Letters*, p. 469: letter to John Crowe Ransom, July 28, 1944)

C 153
"The Figure of the Youth as Virile Poet." *The Sewanee Review*, LII, 4 (Autumn 1944), 508–529.

This essay had been read by WS in the summer of 1943 at the Entretiens de Pontigny, a conference held at Mount Holyoke College, at the invitation of Jean Wahl. In *NA*.

C 154
Two poems. *Accent*, 5, 1 (Autumn 1944), 24–25.

Contents: The Bed of Old John Zeller – Less and Less Human, O Savage Spirit.

"The Bed . . ." in *CP* and *Palm;* "Less and Less Human . . ." in *CP, Poems*, and *Palm*.

C 155
"Wild Ducks, People and Distances." *Arizona Quarterly*, 1, (Spring 1945), 3.

In *CP*.

C 156
"New Poems." *Voices* (Wallace Stevens issue), no. 121 (Spring 1945), 25–29.

Contents: The Pure Good of Theory (I. All the Preludes to Felicity – II. Description of a Platonic Person – III. Fire-Monsters in the Milky Brain – IV. Dry Birds Are Fluttering in Blue Leaves) – A Word with José Rodríguez-Feo – Paisant Chronicle – Flyer's Fall.

Also included in this special issue on WS are four poems from *H-1923*, two poems from *Ideas of Order*, six sections of *The Man with the Blue Guitar*, five sections of *Notes Toward a Supreme Fiction*, and an essay on WS, pp. 30–37, entitled "Plato, Phoebus and the Man from Hartford," by John Malcolm Brinnin. "The Pure Good . . . ," "Paisant Chronicle," and "Flyer's Fall" in *CP* and *Palm;* "A Word . . ." in *CP*.

C 157
"Two Poems." *Briarcliff Quarterly*, II, 6 (July 1945), 84–85.

Contents: Jouga – Debris of Life & Mind.

Both poems in *CP*.

C 158
"Description without Place." *The Sewanee Review*, LIII, 4 (Autumn 1945), 559–565.

In *CP* and *Palm*. See also A 9. This issue of *The Sewanee Review* also contains Hi Simons' "The Genre of Wallace Stevens," pp. 566–579.

Annotations: "I have only one piece of news, and that is that I am going to read a poem before the Phi Beta Kappa at Harvard next June.

"I am about to settle down to my subject: DESCRIPTION WITH-OUT PLACE. Although this is the second or third subject that I have had in mind, unless it develops quickly and easily as I go along, I may change it. It seems to me to be an interesting idea: that is to say, the idea that we live in the description of a place and not in the place itself, and in every vital sense we do. This ought to be a good subject for such an occasion. I suppose there is nothing more helpful to reading a poem than to have someone to read it to, and that particular audience ought to be a good audience." (*Letters*, p. 494: letter to Henry Church, April 4, 1945)

"I am at work on a poem which I am thinking of sending you: DESCRIPTION WITHOUT PLACE. This is going to be read at the Phi Beta Kappa exercises at the Harvard Commencement, if I have vitamins enough in my system to go there with it." (*Letters*, p. 497: letter to Allen Tate, May 2, 1945)

C 159
"Analysis of a Theme." *View*, series V, no. 3 (October 1945), 15.

In *CP*.

C 160
"Two Tales of Liadoff." *Pacific*, I, 1 (November 1945), 20–21.

In *CP*.

C 161
"Attempt to Discover Life." *Origenes*, III, 12 (Winter 1946), 12.

A translation by José Rodríguez-Feo, "Tentativa por Descubrir la Vida," is on p. 13. The poem was also published as part of a group entitled "More Poems for Liadoff" in C 169. In *CP*.

C 162
"Late Hymn from the Myrrh-Mountain." *The Harvard Wake*, no. 5 (Spring 1946), 78.

In *CP* and *Palm*.

C 163
"Four Poems." *The Yale Poetry Review*, I, 3 (Spring 1946), 3–5.

Contents: Man Carrying Things – Pieces – A Completely New Set of Objects – Adult Epigram.

"Man Carrying Thing" in *CP* and *Palm:* remaining three poems in *CP*.

C 164
Reply to a question. *The Yale Literary Magazine*, CXII, 11 (Spring 1946), 17–18.

The question asked was: "What do you believe to be the major problem or problems facing the young writer in America today?"

C 165
"Men Made Out of Words." *Accent*, 6, 3 (Spring 1946), 191.

In *CP* and *Palm*.

C 166
"Two Versions of the Same Poem ('That Which Cannot Be Fixed I and II')." *Contemporary Poetry*, VI, 1 (Spring 1946), 3–4.

In *CP* and *Palm*.

C 167
"Rubbings of Reality." *Briarcliff Quarterly*, III, 11 (October 1946), 201–202.

A tribute to William Carlos Williams; reprinted in *OP* with a minor variation in the text: in the *Briarcliff Quarterly* the first sentence of the last paragraph reads, 'This is an intellectual *tenue.*' In *OP* the same sentence reads, 'There is an intellectual *tenue.*'

C 168
"Four Poems." *Voices*, no. 127 (Autumn 1946), 4–6.

Contents: Thinking of a Relation Between the Images of Metaphors – Chaos in Motion and Not in Motion – The House Was Quiet and the World Was Calm – Continual Conversation with a Quiet Man.

This is the first publication of the four poems in English. They had been published earlier in a Spanish translation by Oscar Rodriguez Feliú in *Origenes,* II, 8 (Winter 1945), 3–6, under the titles, "Unidad de las imagenes," "El caos movil e inmovil," "La casa y el mundo en calma . . . ," and "Conversación con un hombre silencioso." All four poems in *CP;* all but "Continual Conversation . . ." also in *Palm.*

Annotations: "I put off replying to your recent letter until the copies of ORIGENES came. Of course, I know nothing about Spanish and cannot even pronounce it decently; yet it seems to me that Mr. Feliú has caught my particular rhythm. To me this seems to be particularly true in the last few verses of the last poem. I think it was Tasso who delighted to read Greek without having any knowledge whatever of that language. In the same way I take an even greater delight in reading my own poems in Spanish. Please thank Mr. Feliú for me." (*Letters,* p. 524: letter to José Rodríguez-Feo, March 5, 1946)

"The Four Poems will appear in Voices in the late autumn. I shall send you a copy. When I sent the poems to them, I told them that they had been printed in Origenes and I gave them enough information to make it possible for them to say something about it. What they will do remains to be seen. Voices is a little off my circuit. But perhaps it does one more good to appear a little off one's circuit than merely to go round and round and round." (*Letters,* pp. 528–529: letter to José Rodríguez-Feo, May 21, 1946)

C 169
"More Poems for Liadoff." *Quarterly Review of Literature,* III, 2 (Fall 1946), 105–113.

Contents: A Woman Sings a Song for a Soldier Come Home – The Pediment of Appearance – Burghers of Petty Death – Human Arrangement – The Good Man Has No Shape – The Red Fern – From the Packet of Anacharsis – The Dove in the Belly – Mountains Covered with Cats – The Prejudice against the Past – Extraordinary References – Attempt to Discover Life.

"Attempt to Discover Life" had appeared in C 161, with an accompanying translation into Spanish by José Rodríguez-Feo.

All are in *CP;* "A Woman Sings . . . ," "The Good Man . . . ,"
"From the Packet . . . ," "The Dove . . . ," "Mountains . . . ,"
and "The Prejudice . . ." are also in *Palm.*

C 170
"The Pastor Caballero." *Furioso*, II, 2 (Fall 1946), 11.

In *CP.*

C 171
"Memorandum." *Poetry Quarterly*, 8, 3 (Winter 1947), 223.

In *OP.*

C 172
"Three Academic Pieces." *Partisan Review*, XIV, 3 (May–
June 1947), 243–253.

Contents: The Realm of Resemblance – Someone Puts a Pineapple Together – Of Ideal Time and Choice.

Brought together in *Three Academic Pieces*, A 12, and *NA.*
"Someone . . ." and "Of Ideal Time . . ." in *Poems* and *Palm.*

C 173
"Two Poems." *Poetry*, 71, 1 (October 1947), 10–11.

Contents: The Ultimate Poem Is Abstract – Bouquet of Roses
in Sunlight.

Both poems in *CP;* "The Ultimate Poem . . ." also in *Palm.*

C 174
"The Owl in the Sarcophagus." *Horizon*, nos. 93–94 (October
1947), 58–62.

In *CP* and *Palm.*

Annotation: "Recently you spoke of HORIZON. The October
number of HORIZON is to be an American number. I expect to
have a poem in it. The Owl In The Sarcophagus. This was written
in the frame of mind that followed Mr. Church's death. While
it is not personal, I had thought of inscribing it somehow, below
the title, as, for example, Goodbye H.C., but it was hardly written
before I received HORIZON's letter and as it would not have been
easy to talk to you about it at the time I omitted the inscription."
(*Letters*, p. 566: letter to Barbara Church, September 5, 1947)

C 175
"The Beginning." *The Nation*, CLXV, 16 (October 18, 1947),
412.

In *CP*.

C 176
"In the Element of Antagonisms." *Accent*, VIII, 1 (Autumn
1947), 29.

In *CP*.

C 177
"The Auroras of Autumn." *The Kenyon Review*, X, 1 (Winter
1948), 1–10.

In *CP* and *Palm*. See also A 14.

Annotation: "I am going to have a set of poems in the next
number of the Kenyon Review and I expect that I shall receive
from that source within the next month or so a prodigious check,
which, after all, I shall owe to Blackmur [Richard Blackmur
had been an advisory editor of *The Kenyon Review*] and his
associates." (*Letters*, p. 571: letter to José Rodríguez-Feo,
December 15, 1947)

C 178
"Page from a Tale." *Wake*, no. 6 (Spring 1948), 72–73.

In *CP*.

C 179
"Two Poems." *Halcyon*, I, 2 (Spring 1948), 26–27.

Contents: Large Red Man Reading – This Solitude of Cataracts.

Both in *CP* and *Palm*.

C 180
"In a Bad Time." *The Hudson Review*, I, 1 (Spring 1948), 29.

In *CP* and *Palm*.

C 181
"About One of Marianne Moore's Poems." *Quarterly Review of
Literature*, IV, 2 (Summer 1948), 143–149.

This essay is introduced by WS thus: 'My purpose is to bring together one of Miss Moore's poems and a paper, On Poetic Truth,

by H. D. Lewis. The poem, "He 'Digesteth Harde Yron' ", has just been reprinted in the *Partisan Review*. The paper is to be found in the July number (1946) of *Philosophy*, The Journal Of The British Institute Of Philosophy (Macmillan, London).' In *NA*.

C 182
"John Crowe Ransom: Tennessean." *The Sewanee Review*, LVI, 3 (Summer 1948), 367–379.

In *OP*.

C 183
"The State of American Writing, 1948: Seven Questions." *Partisan Review*, XV, 8 (August 1948), 884–886.

Reply to a questionnaire. The only other publication of this reply is in *Letters*, pp. 589–591, in the letter of April 26, 1948, to Delmore Schwartz, then associate editor of *Partisan Review*.

Annotation: "Partisan Review is conducting another catechetical class right now." (*Letters*, p. 585: letter to William Van O'Connor, April 9, 1948)

C 184
"Effects of Analogy." *The Yale Review*, XXXVIII, 1 (September 1948), 29–44.

The Bergen Lecture, delivered at Yale by WS, March 18, 1948. In *NA*.

Annotation: "My prose is not what it ought to be. Last month I gave the Bergen lecture at Yale. This was expected to last the greater part of an hour. As I wrote it, the time was constantly in my mind. This was equally true of the other papers that were read as lectures. And of course one is constantly dealing with questions on which there already exist or may exist huge documentations, which for my part have to be passed up. The lectures were well enough as lectures, notwithstanding all this compromise. There is nothing that I desire more intensely than to make a contribution to the theory of poetry." (*Letters*, p. 585: letter to William Van O'Connor, April 9, 1948)

C 185
On "The Emperor of Ice-Cream." *The Explicator*, VII, 2 (November 1948), [*Explication No.*] 18, p. [15].

Prose. In B 54.

C 186

"Puella Parvula." *Voices*, no. 136 (Winter 1949), 10.

In *CP* and *Palm*.

C 187

"Metaphor as Degeneration." *American Letters*, I, 5 (April 1949), 9.

In *CP* and *Palm*.

C 188

"A Half Dozen Small Pieces." *Botteghe Oscure*, quaderno IV (Autumn 1949), 330–334.

Contents: What We See Is What We Think – A Golden Woman in a Silver Mirror – The Old Lutheran Bells at Home – Questions Are Remarks – Study of Images I – Study of Images II.

Accompanying this issue of *Botteghe Oscure* is a separate pamphlet of 114 pages of translations into Italian. On pages 32–36 of this pamphlet are the Italian translations, by Salvatore Rosati, of "A Half Dozen Small Pieces," entitled: "Mezza Dozzina di Composizioni Brevi" ("I. Quel Che Vediamo e quel Che Pensiamo" – "II. Una Donna Dorata in Uno Specchio d'Argento" – "III. Le Vecchie Campane Luterane in Casa" – "IV. Le Domande Sono Osservazioni" – "V. Studio d'Immagini. I" – "VI. Studio d'Immagini. II").
    All are in *CP;* "The Old Lutheran Bells . . ." also in *Palm;* "Questions . . ." also in *Poems* and *Palm*.

Annotation: "I have just sent off a half dozen short poems to *Botteghe Oscure* of Rome. These were on such things as came into my head. They pleased me. But after a round of this sort of thing I always feel the need of getting some different sort of satisfaction out of poetry. Often when I am writing poetry I have in mind an image of reading a page of a large book: I mean the large page of a book. What I read is what I like. The things I have just sent off to Rome are not the sort of things that one would find on such a page. At least what one ought to find is normal life, insight into the commonplace, reconciliation with every-day reality. The things that it makes me happy to do are things of this sort. However, it is not possible to get away from one's own nature." (*Letters*, pp. 642–643: letter to Barbara Church, July 27, 1949)

C 189
"Things of August." *Poetry*, LXXV, 3 (December 1949), 125–134.

In *CP* and *Palm*.

C 190
"An Ordinary Evening in New Haven." *Transactions of The Connecticut Academy of Arts and Sciences*, 38 (December 1949), 161–172.

'. . . written for the occasion of the Thousandth Meeting of the Connecticut Academy . . .'. Read before the academy at the evening session of its sesquicentennial celebration in New Haven, November 4, 1949. When *The Auroras of Autumn*, A 14, was published, it contained thirty-one sections; the eleven sections of the poem published in *Transactions* . . . appear there in the following order: I, VI, IX, XI, XII, XVI, XXII, XXVIII, XXX, XXXI, and XXIX. These eleven sections were reprinted in *Selected Poems*, A 19. In *CP*, *Poems*, and *Palm*.

Annotation: "At the moment I am at work on a thing called An Ordinary Evening In New Haven. This is confidential and I don't want the thing to be spoken of. But here my interest is to try to get as close to the ordinary, the commonplace and the ugly as it is possible for a poet to get. It is not a question of grim reality but of plain reality. The object is of course to purge oneself of anything false. I have been doing this since the beginning of March and intend to keep studying the subject and working on it until I am quite through with it." (*Letters*, pp. 636–637: letter to Bernard Heringman, May 3, 1949)

C 191
"Angel Surrounded by Paysans." *Poetry London*, 5, 17 (January 1950), 5–6.

In *CP*, *Poems*, and *Palm*.

Annotation: "I am sending you a poem. But there is this string to it: that I am going to include it in the things that I am collecting for the book of which I have just spoken. Will you send me copies of one or two issues of PL. I don't think that I have ever seen it." (*Letters*, p. 650: letter to Nicholas Moore, editor of *Poetry London*, October 13, 1949)

C 192
"The Sick Man." *Accent*, X, 3 (Spring 1950), 156.

In *OP*.

C 193
"Six Poems." *Wake,* no. 9 (Summer 1950), 8–10.

Contents: As at a Theatre – The Desire to Make Love in a Pagoda – Nuns Painting Water-Lilies – The Role of the Idea in Poetry – Americana – The Souls of Women at Night.

All are in *OP;* "As at a Theatre" also in *Palm.*

Annotation: "I have just finished a small group of poems for a magazine at Harvard. As usual, I now want to go on under the impulse of ideas that occurred to me but which I did not use, and I do in fact intend to go on. Probably the book that is coming out about a month from now [*The Auroras of Autumn*] will be my last book, so that the things I do now will probably appear in some general collection." (*Letters,* p. 685: letter to Barbara Church, July 17, 1950)

C 194
"The Rock." *Inventario,* III, 2 (Summer 1950), [1]–4.

Contents: I. Seventy Years Later – II. The Poem as Icon – III. Forms of the Rock in a Night-Hymn.

The first publication in the United States was in the *Trinity Review* (Wallace Stevens number), VIII, 3 (May 1954), 5–9, C 207. In *CP, Poems,* and *Palm.*

Annotation: "Thanks for your note from La Jolla. I have corrected the page proofs and have posted them as you desired.
    "Not having read the poem for some months I was interested to see how the ideas on which it is based came through. They are not quite so well defined as objects seen in the air of Naples, but I think that they do very well. Besides, such ideas are well enough expressed even when there is an amount of uncertainty about them. The last part, which I had liked most, did not please me quite so well as the other parts." (*Letters,* p. 690: letter to Renato Poggioli, August 23, 1950)

C 195
"A Discovery of Thought." *Imagi,* V, 2 (Summer 1950), 5.

In *OP* and *Palm.*

C 196
Two poems. *The Hudson Review,* IV, 1 (Spring 1951), 22–23.

Contents: The Course of a Particular – Final Soliloquy of the Interior Paramour.

"The Course . . ." in *OP*, *Poems*, and *Palm*; "Final Soliloquy . . ."
in *CP*, *Poems*, and *Palm*.

Annotations: "I wish that I could send [the *Hudson Review*]
something but I am not able to do so. Last spring I happened to
meet Mr. [Frederick] Morgan and I told him that I wanted to
send the next thing I did after keeping one or two minor prom-
ises, to you. But I have not done a great deal recently. I greatly
appreciate your kindness in asking me and sooner or later I shall
keep my promise. I know what it is that I want to write about.
The trouble is that I have not particularly felt like writing about
it. Then, too, I have been overwhelmingly busy at the office —
and in consequence too tired to do anything, except to read the
evening paper, at home." (*Letters*, p. 701: letter to Joseph
Bennett, editor of *The Hudson Review*, December 5, 1950)

"I send you a poem after all. I had originally intended to write
a long poem on the subject of the present poem [see HS's footnote at this point, below] but got no farther than the statement
that God and the imagination are one. The implications of this
statement were to follow, and may still. As I said in my note of
December 5th, I have not particularly felt like going on with it
since I started it. After writing to you I looked at the opening
lines which I am now sending you and I thought that they might
do, particularly since I wanted very much to send you something." (*Letters*, pp. 701–702: letter to Joseph Bennett, December 8, 1950)

HS's footnote at the point indicated above in the letter is as
follows: " 'Final Soliloquy of the Interior Paramour', which appeared with 'The Course of a Particular' (sent to Bennett, January 29, 1951) in the *Hudson Review* . . . . In an undated note to
the *Hudson Review*, probably accompanying corrected proofs
of the poem, Stevens wrote:

" 'In *Final Soliloquy* instead of
     We say God and the imagination are one .
     How high thaᵢ highest candle lights the world!
say
     We say God and the imagination are one.
     How high that highest candle lights the world .

This eliminates the exclamation point, which I dislike.
Sorry to trouble you.'
"As printed in *C.P.*, 524, these lines read:

     'We say God and the imagination are one . . .
     How high that highest candle lights the dark.'

"A subsequent note to Ellen St. Sure at the *Hudson Review*, March 12, 1951, said:

'Dark is the word that I intended to use, not world.' " (*Letters*, p. 701)

C 197
"Madame La Fleurie." *Accent*, XI, 4 (Autumn 1951), 193.

In *CP* and *Palm*.

C 198
"A Quiet Normal Life." *Voices*, no. 147 (January–April 1952), 9.

In *CP, Poems,* and *Palm*.

C 199
"How Now, O Brightener." *Shenandoah*, III, 1 (Spring 1952), 21.

In *OP*.

C 200
"Long and Sluggish Lines." *Origin* 5, vol. 2, no. 1 (Spring 1952), 2.

In *CP* and *Palm*.

C 201
"St. Armorer's Church from the Outside." *Poetry*, LXXXI, 1 (October 1952), 72–73.

In *CP*.

C 202
"Note on Moonlight." *Shenandoah*, III, 3 (Autumn 1952), 21.

In *CP*.

C 203
"Eight Poems." *The Hudson Review*, V, 3 (Autumn 1952), 325–334.

Contents: To an Old Philosopher in Rome – The Poem That Took the Place of a Mountain – Vacancy in the Park – Two Illustrations That the World Is What You Make of It (I. The Constant Disquisition of the Wind – II. The World Is Larger in Summer) – Prologues to What Is Possible – Looking across the Fields and Watching the Birds Fly – Song of Fixed Accord – The World as Meditation.

All in *CP;* "The Poem . . . ," "Two Illustrations . . . ," and "Looking across Fields . . ." also in *Palm;* "To an Old Philosopher . . . ," "Prologues . . . ," and "The World as Meditation" also in *Poems* and *Palm.*

Annotation: "At the beginning of the month I sent Mr. [William] Arrowsmith, who had written to me, a poem and said that I should send others. Here are the others. You are welcome to any or all of them. If you use them all, I should like them to be printed in the following order:

1. TO AN OLD PHILOSOPHER IN ROME.
2. THE POEM THAT TOOK THE PLACE OF A MOUNTAIN.
3. VACANCY IN THE PARK.
4. TWO ILLUSTRATIONS THAT THE WORLD IS WHAT YOU MAKE OF IT.
5. PROLOGUES TO WHAT IS POSSIBLE.

In TO AN OLD PHILOSOPHER IN ROME the following changes should be made in the manuscript. On page 2 in the fourth stanza, the first line, which reads:

> So that we feel, in this augustest large,

should be changed to read—

> So that we feel, in this illumined large,

In the next verse the last line, which reads—

> Impatient of the grandeur that you need

should be changed to

> Impatient for the grandeur that you need

On page 3 in the fourth stanza on that page, the two lines which now read—

> The life of the city never lets go, nor do
> You want it to. It is part of the life in your room.

should be changed to read—

> The life of the city never lets go, nor do you
> Ever want it to. It is part of the life in your room.

In the last poem, PROLOGUES TO WHAT IS POSSIBLE, the long lines seem to straggle a bit now that they have been typed. In any event, there is no particular point to the way the last part of each line has been carried over into another line. Thus, for example, the first line which now reads:

> There was an ease of mind that was like being
> alone in a boat at sea,

might just as well read:

> There was an ease of mind that was like being alone
> in a boat at sea,

These lines might look less straggling if they were set in a different manner from the way in which they have been typed. But I am satisfied with the way in which they have been typed, if you don't want to change them. And this is true even as to lines that have been divided into syllables, as, for example, the line containing the word unaccustomed. But you may have your own ideas about the setting of this particular poem and, if so, I shall be glad to have the benefit of them.

"After these have been printed I expect to ask for an assignment of the copyright, having in mind that these may be included in some volume to be published by and by." (*Letters*, pp. 744-746: letter to Joseph Bennett, March 25, 1952)

C 204
"Poems." *The Nation*, 175, 23 (December 6, 1952), 519-520.

Contents: An Old Man Asleep—The Irish Cliffs of Moher—The Plain Sense of Things—One of the Inhabitants of the West—Lebensweisheitspielerei—The Hermitage at the Center—The Green Plant.

All in *CP;* "An Old Man Asleep," "The Plain Sense . . . ," "Lebensweisheitspielerei," and "The Hermitage . . ." also in *Palm;* "The Irish Cliffs . . ." also in *Poems* and *Palm.*

Annotation: "It was easier for me to do a group of short poems than a long one, and here they are. There are 115 lines, to which there must be added lines for title and title spaces, so that this is a little more than you asked for. You are free, of course, to use all or any of these as the available space permits.

"I have used the words savoir in one poem and banlieus in another without italicizing them. I don't know what I should find in respect to savoir in the Oxford Dictionary if I had one, but everyone knows the word. Banlieus has been used as an English word which is the justification for the final s instead of x.

"Now that these poems have been completed they seem to have nothing to do with anything in particular, except poetry, and you will have to determine for yourself whether they are appropriate for use in The Nation." (*Letters*, p. 764: letter to Margaret Marshall, November 12, 1952)

C 205
"The Planet on the Table." *Accent*, XIII, 3 (Summer 1953), 131.

In *CP* and *Palm*.

C 206
"The River of Rivers in Connecticut." *Inventario*, V, 1–4 (September 1953), [64].

A translation by Renato Poggioli, entitled "Il Fiume di Fiumi in Connecticut," is on p. [65]. In *CP*, *Poems*, and *Palm*.

C 207
"Two New Poems." *Trinity Review*, VIII, 3 (May 1954), 5–9.

Contents: Not Ideas about the Thing but the Thing Itself – The Rock (I. Seventy Years Later – II. The Poem as Icon – III. Forms of the Rock in a Night-Hymn).

This issue of the *Trinity Review* celebrated WS's seventy-fifth birthday; in addition to "The Rock" and "Not Ideas about the Thing but the Thing Itself," which was written especially for this issue, there are contributions from friends, other poets, and critics; on the cover is a reproduction of a scratch-board portrait of WS by Inez Campo.

"Not Ideas . . ." in *CP*, *Poems*, and *Palm*. "The Rock" is reprinted from C 194.

Annotations: "Trinity College here in Hartford is going to start a literary magazine. One of its numbers, I believe the first, is to consist of papers about my poetry. The first number is to come out in June, probably late in the month, but, in any event, before vacation time. They want me to do a poem for this magazine just as you wanted a poem for our book. I have been putting them off because, as you know, I have not been writing many things. They have now found out about *The Rock* which has never been published in this country except in *Inventario*. I told them that I would try to do something for them. But day after day is passing with everything piling up. It would be a solution for my difficulty if they could use *The Rock*. Will you ask *Inventario* for permission. I am going to make a real effort to send a new poem to this magazine but it would help to be able to use *The Rock* also. I am going to have a meeting with the editor on March 12. It is conceivable that you could have a reply here by that time or shortly after. Permission to use this poem would be very much appreciated." (*Letters*, pp. 823–824: letter to Renato Poggioli, March 4, 1954)

"The TRINITY REVIEW is like a very rich chocolate cake. It would have been quite possible for me to sit down and devour the whole thing but I took a little of it here and there and then put it away. I don't suppose that you will believe that either, but so help me God." (*Letters*, p. 835: letter to Babette Deutsch, June 2, 1954)

C 208
"Presence of an External Master of Knowledge." *Times Literary Supplement*, September 17, 1954, xx.

In *OP*.

C 209
"A Child Asleep in its Own Life." *Times Literary Supplement*, September 17, 1954, xliv.

In *OP*, *Poems*, and *Palm*.

C 210
"Two Letters." *Vogue*, 124, 6, Whole No. 1936 (October 1, 1954), 126.

Contents: A Letter From – A Letter To.

'Published for the first time in celebration of his 75th birthday, October 2, two new poems by Wallace Stevens – brief, lovely, surprising.' On p. 127 is a photograph of WS by R. (Rollie) Thorne McKenna and a biographical sketch entitled "Wallace Stevens: Lyric Poet." In *OP*.

C 211
"Talk With Mr. Stevens." *New York Times Book Review*, October 3, 1954, section 7, pp. 3, 31.

An interview with WS conducted by Lewis Nichol. On p. 3 is a photograph of WS by Rollie McKenna.

C 212
"Wallace Stevens: Walker." *New York Herald Tribune Book Review*, October 24, 1954, section 6, p. 10.

Autobiographical statement. The photograph of WS on the front page of the *Book Review* is by Rollie McKenna.

Annotation: "I have your letter of September 9. [Mrs. Van Doren had requested a photograph and an autobiographical sketch for a forthcoming issue.]

"I am afraid that you will have to use the photograph that Knopf is using on the cover of my new book. I am not even able to send you snapshots because in recent years Mrs. Stevens has gone in for color. The only thing I could do would be to ask someone from one of the local papers to come out and take a few pictures. But, since I don't have either a dog or a cat, you would not be getting much that Knopf does not already have. Besides, I am embarrassed at the idea of asking these people to take pictures of me.

"The simplest way of giving you a brief autobiographical sketch seems to be to write you this letter.

"[The two paragraphs that follow are the same as those printed in the *Book Review,* with one change: in the printed version, the first sentence of the second paragraph begins: "For relaxation I like most to go to New York for a day . . . ." In the letter, the same sentence begins: "When you speak of play, I should speak of relaxation. I like most to go to New York for a day . . . ."]

"I hope that these notes will, with the aid of your scissors or blue pencil, give you what you want." (*Letters,* pp. 844–845: letter to Irita Van Doren, editor of the *New York Herald Tribune Book Review,* September 20, 1954)

C 213
"Conversation with Three Women of New England." *Accent,* XIV, 4 (Autumn 1954), 227–228.

In *OP.*

C 214
Two poems. *Perspective,* 7, 3 (Autumn 1954), 111–112.

Contents: Dinner Bell in the Woods – Reality Is an Activity of the Most August Imagination.

Both poems in *OP;* "Reality . . ." also in *Poems* and *Palm.*

C 215
"The Whole Man: Perspectives, Horizons." *Yale Review,* XLIV, 2 (Winter 1955), 196–201.

This paper was presented by WS on October 21, 1954, before the delegates attending the Forty-fifth Anniversary Convention of the American Federation of Arts in New York City. In *OP*.

C 216
"Four Poems." *The Sewanee Review*, LXIII, 1 (Winter 1955), 72–74.

Contents: I. Solitaire under the Oaks – II. Local Objects – III. Artificial Populations – IV. A Clear Day and No Memories.

All in *OP*; "A Clear Day . . ." also in *Poems* and *Palm*.

C 217
Excerpt from speech. *Publishers Weekly*, 167, 6 (February 5, 1955), 876.

An excerpt from WS's speech, January 25, 1955, at the Hotel Commodore, New York, N.Y., accepting the sixth annual National Book Award for poetry, given for *Collected Poems*.

C 218
"Banjo Boomer." *Atlantic Monthly*, 195, 3 (March 1955), 66.

In *OP*.

C 219
"July Mountain." *Atlantic Monthly*, 195, 4 (April 1955), 42.

In *OP*.

C 220
"An Interview with Wallace Stevens. One Angry Day-Son," by Signe Culbertson. *In Context*, III, 3 (May 1955), 11–13.

In Context was the student magazine of the Yale Divinity School. On p. 13 is the footnote: '. . . the interviewer wishes to caution that the words put in Mr. Stevens' mouth are not necessarily the exact words he used. Some re-arrangement and interpretation has been given.'

C 221
"Letter." *Nocturne*, VII (Spring 1955), 15.

C 222
"A Footnote to Saul Bellow's 'Pains and Gains'." *Semi-Colon*, I, 3 (Spring 1955), 3.

C 223
"This Is Connecticut." *The Hartford Courant*, July 21, 1955, p. 10.

This is the text of the script which WS prepared for a Voice of America broadcast series under the general title of "This Is America." It appeared in other Connecticut newspapers at about the same time and was reprinted in *OP* as "Connecticut." See also A 25.

C 224
"Poetic Acts." *Quarterly Review of Literature*, VIII, 3 (Fall 1955), 161–163.

A speech accepting an honorary degree from Bard College in 1948. Reprinted as Part I of "Honors and Acts" in *OP*.

C 225
"The Region November." *Zero*, II, 7 (Spring 1956), 28.

C 226
"From the 'Adagia'." *Poetry*, 90, 1 (April 1957), 40–44.

Sixty-two of the adages. On pp. 45–46 is "A Note on the 'Adagia' " by S. F. Morse.

C 227
"Adagia." *The Saturday Review*, XL, 29 (July 20, 1957), 14.

Twenty-one of the adages.

C 228
Three letters. *The Kenyon Review*, XX, 3 (Summer 1958), 454–455.

Excerpts from three letters by WS to Paule Vidal, September 30, October 5, and October 31, 1949. In S. F. Morse's "The Native Element," pp. [446]–465, a paper delivered at The English Institute, September 1957, as part of a conference on WS, and first published here. In *Letters*.

C 229
Excerpt from letter. *Comparative Literature*, XI, 1 (Winter 1959), 49–50.

Brief excerpt from a letter by WS to Paule Vidal, January 30, 1948. In Michel Benamou's "Wallace Stevens: Some Relations

Between Poetry and Painting," pp. 47–60, a paper delivered at The English Institute, September 1957, as part of a conference on WS, and first published here. In *Letters.*

C 230
"Encounters and Letters, Richard Eberhart and Wallace Stevens." *Dartmouth College Library Bulletin,* IV (NS), 3 (December 1961), 57–60.

Two letters by WS to Richard Eberhart, dated December 1, 1950, and January 15, 1954; in addition, there is a letter by Eberhart to WS and excerpts from a lecture, "Emerson and Stevens," delivered by Eberhart at the University of Cincinnati, March 21, 1961. In *Letters.*

C 231
Letters. *ELH* [*English Literary History*], 31, 1 (March 1964), 1–34, 35–63.

Pp. 1–34 contain S. F. Morse's "Wallace Stevens, Bergson, Pater." In this essay are excerpts, varying from single sentences to complete letters, from the following previously unpublished letters by WS:

> To his wife, Elsie Stevens, April 18, 1918
> To his wife, Elsie Stevens, April 19, 1918
> To his wife, Elsie Stevens, April 20, 1918 (The dates of these first three letters are uncertain since the first one when published in *Letters* bears the date 'April 27, 1918? [*sic*]'. The second and third letters do not appear in *Letters.*)
> To Harriet Monroe, August 27, 1919 (This letter does not appear in *Letters.*)
> To Harriet Monroe, August 27, 1919 (This letter does not appear in *Letters.*)
> To Harriet Monroe, December 16, 1919 (The date of this letter, when published in *Letters,* appears as 'August 16? [*sic*], 1919'.)
> To Harriet Monroe, April 25, 1920
> To Harriet Monroe, December 2, 1920
> To Harriet Monroe, October 29, 1921
> To William Stanley Braithwaite, December 5, 1921
> To Harriet Monroe, December 21, 1921
> To Harriet Monroe, April 6, 1922
> To Harriet Monroe, August 24, 1922
> To Harriet Monroe, September 23, 1922
> To Harriet Monroe, October 28, 1922
> To Harriet Monroe, February 12, 1934

To Delmore Schwartz, October 9, 1950
To Thomas McGreevy, November 5, 1950
To Oscar Williams, March 14, 1955 (This letter does not appear in *Letters*.)

Pages 35–63 contain Michel Benamou's "Wallace Stevens and the Symbolist Imagination," with excerpts from the following previously unpublished letters by WS:

To Henry Church, October 28, 1942
To Sister M. Bernetta Quinn, April 7, 1949 (This letter does not appear in *Letters*.)

All in *Letters* except those indicated above.

C 232
"Some Letters." *Encounter*, XXVII, 4 (October 1966), 25–37.

Preceding by one month the publication of *Letters*, where all of them appear, these excerpts from twenty letters by WS are published here for the first time; there is also a brief biography of WS and introductions to the letters by Frank Kermode.

C 233
"Wallace Stevens in Connecticut to Leonard van Geyzel in Ceylon," by John Lucas. *Dartmouth College Library Bulletin*, VII (NS), 2 (April 1967), 38–43.

Excerpts, pp. 39–40, from two previously unpublished letters by WS to Leonard van Geyzel, dated September 13, 1938, and May 27, 1948.

C 234
"Bowl, Cat and Broomstick." *Quarterly Review of Literature* (25th anniversary double poetry issue), XVI, 1–2 (1969), 236–247.

Play. 'Printed here for the first time, from a typescript in the possession of Holly Stevens', with an introduction by A. W. Litz, pp. 230–235. In *Palm*.

Also issued in a hard-cover edition: blue paper over boards; stamped in gold on front and on spine; $8\frac{3}{4} \times 5\frac{1}{2}$ inches; $5.00.

C 235
Letter. *The Wallace Stevens Newsletter*, I, 2 (April 1970), [16].

Letter by WS to Hayden Carruth, editor of *Poetry*, July 21, 1949; first published here.

D. Miscellany

D 1
Dust jacket of *Ideas of Order* (1936).

Contains, on front flap, a statement by WS. See A 2.b.

D 2
Dust jacket of *The Man with the Blue Guitar* (1937 and 1945).

Contains, on front flap, a statement by WS. See A 4.a and A 4.b.

D 3
Jarrell, Randall. *Pictures From An Institution*. New York: Knopf, 1954.

Contains, on front flap of dust jacket, a statement by WS: 'A most literate account of a group of most literate people by a writer of power . . . a delight of true understanding.' See *Letters,* p. 818, letter to Babette Deutsch of February 15, 1954, and footnote 3 containing letter of February 8, 1954, to William Cole, at Alfred A. Knopf, Inc., for full text of WS's note.

D 4
Advertisement flier for *The Hudson Review* (1955).

Contains, on front of flier, a statement by WS: 'Reviews sometimes seem merely to continue. But *The Hudson Review* is young and nimble and enjoys being itself and its readers enjoy it too.' This statement is from an unpublished letter of June 14, 1945, from WS to Joseph Bennett. In the whole the letter reads: 'Dear Mr. Bennett: / You may or may not like the following: / The specific quality of the Hudson Review is that it goes on because it wants to go on. Reviews sometimes seem merely to continue. But the Hudson Review is young and nimble and enjoys being itself and its readers enjoy it too. / I hope to be able to do a few poems this summer. / With best wishes, I am / Sincerely yours,'.

D 5
Statement by WS on an advertisement flyer for books by John Varney (ca. 1960).

243

Contains, p. 2, a one-sentence quotation from an unpublished letter of June 1943 by WS to John Varney about Varney's *Stalingrad, New years 1943* (New York: The Liberal Press, 1943).

D 6
Catalogue Number Nine. Henry W. Wenning, Modern Rare Books, 282 York Street, New Haven, Conn. 06511. February 1965.

Contains, p. 35, a quotation from an unpublished letter by WS to Leonie Adams.

D 7
Catalogue. House of Books, Ltd., 18 East Sixtieth Street, New York, N.Y., 10022. November 1965.

Contains, p. 67, a quotation from an unpublished letter by WS to Murray Welsh, 1937.

D 8
Pivot, IV, 15 and 16 (1965).

Contains, on the back cover of this magazine published by the Poetry Workshop (English 113), directed by Joseph Leonard Grucci at Pennsylvania State University, a one-sentence statement by WS: '*Time of Hawks* is full of extraordinary experience.' Joseph Leonard Grucci, *Time of Hawks. Poems and Translations* (Pittsburgh, Pa.: Mayer Press, 1955).

D 9
Catalogue. House of Books, Ltd., 667 Madison Avenue, New York, N.Y., 10022. November 1968.

Contains, p. 67, a quotation from an unpublished letter by WS to Harvey Breit, October 5, 1942.

D 10
Wallace, Emily Mitchell. *A Bibliography of William Carlos Williams*. Middletown, Conn.: Wesleyan University Press, 1968.

Contains, p. x, the first sentence of a letter by WS to J. Ronald Lane Latimer, November 28, 1934. This sentence was not included when the remainder of the letter was published in *Letters,* p. 271.

D 11
Catalogue. Parke-Bernet Galleries, Inc. Sale No. 3103, 2d Session, Lot 243, October 29, 1970.

Contains a quotation from an unpublished letter by WS to Oscar Williams, January 11, 1943.

E. Translations

ARABIC

ANTHOLOGY

E 1
Sayegh, Tawfig, ed. [*Fifty Poems from Contemporary American Poetry*]. Beirut: Dar El-Yaqza, 1963.

Contains translation by Tawfiq Sayegh of "Esthétique du Mal."

BENGALI

PERIODICALS

E 2
Kavita (special bilingual issue), XVI, I, series 67 (December 1950), 34–37.

Contains translations by Buddhadera Bose of "Gallant Chateau" and "The House Was Quiet and the World Was Calm."

CZECHOSLOVAKIAN

PERIODICAL

E 3
Svetova Literatura: Revue Zahranicnich Literatur, 10, 5 (Prague, 1965), 60–70.

Contains translations by Jirina Haukova of "A Rabbit as King of the Ghosts," "Snow Man," "Thirteen Ways of Looking at a Blackbird," "Domination of Black," "Death of a Soldier," "No Possum, No Sop, No Taters," "Asides on the Oboe," "Human Arrangement," "The House Was Quiet and the World Was Calm," "Vacancy in the Park," and "The Rock"; in addition there is an article on WS by Zdenek Vancura.

247

DANISH

E 4
Digte. Edited by Bent Irve. Copenhagen: Fisker-Nielsen & Lokkes Forlag, 1960. 40 pp.

Contains translations by Per Dorph-Petersen, Niels Barfoed, and Bent Irve of "Ploughing on Sunday," "Fabliau of Florida," "The Paltry Nude Starts on a Spring Voyage," "Homunculus et La Belle Etoile," "The Curtains in the House of the Metaphysician," "Colloquy with a Polish Aunt," "Postcard from a Volcano," "The Glass of Water," "Of the Surface of Things," "Thirteen Ways of Looking at a Blackbird," "The Worms at Heaven's Gate," "Lunar Paraphrase," "The Death of a Soldier," "Another Weeping Woman," "Tea," "The House Was Quiet and the World Was Calm," "Tea at the Palaz of Hoon," "Peter Quince at the Clavier," "Disillusionment of Ten O'Clock," "The Reader," "Poetry Is a Destructive Force," "The Poem That Took the Place of a Mountain," "Lebensweisheitspielerei," "Vacancy in the Park," "The Planet on the Table," "Dry Loaf," and "Sunday Morning."

E 5
Nyholm, Jens, trans. *Amerikanske Stemmer*. Copenhagen: Arene-Frost—Hansens Forlag, 1968.

Contains, pp. 88–97, "Thirteen Ways of Looking at a Blackbird," "Peter Quince at the Clavier," and "Domination of Black."

FRENCH

E 6
Poèmes. Translated by Marie-Jean Beraud-Villars and André Ravaute. Introduction by Bernard Delvaille. Autour du Monde, 71. Paris: Pierre Seghers, 1963. 85 pp.

Contains "Sunday Morning," "The Man with the Blue Guitar," "The Pleasures of Merely Circulating," "The Woman That Had More Babies Than That," "A Postcard from the Volcano," "Au-

tumn Refrain," "Parochial Theme," "Cuisine Bourgeoise,"
"Whistle Aloud, Too Weedy Wren," "Domination of Black,"
"Tattoo," "Annual Gaiety," "Gallant Chateau," "The Motive for
Metaphor," and "Homunculus et la Belle Etoile."

Note: "Whistle Aloud, Too Weedy Wren" consists of the first
five stanzas from the ninth section of the last part of *Notes Toward a Supreme Fiction.*

ANTHOLOGIES

E 7
Jolas, Eugène. *Anthologie de la Nouvelle Poésie Américaine.*
Paris: Kra, 1928.

Contains, pp. 219–222, translation by Eugène Jolas of "Peter
Quince at the Clavier."

Note: There are one hundred numbered copies "sur vélin."

E 8
Bosquet, Alain. *Anthologie de la Poésie Américaine des Ori-
gines à Nos Jours.* Paris: Librairie Stock, 1956.

Contains, pp. 134–141, translations by Alain Bosquet of "Sea
Surface Full of Clouds," "Domination of Black," and "For [*sic*]
an Old Philosopher in Rome."

PERIODICALS

E 9
Mesures, V, 3 (Paris, July 15, 1939), [329]–343.

Contains translations by Pierre Leyris of "Ploughing on Sunday," by Raymond Queneau of "Disillusionment of Ten O'Clock"
and "The Emperor of Ice-Cream," and by Marc Le Templier of
"Thirteen Ways of Looking at a Blackbird."

E 10
Profils, no. 3 (Paris, April 1953), [70]–75.

Contains translation by Alain Bosquet of "To an Old Philosopher
in Rome."

E 11
Profils, no. 8 (Paris, Summer 1954) [30]–45.

Contains translations by "J.D." of "Sunday Morning," "Anecdote of the Jar," "Less and Less Human, O Savage Spirit," "Men Made Out of Words," "The House Was Quiet and the World Was Calm," "Dance of the Macabre Mice," and "This Solitude of Cataracts."

E 12
Europe, XXXVII, 358–359 (Paris, February–March 1959), 114–115.

Contains translations by Renaud de Jouvenal of "Of Modern Poetry" and "Martial Cadenza."

E 13
La Nouvelle Revue Francaise, VII, 83 (Paris, November 1959), 952–960.

Contains translation by Michel Benamou of "Notes Toward a Supreme Fiction."

GERMAN

BOOK

E 14
Der Planet Auf Dem Tisch: Gedichte und Adagia. Translated and edited by Kurt Heinrich Hansen. Hamburg: Claassen Verlag, 1961, 231 pp.

Contains "Infanta Marina," "Domination of Black," "Metaphors of a Magnifico," "World without Peculiarity," "The Load of Sugar-cane," "The Apostrophe to Vincentine," "Two at Norfolk," "Polo Ponies Practicing," "Lunar Paraphrase," "In the Northwest" from "Primordia," "The Death of a Soldier," "The Indigo Glass in the Grass," "The Region November," "Arcades of Philadelphia the Past," "The Silver Plough-Boy," "To the Roaring Wind," "Of Mere Being," "Sailing After Lunch," twelve stanzas from "The Man with the Blue Guitar," "Sunday Morning," "The River of Rivers in Connecticut," "The Planet on the Table," "Vacancy in the Park," "Thirteen Ways of Looking at a Blackbird," "On the Road Home," "Six Significant Landscapes," "How to Live, What to Do," "A Dish of Peaches in Russia," "Re-statement of Romance," "Burghers of Petty Death," "Secret Man," "Earthy Anecdote," "In a Bad Time," four stanzas from "Peter

Quince at the Clavier," "Debris of Life and Mind," "The Sick Man," "A Weak Mind in the Mountains," seventeen stanzas from "Like Decorations in a Nigger Cemetery," "Yellow Afternoon," "In the Carolinas," "The Paltry Nude Starts on a Spring Voyage," "The Wind Shifts," "Of the Surface of Things," "Anecdote of Men by the Thousand," "The Snow Man," "Dance of the Macabre Mice," "Tattoo," five stanzas from "The Idea of Order at Key West," "A Woman Sings a Song for a Soldier Come Home," "Bouquet of Roses in Sunlight," stanza I from "Connoisseur of Chaos," "Gallant Chateau," "Ghosts as Cocoons," "Ploughing on Sunday," "Tea at the Palaz of Hoon," "The House Was Quiet and the World Was Calm," "Martial Cadenza," "The Men That Are Falling," "Girl in a Nightgown," "Life Is Motion," "Disillusionment of Ten O'Clock," "Fabliau of Florida," "Theory," "Cuisine Bourgeoise," "The Brave Man," "Two Figures in Dense Violet Light," "Gray Stones and Gray Pigeons," "The Sense of the Sleight-of-Hand Man," "Farewell to Florida," "A Postcard from the Volcano," "Continual Conversation with a Silent Man," "The Green Plant," "The Well Dressed Man with a Beard," "Poem with Rhythms," "The Candle a Saint," "Of Modern Poetry," "Adagia"; pp. 213–226 contain "Nachwort" by Kurt Heinrich Hansen.

PERIODICALS

E 15
Das Lot, I (Berlin, October 1947), 59–60.

Contains translation by Alexander Koval of "Peter Quince at the Clavier."

E 16
Perspektiven, no. 3 (Frankfurt, May 1953), [56]–61.

Contains translation by Alexander Koval of "To an Old Philoso pher in Rome."

E 17
Perspektiven, no. 8 (Frankfurt, Summer 1954), [26]–45.
[26]–45.

Contains translations by Kurt Heinrich Hansen of "Lunar Paraphrase," a short section from "Peter Quince at the Clavier," "Thirteen Ways of Looking at a Blackbird," "Dance of the Macabre Mice," and "Sunday Morning."

ITALIAN

E 18

Mattino Domenicale ed Altre Poesie. Edited by Renato Poggioli. Turin: Giulio Einaudi Editore, 1954. 185 pp.

See A 21.

E 19

Baldini, Gabriele, ed. *Poeti Americani, 1662–1945.* Maestri e compagni, biblioteca di studi critici e morali (5). Turin: De Silva, 1949.

Contains translation by Gabriele Baldini of "Peter Quince at the Clavier."

E 20

Izzo, Carlo, ed. *Poesia Contemporanea e Poesia Negra.* Parma: Guanda, 1949.

Contains translations by Carlo Izzo of "Peter Quince at the Clavier," "Domination of Black," and "Two Figures in Dense Violet Light."

E 21

Rizzardi, Alfredo, ed. *Lirici Americani.* Caltanissetta and Rome: S. Sciascia, 1955.

Contains translations by Alfredo Rizzardi of "To the Roaring Wind," "The Green Plant," "Lebensweisheitspielerei," "The Plain Sense of Things," and "The Ocean" (i.e., "Somnambulisma").

E 22

Sanesi, Roberto. *Poeti Americani da E. A. Robinson a W. S. Merwin, 1900–1956.* Milan: Feltrinelli, 1958.

Contains, pp. 203–253, translations by Roberto Sanesi of "Fabliau of Florida," "Anecdote of Men by the Thousand," "Of the Surface of Things," "The Emperor of Ice-Cream," "Six Significant Landscapes," "Sea Surface Full of Clouds," "Poetry Is a De-

structive Force," stanza VI of "Esthétique du Mal," "Notes Toward a Supreme Fiction" ("It Must Be Abstract," I, IV, X; "It
Must Change," VI, IX; "It Must Give Pleasure," V, IX); there is
in addition a three-page essay on WS by Sanesi and a three-page
bibliography of WS.

E 23
Izzo, Carlo, ed. *Poesia Americana del '900*. Parma: Guanda,
1963.

Contains, pp. 116–133, translations by Carlo Izzo of "Peter
Quince at the Clavier," "Domination of Black," stanzas II and
VIII of "Things of August," and "Reply to Papini."

PERIODICALS

E 24
Botteghe Oscure, IV (Rome, 1949), 330–334.

See C 188. Accompanying this issue of *Botteghe Oscure* is a
separate pamphlet of translations: pp. 32–36 contain translations
by Salvatore Rosati of "What We See Is What We Think," "A
Golden Woman in a Silver Mirror," "The Old Lutheran Bells at
Home," "Questions Are Remarks," "Study of Images I," and
"Study of Images II."

E 25
Prospetti, no. 3 (Rome, Spring 1953), [76]–81.

Contains translation by Ann Maria Crino of "To an Old Philosopher in Rome."

E 26
Prospetti, no. 8 (Rome, Summer 1954), [26]–39.

Contains translations by Alfredo Rizzardi of "Sunday Morning,"
"This Solitude of Cataracts," "The Idea of Order at Key West,"
and "Lunar Paraphrase." Despite the title "Cinque Poesie" at the
beginning of the section, there are only these four poems.

E 27
Letteratura, II (Rome, September–December 1954), 65–87.

Contains translation by Glauco Cambon of "Notes Toward a Supreme Fiction."

JAPANESE

The following notations of translations of WS's works are taken from citations in Naomi Fukuda, *A Bibliography of Translations, American Literary Works Into Japanese, 1868–1967* (Tokyo: Hara Shobo, 1968). They have not been seen by me.

BOOKS

E 28
Ashibumi orugan. Translated by Rikutaro Fukuda. Tokyo: Heibon-sha, 1959.

Contains excerpts from *Harmonium*.

E 29
Bi to chitsujo no rinen [*The Idea of Order and Beauty: Poems*]. Translated by Toshitada Iketani. Nagoya: Uchū Jidai Shuppan-bu, 1963.

E 30
Sekai shiron takei [*Adagia*]. Translated by Yuzuru Katagiri. Tokyo: Shichō-sha, 1964.

E 31
Ruisui no imi [*Effects of Analogy*]. Translated by Yukio Matsuda. Tokyo: Shichō-sha, 1964.

NORWEGIAN

PERIODICAL

E 32
Vinduet, XXIV (Oslo, 1970), 72–73.

Contains translation by Jan Erik Vold of "Thirteen Ways of Looking at a Blackbird."

PERSIAN

ANTHOLOGY

E 33
Shafā, Shujā' al-Dīn, trans. [*Selections from the Best American Poetry*]. Teheran, 1955.

Contains a prose version of "Peter Quince at the Clavier."

POLISH

BOOK

E 34
Wiersze. Selected and translated, with an introduction, by Jaroslaw Marek Rymkiewicz. Warsaw: Panstwowy Institut Wydawniczy, 1969. 50 pp.

Contains "The Emperor of Ice-Cream," "Sunday Morning," "Lunar Paraphrase," "Dance of the Macabre Mice," "Evening Without Angels," stanza XXII of "The Man with the Blue Guitar," "Parochial Theme," "The Poems of Our Climate," "The Glass of Water," "Dry Loaf," "Connoisseur of Chaos," "The Sense of the Sleight-of-Hand Man," "The Candle A Saint," "On an Old Horn," "Of Modern Poetry," "The Well Dressed Man with a Beard," "Less and Less Human, O Savage Spirit," "Notes Toward a Supreme Fiction," "Puella Parvula," "Angel Surrounded by Paysans," "The World as Meditation," and a portion of "The Sail of Ulysses" entitled "Ulisses."

ANTHOLOGY

E 35
Elektorowicz, Leszek. *Przedmowy do Cisny*. Cracow: Wydawnictwo Literackie, 1968.

Contains, pp. 52–57, "Variations on a Summer Day" and "Soldier, there is a war between the mind."

PERIODICALS

E 36
Kultura, no. 7/69–8/70 (Paris, July–August 1953), 86–89.

Contains translations by Czeslava Milosza of "The Poem That Took the Place of the Mountain" and "Vacancy in the Park."

E 37
Tworczose, XVII, 10 (Warsaw, October 1961), 52–55.

Contains translations by Jaroslaw Marek Rymkiewicz of "The

World as Meditation," "The Candle A Saint," and "Of Modern Poetry" and by Leszek Elektorowicz of "Soldier, there is a war" and "Crude Foyer."

E 38
Wspolczesnosc, IX, 5/157 (Warsaw, February 26–March 11, 1964), 3.

Contains translations by Jaroslaw Marek Rymkiewicz of selections from *Notes Toward a Supreme Fiction, Parts of a World,* and *Transport to Summer.*

ROMANIAN

BOOK

E 39
Lumea ca Meditatie. Translated by Constantin Abaluta and Stefan Stoenescu, with a Preface by Stoenescu. Bucharest: Editura Univers, 1970. 309 pp.

Contains "Domination of Black," "The Snow Man," "The Load of Sugar-Cane," "Le Monocle de Mon Oncle," "Nuances of a Theme by Williams," "Metaphors of a Magnifico," "Ploughing on Sunday," "Cy Est Pourtraicte, Madame Ste Ursule, et Les Unze Mille Vierges," "The Worms at Heaven's Gate," "Of Heaven Considered as a Tomb," "Of the Surface of Things," "Anecdote of the Prince of Peacocks," "The Place of the Solitaires," "The Weeping Burgher," "The Curtains in the House of the Metaphysician," "Banal Sojourn," "Depression Before Spring," "The Emperor of Ice-Cream," "The Cuban Doctor," "Tea at the Palaz of Hoon," "Disillusionment of Ten O Clock," "Sunday Morning," "On the Adequacy of Landscape," "Anecdote of the Jar," "Cortège for Rosenbloom," "Tattoo," "The Wind Shifts," "Life Is Motion," "Colloquy with a Polish Aunt," "Gubbinal," "Theory," "Peter Quince at the Clavier," "Thirteen Ways of Looking at a Blackbird," "The Man Whose Pharynx Was Bad," "The Death of a Soldier," "Negation," "The Surprises of the Superhuman," "Lunar Paraphrase," "Anatomy of Monotony," "Sonatina to Hans Christian Andersen," "Tea," "To the Roaring Wind," "Sad Strains of a Gay Waltz," "Dance of the Macabre Mice," "Lions in Sweden," "The Idea of Order at Key West," "The American Sublime," "The Sun This March," "Gray Stones and Gray Pigeons," "Winter Bells," "The Reader," "Mud Master," "Anglais mort à Florence," "The Pleasures of Merely Circu-

lating," "A Postcard from the Volcano," "Autumn Refrain," "A
Fish-Scale Sunrise," "Gallant Chateau," "Delightful Evening,"
a section from "The Man with the Blue Guitar," "Poetry Is a
Destructive Force," "Poems of Our Climate," "Study of Two
Pears," "The Glass of Water," "Idiom of the Hero," "The Man on
the Dump," "On the Road Home," "The Latest Freed Man,"
"A Rabbit as King of the Ghosts," "Loneliness in Jersey City,"
"A Weak Mind in the Mountains," "Girl in a Nightgown," "Con-
noisseur of Chaos," "Dezembrum," "The Common Life," "The
Sense of the Sleight-of-Hand Man," "The Candle A Saint," "Of
Hartford in a Purple Light," "Cuisine Bourgeoise," "On an Old
Horn," "Bouquet of Belle Scavoir," "Variations on a Summer
Day," "Martial Cadenza," "Landscape with Boat," "Les Plus
Belle Pages," "Poem with Rhythms," "Woman Looking at a
Vase of Flowers," "The Well Dressed Man with a Beard," "Mrs.
Alfred Uruguay," "Asides on the Oboe," "Metamorphosis,"
"Contrary Theses (I)," "Phosphor Reading by His Own Light,"
"The Search for Sound Free from Motion," "Contrary Theses
(II)," "The Hand as a Being," "Oak Leaves Are Hands," "God Is
Good. It Is a Beautiful Night," "No Possum, No Sop, No Taters,"
"So-And-So Reclining on Her Couch," "Somnambulisma,"
"Crude Foyer," "The Bed of Old John Zeller," "Less and Less
Human, O Savage Spirit," "Debris of Life and Mind," "Man
Carrying Thing," "Men Made Out of Words," "Chaos in Motion
and Not in Motion," "The House Was Quiet and the World Was
Calm," "Continual Conversation with a Silent Man," "A Woman
Sings a Song for a Soldier Come Home," "The Good Man Has No
Shape," "The Prejudice against the Past," "The Auroras of Au-
tumn," "Large Red Man Reading," "This Solitude of Cataracts,"
"The Owl in the Sarcophagus," "A Primitive like an Orb," "Meta-
phor as Degeneration," "The Woman in Sunshine," "World
without Peculiarity," "Puella Parvula," "What We See Is What
We Think," "Questions Are Remarks," "Study of Images I,"
"An Old Man Asleep," "The Irish Cliffs of Moher," "The Plain
Sense of Things," "One of the Inhabitants of the West," "Leben-
sweisheitspielerei," "The Hermitage at the Center," "Madame
La Fleurie," "To an Old Philosopher in Rome," "Vacancy in the
Park," "The Poem That Took the Place of a Mountain," "Two
Illustrations That the World Is What You Make of It," "Prologues
to What Is Possible," "The World as Meditation," "A Quiet Nor-
mal Life," "Final Soliloquy of the Interior Paramour," "The
Rock," "Note on Moonlight," "The Planet on the Table," "The
River of Rivers in Connecticut," "Not Ideas about the Thing
but the Thing Itself," "The Indigo Glass in the Grass," "The
Course of a Particular," "The Sail of Ulysses," "A Child

sand," "Disillusionment of Ten O'Clock," "Sunday Morning," "Six Significant Landscapes," "Anecdote of the Jar," "Two Figures in Dense Violet Light," "Thirteen Ways of Looking at a Blackbird," a selection from "Sea Surface Full of Clouds," "The Sun This March," a selection from "The Man with the Blue Guitar," "Poetry Is a Destructive Force," "Study of Two Pears," "Men Made Out of Words," "The House Was Quiet and the World Was Calm," a selection from "Notes Toward a Supreme Fiction," "This Solitude of Cataracts," and "To an Old Philosopher in Rome."

ANTHOLOGIES

E 42
Weiss, Alfredo, trans. *Poesia Estado Unidense*. Buenos Aires: Ediciones Continental, 1944.

Contains "Of Heaven Considered as a Tomb" and "Peter Quince at the Clavier."

E 43
Florit, Eugenio, trans. *Antologia de la Poesia Norteamericana Contemporanea*. Washington, D.C.: Union Panamericana, 1955.

Contains "Domination of Black," "Tattoo," and "Thirteen Ways of Looking at a Blackbird."

E 44
Urtecho, Coronel, and Cardenal, Ernest, trans. *Antologia de la Poesia Norteamericana*. Madrid: Aguilar, 1963.

Contains "Final Soliloquy of the Interior Paramour," "In the Carolinas," "Metaphors of a Magnifico," "The Snow Man," "Of the Surface of Things," "Anecdote of Men by the Thousand," "Theory," "Domination of Black," "To the Roaring Wind," "Tattoo," "The Mechanical Optimist," and "Peter Quince at the Clavier."

E 45
Novo, Salvador, ed. *101 Poemas, Antologia Bilingue de la Poesia Norteamericana Moderna*. Mexico: Editorial Letras, 1965.

Contains, pp. 246–255, translations by J. A. Shelley of "Domination of Black" and by Toro Concha of "The Emperor of Ice-Cream."

E 46
1929 revista de avance, X, 40 (Havana, November 15, 1929),
326–327.

Contains "Discourse in a Cantina at Havana."

E 47
Sur, XIV (Buenos Aires, March–April 1944), 98–111.

Contains translation by A. Bio y Casares and Jorge Luis Borges of
"Sunday Morning."

E 48
Origenes, II (Havana, Winter 1945), 3–6.

Contains translations by Oscar Rodriguez Feliú of "Thinking
of a Relation between the Images of Metaphors," "Chaos in Motion and Not in Motion," "The House Was Quiet and the World
Was Calm," and "Continual Conversation with a Silent Man."

E 49
Origenes, IX (Havana, Winter 1952), 3–11.

Contains translation by José Rodríguez-Feo of "The Relations
between Poetry and Painting."

E 50
Artes Hispanicas, I, 1 (New York, Spring–Summer 1967),
159–162.

Contains translations by Jorge Guillén of "Study of Two Pears"
and "The House Was Quiet and the World Was Calm."

SWEDISH

BOOK

E 51
Dikter. Translated by Folke Isaksson. Stockholm: Bonniers
Boktryckeri, 1957. 70 pp.

Contains thirty poems. On the copyright page there is a note that
the translations are made from *The Collected Poems of Wallace
Stevens.*

TURKISH

BOOK

E 52
Wallace Stevens: Seçme Siirler. Translated, with an introduction, by Talat Sait Halman. Ankara: Yeditepe Yayinevi, 1970.
80 pp.

Contains forty poems.

ANTHOLOGY

E 53
Nutku, Ozdemir, and Dursun K, Tarik, trans. *Cagdas Amerikan
Surleri.* Ankara: Sairler Tapragi, 1956.

Contains translations by Ozdemir Nutku and Tarik Dursun K. of
Section VII of "Sunday Morning," the Turkish title of which
reads "On a Summer Morn," and of "A Postcard from the Volcano," the Turkish title of which reads "A Postcard Came to the
World."

PERIODICALS

E 54
See *The Wallace Stevens Newsletter,* II, 1 (October 1970),
19–20, for Talat Sait Halman's "Wallace Stevens and Turkish
Poetry" and mention of other periodical appearances.

YIDDISH

PERIODICAL

E 55
Di Tsukunft, LXXIII, 11 (New York, November 1968), 497.

Contains translation by Eliezer Blum-Alquit of "The Dry Loaf."

F. Musical Settings

F 1

"Thirteen Ways of Looking at a Blackbird." Set to music by P. Glanville-Hicks. New York: Weintraub Music Co., 1951. 19 pp.

F 2

"Ideas of Order." Set to music for orchestra by Arthur Berger. New York: Circle Blue Print Co., 1952.

The first page of the score is reproduced on the inside back cover of *Trinity Review* for May 1954.

Reprinted: New York: C. F. Peters Corp., 1956.

F 3

"The Pleasures of Merely Circulating." Set to music by Starling A. Cumberworth. New York: Independent Music Publishers, 1953. 11 pp.

F 4

"Thirteen Ways of Looking at a Blackbird." Set to music by John Gruen, in his *Song Cycles*, Op. 20. New York: John Gruen, 1953. 22 pp.

Recorded on Contemporary Records, AP 121. See G 5.

F 5

"Thirteen Ways of Looking at a Blackbird." Set to music by Boris Blacher under the title *Eine Amsel dreizehnmal gesehen*, from the translation by Kurt Hansen, for voice and string orchestra, Op. 54. Berlin: Bote & Bock, 1958.

Recorded on Deutsche Gramophone LPM 18759. See G 8.

F 6

"Harmonium." A song cycle for soprano and piano by Vincent Persichetti, Op. 50. Philadelphia: Elkan-Vogel Co., 1959. 105 pp.

Includes, along with a frontispiece by Bernard Kohn, "Valley

Candle," "The Place of the Solitaires," "Theory," "Lunar Para-
phrase," "The Death of a Soldier," "The Wind Shifts," "The
Weeping Burgher," "Six Significant Landscapes," "In the Clear
Season of Grapes," "Tea," "The Snow Man," "Tattoo," "Sonatina
to Hans Christian," "Infanta Marina," "Metaphors of a Magni-
fico," "Gubbinal," "Domination of Black," "Earthy Anecdote,"
"Of the Surface of Things," and "Thirteen Ways of Looking at a
Blackbird." Persichetti's "Harmonium" had its premiere on
January 20, 1952, at the Museum of Modern Art, New York City,
under the auspices of a League of Composers program.

F 7
"Peter Quince at the Clavier." A song cycle by Gordon Cyr.
Berkeley: Fantasy Records, 1959.

Recorded on Fantasy Records, no. 5008. See G 6.

F 8
"Infanta Marina." Set to music for viola and piano by Vincent
Persichetti, Op. 83. Philadelphia: Elkan-Vogel Co., 1960. 15 pp.

Commissioned by the Walter W. Naumburg Foundation.

F 9
"The Emperor of Ice-Cream." Set to music by Roger Reynolds
for eight voices, piano, percussion, and double bass. London and
New York: C. F. Peters Corp., 1963. Edition Peters, 6616.

F 10
"From *Harmonium*." A song cycle for high voice and piano by
Donald Lybbert. Bryn Mawr, Pa.: Merion Music, 1970.

F 11
"Thirteen Ways of Looking at a Blackbird." A secular cantata by
Ian Wisse for mezzo-soprano, mixed chorus, and orchestra.
39 pp.

Manuscript score only, written in 1952. In the Yale University
Library.

G. Recordings

G 1

Tape recording of reading made at the University of Massachusetts, Amherst, Mass. March 1954.

G 2

Wallace Stevens "reading his poems at the YMHA Poetry Center, New York City, April 14, 1954." Washington, D.C.: Library of Congress, 1954. LWO 2863, tape-recording reels 1 and 2.

Contains, from *Harmonium*, "Infanta Marina," "Fabliau of Florida," "Bantams in Pine-Woods," "Nomad Exquisite," "Indian River"; from *Transport to Summer*, "Certain Phenomena of Sound" (parts 1–3), "So-And-So Reclining on Her Couch," "Less and Less Human, O Savage Spirit," "Mountains Covered with Cats," "Credences of Summer" (I–X); from *The Auroras of Autumn*, "Imago," "The Novel," "Questions Are Remarks," "An Ordinary Evening in New Haven" (I–XI), "The Course of a Particular," "Two Paraphrases from Léon-Paul Fargue" (I. 'In a quarter made drowsy by the odor of its gardens' and II. 'Between the things of these twenty years').

G 3

The Caedmon Treasury of Modern Poets Reading Their Own Poetry. New York: Caedmon Records, 1957. TC 2006, 2–12, LPs. L.C. R57-256. $13.00.

Record 2, side 2, contains WS reading his "The Idea of Order at Key West."

G 4

Wallace Stevens, Reading His Poems. New York: Caedmon Records, 1957. TC 1068, 1–12, LP. L.C. R66-1780. $6.50.

Contains "The Theory of Poetry" (a prose note), "The Idea of Order at Key West," "Credences of Summer," "The Poem That Took the Place of a Mountain," "Vacancy in the Park," "Large Red Man Reading," "This Solitude of Cataracts," "In the Element of Antagonisms," "Puella Parvulla," "To an Old Philosopher in Rome," "Two Illustrations That the World Is What You Make of It" (I. "The Constant Disquisition of the Wind," II. "The World Is Larger in Summer"), "Prologues to What Is Possible," "Looking Across the Fields and Watching the Birds Fly," "Final Soliloquy of the Interior Paramour," and "The Life of the Poet" (a prose note).

G 5
Thirteen Ways of Looking at a Blackbird. New York: Contemporary Records, 1958. AP 121.

Contains "Thirteen Ways of Looking at a Blackbird," set to music by John Gruen in his *Song Cycles,* Op. 20. See F 4.

G 6
Peter Quince at the Clavier. Composers' forum series. Berkeley: Fantasy Records, 1959. No. 5008.

Song cycle by Gordon Cyr. See F 7.

G 7
20th Century Poetry in English: An Album of Modern Poetry. Edited by Oscar Williams. Washington, D.C.: Library of Congress, Recording Lab, 1959. Three records.

Record 1, side 1, contains WS reading his "So-And-So Reclining on Her Couch" and "Mountains Covered with Cats."

Reissued as part of the three-volume *Album of Modern Poetry: An Anthology Read by the Poets.* New York: Record Collectors Guild, 1964. Gryphon, GR 902/3/4.

G 8
Thirteen Ways of Looking at a Blackbird. New York: Deutsche Gramophone, 1962. LPM 18759.

Contains "Thirteen Ways of Looking at a Blackbird," set to music by Boris Blacher under the title *Eine Amsel dreizehnmal gesehen,* from the translation by Kurt Hansen, for voice and string orchestra, Op. 54. See F 5.

G 9
The Spoken Arts Treasury of 100 Modern American Poets. New York: Spoken Arts, 1969. SA 1041.

Volume 2 contains WS reading his "Infanta Marina," "Fabliau of Florida," "Bantams in Pine Woods," "Nomad Exquisite," "Indian River," "Less and Less Human, O Savage Spirit," "Imago," and "The Novel."

H. Dedicatory Poems and Poems Referring to Stevens

H 1
Berrone, Louis. "Disillusionment at Eleven O'Clock." *Trinity Review*, VIII (May 1954), 18.

H 2
Berryman, John. "So Long? Stevens." In his *The Dream Songs*. New York: Farrar, Straus & Giroux, 1969, p. 238.

H 3
Bly, Robert. "Thinking of Wallace Stevens on the First Snowy Day in December." In his *Silence in the Snowy Fields*. Middletown, Conn.: Wesleyan University Press, 1962, p. 16.

H 4
Brinnin, John Malcolm. "Twelve or Thirteen Ways of Looking at Wallace Stevens." *Trinity Review*, VIII (May 1954), 20.

H 5
Cantwell, Robert. "Wallace Stevens at the Windowsill." *Hika* (Kenyon College), XXIV (Fall 1971), 8.

H 6
Ciardi, John. "A Praise of Good Poets in a Bad Time" ('To the Memory of Wallace Stevens'). *Saturday Review*, XXIX (August 11, 1956), 13.

H 7
Dayton, Irene. "Wallace Stevens." *Adam (International Review)*, XXXV (1970), 21.

H 8
Deutsch, Babette. "Letter to Wallace Stevens." In her *Animal Vegetable Mineral*. New York: Dutton, 1954, pp. 51–52.

Reprinted in *Trinity Review*, VIII (May 1954), 23.

H 9
Eberhart, Richard. "Two Poems 'Closing Off the View' and 'The Meaning of Indian Summer'" ('For Wallace Stevens'). *Trinity Review*, VIII (May 1954), 24.

H 10
Eberhart, Richard. "At the Canoe Club" ('For Wallace Stevens'). In his *Collected Poems 1930–1960*. New York: Oxford University Press, 1960, p. 217.

H 11
Friedman, Phillip A. "Epitaph for Wallace Stevens." *College English*, XXIV (April 1963), 559.

H 12
Fulton, Robin. "Wallace Stevens – in reply to R. S. Thomas –." In his *Instances*. Edinburgh: Macdonald, 1967.

Reprinted in *WSN* (October 1969), p. 7.

H 13
Gitin, David. "In Which Wallace Stevens Meets Mario Giacomelli." *Western Humanities Review*, XXV (Summer 1971), 242.

H 14
Kreymborg, Alfred. "Premonition" ('To Wallace Stevens'). *Trinity Review*, VIII (May 1954), 12.

H 15
Kummings, David D. "The Invention of Contests and Harmonies." *The CEA Critic*, XXXI (November 1968), 7.

H 16
Lowell, Amy. *A Critical Fable*. Boston: Houghton, Mifflin, 1922, p. 27.

Reprinted in *The Complete Poetical Works of Amy Lowell*. Boston: Houghton Mifflin, 1955, p. 433.

H 17
MacLeish, Archibald. "Reasons for Music" ('For Wallace Stevens'). *Trinity Review*, VIII (May 1954), 9.

Reprinted in his *Songs for Eve*. Boston: Houghton Mifflin, 1954, pp. 57–58.

H 18
Magner, Gene. "Au Le Plus Grand Interpreteur Wallace Stevens." *Trinity Review*, VIII (May 1954), 32.

H 19
Morris, Herbert. "Mr. Stevens Out Into the Night." *Western Review*, XX (Winter 1956), 145–146.

H 20
Morse, Samuel French. "The Poet Who Lived with His Work" ('For Wallace Stevens'). *Saturday Review*, XXIX (August 11, 1956), 11.

H 21
Nathan, Leonard. "The Master of the Winter Landscape." In his *The Day the Perfect Speakers Left*. Middletown, Conn.: Wesleyan University Press, 1969, p. 50.

Reprinted in *WSN* (October 1969), p. 5.

H 22
Noll, Bink. "For Wallace Stevens." *Dartmouth College Library Bulletin*, n.s. IV (December 1961), 34.

H 23
Park, Herbert. "To the Poet." *Trinity Review*, VIII (May 1954), 34.

H 24
Reiss, James. "Homage to Stevens." *College English*, XXV (November 1964), 167.

Reprinted in *WSN* (April 1970), p. 11.

H 25
Roethke, Theodore. "A Rouse for Stevens." 7 *Arts*, no. 3 (1955), 117.

H 26
Salomon, I. L. "Hartford Poet (Essence of an Encounter)." *Trinity Review*, VIII (May 1954), 40.

H 27
Scott, Winfield Townley. "Conversation with Stevens." *Saturday Review*, LII (January 11, 1969), 104.

H 28
Searcy, David. *"J'Accuse* Wallace Stevens." *Southwest Review,*
LVI (Spring 1971), 125.

H 29
Thomas, R. S. "Wallace Stevens." In his *The Bread of Truth.*
London: R. Hart-Davis, 1963, pp. 25–26.

H 30
Updike, John. "An Imaginable Conference. Mr. Henry Green,
Industrialist, and Mr. Wallace Stevens, Vice-President of the
Hartford Accident & Indemnity Co., Meet in the Course of Busi-
ness." In his *The Carpentered Hen and Other Tame Creatures.*
New York: Harper, 1958, p. 25.

H 31
Wilbur, Richard. "Mind." *Trinity Review,* VIII (May 1954),
46.

I. Books About Stevens

This section contains books devoted entirely to Stevens, arranged chronologically.

I 1
O'Connor, William Van. *The Shaping Spirit: A Study of Wallace Stevens*. Chicago: Henry Regnery Co., 1950. 146 pp. $2.75.

Contains, pp. [141]–146, "Bibliography."

Reprinted: New York: Russell and Russell, 1964.

I 2
Morse, Samuel French. *Wallace Stevens: A Preliminary Check-list of His Published Writings: 1898–1954*. New Haven: Yale University Library, 1954. 66 pp. $2.50.

Published in connection with an exhibition held in honor of the poet's seventy-fifth birthday, October 2, 1954.

Revised and expanded: Morse, Samuel French; Bryer, Jackson R.; and Riddel, Joseph N. *Wallace Stevens Checklist and Bibliography of Stevens Criticism*. Denver: Alan Swallow, 1963. 98 pp. $3.50.

I 3
Pack, Robert. *Wallace Stevens — An Approach to His Poetry and Thought*. New Brunswick, N.J.: Rutgers University Press, 1958. 203 pp. $4.50.

I 4
Kermode, Frank. *Wallace Stevens*. Writers and Critics series. Edinburgh and London: Oliver and Boyd, 1960. 134 pp. 3s. 6d.

Contains, pp. [131]–134, "Bibliography."

I 5
Tindall, William York. *Wallace Stevens*. University of Minnesota Pamphlets on American Writers, no. 11. Minneapolis: University of Minnesota Press, 1961. 47 pp. 65¢.

Contains, pp. 46–47, "Selected Bibliography." See J 147.

16

Brown, Ashley, and Haller, Robert S., eds. *The Achievement of Wallace Stevens*. Philadelphia and New York: J. B. Lippincott Co., 1962. 287 pp. $5.00.

Contains, pp. 9–17, "Introduction" by Ashley Brown and Robert S. Haller; pp. 19–20, "From 'Mr. Yeats and the Poetic Drama'" by Harriet Monroe (comments on WS's *Three Travelers Watch a Sunrise*, first published in *Poetry*, 1920 [K 276]); pp. 21–28, "Well Moused Lion" by Marianne Moore (a review of the 1923 *Harmonium*, first published in *The Dial*, 1924 [K 279], and reprinted in William Wasserstrom, ed., *A Dial Miscellany* [see J 102]); pp. 29–34, "The Thirteenth Way" by Llewelyn Powys (first published in *The Dial*, 1924 [K 329]); pp. 35–40, "Wallace Stevens" by Paul Rosenfeld (reprinted from his *Men Seen — Twenty-Four Modern Authors* [J 132]); pp. 41–45, "The Dandyism of Wallace Stevens" by Gorham B. Munson (first published in *The Dial*, 1925 [K 294], and reprinted in his *Destinations — A Canvass of American Literature Since 1900* [J 106]); pp. 46–51, "The Harmonium of Wallace Stevens" by Morton Dauwen Zabel (a review of the 1931 *Harmonium*, first published in *Poetry*, 1931 [K 440]); pp. 52–80, "Examples of Wallace Stevens" by Richard P. Blackmur (first published in *The Hound and Horn*, 1932 [K 36], and reprinted in his *The Double Agent* [J 15], in his *Language as Gesture: Essays in Poetry* [see J 15], and in his *Form and Value in Modern Poetry* [see J 15]); pp. 81–96, "Wallace Stevens" by Howard Baker (first published as part of an omnibus review called "Wallace Stevens and Other Poets" in *The Southern Review*, 1935 [K 16]); pp. 97–113, "'The Comedian as the Letter C': Its Sense and Its Significance" by Hi Simons (first published in *The Southern Review*, 1940 [K 376]); pp. 114–122, "A Short View of Wallace Stevens" by Julian Symons (first published in *Life and Letters Today*, 1940 [K 401]); pp. 123–140, "Tradition and Modernity: Wallace Stevens" by J. V. Cunningham (first published in *Poetry*, 1949 [K 87], under the title "The Poetry of Wallace Stevens"; reprinted in Irving Howe, ed., *Modern Literary Criticism* [see J 35], under the title in Brown and Haller; and reprinted in J. V. Cunningham, *Tradition and the Poetic Structure* [J 35], under the title in *Poetry*); pp. 141–161, "The Poetry of Wallace Stevens" by Marius Bewley (first published in *Partisan Review*, 1940 [K 33], and reprinted in his *The Complex Fate* [J 12]); pp. 162–165, "'The World Imagined . . . Since We Are Poor'" by Marianne Moore (first published as a review of *The Auroras of Autumn* in *Poetry-New York*, 1951 [K 280]); pp. 166–178,

"The Auroras of Autumn" by Donald Davie (first published in
Perspective, 1954 [K 91]); pp. 179-192, "The Collected Poems
of Wallace Stevens" by Randall Jarrell (first published in *The
Yale Review*, 1955 [K 199], and reprinted in his *The Third Book
of Criticism* [see J 72]); pp. 193-210, "The Native Element"
by Samuel French Morse (first published in *The Kenyon Review*,
1958 [K 287]); pp. 211-231, "Wallace Stevens: The World as
Meditation" by Louis L. Martz (first published in *The Yale
Review*, 1958 [K 255], and reprinted in M. H. Abrams, ed.,
Literature and Belief: English Institute Essays, 1957 [J 87]
and in Borroff [I 7]); pp. 232-248, "Wallace Stevens: Some Relations Between Poetry and Painting" by Michel Benamou (first
published in *Comparative Literature*, 1959 [K 25]); pp. 249-
270, "Wallace Stevens: A Hero of Our Time" by Goeffrey Moore
(first published in Carl Bode, ed., *The Great Experiment in
American Literature* [J 98]); pp. 271-287, "For Further Reading: A Bibliography of Books and Articles about Wallace Stevens
and Selected Reviews of His Work." Cf. B 54.

I 7
Borroff, Marie, ed. *Wallace Stevens: A Collection of Critical
Essays*. A Spectrum Book: Twentieth Century Views, S-TC-33.
Englewood Cliffs, N.J.: Prentice-Hall, Inc., 1963. 181 pp. $3.95
clothbound; $1.95 paperbound.

Contains, pp. 1-23, "Introduction, Wallace Stevens: The World
and the Poet" by Marie Borroff; pp. 24-29, "Three Academic
Pieces: I" by Wallace Stevens (a reprint from *NA*, 1951, pp. 71-
82); pp. 30-42, "Walt Whitman and Wallace Stevens: Functions
of a 'Literatus'" by Joseph N. Riddel (first published in *The South
Atlantic Quarterly*, 1962 [K 349]); pp. 43-53, "The Genre of
Wallace Stevens" by Hi Simons (first published in *The Sewanee
Review*, 1945 [K 377]); pp. 54-70, "Metamorphosis in Wallace
Stevens" by Sister M. Bernetta Quinn (first published in *The
Sewanee Review*, 1952 [K 332], and reprinted in a different
form in her *The Metamorphic Tradition in Modern Poetry*
[J 118], under the title "Wallace Stevens: His 'Fluent Mundo'");
pp. 71-75, "A Central Poetry" by C. Roland Wagner (first pub-
lished as a review of *NA* in *The Hudson Review*, 1952 [K 425]);
pp. 76-95, "*Notes toward a Supreme Fiction: A Commentary*"
by Harold Bloom (first published here and reprinted in his *The
Ringers in the Tower. Studies in Romantic Tradition* [see
J 19]); pp. 96-110, "Wallace Stevens: The Image of the Rock"
by Ralph J. Mills, Jr. (first published in *Accent*, 1958 [K 267]);
pp. 111-132, "Wallace Stevens: The Life of the Imagination"

by Roy Harvey Pearce (first published in *Publications of the Modern Language Association,* 1951 [K 319], and reprinted in a different form as chapter 9 in his *The Continuity of American Poetry* [see J 116]); pp. 133–150, "Wallace Stevens: The World as Meditation" by Louis L. Martz (see Brown and Haller [I 6], pp. 211–231); pp. 151–160, "Wallace Stevens and the Image of Man" by Morton Dauwen Zabel (first published in *The Harvard Advocate,* 1940 [K 441], and reprinted in a different version as "Wallace Stevens" in Ray B. West, Jr., *Essays in Modern Literary Criticism* [J 170]); pp. 161–176, "The Realistic Oriole: A Study of Wallace Stevens" by Northrop Frye (first published in *The Hudson Review,* 1957 [K 152], and reprinted in his *Fables of Identity: Studies in Poetic Mythology* [J 53] and in John Hollander, ed., *Modern Poetry—Essays in Criticism* [see J 53]); p. 177, "Chronology of Important Dates"; p. 179, "Notes on the Editor and Authors"; p. 181, "Selected Bibliography."

I 8
Fuchs, Daniel. *The Comic Spirit of Wallace Stevens.* Durham, N.C.: Duke University Press, 1963. 201 pp. $6.00.

Contains, pp. [193]–196, "Selected Bibliography."

I 9
Morse, Samuel French; Bryer, Jackson R.; and Riddel, Joseph N. *Wallace Stevens Checklist and Bibliography of Stevens Criticism.* See I 2.

I 10
Walsh, Thomas F. *Concordance to the Poetry of Wallace Stevens.* University Park, Pa.: Pennsylvania State University Press, 1963. 341 pp. Double columns. $12.50.

I 11
Enck, John J. *Wallace Stevens: Images and Judgments.* With a Preface by Harry T. Moore. Crosscurrents; Modern Critiques series. Carbondale: Southern Illinois University Press, 1964. 258 pp. $4.50.

I 12
Wells, Henry W. *Introduction to Wallace Stevens.* Bloomington: Indiana University Press, 1964. 218 pp. $6.00.

I 13
Fowler, Austin. *The Poetry of Wallace Stevens.* Monarch Notes

and Study Guides, 790-6. New York: Monarch Press, 1965. 80 pp. $1.00 paperbound.

I 14

Galilea, Hernan. *El Mundo Impresionista de Wallace Stevens.* El Espejo de Papel. Caudernos de Centro de Investigaciones de Literatura Comparada Universidad de Chile. Santiago de Chile: Editorial Universitaria, 1965. 118 pp.

Cf. E 40.

I 15

Nassar, Eugene Paul. *Wallace Stevens: An Anatomy of Figuration.* Philadelphia: University of Pennsylvania Press, 1965. 229 pp. $5.00.

Contains, pp. 227-229, "Bibliography."

I 16

Pearce, Roy Harvey, and Miller, J. Hillis, eds. *The Act of the Mind: Essays on the Poetry of Wallace Stevens.* Baltimore: The Johns Hopkins Press, 1965. 287 pp. $5.95.

Contains, pp. 1-12, "Wallace Stevens: The Use of Poetry" by Bernard Heringman (first published in *ELH*, 1949 [K 184]); pp. 13-28, "This Invented World: Stevens' 'Notes Toward a Supreme Fiction' " by Frank Doggett (first published in *ELH*, 1961 [K 102]); pp. 29-57, "Wallace Stevens at Harvard: Some Origins of His Theme and Style" by Robert Buttel (first published in *ELH*, 1962 [K 69]); pp. 58-91, "Wallace Stevens, Bergson, Pater" by Samuel French Morse (first published in *ELH*, 1964 [K 289]); pp. 92-120, "Wallace Stevens and the Symbolist Imagination" by Michel Benamou (first published in *ELH*, 1964 [K 24]); pp. 121-142, "Wallace Stevens: The Last Lesson of the Master" by Roy Harvey Pearce (first published in *ELH*, 1964 [K 318], and reprinted in his *Historicism Once More* [see J 115]); pp. 143-162, "Wallace Stevens' Poetry of Being" by J. Hillis Miller (first published in *ELH*, 1964 [K 265], and reprinted in shorter form in his *Poets of Reality: Six Twentieth Century Writers* [see J 91] and in Jerome Mazzaro, ed., *Modern American Poetry. Essays in Criticism* [see J 91]); pp. 163-178, "The Qualified Assertions of Wallace Stevens" by Helen Hennessy Vendler (first published here); pp. 179-184, "On the Grammar of Wallace Stevens" by Mac Hammond (first published here); pp. 185-223, "The Climates of Wallace Stevens" by Richard A. Macksey (first published here); pp. 224-242, "Nuances of a Theme by Stevens" by Denis Donoghue (first published here); pp. 243–276, "The Contours of Stevens Criticism" by Joseph N. Riddel (first published in *ELH*, 1964 [K 340]); p. 277, "Notes on Contributors"; p. 278, "A Note on the Essays"; pp. 279–287, "Index." Cf. B 56.

I 17
Riddel, Joseph N. *The Clairvoyant Eye: The Poetry and Poetics of Wallace Stevens*. Baton Rouge: Louisiana State University Press, 1965. 308 pp. $7.50 clothbound; $2.25 paperbound.

Cf. B 55.

I 18
Doggett, Frank. *Stevens' Poetry of Thought*. Baltimore: The Johns Hopkins Press, 1966. 223 pp. $7.50 clothbound; $2.25 paperbound.

I 19
Stern, Herbert J. *Wallace Stevens: Art of Uncertainty*. Ann Arbor: University of Michigan Press, 1966. 206 pp. $5.95.

I 20
Buttel, Robert. *Wallace Stevens: The Making of Harmonium*. Princeton: Princeton University Press, 1967. 269 pp. $6.95.

Cf. B 58.

I 21
Sukenick, Ronald. *Wallace Stevens: Musing the Obscure. Readings, an Interpretation and a Guide to the Collected Poetry*. New York: New York University Press, 1967. 234 pp. $8.00 clothbound; $2.45 paperbound.

I 22
Baird, James. *The Dome and the Rock: Structure in the Poetry of Wallace Stevens*. Baltimore: The Johns Hopkins Press, 1968. 334 pp. $8.95.

Cf. B 59.

I 23
Burney, William. *Wallace Stevens*. Twayne's United States Authors Series, 127. New York: Twayne Publishers, Inc., 1968. 190 pp. $3.95.

I 24
Vendler, Helen Hennessy. *On Extended Wings: Wallace Ste-*

vens' Longer Poems. Cambridge, Mass.: Harvard University Press, 1969. 334 pp. $7.50.

I 25
Blessing, Richard Allen. *Wallace Stevens' "Whole Harmonium."* Syracuse, N.Y.: Syracuse University Press, 1970. 185 pp. $7.50.

I 26
Huguelet, Theodore L. *The Merrill Checklist of Wallace Stevens*. Charles E. Merrill Checklists. Columbus, Ohio: Charles E. Merrill Publishing Co., 1970. 35 pp. 75¢ paperbound.

I 27
Morse, Samuel French. *Wallace Stevens: Poetry as Life*. New York: Pegasus, 1970. 232 pp. $6.95.

Cf. B 60.

I 28
Brown, Merle E. *Wallace Stevens: The Poem as Act*. Detroit: Wayne State University Press, 1971. 219 pp. $8.50.

I 29
Kessler, Edward. *Images of Wallace Stevens*. New Brunswick, N.J.: Rutgers University Press, 1972. 267 pp. $10.00.

I 30
Litz, A. Walton. *Introspective Voyager: The Poetic Development of Wallace Stevens*. New York: Oxford University Press, 1972. 326 pp. $8.50.

I 31
McNamara, Peter L., ed. *Critics on Wallace Stevens*. Readings in Literary Criticism: 19. Coral Gables, Fla.: University of Miami Press, 1972. 128 pp. $3.95.

* * *

Note

Ford, William T., ed. *Wallace Stevens Newsletter*. Chicago and Evanston, Ill., 1969–.

A newsletter entirely devoted to WS.

J. Books Partially About Stevens and Articles in Books

J 1
Aiken, Conrad. *Scepticisms: Notes on Contemporary Poetry.*
New York: Alfred A. Knopf, Inc., 1919, pp. 62, 127, 129, 161,
162, 176, 238, 241, 267, 268, 292–293.

J 2
Alvarez, Alfred. "Wallace Stevens: Platonic Poetry." In his
*Stewards of Excellence: Studies in Modern English and Amer-
ican Poets.* New York: Charles Scribner's, 1958, pp. 124–139.

This book was also published in England under the title *The
Shaping Spirit: Studies in Modern English and American
Poets.* London: Chatto and Windus, 1958.

J 3
Arms, George, and Kuntz, Joseph M. *Poetry Explication: A
Checklist of Interpretation Since 1925 of British and Amer-
ican Poems Past and Present.* Contemporary Critics Series.
New York: Swallow Press and Morrow, 1950, pp. 141–146.

Revised edition, with additional entries, compiled solely by
Joseph M. Kuntz. Denver: Alan Swallow, 1962, pp. [242]–[246].

J 4
Arnavon, Cyrille. *Histoire Littéraire des États-Unis.* Paris:
Hachette, 1953, p. 372.

J 5
Baird, James. "Transvaluation in the Poetics of Wallace Ste-
vens." In *Studies in Honor of John C. Hodges and Alwin Thaler.*
Edited by Richard B. Davis and John L. Lievsay. Tennessee
Studies in English, special number. Knoxville: University of
Tennessee Press, 1961, pp. 163–173.

J 6
Baker, Howard. "Wallace Stevens." In Brown and Haller (I 6),
pp. 81–96.

First published as "Wallace Stevens and Other Poets" in *The Southern Review*, 1935 (K 16).

J 7
Balakian, Anna. *The Symbolist Movement. A Critical Appraisal.* Studies in Language and Literature. New York: Random House, 1967, passim.

J 8
Beach, Joseph Warren. *Obsessive Images: Symbolism in Poetry of the 1930's and 1940's.* Edited by William Van O'Connor. Minneapolis: University of Minnesota Press, 1960, pp. 95–96, 132–133, 209–213, 338–340, and passim.

J 9
Benamou, Michel. "Wallace Stevens and the Symbolist Imagination." In Pearce and Miller (I 16), pp. 92–120.

First published in *ELH*, 1964 (K 24).

J 10
Benamou, Michel. "Wallace Stevens: Some Relations Between Poetry and Painting." In Brown and Haller (I 6), pp. 232–248.

First published in *Comparative Literature*, 1959 (K 25).

J 11
Benziger, James. *Images of Eternity, Studies in the Poetry of Religious Vision from Wordsworth to T. S. Eliot.* Carbondale: Southern Illinois University Press, 1962, pp. 235–243 and passim.

J 12
Bewley, Marius. "The Poetry of Wallace Stevens." In his *The Complex Fate.* London: Chatto and Windus, 1952, pp. 171–192.

Reprinted in Brown and Haller (I 6), pp. 141–161. First published in *Partisan Review*, 1949 (K 33).

J 13
Bewley, Marius. "Wallace Stevens and Emerson." In his *Masks and Mirrors, Essays in Criticism.* New York: Atheneum, 1970, pp. 271–280.

J 14
Blackmur, Richard P. "An Abstraction Blooded." In his *Lan-*

guage as Gesture: Essays in Poetry. New York: Harcourt, Brace and Company, 1952, pp. 250–254.

Reprinted as "Wallace Stevens: An Abstraction Blooded." In his *Form and Value in Modern Poetry.* Garden City: N.Y., Doubleday, 1957, pp. 213–217. First published in *Partisan Review,* 1943 (K 34).

J 15
Blackmur, Richard P. "Examples of Wallace Stevens." In his *The Double Agent.* New York: Arrow Editions, 1935, pp. 68–102.

Reprinted in his *Language as Gesture: Essays in Poetry* (see J 14), pp. 221–249; in his *Form and Value in Modern Poetry* (see J 14), pp. 183–212; and in Brown and Haller (I 6), pp. 52–80. First published in *The Hound and Horn,* 1932 (K 36).

J 16
Blackmur, Richard P. "Poetry and Sensibility: Some Rules of Thumb." In his *Language as Gesture: Essays in Poetry* (see J 14), pp. 255–259.

Reprinted in his *Form and Value in Modern Poetry* (see J 14), with the title "On Herbert Read and Wallace Stevens," pp. 219–223. First published in *Poetry,* 1948 (K 37).

J 17
Block, Haskell M. "The Impact of French Symbolism on Modern American Poetry." In *The Shaken Realist: Essays in Modern Literature in Honor of Frederick J. Hoffman.* Edited by Melvin J. Friedman and John B. Vickery. Baton Rouge: Louisiana State University Press, 1970, pp. 165–217.

J 18
Bloom, Harold. "The Central Man: Emerson, Whitman, Wallace Stevens." In his *The Ringers in the Tower. Studies in Romantic Tradition.* Chicago and London: The University of Chicago Press, 1971, pp. 217–233.

First published in the *Massachusetts Review,* 1966 (K 40).

J 19
Bloom, Harold. *"Notes toward a Supreme Fiction:* A Commentary." In Borroff (I 7), pp. 76–95.

Reprinted in his *The Ringers in the Tower. Studies in Romantic Tradition* (see J 18), pp. 235–255.

J 20
Bogan, Louise. *Achievement in Modern Poetry, 1900–1950.*
Chicago: Henry Regnery Co., 1951, passim.

J 21
Bogan, Louise. "The Auroras of Autumn." In her *Selected Criticism*. New York: Noonday, 1955, pp. 363–364.

First published in *The New Yorker,* 1950 (K 41).

J 22
Bogan, Louise. "The Imaginative Direction of Our Time." In
EΣTI: *eec: E. E. Cummings and the Critics.* Edited by Stanley
Vergil Baum. East Lansing: Michigan State University Press,
1962, pp. 193–194.

J 23
Bradbury, Malcolm. "An Ironic Romantic: Three Readings of
Wallace Stevens." In *American Poetry.* Edited by John R. Brown,
Irvin Ehrenpreis, and Bernard Harris. New York: St. Martin's
Press, 1965, pp. 155–173.

J 24
Brown, John. *Panorama de la Littérature Contemporaine aux
États-Unis.* Paris: Gallimard, 1954, pp. 288–289.

J 25
Burke, Kenneth. *A Grammar of Motives.* New York: Prentice-
Hall, Inc., 1945, pp. 224–226.

J 26
Buttell, Robert. "Wallace Stevens at Harvard: Some Origins of
His Theme and Style." In Pearce and Miller (I 16), pp. 29–57.

First published in *ELH,* 1962 (K 69).

J 27
Cambon, Glauco. "Wallace Stevens: *Notes Toward a Supreme
Fiction.*" In his *The Inclusive Flame: Studies in American
Poetry.* Bloomington: Indiana University Press, 1963, pp.
79–119.

J 28
Cargill, Oscar. *Intellectual America: Ideas on the March.* New
York: Macmillan, 1941, pp. 255–258.

J 29
Carrier, Warren. "Wallace Stevens' 'Study of Images I.'" In

Reading Modern Poetry. Edited by Paul Engle and Warren Carrier. Glenview, Ill.: Scott, Foresman & Co., 1968, pp. 260–363.

First published as "Wallace Stevens' Pagan Vantage" in *Accent*, 1953 (K 74).

J 30
Chase, Stanley P. "Dionysus in Dismay." In *Humanism and America*. Edited by Norman Foerster. New York: Farrar & Rinehart, 1930, pp. 205–230.

J 31
Ciardi, John. "Dialogue with the Audience." In his *Dialogue with an Audience*. New York: J. B. Lippincott Co., 1963, pp. 22–37.

First published in *Saturday Review*, 1958 (K 79).

J 32
Coffman, Stanley K. *Imagism: A Chapter for the History of Modern Poetry*. Norman: University of Oklahoma Press, 1951, p. 223.

J 33
Cohen, John Michael. *Poetry of This Age: 1908–1958*. London: Hutchinson, 1960, pp. 215–218.

J 34
Cunliffe, Marcus. *The Literature of the United States*. Harmondsworth, Middlesex: Penguin Books, 1954, pp. 257–260.

J 35
Cunningham, J. V. "The Poetry of Wallace Stevens." In his *Tradition and Poetic Structure*. Denver: Alan Swallow, 1960, pp. 106–124.

Reprinted in revised form in Brown and Haller (I 6), pp. 123–140, under the title "Tradition and Modernity: Wallace Stevens." First published in *Poetry*, 1949 (K 87).

J 36
Davie, Donald. "The Auroras of Autumn." In Brown and Haller (I 6), pp. 166–178.

First published in *Perspective*, 1954 (K 91).

J 37
Dembo, L. S. "Wallace Stevens: Meta-men and Para-things." In his *Conceptions of Reality in Modern American Poetry.* Berkeley and Los Angeles: University of California Press, 1966, pp. 81–107.

J 38
Deutsch, Babette. "The Ghostly Member." In her *Poetry in Our Time.* New York: Henry Holt, 1952, pp. 241–253.

J 39
Doggett, Frank. "Our Number Is Her Nature." In *The Twenties: Poetry and Prose; 20 Critical Essays.* Edited by Richard E. Langford and William Edwards Taylor. Deland, Fla.: Everett-Edwards, 1966, pp. 36–41.

J 40
Doggett, Frank. "This Invented World: Stevens' 'Notes Toward a Supreme Fiction.'" In Pearce and Miller (I 16), pp. 13–28.

First published in *ELH,* 1961 (K 102).

J 41
Donoghue, Denis. "Nuances of a Theme by Stevens." In Pearce and Miller (I 16), pp. 224–242.

J 42
Donoghue, Denis. "On Notes Toward a Supreme Fiction." In his *The Ordinary Universe: Soundings in Modern Literature.* New York: Macmillan, 1968, pp. 267–290.

J 43
Donoghue, Denis. *The Third Voice: Modern British and American Verse Drama.* Princeton: Princeton University Press, 1959, pp. 193–194 and passim.

J 44
Donoghue, Denis. "Wallace Stevens." In his *Connoisseurs of Chaos: Ideas of Order in Modern American Poetry.* New York: Macmillan, 1965, pp. 190–215.

J 45
Drew, Elizabeth, in collaboration with John L. Sweeney. *Directions in Modern Poetry.* New York: W. W. Norton, 1940, pp. 58, 69, 72–75, 200, 201, 227, 257, 263.

J 46
Duncan, Joseph E. *The Revival of Metaphysical Poetry: The History of a Style, 1800 to the Present.* Minneapolis: University of Minnesota Press, 1959, pp. 182–186.

J 47
Eberhart, Richard. "Preface: Attitudes to War." In *War and the Poet: An Anthology of Poetry Expressing Man's Attitudes to War from Ancient Times to the Present.* Edited by Richard Eberhart and Selden Rodman. New York: Devin-Adair, 1945, pp. v–xv.

J 48
Ellmann, Richard. "Wallace Stevens' Ice-Cream." In *Aspects of Modern Poetry — Essays Presented to Howard Mumford Jones.* Edited by Richard M. Ludwig. Columbus: Ohio State University Press, 1963, pp. 203–222.

First published in *The Kenyon Review*, 1957 (K 121).

J 49
Feidelson, Charles, Jr. *Symbolism and American Literature.* Chicago: University of Chicago Press, 1953, p. 73.

J 50
Frankenberg, Lloyd. "Variations on Wallace Stevens." In his *Pleasure Dome — On Reading Modern Poetry.* Boston: Houghton Mifflin, 1949, pp. 197–267.

J 51
Fraser, G. S. "E. E. Cummings and Wallace Stevens: The Sensationalist and the Aesthete." In his *Vision and Rhetoric — Studies in Modern Poetry.* London: Faber & Faber Limited, 1959, pp. 125–134.

First published as "The Aesthete and the Sensationalist" in *Partisan Review*, 1955 (K 148).

J 52
Freedman, Ralph. "Wallace Stevens and Rainer Maria Rilke: Two Versions of a Poetic." In *The Poet as Critic.* Edited by Frederick P. W. McDowell. Evanston, Ill.: Northwestern University Press, 1967, pp. 60–80.

J 53
Frye, Northrop. "The Realistic Oriole: A Study of Wallace Ste-

vens." In his *Fables of Identity: Studies in Poetic Mythology*. New York: Harcourt, Brace, and World, 1963, pp. 238–255.

Reprinted in John Hollander, ed. *Modern Poetry—Essays in Criticism*. New York: Oxford University Press, 1968, pp. 267–284, and in Borroff (I 7), pp. 161–176. First published in *The Hudson Review*, 1957 (K 152).

J 54
Fuchs, Daniel. "Wallace Stevens and Santayana." In *Patterns of Commitment in American Literature*. Edited by Marston LaFrance. Toronto: University of Toronto Press, 1967, pp. 135–164.

J 55
Gilbert, Katharine. "Recent Poets on Man and His Place." In her *Aesthetic Studies: Architecture and Poetry*. Durham, N.C.: Duke University Press, 1952, pp. 49–81.

First published in *Philosophical Review*, 1947 (K 157).

J 56
Gregory, Horace, and Zaturenska, Marya. "The Harmonium of Wallace Stevens." In their *A History of American Poetry*. New York: Harcourt, Brace and Co., 1942, pp. 326–335.

J 57
Gross, Harvey S. "Hart Crane and Wallace Stevens." In his *Sound and Form in Modern Poetry: A Study of Prosody from Thomas Hardy to Robert Lowell*. Ann Arbor: University of Michigan Press, 1964, pp. 215–246.

J 58
Hamburger, Michael. *The Truth of Poetry. Tensions in Modern Poetry from Baudelaire to the 1960s*. London: Weidenfeld & Nicolson, 1969, pp. 28, 33–34, 37–38, 70, 85, 99, 102, 104–111, 113, 115, 128, 208, 234, 265.

J 59
Hammond, Mac. "On the Grammar of Wallace Stevens." In Pearce and Miller (I 16), pp. 179–184.

J 60
Heringman, Bernard. "Wallace Stevens: The Use of Poetry." In Pearce and Miller (I 16), pp. 1–12.

First published in *ELH*, 1949 (K 184).

J 61
Hillyer, Robert. *In Pursuit of Poetry*. New York: McGraw-Hill, 1960, pp. 197–200.

J 62
Hoffman, Frederick J. *Conrad Aiken*. New York: Twayne Publishers, Inc., 1962, pp. 96–97, 135–137, and passim.

J 63
Hoffman, Frederick J. *The Imagination's New Beginning*. Notre Dame: University of Notre Dame Press, 1967, passim.

J 64
Hoffman, Frederick J. "Mortality and Modern Literature." In *The Meaning of Death*. Edited by Herman Feifel. New York: McGraw-Hill, 1959, pp. 133–156.

J 65
Hoffman, Frederick J. *The Mortal No: Death and the Modern Imagination*. Princeton: Princeton University Press, 1964, passim.

J 66
Hoffman, Frederick J. *The Twenties*. New York: Viking Press, 1955, pp. 182–186 and passim.

J 67
Hopper, Stanley R. "Wallace Stevens: The Sundry Comforts of the Sun." In *Four Ways of Modern Poetry: Wallace Stevens, Robert Frost, Dylan Thomas, W. H. Auden*. Edited by Nathan A. Scott, Jr. Chime Paperbacks. Richmond, Va.: John Knox Press, 1965, pp. 13–31.

J 68
Howard, Leon. *Literature and the American Tradition*. Garden City, N.Y.: Doubleday, 1960, pp. 315–318.

J 69
Howe, Irving. "Another Way of Looking at the Blackbird." In *Identity and Anxiety: Survival of the Person in Mass Society*. Edited by Maurice R. Stein, Arthur J. Vidich, and David M. White. New York: Free Press, 1960, pp. 533–539.

Reprinted as "Wallace Stevens: Another Way of Looking at the Blackbird." In his *A World More Attractive: A View of Modern Literature and Politics*. New York: Horizon Press, 1963, pp. 158–167. First published in *The New Republic*, 1957 (K 193).

J 70
Hunter, Jim. "Wallace Stevens." In his *Modern Poets One.* London: Faber and Faber Limited, 1968, pp. 86–109.

J 71
Izzo, Carlo. *Storia della Letteratura Nord-Americana.* Milan: Nuova Accademia, 1957, pp. 569–571.

J 72
Jarrell, Randall. "The Collected Poems of Wallace Stevens." In Brown and Haller (I 6), pp. 179–192.

Reprinted in his *The Third Book of Criticism* (New York: Farrar, Straus & Giroux, 1969), pp. 55–73. First published in *The Yale Review,* 1955 (K 199).

J 73
Jarrell, Randall. "Reflections on Wallace Stevens." In his *Poetry and the Age.* New York: Alfred A. Knopf, Inc., 1953, pp. 133–148.

Reprinted in William Phillips and Philip Rahv, eds. *The New Partisan Reader, 1945–1953.* New York: Harcourt, Brace and Co., 1953, pp. 408–417. First published in *Partisan Review,* 1951 (K 201).

J 74
Jennings, Elizabeth. "Vision Without Belief – A Note on the Poetry of Wallace Stevens." In her *Every Changing Shape.* London: Andre Deutsch, 1961, pp. 201–212.

J 75
Johnson, Carol. *Reason's Double Agents.* Chapel Hill: University of North Carolina Press, 1964, pp. 33, 35–36.

J 76
Kermode, Frank. "Afterthoughts on Wallace Stevens." In his *Continuities.* New York: Random House, 1968, pp. 77–91.

J 77
Kermode, Frank. *Romantic Image.* London: Routledge & Kegan Paul, 1957, pp. 47–48, 153–154.

J 78
Kreymborg, Alfred. *Our Singing Strength: An Outline of American Poetry (1620–1930).* New York: Coward, McCann, 1929, pp. 500–504 and passim.

J 79
Kreymborg, Alfred. *Troubadour—An Autobiography*. New York: Liveright, 1925, passim.

J 80
Kunitz, Stanley J., and Haycraft, Howard, eds. *Twentieth Century Authors*. New York: H. W. Wilson, 1942, pp. 1344-1345.

First supplement, 1955, pp. 958-959.

J 81
Lensing, George S. "Wallace Stevens' Letters of Rock and Water." In *Essays in Honor of Esmond Linworth Marilla*. Edited by Thomas A. Kirby and William J. Olive. Baton Rouge: Louisiana State University Press, 1970, pp. 320-330.

J 82
Lentricchia, Frank. *The Gaiety of Language: An Essay on the Radical Poetics of W. B. Yeats and Wallace Stevens*. Perspectives in Criticism, 19. Berkeley and Los Angeles: University of California Press, 1968, pp. 119-192 and passim.

J 83
Levi, Albert William. "Three." In *The Hidden Harmony: Essays in Honor of Philip Wheelwright*. Edited by Oliver Johnson, David Harrah, Peter Fuss, and Theodore Guleserian. New York: Odyssey, 1966, pp. 73-91.

J 84
McGill, Arthur C. "Artificial Speech: Wallace Stevens." In his *The Celebration of Flesh—Poetry in Christian Life*. New York: Association Press, 1964, pp. 126-186.

J 85
Macksey, Richard A. "The Climates of Wallace Stevens." In Pearce and Miller (I 16), pp. 185-223.

J 86
Martz, Louis L. "Wallace Stevens." In his *Poem of the Mind. Essays on Poetry English and American*. New York: Oxford University Press, 1966, pp. 183-223.

J 87
Martz, Louis L. "Wallace Stevens: The World as Meditation." In *Literature and Belief: English Institute Essays, 1957.*

Edited by M. H. Abrams. New York: Columbia University Press, 1958, pp. 139-165.

Reprinted in Brown and Haller (I 6), pp. 211-231, and in Borroff (I 7), pp. 133-150. First published in *The Yale Review*, 1958 (K 255).

J 88
Martz, Louis L. "The World of Wallace Stevens." In *Modern American Poetry: Focus Five*. Edited by B. Rajan. London: Dennis Dobson Ltd, 1950, pp. 94-109.

J 89
Matthiessen, Francis O. "Late Summer Wine: Wallace Stevens." In his *The Responsibilities of the Critic*. Selected by John Rackliffe. New York: Oxford University Press, 1952, pp. 71-74.

First published as "Wallace Stevens at 67" in the *New York Times Book Review*, 1947 (K 257).

J 90
Miles, Josephine. *The Continuity of Poetic Language*. Berkeley and Los Angeles: University of California Press, 1951, pp. 393, 403-409, and passim.

J 91
Miller, J. Hillis. "Wallace Stevens' Poetry of Being." In Pearce and Miller (I 16), pp. 143-162.

Reprinted in shorter form as "Wallace Stevens" in his *Poets of Reality: Six Twentieth Century Writers*. Cambridge, Mass.: Harvard University Press, Belknap Press, 1965, pp. 217-284. Reprinted in Jerome Mazzaro, ed. *Modern American Poetry. Essays in Criticism*. New York: David McKay, 1970, pp. 93-115. First published in *ELH*, 1964 (K 265).

J 92
Millett, Fred B. *Contemporary American Authors, A Critical Survey and 219 Bibliographies*. New York: Harcourt, Brace and Company, 1940, pp. 597-598.

J 93
Mills, Ralph J., Jr. *Contemporary American Poetry*. New York: Random House, 1965, passim.

J 94
Mills, Ralph J., Jr. "Wallace Stevens: The Image of the Rock." In Borroff (I 7), pp. 96-110.

First published in *Accent*, 1958 (K 267).

J 95
Monroe, Harriet. "From 'Mr. Yeats and the Poetic Drama.'" In Brown and Haller (I 6), pp. 19-20.

First published in *Poetry*, 1920 (K 276).

J 96
Monroe, Harriet. *A Poet's Life*. New York: Macmillan, 1938, pp. 342-343, 390-391, and passim.

J 97
Monroe, Harriet. "Wallace Stevens." In her *Poets and Their Art*. New York: Macmillan, 1926, pp. 39-45.

First published as "A Cavalier of Beauty" in *Poetry*, 1924 (K 274).

J 98
Moore, Geoffrey. "Wallace Stevens: A Hero of Our Time." In *The Great Experiment in American Literature*. Edited by Carl Bode. New York: Praeger, 1961, pp. 103-132.

Reprinted in Brown and Haller (I 6), pp. 249-270.

J 99
Moore, Marianne. "A Bold Virtuoso." In her *Predilections*. New York: Viking Press, 1955, pp. 42-46.

J 100
Moore, Marianne. "The Poetry of Wallace Stevens." In *Literary Opinion in America*. Edited by Morton D. Zabel. New York: Harper, 1937, pp. 233-236.

Reprinted as "Conjuries That Endure" in her *Predilections* (J 99), pp. 32-36. First published as "Unanimity and Fortitude" in *Poetry*, 1937 (K 278).

J 101
Moore, Marianne. "There Is a War That Never Ends." In her *Predilections* (J 99), pp. 36-41.

First published in *The Kenyon Review*, 1943 (K 277).

J 102
Moore, Marianne. "Well Moused Lion." In Brown and Haller (I 6), pp. 21-28.

First published in *The Dial,* 1924 (K 279), and reprinted in William Wasserstrom, ed. *A Dial Miscellany.* Syracuse: Syracuse University Press, 1963, pp. 196–203.

J 103
Moore, Marianne. "'The World Imagined . . . Since We Are Poor.'" In Brown and Haller (I 6), pp. 162–165.

First published in *Poetry – New York,* 1951 (K 280).

J 104
Morse, Samuel French. "The Native Element." In Brown and Haller (I 6), pp. 193–210.

First published in *The Kenyon Review,* 1958 (K 287).

J 105
Morse, Samuel French. "Wallace Stevens, Bergson, Pater." In Pearce and Miller (I 16), pp. 58–91.

First published in *ELH,* 1964 (K 289).

J 106
Munson, Gorham. "The Dandyism of Wallace Stevens." In his *Destinations – A Canvass of American Literature Since 1900.* New York: J. H. Sears, 1928, pp. 75–89.

Reprinted in Brown and Haller (I 6), pp. 41–45. First published in *The Dial,* 1925 (K 294).

J 107
Nassar, Eugene P. "Wallace Stevens' 'Sunday Morning.'" In his *The Rape of Cinderella: Essays in Literary Continuity.* Bloomington: Indiana University Press, 1970, pp. 46–57.

J 108
Nemerov, Howard. "The Poetry of Wallace Stevens." In his *Poetry and Fiction: Essays.* New Brunswick, N.J.; Rutgers University Press, 1963, pp. 75–85.

First published in *The Sewanee Review,* 1957 (K 302).

J 109
Nilsen, Helge Norman. "The Quest for Reality. A Study in the Poetry of Wallace Stevens." In Sigmund Skard, ed., *Americana Norvegica: Norwegian Contributions to American Studies.* Vol. II. Philadelphia: University of Pennsylvania Press; Oslo:

Gyldendal Norsk Forlag; London: Oxford University Press, 1968, pp. 219–298.

J 110
Noon, William T. "Wallace Stevens." In his *Poetry and Prayer*. New Brunswick, N.J.: Rutgers University Press, 1967, pp. 157–192.

J 111
O'Connor, William Van. *Sense and Sensibility in Modern Poetry*. Chicago: University of Chicago Press, 1948, pp. 10, 40, 76, 78, 83–84, 115–116, 124, 129, 130, 138, 149–150, 167, 233, 259.

J 112
O'Connor, William Van. "Wallace Stevens and Imagined Reality." In his *The Grotesque: An American Genre and Other Essays*. Carbondale: Southern Illinois University Press, 1962, pp. 128–136.

First published in *Western Review*, 1948 (K 306).

J 113
Pearce, Roy Harvey. "The Modern Age (3): Wallace Stevens and the Ultimate Poem." In his *The Continuity of American Poetry*. Princeton: Princeton University Press, 1961, pp. 376–419 and passim.

J 114
Pearce, Roy Harvey. "Stevens Posthumous." In *International Literary Annual*, no. 2. Edited by John Wain. London: John Calder, 1959, pp. 65–89.

J 115
Pearce, Roy Harvey. "Wallace Stevens: The Last Lesson of the Master." In Pearce and Miller (I 16), pp. 121–142.

Reprinted in his *Historicism Once More*. Princeton: Princeton University Press, 1969, pp. 261–293. First published in *ELH*, 1964 (K 318).

J 116
Pearce, Roy Harvey. "Wallace Stevens: The Life of the Imagination." In Borroff (I 7), pp. 111–132.

First published in *PMLA*, 1951 (K 319), and printed in a different form as chapter 9 in his *The Continuity of American Poetry* (Princeton: Princeton University Press, 1961).

J 117
Powys, Llewelyn. "The Thirteenth Way." In Brown and Haller
(I 6), pp. 29–34.

First published in *The Dial,* 1924 (K 329).

J 118
Quinn, Sister M. Bernetta. "Wallace Stevens: His 'Fluent
Mundo.'" In her *The Metamorphic Tradition in Modern Poetry.*
New Brunswick, N.J.: Rutgers University Press, 1955, pp. 49–88.

Reprinted in Borroff (I 7), pp. 54–70. First published as "Metamorphosis in Wallace Stevens" in *The Sewanee Review,* 1952
(K 332).

J 119
Raghavacharyulu, D. V. K. "The Well-Wrought Jar of Wallace
Stevens." In *The Unpunctual Pen.* Hyderabad: Maruthi Book
Depot, 1968, pp. 29–32.

J 120
Raiziss, Sona. "Wallace Stevens." In her *La Poésie Américaine
"Moderniste" 1910–1940.* Paris: Mercure de France, 1948, pp.
96–100.

J 121
Ramsey, Paul. "The Longer Kinds." In his *The Lively and the
Just: An Argument for Propriety.* University, Ala.: University
of Alabama Press, 1962, pp. 104–117.

J 122
Ransom, John Crowe. *The World's Body.* New York: Charles
Scribner's, 1938, pp. 55–75.

J 123
Richardson, Kenneth, ed. *Twentieth Century Writing. A
Reader's Guide to Contemporary Literature.* London and New
York: Newnes Books, 1969, pp. 588–590.

J 124
Riddel, Joseph N. "The Contours of Stevens Criticism." In
Pearce and Miller (I 16), pp. 243–276.

First published in *ELH,* 1964 (K 340).

J 125
Riddel, Joseph N. "Stevens on Imagination – the Point of De-

parture." In *The Quest for Imagination*. Edited by O. B. Hardison, Jr. Cleveland: Press of Case Western Reserve University, 1971, pp. 55–85.

J 126
Riddel, Joseph N. "Wallace Stevens." In *Fifteen Modern American Authors. A Survey of Research and Criticism*. Edited by Jackson R. Bryer. Durham, N.C.: Duke University Press, 1969, pp. 389–423.

J 127
Riddel, Joseph N. "Walt Whitman and Wallace Stevens: Functions of a 'Literatus.'" In Borroff (I 7), pp. 30–42.

First published in *The South Atlantic Quarterly*, 1962 (K 349).

J 128
Riding, Laura, and Graves, Robert. *A Survey of Modernist Poetry*. London: William Heinemann, 1927, pp. 166, 216, 217, 289.

J 129
Rizzardi, Alfredo. "Creazione e Distruzione del Mondo Fantastico di Wallace Stevens." In his *La Condizione Americana*. Rome: Capelli, 1959, pp. 71–83.

First published in *Nuova Corrente*, 1955 (K 354).

J 130
Rosati, Salvatore. *L'Ombra dei Padri — Studi sulla Letteratura Americana*. Rome: Edizioni di Storia e Letteratura, 1958, pp. 165–169.

J 131
Rosati, Salvatore. *Storia della Letteratura Americana*. Torino: Radio Italiana, 1956, pp. 216–217.

J 132
Rosenfeld, Paul. "Wallace Stevens." In his *Men Seen — Twenty-Four Modern Authors*. New York: The Dial Press, 1925, pp. 151–162.

Reprinted in Brown and Haller (I 6), pp. 35–40.

J 133
Rosenthal, M. L. *The Modern Poets — A Critical Introduction*. New York: Oxford University Press, 1960, pp. 121–131.

J 134
Sheehan, Donald. "The Ultimate Plato: A Reading of Wallace Stevens' *Notes Toward a Supreme Fiction.*" In *The Forties: Fiction, Poetry, Drama.* Edited by Warren French. Deland, Fla.: Everett-Edwards, 1969, pp. 165–177.

J 135
Sheehan, Donald. "Wallace Stevens in the 30s: Gaudy Bosh and the Gesture's Whim." In *The Thirties: Fiction, Poetry, Drama.* Edited by Warren French. Deland, Fla.: Everett-Edwards, 1967, pp. 149–157.

J 136
Sheehan, Donald. "The Whole of Harmonium: Poetic Technique in Wallace Stevens." In *The Fifties: Fiction, Poetry, Drama.* Edited by Warren French. Deland, Fla.: Everett-Edwards, Inc., 1970, pp. 175–186.

J 137
Simons, Hi. "'The Comedian as the Letter C': Its Sense and Its Significance." In Brown and Haller (I 6), pp. 97–113.

First published in *The Southern Review,* 1940 (K 376).

J 138
Simons, Hi. "The Genre of Wallace Stevens." In Borroff (I 7), pp. 43–53.

First published in *The Sewanee Review,* 1945 (K 377).

J 139
Southworth, James G. "Wallace Stevens." In his *Some Modern American Poets.* Oxford: Basil Blackwell, 1950, pp. 88–106.

J 140
Spiller, Robert E., et al., eds. *Literary History of the United States.* 3d rev. ed. New York and London: Macmillan, 1963; vol. 1: pp. 355, 1120, 1174, 1354–1355, 1410, 1411, 1413, 1471, 1479; vol. 2: pp. 732–734; Bibliography Supplement: pp. 193–195.

J 141
Symons, Julian. "A Short View of Wallace Stevens." In Brown and Haller (I 6), pp. 114–122.

First published in *Life and Letters Today,* 1940 (K 401).

J 142
Tate, Allen. *Sixty American Poets, 1896–1944*. Rev. ed. Washington, D.C.: Library of Congress, 1954, pp. 127–129.

J 143
Taupin, René. *L'Influence du Symbolisme Francais sur la Poésie Américaine*. Paris: H. Champion, 1929, pp. 276–277 and passim.

J 144
Taylor, Walter F. *The Story of American Letters*. Chicago: Henry Regnery Co., 1956, pp. 427–430.

J 145
Thorp, Willard. *American Writing in the Twentieth Century*. Cambridge, Mass.: Harvard University Press, 1960, pp. 225–232 and passim.

J 146
Tindall, William York. *The Literary Symbol*. New York: Columbia University Press, 1955, pp. 214–217, 258–261, and passim.

J 147
Tindall, William York. "Wallace Stevens." In *Seven Modern American Poets: An Introduction*. Edited by Leonard Unger. Minneapolis: University of Minnesota Press, 1967, pp. 45–82.

This is a reprint of Tindall's pamphlet on WS; see I 5.

J 148
Unger, Leonard, and O'Connor, William Van. "Wallace Stevens." In their *Poems for Study*. New York: Rinehart, 1953, pp. 604–617.

J 149
Untermeyer, Louis. *American Poetry Since 1900*. New York: Henry Holt, 1923, pp. 323–328 and passim.

J 150
Untermeyer, Louis. *The New Era in American Poetry*. New York: Henry Holt, 1919, pp. 317–318.

J 151
Untermeyer, Louis. "Wallace Stevens." In his *Lives of the Poets*. New York: Simon and Schuster, 1959, pp. 696–699.

J 152
Untermeyer, Louis. "Wallace Stevens." In his *Modern American Poetry*. New York: Harcourt, Brace, 1950, pp. 258–260. Revised and enlarged edition, 1962, pp. 237–253.

J 153
Vendler, Helen Hennessy. "The Qualified Assertions of Wallace Stevens." In Pearce and Miller (I 16), pp. 163–178.

J 154
Waggoner, Hyatt. "The Idea of Order: Fictive Music – Wallace Stevens." In his *American Poets from the Puritans to the Present*. Boston: Houghton Mifflin, 1968, pp. 428–442.

J 155
Wagner, C. Roland. "A Central Poetry." In Borroff (I 7), pp. 71–75.

First published in *The Hudson Review*, 1952 (K 425).

J 156
Wahl, Jean. *Poésie, Pensée, Perception*. Paris: Calmann-Lévy, 1948, p. 25.

J 157
Watts, Harold H. "Wallace Stevens and the Rock of Summer." In his *Hound and Quarry*. London: Routledge & Kegan Paul, 1953, pp. 41–61.

First published in *The Kenyon Review*, 1952 (K 430).

J 158
Whitaker, Thomas R. "Of Speaking Humanly." In *The Philosopher Critic*. Edited by Robert Scholes. Monograph series, no. 10. Tulsa, Okla.: University of Tulsa, 1970, pp. 67–88.

J 159
Whitbread, Thomas B. "The Poet-Readers of Wallace Stevens." In *In Defense of Reading*. Edited by Reuben A. Brower and Richard Poirier. New York: Dutton, 1962, pp. 94–109.

J 160
Wilder, Amos Niven. *Modern Poetry and the Christian Tradition: A Study in the Relation of Christianity to Culture*. New York: Charles Scribner's, 1952, pp. 239–242.

J 161
Wilder, Amos Niven. "Protestant Orientation in Contemporary
Literature." In *Spiritual Problems in Contemporary Literature.* Edited by Stanley R. Hopper. New York, Harper, 1957,
pp. 243-259.

J 162
Williams, William Carlos. *Kora in Hell.* Boston: The Four Seas
Company, 1920, pp. 16-18.

J 163
Williams, William Carlos. *The Selected Letters of William
Carlos Williams.* New York: McDowell, Obolensky, 1957,
passim.

J 164
Wilson, Edmund. "Wallace Stevens and E. E. Cummings." In
his *The Shores of Light.* New York: Farrar, Straus and Young,
1952, pp. 49-56.

J 165
Winters, Yvor. "Poetic Styles, Old and New." In *Four Poets on
Poetry.* Edited by Don Cameron Allen. Baltimore: The Johns
Hopkins University Press, 1959, pp. 44-75.

J 166
Winters, Yvor. "Postscript to 'Wallace Stevens or the Hedonist's
Progress.'" In his *On Modern Poets.* New York: Meriden Books,
1959, pp. 34-35.

Reprinted in his *In Defense of Reason.* Denver: Alan Swallow,
1960, p. 459. See J 168.

J 167
Winters, Yvor. *Primitivism and Decadence — A Study of American Experimental Poetry.* New York: Arrow Editions. 1937,
pp. 57-58, 82, 84-85, 94-95, 117-118.

J 168
Winters, Yvor. "Wallace Stevens or the Hedonist's Progress."
In his *The Anatomy of Nonsense.* Norfolk, Conn.: New Direc-
tions, 1943, pp. 88-119.

Reprinted in his *In Defense of Reason.* New York: Swallow
Press and William Morrow, 1947, and Denver: Alan Swallow,

1960, pp. 431–459. Also reprinted in his *On Modern Poets*. New York: Meriden Books, 1959, pp. 11–34.

J 169
Zabel, Morton Dauwen. "The Harmonium of Wallace Stevens." In Brown and Haller (I 6), pp. 46–51.

First published in *Poetry,* 1931 (K 440).

J 170
Zabel, Morton Dauwen. "Wallace Stevens." In *Essays in Modern Literary Criticism*. Edited by Ray B. West, Jr. New York: Rinehart, 1952, pp. 411–417.

First published as "Wallace Stevens and the Image of Man" in *The Harvard Advocate,* 1940 (K 441), and reprinted in Borroff (I 7), pp. 151–160. The West version is different from the other two.

K. Articles About Stevens in Periodicals

This section lists, alphabetically by author, articles about Stevens in periodicals and newspapers. Reviews of more than average substance are found here as well as in Section L, "Book Reviews."

K 1

Abel, Lionel. "In the Sacred Park." *Partisan Review,* XXV (Winter 1958), 86–98.

K 2

Ackerman, Harold C. "Notes Toward an Explication of 'Sea Surface Full of Clouds.'" *Concerning Poetry,* II (Spring 1969), 73–78.

K 3

Ackerman, R. D. "Stevens' 'Arcades of Philadelphia the Past.'" *The Explicator,* XXIV (May 1966), item 80.

K 4

Adams, Richard P. "'The Comedian as the Letter C': A Somewhat Literal Reading." *Tulane Studies in English,* XVIII (1970), 95–114.

K 5

Aiken, Conrad. Untitled statement. *Trinity Review,* VIII (May 1954), 16.

K 6

Amacher, Richard E. "Stevens' 'To the One of Fictive Music.'" *The Explicator,* XI (April 1953), item 43.

K 7

Anonymous. "Chicago Poets and Poetry." *Minaret,* I (February 1916), 26.

K 8

Anonymous. "The Laureate of Hartford." *Business Week,* no. 1075 (April 8, 1950), 94.

K 9

Anonymous. "The Laurels." *Time,* LV (April 10, 1950), 36.

K 10
Anonymous. "La Place de Wallace Stevens dans la Poésie Américaine." *Critique*, XX (Paris, October 1964), 836–850.

K 11
Anonymous. "The Poetry of Wallace Stevens." *Times Literary
Supplement,* June 19, 1953, p. 396.

Review article of *Selected Poems*, 1953, partially reprinted in
Trinity Review, VIII (May 1954), 46–48.

K 12
Anonymous. "Stevens' 'Anecdote of the Jar.'" *The Explicator,*
III (November 1944), item 16.

K 13
Anonymous. "A Supplementing List of Items in the Wallace
Stevens Collection at Dartmouth College." *Dartmouth College
Library Bulletin*, n.s. IV (December 1961), 67–71.

K 14
Anonymous. "The Vice President of Shapes." *Time*, LXVI
(August 15, 1955), 12.

K 15
Baker, Howard. "Add This to Rhetoric." *The Harvard Advocate*,
CXXVII (December 1940), 16–18.

K 16
Baker, Howard. "Wallace Stevens and Other Poets." *The Southern Review,* I (Autumn 1935), 373–396.

See I 6.

K 17
Baym, Max I. "Three Moths and a Candle: A Study of the Impact
of Pascal on Walter Pater, Henry Adams and Wallace Stevens."
Comparative Literature: Proceedings of the Second Congress,
II (University of North Carolina, 1959), 336–348.

K 18
Benamou, Michel. "Beyond Emerald or Amethyst — Wallace
Stevens and the French Tradition." *Dartmouth College Library
Bulletin,* n.s. IV (December 1961), 60–66.

K 19
Benamou, Michel. "Jules Laforgue and Wallace Stevens." *Romanic Review*, L (April 1959), 107-117.

K 20
Benamou, Michel. "Le Prétendu 'Symbolisme' de Wallace Stevens." *Critique*, XVII (Paris, December 1961), 1029-1045.

K 21
Benamou, Michel. "The Structures of Wallace Stevens' Imagination." *Mundus Artium*, I (Winter 1967), 73-84.

K 22
Benamou, Michel. "Le Thème du Héros dans la Poésie de Wallace Stevens." *Études Anglaises*, XII (July–September 1959), 222-230.

K 23
Benamou, Michel. "Wallace Stevens and Apollinaire." *Comparative Literature*, XX (Fall 1968), 289-300.

K 24
Benamou, Michel. "Wallace Stevens and the Symbolist Imagination." *ELH*, XXXI (March 1964), 35-63.

See I 16.

K 25
Benamou, Michel. "Wallace Stevens: Some Relations Between Poetry and Painting." *Comparative Literature*, XI (Winter 1959), 47-60.

See I 6.

K 26
Benét, William Rose. "The Phoenix Nest." *Saturday Review of Literature*, XV (January 16, 1937), 18.

Review article of *Owl's Clover*.

K 27
Bennett, Joseph. "Five Books, Four Poets." *The Hudson Review*, IV (Spring 1951), 134-137.

Contains review of *The Auroras of Autumn*.

K 28
Berger, Arthur. *"Ideas of Order."* *Trinity Review*, VIII (May 1954), 17.

K 29
Betar, George. "Stevens' 'Earthy Anecdote.'" *The Explicator*, XXII (February 1964), item 43.

K 30
Bevis, William W. "The Arrangement of *Harmonium*." *ELH*, XXXVII (September 1970), 456–473.

K 31
Bevis, William W. "Metaphor in Wallace Stevens." *Shenandoah*, XV (Winter 1964), 35–48.

K 32
Bewley, Marius. "The Poetry of Wallace Stevens." *Commonweal*, LXII (September 23, 1955), 617–622.

K 33
Bewley, Marius. "The Poetry of Wallace Stevens." *Partisan Review*, XVI, (September 1949), 895–915.

See I 6.

K 34
Blackmur, Richard P. "An Abstraction Blooded." *Partisan Review*, X (May–June 1943), 297–301.

Contains reviews of *Parts of a World* and *Notes Toward a Supreme Fiction*. See J 14.

K 35
Blackmur, Richard P. "The Composition in Nine Poets." *The Southern Review*, II (Winter 1937), 572–576.

Contains review of *Ideas of Order*.

K 36
Blackmur, Richard P. "Examples of Wallace Stevens." *The Hound and Horn*, V (January–March 1932), 223–255.

See I 6.

K 37
Blackmur, Richard P. "Poetry and Sensibility: Some Rules of Thumb." *Poetry*, LXXI (February 1948), 271–276.

Contains review of *Transport to Summer*. See J 16.

K 38
Blackmur, Richard P. "The Substance That Prevails." *The Kenyon Review*, XVII (Winter 1955), 94–110.

K 39
Blake, Howard. "Thoughts on Modern Poetry." *The Sewanee Review*, XLIII (Spring 1935), 187–196.

K 40
Bloom, Harold. "The Central Man: Emerson, Whitman, Wallace Stevens." *Massachusetts Review*, VII (Winter 1966), 23–42.

See J 18.

K 41
Bogan, Louise. "The Auroras of Autumn." *The New Yorker*, XXVI (October 28, 1950), 129–130.

See J 21.

K 42
Bogan, Louise. "*Harmonium* and the American Scene." *Trinity Review*, VIII (May 1954), 18–20.

K 43
Bolt, Sydney. "The Impropriety of Wallace Stevens." *Delta*, no. 37 (Autumn 1965), 9–14.

K 44
Bosquet, Alain. "Deux Poètes Philosophes: Wallace Stevens et Conrad Aiken." *La Table Ronde*, no. 105 (September 1956), 129–131.

K 45
Bosquet, Alain. "Tendances Actuelles de la Poésie Américaine." *L'Age Nouveau*, no. 96 (March 1956), 66–70.

K 46
Bosquet, Alain. "Wallace Stevens (1879–1955)." *Nouvelle Revue Francaise*, III (October 1, 1955), 777–779.

K 47
Botsford, Keith. *"Esthétique du Mal* by Wallace Stevens." *The Yale Poetry Review,* I (Spring 1946), 34–37.

Contains review of *Esthétique du Mal.*

K 48
Bradbury, Malcolm, and Cook, F. W. *"Whose Hoo?* A Reading of Wallace Stevens' 'Bantams in Pine Woods.'" *British Association for American Studies Bulletin,* no. 4 (August 1962), 36–41.

K 49
Bradley, Ardyth. "Wallace Stevens' Decorations." *Twentieth Century Literature,* VII (October 1961), 114–117.

K 50
Breit, Harvey. "Poet's Poet." *New York Times Book Review,* August 14, 1955, p. 8.

K 51
Brinnin, John Malcolm. "Plato, Phoebus and the Man from Hartford." *Voices,* no. 121 (Spring 1945), 30–37.

K 52
Brooks, Cleanth. "Poetry since *The Waste Land." The Southern Review,* n.s. I (Summer 1965), 487–500.

K 53
Brooks, Cleanth. "Wallace Stevens: An Introduction." *McNeese Review,* XIV (1963), 3–13.

K 54
Brooks, Cleanth. Untitled statement. *The Harvard Advocate,* CXXVII (December 1940), 29–30.

K 55
Brown, Merle E. "Concordia Discors in the Poetry of Wallace Stevens." *American Literature,* XXXIV (May 1962), 246–269.

K 56
Brown, Merle E. "A Critical Performance of 'Asides on the Oboe.'" *Journal of Aesthetics and Art Criticism,* XXIX (Fall 1970), 121–128.

K 57
Browne, Robert M. "Grammar and Rhetoric in Criticism." *Texas*

Studies in Literature and Language, III (Spring 1961), 144–157.

K 58
Bruns, Gerald L. "Poetry as Reality: The Orpheus Myth and Its Modern Counterparts." *ELH,* XXXVII (June 1970), 263–286.

K 59
Bryer, Jackson R., and Riddel, Joseph N. "A Checklist of Stevens Criticism." *Twentieth Century Literature,* VIII (October 1962–January 1963), 124–142.

K 60
Buchwald, Emilie. "Wallace Stevens: The Delicatest Eye of the Mind." *American Quarterly,* XIV (Summer 1962), 185–196.

K 61
Buddingh', C. "Wallace Stevens." *Tirade,* VIII (Amsterdam, 1964), 258–266.

K 62
Buhr, Marjorie. "The Impossible Possible Philosopher's Man: Wallace Stevens." *Carrell,* VI (June 1965), 7–13.

K 63
Buhr, Marjorie. "When Half-Gods Go: Stevens' Spiritual Odyssey." *WSN,* I (April 1970), [9]–11.

K 64
Burckhardt, Sigurd, and Pearce, Roy Harvey. "Poetry, Language and the Condition of Modern Man." *The Centennial Review of Arts and Sciences,* IV (Winter 1960), 1–31.

K 65
Burns, Charles R. "The Two Worlds of Wallace Stevens." *Trace,* LI (Winter 1965), 295–296, 336–338.

K 66
Burnshaw, Stanley. "Turmoil in the Middle Ground." *New Masses,* XVII (October 1, 1935), 41–42.

Contains review of *Ideas of Order.*

K 67
Burnshaw, Stanley. "Wallace Stevens and the Statue." *The Sewanee Review,* LXIX, (Summer 1961), 355–366.

K 68
Buttel, Robert W. "Stevens' 'Two Figures in Dense Violet Light.'"
The Explicator, IX (May 1951), item 45.

K 69
Buttel, Robert W. "Wallace Stevens at Harvard: Some Origins
of His Theme and Style." *ELH,* XXIX (March 1962), 90–119.

See I 16.

K 70
Cambon, Glauco. "Le 'Notes toward a Supreme Fiction' di
Wallace Stevens." *Studi Americani,* I (Rome, 1955), 205–233.

K 71
Cambon, Glauco. "Nothingness as Catalyst: An Analysis of Three
Poems by Ungaretti, Rilke and Stevens." *Comparative Litera-
ture Studies* (special advance issue), (1963), 91–99.

K 72
Cambon, Glauco. "Wallace Stevens Acrobata Interiore." *La Fiera
Letteraria,* (Rome, June 13, 1954), 4–6.

K 73
Campo, Michael. "Mattino Domenicale." *Trinity Review,* VIII
(May 1954), 21–22.

K 74
Carrier, Warren. "Wallace Stevens' Pagan Vantage." *Accent,*
XIII (Summer 1953), 165–168.

See J 29.

K 75
Carruth, Hayden. "Ideality and Metaphor." *Poetry,* LXXII (August 1948), 270–273.

K 76
Carruth, Hayden. "Without the Inventions of Sorrow." *Poetry,*
LXXXV (February 1955), 288–293.

Review article of *CP.*

K 77
Cavitch, David. "Stevens' 'The Man With the Blue Guitar.'"
The Explicator, XXVII (December 1968), item 30.

K 78
Cecil, C. D. "An Audience for Wallace Stevens." *Essays in Criticism,* XV (April 1965), 193-206.

K 79
Ciardi, John. "Dialogue with the Audience." *Saturday Review,* XLI (November 22, 1958), 10-12, 42.

See J 31.

K 80
Ciardi, John. "Wallace Stevens: 1879-1955." *The Nation,* CLXXXI (October 22, 1955), 335-336.

K 81
Ciardi, John. "Wallace Stevens's 'Absolute Music.'" *The Nation,* CLXXIX (October 16, 1954), 346-347.

Review article of *CP*.

K 82
Clough, Wilson O. "Stevens' 'Notes Toward a Supreme Fiction, Part III, Section III.'" *The Explicator,* XXVIII (November 1969), item 24.

K 83
Collie, M. J. "The Rhetoric of Accurate Speech, A Note on the Poetry of Wallace Stevens." *Essays in Criticism,* XII (January 1962), 54-66.

K 84
Corman, Cid. "The Angel of Necessity." *Caterpillar,* 1 (October 1967), 103-130.

Review article of *Letters*.

K 85
Corrington, John William. "Wallace Stevens and the Problem of Order: A Study of Three Poems." *Arlington Quarterly,* I (Summer 1968), 50-63.

K 86
Culbert, Taylor, and Violette, John M. "Wallace Stevens' Emperor." *Criticism,* II (Winter 1960), 38-47.

K 87
Cunningham, J. V. "The Poetry of Wallace Stevens." *Poetry,* LXXV (December 1949), 149-165.

See I 6.

K 88
Cunningham, J. V. "The Styles and Procedures of Wallace Stevens." *University of Denver Quarterly*, I (Spring 1966), 8–28.

K 89
Daiches, David. "Some Recent Poetry." *The Yale Review*, n.s. XL (December 1950), 355–356.

Contains review of *The Auroras of Autumn*.

K 90
Davenport, Guy. "Spinoza's Tulips, A Commentary on 'The Comedian as the Letter C.'" *Perspective*, VII (Autumn 1954), 147–154.

K 91
Davie, Donald. "The Auroras of Autumn." *Perspective*, VII (Autumn 1954), 125–136.

See I 6.

K 92
Davie, Donald. "'Essential Gaudiness': The Poems of Wallace Stevens." *Twentieth Century*, CLIII (June 1953), 455–462.

Review article of *The Selected Poems*, 1952 and 1953.

K 93
Davie, Donald. "Notes on the Later Poems of Stevens." *Shenandoah*, VII (Summer 1956), 40–41.

K 94
Deen, Rosemary F. "Wonder and Mystery of Art." *Commonweal*, LXVI (September 20, 1957), 620–621.

Contains review of *OP*.

K 95
Deutsch, Babette. "Contemporary Portrait No. 2: Wallace Stevens." *Poetry: London–New York*, I (Winter 1956), 42–47.

K 96
Dietrichson, Jan W. "Wallace Stevens' 'Sunday Morning.'" *Edda*:

Nordisk Tidsskrift for Litteraturforskning, sec. 2 (1970), 105–116.

K 97
Dillon, George. "A Blue Phenomenon." *Poetry,* LXVIII (May 1946), 97–100.

Contains review of *Esthétique du Mal.*

K 98
Doggett, Frank. "Abstraction and Wallace Stevens." *Criticism,* II (Winter 1960), 23–37.

K 99
Doggett, Frank. "The Poet of Earth: Wallace Stevens." *College English,* XXII (March 1961), 373–380.

K 100
Doggett, Frank. "Stevens' 'It Must Change, VI.'" *The Explicator,* XV (February 1957), item 30.

K 101
Doggett, Frank. "Stevens' 'Woman Looking at a Vase of Flowers.'" *The Explicator,* XIX (November 1960), item 7.

K 102
Doggett, Frank. "This Invented World: Stevens' 'Notes toward a Supreme Fiction.'" *ELH,* XXVIII (September 1961), 284–299.

See I 16.

K 103
Doggett, Frank. "Wallace Stevens and the World We Know." *English Journal,* XLVIII (October 1959), 365–373.

K 104
Doggett, Frank. "Wallace Stevens' Later Poetry." *ELH,* XXV (June 1958), 137–154.

K 105
Doggett, Frank. "Wallace Stevens' River That Flows Nowhere." *Chicago Review,* XV (Summer-Autumn 1962), 67–80.

K 106
Doggett, Frank. "Wallace Stevens' Secrecy of Words: A Note on

Import in Poetry." *New England Quarterly*, XXXI (September 1958), 375–391.

K 107
Doggett, Frank. "Why Read Wallace Stevens?" *Emory University Quarterly*, XVII (Summer 1962), 81–91.

K 108
Donoghue, Denis. "The Sacred Rage: Three American Poets." *The Listener*, LXIX (June 6, 1963), 965–967.

K 109
Donoghue, Denis. "Wallace Stevens and the Abstract." *Studies: An Irish Quarterly Review*, XLIX (Winter 1960), 389–406.

K 110
Dune, Edmond. "La Place de Wallace Stevens dans la Poésie Américaine." *Critique*, XX (Paris, October 1964), 836–850.

K 111
Eberhart, Richard. "Emerson and Wallace Stevens." *Literary Review*, VII (Autumn 1963), 51–71.

K 112
Eberhart, Richard. "The Stevens Prose." *Accent*, XII (Spring 1952), 122–125.

Contains review of *NA*.

K 113
Eddins, Dwight. "Wallace Stevens: America the Primordial." *Modern Language Quarterly*, XXXII (March 1971), 73–88.

K 114
Eder, Doris L. "The Meaning of Wallace Stevens' Two Themes." *Critical Quarterly*, XI (Summer 1969), 181–190.

K 115
Eder, Doris L. "A Review of Stevens' Criticism to Date." *Twentieth Century Literature*, XV (April 1969), 3–18.

K 116
Eder, Doris L. "Wallace Stevens: Heritage and Influences." *Mosaic*, IV (Fall 1970), 49–61.

K 117
Eder, Doris L. "Wallace Stevens' Landscapes and Still Lifes."
Mosaic, IV (Summer 1971), 1–5.

K 118
Eder, Doris L. "Wallace Stevens: The War Between the Mind and
the Eye." *The Southern Review*, VII (July 1971), 749–764.

K 119
Eder, Doris. Review of Helen Vendler's *On Extended Wings:
Wallace Stevens' Longer Poems. WSN*, I (April 1970), 12.

K 120
Eliot, T. S. Untitled statement. *Trinity Review*, VIII (May
1954), 9.

K 121
Ellmann, Richard. "Wallace Stevens' Ice-Cream." *The Kenyon
Review*, XIX (Winter 1957), 89–105.

See J 48.

K 122
Emerson, Dorothy. "Poetry Corner: Wallace Stevens." *Scho-
lastic*, XXIV (February 3, 1934), 11.

K 123
Empson, William. "An American Poet." *The Listener*, XLIX
(March 26, 1953), 521.

Review article of *The Selected Poems*, 1953, reprinted in *Trinity
Review*, VIII (May 1954), 25.

K 124
Enck, John J. "Stevens' Crispin as the Clown." *Texas Studies
in Literature and Language*, III (Autumn 1961), 389–398.

K 125
Engel, Bernard. "A Democratic Vista of Religion." *Georgia
Review*, XX (Spring 1966), 84–89.

K 126
Exner, Richard. "Wallace Stevens: Die Welt als Meditation."
Text und Zeichen, III (July 1957), 526–528.

K 127
Fahey, William. "Stevens' 'Le Monocle de Mon Oncle.'" *The Explicator*, XV (December 1956), item 16.

K 128
Farnsworth, Robert M. "Stevens' 'So-and-So Reclining on Her Couch,'" *The Explicator*, X (June 1952), item 60.

K 129
Feldman, Steve. "Reality and the Imagination: The Poetic of Wallace Stevens' 'Necessary Angel.'" *University of Kansas City Review*, XXI (Autumn 1954), 35-43.

K 130
Feldman, Steve. "Wallace Stevens." *The Nation*, CLXXIX (November 20, 1954), inside front cover.

Letter to the editor.

K 131
Ferrán, Jaime. "El Poeta Wallace Stevens." *Atlántico*, no. 5 (April 1957), 17-32.

K 132
Ferry, David R. "Stevens' 'Sea Surface Full of Clouds,'" *The Explicator*, VI (June 1948), item 56.

K 133
Feshbach, Sidney. "Criticism as Act." *WSN*, II (April 1971), [25]-27.

Review article of Merle E. Brown's *Wallace Stevens: The Poem as Act.*

K 134
Feshbach, Sidney. "A Note on Mapping Stevens' Development." *WSN*, II (October 1970), 22-23.

Comment on Marjorie Buhr's article, "When Half-Gods Go: Stevens' Spiritual Odyssey," *WSN*, I (April 1970), 9-13.

K 135
Feshbach, Sidney. "Wallace Stevens and Erik Satie: A Source for 'The Comedian as the Letter C.'" *Texas Studies in Literature and Language*, XI (Spring 1969), 811-818.

K 136
Fields, Kenneth W. "Postures of the Nerves: Reflections of the Nineteenth Century in the Poems of Wallace Stevens." *The Southern Review*, VII (July 1971), 778–824.

K 137
Finch, John. "North and South in Stevens' America." *The Harvard Advocate*, CXXVII (December 1940), 23–26.

K 138
Fitzgerald, Robert. "Thoughts Resolved." *Poetry*, LI (December 1937), 153–157.

Contains review of *The Man with the Blue Guitar*.

K 139
Fletcher, John Gould. "Some Contemporary American Poets." *The Chapbook*, II (May 1920), 1–31.

K 140
Flint, F. Cudworth. "The Poem as It Is." *Dartmouth College Library Bulletin*, n.s. IV (December 1961), 51–56.

K 141
Flint, F. Cudworth. "Whether of Bronze or Glass." *Trinity Review*, VIII (May 1954), 26–27.

K 142
Ford, Charles Henri. "Verlaine in Hartford." *View*, I (September 1940), 6.

K 143
Ford, Newell F. "Peter Quince's Orchestra." *Modern Language Notes*, LXXV (May 1960), 405–411.

K 144
[Ford, William T.]. "Some Notes on Stevens' Foreign Bibliography." *WSN*, I (October 1969), [1]–3.

K 145
[Ford, William T.]. Review of Richard Blessing's *Wallace Stevens' "Whole Harmonium." WSN*, I (April 1970), 13.

K 146
Foster, Steven. "The *Gestalt* Configurations of Wallace Stevens." *Modern Language Quarterly*, XXVIII (March 1967), 60–76.

K 147
Fowler, Helen. "Three Debts to Wallace Stevens." *Poetry Digest,*
IV (February–March 1957), 6–12.

K 148
Fraser, G. S. "The Aesthete and the Sensationalist." *Partisan Review,* XXII (Spring 1955), 265–272.

Contains review of *CP.* See J 51.

K 149
Fraser, G. S. "Mind All Alone." *New Statesman and Nation,*
n.s. LIX (January 9, 1960), 43–44.

Review article of *OP.*

K 150
Frederick, John T. "Wallace Stevens: A Classroom Approach."
The CEA Critic, XXXI (November 1968), 6–7.

K 151
French, Warren G. "Stevens' 'The Glass of Water,'" *The Explicator,* XIX (January 1961), item 23.

K 152
Frye, Northrop. "The Realistic Oriole: A Study of Wallace Stevens." *The Hudson Review,* X (Autumn 1957), 353–370.

See I 7.

K 153
Fuller, Roy. "Both Pie and Custard." *Shenandoah,* XXI (Spring 1970), 61–76.

Review articles of *Letters.* See L 17.a; the *Times Literary Supplement* review would seem to be an earlier or abridged version of this review.

K 154
Gaskins, Avery F. "The Concept of Correspondence in the Works of Wallace Stevens and Ralph Waldo Emerson." *Philological Papers. West Virginia University Bulletin,* XV (June 1966), 62–69.

K 155
Gay, R. M. "Stevens' 'Le Monocle de Mon Oncle.'" *The Explicator,* VI (February 1948), item 27.

K 156
Geiger, Don. "Wallace Stevens' Wealth." *Perspective*, VII (Autumn 1954), 155–166.

K 157
Gilbert, Katharine. "Recent Poets on Man and His Place." *Philosophical Review*, LVI (September 1947), 469–490.

See J 55.

K 158
Gollin, Richard M. "Wallace Stevens: The Poet in Society." *Colorado Quarterly*, IX (Summer 1960), 47–58.

K 159
Gorlier, Claudia. "Wallace Stevens: Una Rhetorica della Poesia." *Paragone: Letteratura*, V (Florence, 1954), 73–78.

K 160
Green, Elizabeth. "The Urbanity of Stevens." *Saturday Review*, XXXIX (August 11, 1956), 11–13.

K 161
Greenhut, Morris. "Sources of Obscurity in Modern Poetry: The Examples of Eliot, Stevens, and Tate." *The Centennial Review of Arts and Sciences*, VII (Spring 1963), 171–190.

K 162
Gregory, Horace. "An Examination of Wallace Stevens in a Time of War." *Accent*, III (Autumn 1942), 57–61.

K 163
Griffith, Clark. "Stevens' 'The Men That Are Falling.' " *The Explicator*, XXIII (January 1955), item 41.

K 164
Grube, John. "Stevens' 'Theory.' " *The Explicator*, XXV (November 1966), item 26.

K 165
Gruen, John. "Thirteen Ways of Looking at a Blackbird: A Song Cycle." *Trinity Review*, VIII (May 1954), 28–29.

K 166
Guereschi, Edward F. " 'The Comedian as the Letter C': Wallace

Stevens' Anti-Mythological Poem." *The Centennial Review of Arts and Science*, VIII (Fall 1964), 465–477.

K 167
Gustafson, Richard. "The Practick of the Maker in Wallace Stevens." *Twentieth Century Literature*, IX (July 1963), 83–88.

K 168
Guthrie, Ramon. "Stevens' 'Lions in Sweden,' 18." *The Explicator*, XX (December 1961), item 32.

K 169
Hafner, John H. "One Way of Looking at 'Thirteen Ways of Looking at a Blackbird.'" *Concerning Poetry*, III (Spring 1970), 61–65.

K 170
Hagopian, John V. "Thirteen Ways of Looking at a Blackbird." *American Notes and Queries*, I (February 1963), 84–85.

K 171
Halman, Talat S. "Wallace Stevens and Turkish Poetry." *WSN*, II (October 1970), 19–20.

K 172
Hansen-Löve, Friedrich. "Wallace Stevens oder die 'Romantische Agonie.'" *Wort und Wahrheit*, VIII (July 1953), 558–559.

K 173
Hartley, Anthony. "The Minimum Myth." *Twentieth Century*, CLXVII (June 1960), 545–549.

K 174
Hartsock, Mildred E. "Image and Idea in the Poetry of Stevens." *Twentieth Century Literature*, VII (April 1961), 10–21.

K 175
Hartsock, Mildred E. "Stevens' 'Bantams in Pine Woods.'" *The Explicator*, XVIII (March 1960), item 33.

K 176
Hartsock, Mildred E. "Wallace Stevens and the 'Rock.'" *Personalist*, XLII (Winter 1961), 66–76.

K 177
Hatfield, Jerald E. "More About Legend." *Trinity Review*, VIII (May 1954), 29–31.

K 178
Hays, H. R. "Laforgue and Wallace Stevens." *Romanic Review*, XXV (July–September 1934), 242–248.

K 179
Heath, William W. "Stevens' 'Certain Phenomena of Sound,'" *The Explicator*, XII (December 1953), item 16.

K 180
Hennecke, Hans. "Wallace Stevens und die Dichterische Ein-bildungskraft." *Perspektiven* (1956), 161–179.

K 181
Heringman, Bernard. "The Critical Angel." *The Kenyon Review*, XIV (Summer 1952), 520–523.

Contains review of *NA*.

K 182
Heringman, Bernard. "The Poetry of Synthesis." *Perspective*, VII (Autumn 1954), 167–174.

K 183
Heringman, Bernard. "Two Worlds and Epiphany." *Bard Review*, II (May 1948), 156–159.

K 184
Heringman, Bernard. "Wallace Stevens: The Use of Poetry." *ELH*, XVI (December 1949), 325–336.

See I 16.

K 185
Hess, M. Whitcomb. "Wallace Stevens and the 'Shaping Spirit.'" *Personalist*, XLII (Spring 1961), 207–212.

K 186
Heyen, William. "The Text of *Harmonium*." *Twentieth Century Literature*, XII (October 1966), 147–148.

K 187
Hobsbaum, Philip. "The Critics at the Harmonium: Blackmur and Winters on Stevens." *British Association for American Studies Bulletin*, no. 11 (December 1965), 43–57.

K 188
Hoffman, Frederick J. "*Symbolisme* and Modern Poetry in the

United States." *Comparative Literature Studies*, IV (1967), 193–199.

K 189
Honig, Edwin. "Continual Conversation with a Silent Man—Wallace Stevens' The Necessary Angel." *Voices*, no. 160 (May–August 1960), 32–36.

K 190
Honig, Edwin. "Meeting Wallace Stevens." *WSN*, I (April 1970), 11–12.

K 191
Hough, Graham. "The Poetry of Wallace Stevens." *Critical Quarterly*, II (Autumn 1960), 201–218.

K 192
Howard, Richard. "Tireless Conscience." *Poetry*, CXI (October 1967), 39–40.

Contains review of *Letters*.

K 193
Howe, Irving. "Another Way of Looking at the Blackbird." *The New Republic*, CXXXVII (November 4, 1957), 16–19.

Review article of *OP*. See J 69.

K 194
Hudson, Deatt. "Wallace Stevens." *Twentieth Century Literature*, I (October 1955), 135–138.

K 195
Huston, J. Dennis. "'Credences of Summer': An Analysis." *Modern Philology*. LXVII (February 1970), 263–272.

K 196
Ingalls, Jeremy. "The Poetry of Wallace Stevens: A Christian Context." *Religion in Life*, XXXI (Winter 1961–1962), 118–130.

K 197
Isaacs, Neil D. "The Autoerotic Metaphor in Joyce, Sterne, Lawrence, Stevens and Whitman." *Literature and Psychology*, XV (Winter 1965), 92–106.

K 198
Jäger, Dietrich. "Sas Verhältnis Zweischen Wirklichkeit und

menschlicher Ordnung als Thema der Lyrik: Robert Frost und Wallace Stevens im vergelich mit europäischen Dichten." *Die Neueren Sprachen,* XXVII (February 1968), 65–83.

K 199
Jarrell, Randall. "The Collected Poems of Wallace Stevens." *The Yale Review,* n.s. XLIV (March 1955), 340–353.

See I 6.

K 200
Jarrell, Randall. "Fifty Years of American Poetry." *Prairie Schooner,* XXXVII (Spring 1963), 1–27.

K 201
Jarrell, Randall. "Reflections on Wallace Stevens." *Partisan Review,* XVIII (May–June 1951), 335–344.

See J 73.

K 202
Johnson, Wendell Stacy. "Some Functions of Poetic Form." *Journal of Aesthetics and Art Criticism,* XIII (June 1955), 496–506.

K 203
Jumper, Will C. "The Language of Wallace Stevens." *Iowa English Yearbook,* no. 6 (Fall 1961), 23–24.

K 204
Kalb, Bernard. "The Author." *Saturday Review,* XXXVII (December 4, 1954), 26.

K 205
Kammer, Alfred S. "Wallace Stevens and Christopher Morley." *Furioso,* III (Winter 1947), 56–57.

K 206
Kato, Kikuo. "On Fluent Mundo in the Poetry of Wallace Stevens." *Bulletin,* XIII (Tokyo Gakugei University, 1962), 11–18.

K 207
Kaul, A. N. " 'So-and-So Reclining on Her Couch': A Late Poem of Wallace Stevens." *An English Miscellany,* no. 2 (St. Stephen's College, Delhi, 1963), 63–67.

K 208
Keast, W. R. "Wallace Steven's [*sic*] 'Thirteen Ways of Looking at a Blackbird.'" *Chicago Review,* VIII (Winter–Spring 1954), 48–63.

K 209
Kermode, Frank. "The Gaiety of Language." *Spectator,* CCI (October 3, 1958), 454–455.

Review article of *NA* and *OP*.

K 210
Kermode, Frank. "*Notes toward a Supreme Fiction:* A Commentary." *Annali dell'Istituto Universitario Orientale: Sezione Germanica,* IV (Naples, 1961), 173–201.

K 211
Kermode, Frank. "Strange Contemporaries: Wallace Stevens and Hart Crane." *Encounter,* XXVIII (May 1967), 65–70.

Contains review of *Letters.*

K 212
Kermode, Frank. "The Words of the World: On Wallace Stevens." *Encounter,* XIV (April 1960), 45–50.

K 213
King, Bruce. "Wallace Stevens' 'Metaphors of a Magnifico.'" *English Studies,* XLIX (October 1968), 450–452.

K 214
King, Montgomery W. "The Two Worlds of Wallace Stevens." *College Language Association Journal,* VIII (December 1964), 141–148.

K 215
Knox, George. "Stevens' Verse Plays: Fragments of a Total Agon." *Genre,* I (April 1968), 124–140.

K 216
Koch, Vivienne. "Poetry in World War II." *Briarcliff Quarterly,* III (April 1946), 3–24.

Contains review of *Esthétique du Mal.*

K 217
Kocher, Annis C. "The Jar of a Wallace Stevens' Anecdote." *California English Journal,* II (Summer 1966), 56–59.

K 218

Kreymborg, Alfred. "An Early Impression of Wallace Stevens."
Trinity Review, VIII (May 1954), 12–16.

K 219

Kunitz, Stanley. "Hartford Walker." *The New Republic*, CLV
(November 12, 1966), 23–26.

Review article of *Letters*.

K 220

Lafferty, Michael. "Wallace Stevens: A Man of Two Worlds."
Historical Review of Berks County, XXIV (Fall 1959), 109–113,
130–132.

K 221

Langbaum, Robert. "The New Nature Poetry." *American
Scholar*, XXVIII, (Summer 1959), 323–340.

K 222

Laros, Fred. "Wallace Stevens Today." *Bard Review*, II (Spring
1947), 8–15.

K 223

Lash, Kenneth, and Thackaberry, Robert. "Stevens' 'The Emperor of Ice-Cream.' " *The Explicator*, VI (April 1948), item 36.

K 224

Lask, Thomas. "Poetry of Stevens." *New York Times*, February
9, 1958, sec. II, p. 9.

K 225

Lawler, Justus George. "The Poet, the Metaphysician and the
Desire for God." *Downside Review*, LXXXIV (July 1966),
288–304.

K 226

LeBrun, P. "Duologue of Two O'Clock." *Essays in Criticism*,
XI (April 1961), 226–232.

Review article of *NA*.

K 227

Leiter, Louis H. "Sense in Nonsense: Wallace Stevens' 'The Bird
with the Coppery, Keen Claws.' " *College English*, XXVI (April
1965), 551–554.

K 228
Lensing, George S. "Mere Facts and the Biography of Wallace
Stevens." *WSN*, II (October 1970), [17]-18.

Review article of Samuel French Morse's *Wallace Stevens:
Poetry as Life*.

K 229
Lensing, George S. "Robinson and Stevens: Some Tangential
Bearings." *The Southern Review*, III (Spring 1967), 505-513.

K 230
Lensing, George S. "Wallace Stevens and the State of Winter
Simplicity." *The Southern Review,* VII (July 1971), 765-777.

K 231
Lentricchia, Frank. "Wallace Stevens: Emergence of the Poet."
Poetry, CIX (December 1966), 201-203.

K 232
Lentricchia, Frank. "Wallace Stevens: The Ironic Eye." *The
Yale Review,* LVI (Spring 1967), 336-353.

K 233
Levi, Albert William. "A Note on Wallace Stevens and the Poem
of Perspective." *Perspective,* VII (Autumn 1954), 137-146.

K 234
Levin, Harry. Untitled statement. *The Harvard Advocate,*
CXXVII (December 1940), 30.

K 235
Liddie, Alexander. "Stevens' 'Metaphors of a Magnifico.'" *The
Explicator,* XXI (October 1962), item 15.

K 236
Linebarger, J. M. "Wallace Stevens' 'Gubbinal.'" *WSN*, II (April
1971), [25].

K 237
Linebarger, J. M. "Wallace Stevens' 'Paltry Nude Starts on a
Spring Voyage.'" *The Laurel Review,* VII (Spring 1967), 55-56.

K 238
Linebarger, J. M. "Wallace Stevens' 'The Good Man Has No
Shape.'" *The Laurel Review,* IX (Spring 1969), 47-49.

K 239
Linneman, Sister M. Rose Ann. "Donne as Catalyst in the Poetry of Elinor Wylie, Wallace Stevens, Herbert Read, and William Empson." *Xavier University Studies*, I (Summer–Fall 1962), 264–272.

K 240
Liss, Marion. "Wallace Stevens' 'Sunday Morning': Eine Interpretation." *Kleine Beitrage*, 21 (1960), 67–74.

K 241
Litz, A. Walton. "Wallace Stevens: Business and a Sonnet." *The Nation*, CCIV (January 16, 1967), 85–87.

Review article of *Letters*.

K 242
Logan, John. "John Gruen's Settings for Wallace Stevens." *The Hudson Review*, IX (Summer 1956), 273–276.

K 243
Lowell, Robert. "Imagination and Reality." *The Nation*, CLXIV (April 5, 1947), 400–402.

Review article of *Transport to Summer*.

K 244
Lucas, John. "Wallace Stevens in Connecticut to Leonard van Geyzel in Ceylon." *Dartmouth College Library Bulletin*, VII (April 1967), 38–43.

K 245
MacCaffrey, Isabel G. "The Other Side of Silence: 'Credences of Summer' as an Example." *Modern Language Quarterly*, XXX (September 1969), 417–438.

K 246
McFadden, George. "Poet, Nature, and Society in Wallace Stevens." *Modern Language Quarterly*, XXII (September 1962), 263–271.

K 247
McFadden, George. "Probings for an Integration: Color Symbolism in Wallace Stevens." *Modern Philology*, LVII (February 1961), 186–193.

K 248
McGrory, Kathleen. "Wallace Stevens as a Romantic Rebel."
Connecticut Review, IV (October 1970), 59–64.

K 249
Macksey, Richard. "The Old Poets." *The Johns Hopkins Magazine,* XIX (Spring 1968), 42–48.

K 250
McNamara, Peter L. "The Multi-Faceted Blackbird and Wallace
Stevens' Poetic Vision." *College English,* XXV (March 1964),
446–448.

K 251
Mangalam, N. "Island Solitudes: A Study of Human Values in
the Poetry of Wallace Stevens." *Osmania Journal of English
Studies for 1967,* VI (1967), 55–63.

K 252
Mariani, Paul. "The Critic as Friend from Pascagoula." *Massachusetts Review,* XII (Winter 1971), 215–227.

Review article of Helen Vendler's *On Extended Wings: Wallace
Stevens' Longer Poems* and Richard Blessing's *Wallace Stevens' Whole Harmonium.*

K 253
Martz, Louis L. "Recent Poetry." *The Yale Review,* n.s. XXXVII
(December 1947), 339–341.

Contains review of *Transport to Summer.*

K 254
Martz, Louis L. "Wallace Stevens: The Romance of the Precise."
The Yale Poetry Review, II (Autumn 1946), 13–20.

K 255
Martz, Louis L. "Wallace Stevens: The World as Meditation."
The Yale Review, n.s. XLVII (Summer 1958), 517–536.

See I 6 and I 7.

K 256
Matthiessen, Francis O. "Society and Solitude in Poetry." *The
Yale Review,* n.s. XXV (March 1936), 605–607.

Contains review of *Ideas of Order.*

K 257
Matthiessen Francis O. "Wallace Stevens at 67." *New York Times Book Review,* April 20, 1947, pp. 4, 26.

Review article of *Transport to Summer.* See J 89.

K 258
Matthiessen, Francis O. Untitled statement. *The Harvard Advocate,* CXXVII (December 1940), 31.

K 259
Mayhead, Robin. "The Poetry of Wallace Stevens." *Community,* I (April 1954), 28–36.

K 260
Merivale, Patricia. "Wallace Stevens' 'Jar': The Absurd Detritus of Romantic Myth." *College English,* XXVI (April 1965), 527–532.

K 261
Meyer, Gerard P. "Actuary Among the Spondees." *Saturday Review,* XXXVII (December 4, 1954), 26–27.

Review article of *CP.*

K 262
Meyer, Gerard P. "Bollingen Winner." *Saturday Review of Literature,* XXXIII (July 1, 1950), 19.

K 263
Meyer, Gerard P. "Wallace Stevens: Major Poet." *Saturday Review of Literature,* XXIX (March 23, 1946), 7–8.

Review article of *Esthétique du Mal.*

K 264
Miller, J. Hillis. "An Exercise in Discrimination." *The Yale Review,* LIX (Winter 1970), 281–289.

Review article of Helen Vendler's *On Extended Wings: Wallace Stevens' Longer Poems.*

K 265
Miller, J. Hillis. "Wallace Stevens' Poetry of Being." *ELH,* XXXI (March 1964), 86–105.

See I 16.

K 266
Mills, Ralph J., Jr. "Wallace Stevens and the Poem of Earth."
Gemini/Dialogue, III (January 1960), 20–30.

K 267
Mills, Ralph J., Jr. "Wallace Stevens: The Image of the Rock."
Accent, XVIII (Spring 1958), 75–89.

See I 7.

K 268
Miner, Earl R. "Stevens' 'Le Monocle de Mon Oncle, III.' " *The
Explicator*, XIII (March 1955), item 28.

K 269
Mitchell, Roger S. "Wallace Stevens: A Checklist of Criticism."
Bulletin of Bibliography, XXIII (September–December 1962),
208–211.

K 270
Mitchell, Roger S. "Wallace Stevens: A Checklist of Criticism,
Part II." *Bulletin of Bibliography*, XXIII (January–April 1963),
232–233.

K 271
Mitchell, Roger S. "Wallace Stevens' 'Spaniard of the Rose':
William Carlos Williams." *Notes and Queries*, X (September
1963), 381–382.

K 272
Mitchell, Roger S. "Wallace Stevens: The Dedication to *Notes
toward a Supreme Fiction*." *Notes and Queries*, XIII (November 1966), 417–418.

K 273
Mizener, Arthur. "Not in Cold Blood." *The Kenyon Review*,
XIII (Spring 1951), 218–225.

K 274
Monroe, Harriet. "A Cavalier of Beauty." *Poetry*, XXIII (March
1924), 322–327.

Contains review of *Harmonium*. See J 97.

K 275
Monroe, Harriet. "The Free-Verse Movement in America."
English Journal, XIII (December 1924), 691–705.

K 276
Monroe, Harriet. "From 'Mr. Yeats and the Poetic Drama.'"
Poetry, XVI (April 1920), 32–38.

Review article of *Three Travelers Watch a Sunrise*. See I 6.

K 277
Moore, Marianne. "There Is a War That Never Ends." *The Kenyon Review*, V (Winter 1943), 144–147.

Review article of *Parts of a World* and *Notes Toward A Supreme Fiction*. See J 101.

K 278
Moore, Marianne. "Unanimity and Fortitude." *Poetry*, XLIX (February 1937), 268–272.

Review article of *Ideas of Order* and *Owl's Clover*. See J 100.

K 279
Moore, Marianne. "Well Moused Lion." *The Dial*, LXXVI (January 1924), 84–91.

Review article of *Harmonium*. See I 6.

K 280
Moore, Marianne. "'The World Imagined . . . Since We Are Poor.'" *Poetry–New York*, no. 4 (1951), 7–9.

Review article of *The Auroras of Autumn*. See I 6.

K 281
Moore, Marianne. Untitled statement. *The Harvard Advocate*, CXXVII (December 1940), 31.

K 282
Moore, Marianne. Untitled statement. *Trinity Review*, VIII (May 1954), 11.

K 283
Moorman, Charles. "Stevens' 'Six Significant Landscapes.'"
The Explicator, XVII (October 1958), item 1.

K 284
Morse, Samuel French. "Agenda: A Note on Some Uncollected Poems." *Trinity Review*, VIII (May 1954), 32–34.

K 285
Morse, Samuel French. "'Lettres d'un Soldat.'" *Dartmouth*

College Library Bulletin, n.s. IV (December 1961), 44-50.

K 286
Morse, Samuel French. "The Motive for Metaphor—Wallace Stevens: His Poetry and Practice." *Origin V,* II (Spring 1952), 3-65.

K 287
Morse, Samuel French. "The Native Element." *The Kenyon Review,* XX (Summer 1958), 446-465.

See I 6.

K 288
Morse, Samuel French. "A Note on the 'Adagia.' " *Poetry,* XC (April 1957), 45-46.

K 289
Morse, Samuel French. "Wallace Stevens, Bergson, Pater." *ELH,* XXXI (March 1964), 1-34.

See I 16.

K 290
Morse, Samuel French. "Wallace Stevens: Some Ideas About the Thing Itself." *Boston University Studies in English,* II (Spring 1956), 55-64.

K 291
Morse, Samuel French. "Wallace Stevens: The Poet and the Critic." *The Southern Review,* I (Spring 1965), 430-446.

K 292
Mulqueen, James E. "A Reading of Wallace Stevens' 'The Comedian As the Letter C.' " *Cimarron Review,* no. 13 (October 1970), 35-42.

K 293
Mulqueen, James E. "Wallace Stevens: Radical Transcendentalist." *Midwest Quarterly,* XI (April 1970), 329-340.

K 294
Munson, Gorham. "The Dandyism of Wallace Stevens." *The Dial,* LXXIX (November 1925), 413-417.

See I 6.

K 295
Murphy, Francis E. " 'The Comedian as the Letter C.' " *Wisconsin Studies in Contemporary Literature,* III (Spring–Summer 1962), 79–99.

K 296
Nash, Ralph. "About 'The Emperor of Ice-Cream.' " *Perspective,* VII (Autumn 1954), 122–124.

K 297
Nash, Ralph. "Wallace Stevens and the Point of Change." *Perspective,* VII (Autumn 1954), 113–121.

K 298
Nassar, Eugene P. "Wallace Stevens: 'Peter Quince at the Clavier.' " *College English,* XXVI (April 1965), 549–551.

K 299
Nassar, Eugene P. "Reply." *College English,* XXVII (February 1966), 431.

See Perrine's article in the same issue (K 322).

K 300
Nathan, Leonard. "Wallace Stevens and Modern Poetry." *Indian Literature,* X (January–March 1967), 82–101.

K 301
Nelson, Phyllis E. "Stevens' 'Peter Quince at the Clavier.' " *The Explicator,* XXIV (February 1966), item 52.

K 302
Nemerov, Howard. "The Poetry of Wallace Stevens." *The Sewanee Review,* LXV (Winter 1957), 1–14.

See J 108.

K 303
Nemerov, Howard. "Wallace Stevens and the Voices of Imagination." *Carleton Miscellany,* IV (Spring 1963), 90–97.

K 304
O'Connor, William Van. "The Politics of a Poet." *Perspective,* I (Summer 1948), 204–207.

K 305
O'Connor, William Van. "Tension and Structure in Poetry." *The Sewanee Review*, LI (Autumn 1943), 555–573.

K 306
O'Connor, William Van. "Wallace Stevens and Imagined Reality." *Western Review*, XII (Spring 1948), 156–163.

See J 112.

K 307
O'Connor, William Van. "Wallace Stevens: Impressionism in America." *Revue des Langues Vivantes*, XXXII (Brussels, January–February 1966), 66–77.

K 308
O'Connor, William Van. "Wallace Stevens on 'The Poems of Our Climate.'" *University of Kansas City Review*, XV (Winter 1948), 105–110.

K 309
Olson, Elder. "The Poetry of Wallace Stevens." *College English*, XVI (April 1955), 395–402.

K 310
Otake, Masaru V. "The Haiku Touch in Wallace Stevens and Some Imagists." *East-West Review*, II (Dosgisha University, Kyoto, Winter 1966), 152–164.

K 311
Owen, David H. "'The Glass of Water.'" *Perspective*, VII (Autumn 1954), 175–183.

K 312
Pack, Robert. "The Abstracting Imagination of Wallace Stevens: Nothingness and the Hero." *Arizona Quarterly*, XI (Autumn 1955), 197–209.

K 313
Pack, Robert. "Wallace Stevens: The Secular Mystery and the Comic Spirit." *Western Review*, XX (Autumn 1955), 51–62.

K 314
Pauker, John. "A Discussion of 'Sea Surface Full of Clouds.'" *Furioso*, V (Fall 1950), 34–36.

K 315
Pearce, Roy Harvey. "On the Continuity of American Poetry."
The Hudson Review, X (Winter 1958), 518–539.

K 316
Pearce, Roy Harvey. "The Poet as Person." *The Yale Review*,
n.s. XLI (March 1952), 421–440.

K 317
Pearce, Roy Harvey. "Stevens Posthumous." *International
Literary Annual*, II (1959), 65–89.

K 318
Pearce, Roy Harvey. "Wallace Stevens: The Last Lesson of the
Master." *ELH*, XXXI (March 1964), 64–85.

See I 16.

K 319
Pearce, Roy Harvey. "Wallace Stevens: The Life of the Imagination." *PMLA*, LXVI (September 1951), 561–582.

See I 7.

K 320
Pearson, Norman Holmes. "Wallace Stevens and 'Old Higgs.'"
The Trinity Review, VIII (May 1954), 35–36.

K 321
Perloff, Marjorie. "Irony in Wallace Stevens's *The Rock*." *American Literature*, XXXVI (November 1964), 327–342.

K 322
Perrine, Laurence N. " 'Peter Quince at the Clavier': A Protest."
College English, XXVII (February 1966), 430.

See Nassar's article in the same issue (K 299).

K 323
Peterson, Margaret L. W. *"Harmonium* and William James."
The Southern Review, VII (July 1971), 658–682.

K 324
Petitt, Dorothy. "'Domination of Black': A Study of Involve-
ment." *English Journal*, LI (May 1962), 347–348.

K 325
Pinkerton, Jan. "Wallace Stevens in the Tropics: A Conservative
Protest." *The Yale Review*, LX (December 1970), 215–227.

K 326
Pinkerton, Jan. Review of Helen Vendler's *On Extended Wings:
Wallace Stevens' Longer Poems. Criticism*, XII (Spring 1970),
161–164.

K 327
Poggenburg, Raymond P. "Baudelaire and Stevens: 'L'Esthétique
du Mal.'" *South Atlantic Bulletin*, XXXIII (November 1968),
14–18.

K 328
Powell, Grosvenor E. "Of Heroes and Nobility: The Personae of
Wallace Stevens." *The Southern Review*, VII (July 1971),
727–748.

K 329
Powys, Llewelyn. "The Thirteenth Way." *The Dial*, LXXVII
(July 1924), 45–50.

See I 6.

K 330
Pritchett, V. S. "Truffles in the Sky." *New Statesman and Nation*, LXXIII (March 31, 1967), 439–440.

Review article of *Letters*.

K 331
Quinn, Sister M. Bernetta. "A Few Steps Toward Reassessing
Wallace Stevens." *Dartmouth College Library Bulletin*, n.s. V
(April 1966), 73–78.

K 332
Quinn, Sister M. Bernetta. "Metamorphosis in Wallace Stevens."
The Sewanee Review, LX (Spring 1952), 230–252.

See I 7.

K 333
Ramsey, Warren. "Some Twentieth Century Ideas of the Verse
Theatre." *Comparative Literature Studies* (special advance
number), (1963), 43–50.

K 334
Ramsey, Warren. "Uses of the Visible: American Imagism, French Symbolism." *Comparative Literature Studies,* IV (1967), 177-191.

K 335
Ramsey, Warren. "Wallace Stevens and Some French Poets." *Trinity Review,* VIII (May 1954), 36-40.

K 336
Ransom, John Crowe. "The Concrete Universal: Observations on the Understanding of Poetry, II." *The Kenyon Review,* XVII (Summer 1955), 383-407.

K 337
Ransom, John Crowe. "The Planetary Poet." *The Kenyon Review,* XXVI (Winter 1964), 233-264.

K 338
Riddel, Joseph N. "The Authorship of Wallace Stevens' 'On Poetic Truth.'" *Modern Language Notes,* LXXVI (February 1961), 126-129.

K 339
Riddel, Joseph N. "Blue Voyager." *Salmagundi,* II (1967-1968), 61-74.

K 340
Riddel, Joseph N. "The Contours of Stevens Criticism." *ELH,* XXXI (March 1964), 106-138.

See I 16.

K 341
Riddel, Joseph N. "'Disguised Pronunciamento': Wallace Stevens' 'Sea Surface Full of Clouds.'" *Texas Studies in English,* XXXVII (1958), 177-186.

K 342
Riddel, Joseph N. "The Metaphysical Changes of Stevens' 'Esthétique du Mal.'" *Twentieth Century Literature,* VII (July 1961), 64-80.

K 343
Riddel, Joseph N. "'Poets' Politics'—Wallace Stevens' *Owl's Clover.*" *Modern Philology,* LVI (November 1958), 118-132.

K 344
Riddel, Joseph N. "Stevens' 'Peter Quince at the Clavier': Immortality as Form." *College English*, XXIII (January 1962), 307–309.

K 345
Riddel, Joseph N. "Wallace Stevens' *Ideas of Order:* The Rhetoric of Politics and the Rhetoric of Poetry." *New England Quarterly*, XXXIV (September 1961), 328–351.

K 346
Riddel, Joseph N. "Wallace Stevens – It Must Be Human." *English Journal*, LVI (April 1967), 525–534.

K 347
Riddel, Joseph N. "Wallace Stevens' 'Notes toward a Supreme Fiction.'" *Wisconsin Studies in Contemporary Literature*, II (Spring–Summer 1961), 20–42.

K 348
Riddel, Joseph N. "Wallace Stevens' 'Visibility of Thought.'" *PMLA*, LXXVII (September 1962), 482–498.

K 349
Riddel, Joseph N. "Walt Whitman and Wallace Stevens: Functions of a 'Literatus.'" *The South Atlantic Quarterly*, LXI (Autumn 1962), 506–520.

See I 7.

K 350
Riddel, Joseph N. Review of Frank Lentricchia's *The Gaiety of Language: An Essay on the Radical Poetics of W. B. Yeats and Wallace Stevens. Journal of Germanic and English Philology*, LXVIII (October 1969), 718–723.

K 351
Riddel, Joseph N. Review of James Baird's *The Dome and the Rock: Structure in the Poetry of Wallace Stevens. American Literature*, XLI (January 1970), 609–611.

K 352
Riddel, Joseph N. Review of Robert Buttel's *Wallace Stevens: The Making of* Harmonium. *American Literature*, XL (March 1968), 102–104.

K 353
Riese, Teut Andreas. "Das Gestaltunsprinzip der Konketion in der Neueren Amerikanischen Lyrik." *Jahrbuch für Amerikastudien,* no. 8 (1963), 136–147.

K 354
Rizzardi, Alfredo. "Creazione e Distruzione del Mondo Fantastico di Wallace Stevens," *Nuova Corrente,* I (Genoa, January 1955), 186–197.

See J 129.

K 355
Rizzardi, Alfredo. "Poesia di Wallace Stevens." *Galleria,* IV (1954), 371–375.

K 356
Rockwell, Eleanor. "Wallace Stevens: Towards a Redefinition of Value." *The Silo,* VII (Bennington College, Winter 1945), 34–37.

K 357
Rooney, William J. "'Spelt from Sibyl's Leaves'—A Study in Contrasting Methods of Evaluation." *Journal of Aesthetics and Art Criticism,* XIII (June 1955), 507–519.

K 358
Rosenthal, M. L. "Stevens in a Minor Key." *The New Republic,* CXXIV, (May 7, 1951), 26–28.

Contains review of *The Auroras of Autumn.*

K 359
Rosenthal, M. L. "Stevens' 'Sea Surface Full of Clouds.'" *The Explicator,* XIX (March 1961), item 38.

K 360
Sanders, Paul. "Stevens' 'Arcades of Philadelphia the Past.'" *The Explicator,* XXV (May 1967), item 72.

K 361
Schulze, F. W. "Begriff und Bild der Wirklichkeit im Werk von Wallace Stevens." *Studium Generale,* XXI (Berlin, 1968), 1–18.

K 362
Schwartz, Delmore. "Instructed of Much Mortality." *The Sewanee Review,* LIV (Summer 1946), 439–448.

K 363
Schwartz, Delmore. "In the Orchards of the Imagination." *The New Republic*, CXXXI (November 1, 1954), 16–18.

Review article of *CP*.

K 364
Schwartz, Delmore. "New Verse." *Partisan Review*, IV (February 1938), 49–52.

Contains review of *The Man with the Blue Guitar*.

K 365
Schwartz, Delmore. "The Ultimate Plato with Picasso's Guitar." *The Harvard Advocate*, CXXVII (December 1940), 11–16.

K 366
Schwartz, Delmore. "Wallace Stevens – An Appreciation." *The New Republic*, CXXXIII (August 22, 1955), 20–22.

K 367
Sellin, Eric. "Stevens' 'The Glass of Water.'" *The Explicator*, XVII (January 1959), item 28.

K 368
Seymour, Charles, Jr. "Wallace Stevens. A Study in Contemporary Minor Poetry." *Harkness Hoot*, IV (November 1933), 26–33.

K 369
Shankar, D. A. "Wallace Stevens: An Ontological Poet." *Literary Criterion*, VI (Summer 1965), 78–82.

K 370
Shapiro, Karl. "Modern Poetry as a Religion." *American Scholar*, XXVIII (Summer 1959), 297–305.

K 371
Shapiro, Karl. "What's the Matter with Poetry?" *New York Times Book Review*, December 13, 1959, pp. 1, 22.

K 372
Sheehan, Donald. "Wallace Stevens' 'Theory of Metaphor.'" *Papers on Language and Literature*, II (Winter 1966), 57–66.

K 373
Silverstein, Norman. "Stevens' 'Homunculus et la Belle Etiole.'" *The Explicator*, XIII (May 1955), item 40.

K 374
Silverstein, Norman. "Stevens' 'Of Hartford in a Purple Light.'"
The Explicator, XVIII (December 1959), item 20.

K 375
Simons, Hi. "Bibliography: October 1937–November 1940–
Work Since 'The Man with the Blue Guitar.'" *The Harvard Advocate*, CXXVII (December 1940), 32–34.

K 376
Simons, Hi. "'The Comedian as the Letter C': Its Sense and Its
Significance." *The Southern Review*, V (Winter 1940), 453–468.

See I 6.

K 377
Simons, Hi. "The Genre of Wallace Stevens." *The Sewanee Review*, LIII (Autumn 1945), 566–579.

See I 7.

K 378
Simons, Hi. "The Humanism of Wallace Stevens." *Poetry*, LXI
(November 1942), 448–452.

Review article of *Parts of a World*.

K 379
Simons, Hi. "Vicissitudes of Reputation, 1914–1940." *The Harvard Advocate*, CXXVII (December 1940), 8–10, 34–44.

K 380
Simons, Hi. "Wallace Stevens and Mallarmé." *Modern Philology*,
XLIII (May 1946), 235–259.

K 381
H.S. [Harrison Smith]. "More Gold Medals." *Saturday Review
of Literature*, XXXIV (March 17, 1951), 22–23.

K 382
Smith, Hugh L. "Stevens' 'Earthy Anecdote.'" *The Explicator*,
XXIV (December 1965), item 37.

K 383
Smith, Hugh L. "Stevens' 'Life Is Motion.'" *The Explicator*,
XIX (April 1961), item 48.

K 384
Smith, William Jay. "Modern Poetry: Texture and Text." *Shenandoah*, VI (Spring 1955), 6–16.

K 385
Spector, Robert D. "Steven's [*sic*] 'Earthy Anecdote': Introduction to a Collection." *History of Ideas News Letter*, V (Spring 1959), 36–38.

K 386
Spencer, Theodore. "The Poetry of Wallace Stevens: An Evaluation." *The Harvard Advocate*, CXXVII (December 1940), 26–29.

K 387
Spycher, Peter. "Wallace Stevens' Gesammelte Gedichte." *Neue Schweizer Rundschau*, XXII (Zurich, July 1955), 757–762.

K 388
Stallknecht, Newton P. "Absence in Reality: A Study in the Epistemology of The Blue Guitar." *The Kenyon Review*, XXI (Autumn 1959), 545–562.

K 389
Stanford, Donald E. "The Well-Kept Life: The Letters of Wallace Stevens." *The Southern Review*, III (Summer 1967), 757–763.

Review article.

K 390
Stevens, Holly. "Bits of Remembered Time." *The Southern Review*, VII (July 1971), 651–657.

K 391
Stocking, Fred H. "Stevens' 'Bantams in Pine Woods.'" *The Explicator*, III (April 1945), item 45.

K 392
Stocking, Fred H. "Stevens' 'The Comedian as the Letter C.'" *The Explicator*, III (March 1945), item 45.

K 393
Stocking, Fred H. "Stevens' 'Peter Quince at the Clavier.'" *The Explicator*, V (May 1947), item 47.

K 394
Stocking, Fred H. "Wallace Stevens' 'The Ordinary Women.'" *The Explicator*, IV (October 1945), item 4.

K 395
Stoenescu, Stefan. "Ecouri Victorienne in Poezia lui Wallace Stevens." *Analele Universitatii Ducuresti: Literatura Universala si Comparata*, XIX (1970), 43–54.

K 396
Storm, Mary Joan. "Stevens' 'Peter Quince at the Clavier.'" *The Explicator*, XIV (November 1955), item 9.

K 397
Straumann, Heinrich. "Der Mann mit der Blauen Gitarre: Zum Tode des Amerikanischen Dichters Wallace Stevens (1879–1955)." *Neue Zücher Zeitung*, August 14, 1955, p. 4.

K 398
Sutherland, Donald. "An Observation on Wallace Stevens in Connection with Supreme Fictions." *Trinity Review*, VIII (May 1954), 41–42.

K 399
Sweeney, John L. "The Stevens Athenaeum." *Trinity Review*, VIII (May 1954), 42–43.

K 400
Sweitzer, Ronald L. "Wallace Stevens: Advocate of the Imagination." *Historical Review of Berks County*, XXIV (Fall 1959), 117–129.

K 401
Symons, Julian. "A Short View of Wallace Stevens." *Life and Letters Today*, XXVI (September 1940), 215–224.

See I 6.

K 402
Symons, Julian. "Stevens in England." *Trinity Review*, VIII (May 1954), 43–45.

K 403
Sypher, Wylie. "Connoisseur in Chaos: Wallace Stevens." *Partisan Review*, XIII (Winter 1946), 83–94.

K 404
Tanner, Tony. Review of *Letters*. *London Magazine*, VII (April 1967), 105–111.

K 405
Tanselle, G. Thomas. "The Text of Stevens's 'Le Monocle de Mon Oncle.'" *The Library* (Transactions of the Bibliographical Society), 3rd Ser. XIX (1964), 246–248.

K 406
Taranath, Rajeev. "Deepening Experience: A Note on 'The Emperor of Ice-Cream.'" *Literary Criterion,* VI (Summer 1965), 68–72.

* K 407
Tate, Allen. "American Poetry Since 1920." *Bookman,* LXVIII (January 1929), 503–508.

K 408
Tate, Allen. Untitled statement. *The Harvard Advocate,* CXXVII (December 1940), 31.

K 409
Thérèse, Sister, S.N.D. "Stevens' 'The Glass of Water.'" *The Explicator,* XXI (March 1963), item 56.

K 410
Tindall, William York. "The Poet Behind the Desk." *Saturday Review,* XLIX (November 19, 1966), 42–43.

Review article of *Letters.*

K 411
Tryford, John. "Wallace Stevens." *Trace,* LXVI (Fall 1967), 339–344.

K 412
Turner, Myron. "The Imagery of Wallace Stevens and Henry Green." *Wisconsin Studies in Contemporary Literature,* VIII (Winter 1967), 60–77.

K 413
Untermeyer, Louis. "The Ivory Tower." *The New Republic,* XIX (May 10, 1919), 60–61.

K 414
Vance, Thomas. "Wallace Stevens and T. S. Eliot." *Dartmouth College Library Bulletin,* n.s. IV (December 1961), 37–44.

K 415
Vance, Will. "Wallace Stevens: Man off the Street." *Saturday Review of Literature*, XXIX (March 23, 1946), 8.

K 416
Van Ghent, Dorothy. "When Poets Stood Alone." *New Masses*, XXVI (January 11, 1938), sec. II, 41–46.

K 417
Van Vechten, Carl. "Rogue Elephant in Porcelain." *Yale University Library Gazette*, XXXVIII (July 1963), 41–50.

K 418
Vazakas, Byron. "Three Modern Old Masters: Moore — Stevens — Williams." *New Mexico Quarterly Review*, XXII (Winter 1952), 434–439.

Contains review of *NA*.

K 419
Vazakas, Byron. "Wallace Stevens: Reading Poet." *Historical Review of Berks County*, III (July 1938), 111–113.

K 420
Vendler, Helen. "Stevens' 'Like Decorations in a Nigger Cemetery.'" *Massachusetts Review*, VII (Winter 1966), 136–146.

K 421
Vendler, Helen. "Wallace Stevens: The False and True Sublime." *The Southern Review*, VII (July 1971), 683–698.

K 422
Viereck, Peter. "Some Notes on Wallace Stevens." *Contemporary Poetry*, VII (Winter 1948), 14–15.

Review article of *Transport to Summer*, reprinted in *Trinity Review*, VIII (May 1954), 45–46.

K 423
Viereck, Peter. "Stevens Revisited." *The Kenyon Review*, X (Winter 1948), 154–157.

Contains reviews of *Harmonium* and *Transport to Summer*.

K 424
Waggoner, Hyatt H. Review of Ronald Sukenick's *Wallace*

Stevens: Musing the Obscure and James Baird's *The Dome and the Rock: Structure in the Poetry of Wallace Stevens. Modern Philology*, LXVII (May 1970), 392–396.

K 425
Wagner, C. Roland. "A Central Poetry." *The Hudson Review*, V (Spring 1952), 144–148.

Review article of *NA*. See I 7.

K 426
Wagner, C. Roland. "The Idea of Nothingness in Wallace Stevens." *Accent*, XII (Spring 1952), 111–121.

K 427
Walcutt, Charles C. "Interpreting the Symbol." *College English*, XIV (May 1953), 446–454.

K 428
Warren, Robert Penn. Untitled statement. *The Harvard Advocate*, CXXVII (December 1940), 32.

K 429
Waterman, Arthur. "Poetry as Play." *The CEA Critic*, XXVI (January 1964), 7.

K 430
Watts, Harold H. "Wallace Stevens and the Rock of Summer." *The Kenyon Review*, XIV (Winter 1952), 122–140.

See J 157.

K 431
Weiss, T. "The Nonsense of Winters' *Anatomy* (Part I: Henry Adams and Wallace Stevens)." *Quarterly Review of Literature*, I (Spring 1944), 212–234.

K 432
Wentersdorf, Karl P. "Wallace Stevens, Dante Alighieri and the Emperor." *Twentieth Century Literature*, XIII (January 1968), 197–204.

K 433
Whitbread, Thomas B. "Wallace Stevens' 'Highest Candle.'" *Texas Studies in Literature and Language*, IV (Winter 1963), 465–480.

K 434
Williams, William Carlos. "Comment: Wallace Stevens." *Poetry*,
LXXXVII (January 1956), 234–239.

K 435
Williams, William Carlos. "Wallace Stevens." *Trinity Review*,
VIII (May 1954), 10–11.

K 436
Williams, William Carlos. Untitled statement. *The Harvard
Advocate*, CXXVII (December 1940), 32.

K 437
Wilson, Edmund. "Wallace Stevens and E. E. Cummings." *The
New Republic*, XXXVIII (March 19, 1924), 102–103.

Review article of *Harmonium*.

K 438
Winters, Yvor. "A Cool Master." *Poetry*, XIX (February 1922),
278–288.

K 439
Young, David P. "A Skeptical Music: Stevens and Santayana."
Criticism, VII (Summer 1965), 263–283.

K 440
Zabel, Morton Dauwen. "The Harmonium of Wallace Stevens."
Poetry, XXXIX (December 1931), 148–154.

Review article. See I 6.

K 441
Zabel, Morton Dauwen. "Wallace Stevens and the Image of
Man." *The Harvard Advocate*, CXXVII (December 1940), 19–23.

See I 7.

K 442
Zimmerman, Michael. "The Pursuit of Pleasure and the Uses of
Death: Wallace Stevens' 'Sunday Morning.'" *University of Kan-
sas City Review*, XXXIII (Winter 1966), 113–123.

K 443
Zimmerman, Michael. "Wallace Stevens' Emperor." *English
Language Notes*, IV (December 1966), 119–123.

K 444
Zolla, Elemire. "Nota su Wallace Stevens." *Letterature Moderne,* VI (March–April 1956), 213–215.

L. Book Reviews

L 1 HARMONIUM
New York: Alfred A. Knopf, 1923

L 1.a
Anonymous. *Bookman*, LVIII (December 1923), 483.

L 1.b
Anonymous. Springfield (Mass.) *Republican*, October 23, 1923, p. 7a.

L 1.c
C.T.C. Boston *Evening Transcript*, December 29, 1923, part 6, p. 5.

L 1.d
Fletcher, John Gould. *Freeman*, VIII (December 19, 1923), 355–356.

L 1.e
Holden, Raymond. *Measure*, IV (March 1924), 17–18.

L 1.f
Jones, Llewellyn. *Chicago Evening Post Literary Review*, December 21, 1923, p. 6.

L 1.g
Josephson, Matthew. *Broom*, V (November 1923), 236–237.

L 1.h
Monroe, Harriet. *Poetry*, XXIII (March 1924), 322–327.

L 1.i
Moore, Marianne. *The Dial*, LXXVI (January 1924), 84–91.

L 1.j
Pendragon. New York *World*, October 28, 1923, p. 7E.

361

L 1.k
Seiffert, Marjorie Allen. *Poetry,* XXIII (December 1923), 154–160.

L 1.l
Untermeyer, Louis. *The Yale Review,* n.s. XIV (October 1924), 159–160.

L 1.m
Van Doren, Mark. *The Nation,* CXVII (October 10, 1923), 400.

L 1.n
Wilson, Edmund. *The New Republic,* XXXVIII (March 19, 1924), 102–103.

L 2 HARMONIUM
New York: Alfred A. Knopf, 1931 and 1947

L 2.a
Anonymous. *Bookman,* LXXIV (October 1931), 207–208.

L 2.b
Anonymous. Boston *Evening Transcript,* September 2, 1931, part 4, p. 3.

L 2.c
Gregory, Horace. *New York Herald Tribune Books,* September 27, 1931, p. 28.

L 2.d
Holmes, John. *Virginia Quarterly Review,* XII (April 1936), 294–295.

L 2.e
Hutchison, Percy. *New York Times Book Review,* August 9, 1931, p. 4.

L 2.f
Larsson, Raymond. *Commonweal,* XV (April 6, 1932), 640–641.

L 2.g
Viereck, Peter. *The Kenyon Review,* X (Winter 1948), 154–157.

L 2.h
Walton, Eda Lou. *The Nation*, CXXXIII (September 9, 1931), 263–264.

L 2.i
Zabel, Morton Dauwen. *Poetry*, XXXIX (December 1931), 148–154.

L 3 IDEAS OF ORDER
New York: The Alcestis Press, 1935
New York: Alfred A. Knopf, 1936

L 3.a
Belitt, Ben. *The Nation*, CXLIII (December 12, 1936), 708.

L 3.b
Benét, William Rose. *North American Review*, CCXLIII (Spring 1937), 195–197.

L 3.c
Blackmur, Richard P. *The Southern Review*, II (Winter 1937), 572–576.

L 3.d
Burnshaw, Stanley. *New Masses*, XVII (October 1, 1935), 41–42.

L 3.e
Deutsch, Babette. *New York Herald Tribune Books*, December 1935, p. 18.

L 3.f
G.E.G. *New Verse*, no. 19 (February–March 1936), 18–19.

L 3.g
Holmes, John. Boston *Evening Transcript*, December 19, 1936, sec. 6, p. 2.

L 3.h
Holmes, John. *Virginia Quarterly Review*, XII (April 1936), 294.

L 3.i
Jack, Peter Monro. *New York Times Book Review*, January 12, 1936, p. 15.

L 3.j
Lechlitner, Ruth. *New York Herald Tribune Books*, December 6, 1936, p. 40.

L 3.k
Matthiessen, Francis O. *The Yale Review*, n.s. XXV (March 1936), 605–607.

L 3.l
Monroe, Harriet. *Poetry*, XLVII (December 1935), 153–157.

L 3.m
Moore, Marianne. *Criterion*, XV (London, January 1936), 307–309.

L 3.n
Moore, Marianne. *Poetry*, XLIX (February 1937), 268–272.

L 3.o
Roethke, Theodore. *The New Republic*, LXXXVII (July 15, 1936), 304–305.

L 3.p
Schneider, Isidor. *New Masses*, XXI (October 27, 1936), 24.

L 3.q
Stone, Geoffrey. *American Review*, VIII (November 1936), 120–125.

L 3.r
Untermeyer, Louis. *American Mercury*, XXXVI (November 1935), 377–378.

L 3.s
Walton, Eda Lou. *New York Times Book Review*, December 6, 1936, p. 18.

L 4 OWL'S CLOVER
New York: The Alcestis Press, 1936

L 4.a
Belitt, Ben. *The Nation*, CXLIII (December 12, 1936), 710.

L 4.b
Benét, William Rose. *Saturday Review of Literature*, XV (January 16, 1937), 18.

L 4.c
Lechlitner, Ruth. *New York Herald Tribune Books*, December 6, 1936, p. 40

L 4.d
Moore, Marianne. *Poetry*, XLIX (February 1937), 268–272.

L 4.e
Walton, Eda Lou. *New York Times Book Review*, December 6, 1936, p. 18.

> L 5 THE MAN WITH THE BLUE GUITAR
> *New York: Alfred A. Knopf, 1937*
> *and*
> THE MAN WITH THE BLUE GUITAR,
> INCLUDING IDEAS OF ORDER
> *New York: Alfred A. Knopf, 1952*

L 5.a
Belitt, Ben. *The Nation*, CXLV (November 6, 1937), 508–509.

L 5.b
Fitzgerald, Robert. *Poetry*, LI (December 1937), 153–157.

L 5.c
Holmes, John. Boston *Evening Transcript*, December 24, 1937, sec. 4, p. 2.

L 5.d
Lechlitner, Ruth. *New York Herald Tribune Books*, November 14, 1937, p. 2.

L 5.e
O'Connor, William Van. *Poetry*, LXXXI (November 1952), 139–143.

L 5.f
Rodman, Selden. *Common Sense*, VII (January 1938), 28.

L 5.g
Schwartz, Delmore. *Partisan Review*, IV (February 1938), 49–52.

L 5.h
Walton, Eda Lou. *New York Times Book Review*, October 24, 1937, p. 5.

L 5.i
Williams, William Carlos. *The New Republic*, XCIII (November 17, 1937), 50.

L 5.j
Zabel, Morton Dauwen. *The Southern Review*, V (Autumn 1939), 603–605.

L 6 PARTS OF A WORLD
New York: Alfred A. Knopf, 1942

L 6.a
Anonymous. *American Mercury*, LV (November 1942), 630.

L 6.b
Anonymous. *Time*, XL (November 2, 1942), 103–104.

L 6.c
Benét, Laura. *Voices*, no. 111 (Autumn 1942), 54.

L 6.d
Blackmur, Richard P. *Partisan Review*, X (May–June 1943), 297–301.

L 6.e
Bogan, Louise. *The New Yorker*, XVIII (October 10, 1942), 61–62.

L 6.f
Colum, Mary L. *New York Times Book Review*, November 29, 1942, p. 12.

L 6.g
Drew, Elizabeth. *Atlantic Monthly*, CLXX (November 1942), 154.

L 6.h
Eaton, Alice R. *Library Journal*, LXVII (September 1, 1942), 738.

L 6.i
Flint, F. Cudworth. *Virginia Quarterly Review*, XIX (Winter 1943), 133–134.

L 6.j
Jones, Frank. *The Nation*, CLV (November 7, 1942), 488.

L 6.k
Kees, Weldon. *The New Republic*, CVII (September 28, 1942), 387–388.

L 6.l
Lechlitner, Ruth. *New York Herald Tribune Books*, November 8, 1942, p. 26.

L 6.m
Moore, Marianne. *The Kenyon Review*, V (Winter 1943), 144–147.

L 6.n
Simons, Hi. *Poetry*, LXI (November 1942), 448–452.

L 6.o
Tindall, William York. *American Mercury*, LVI (January 1943), 119–120.

L 6.p
Untermeyer, Louis. *Saturday Review of Literature*, XXV (December 19, 1942), 11.

L 6.q
Weiss, T. *Quarterly Review of Literature*, I (Summer 1944), 326–327.

L 7 NOTES TOWARD A SUPREME FICTION
Cummington, Mass.: The Cummington Press, 1942

L 7.a
Anonymous. *New York Herald Tribune Weekly Book Review*, February 28, 1943, p. 14.

L 7.b
Anonymous. *Virginia Quarterly Review*, XIX (Winter 1943), xiv.

L 7.c
Blackmur, Richard P. *Partisan Review*, X (May–June 1943), 297–301.

L 7.d
Breit, Harvey. *Poetry*, LXII (April 1943), 48–50.

L 7.e
Fitts, Dudley. *Saturday Review of Literature*, XXVI (August 28, 1943), 8–9.

L 7.f
Gregory, Horace. *The Sewanee Review*, LII (Autumn 1944), 584.

L 7.g
Moore, Marianne. *The Kenyon Review*, V (Winter 1943), 144–147.

L 7.h
Ritchey, John. *Voices*, no. 113 (Spring 1943), 42–43.

L 7.i
Weiss, T. *Quarterly Review of Literature*, I (Summer 1944), 328.

L 8 ESTHÉTIQUE DU MAL
Cummington, Mass.: The Cummington Press, 1945

L 8.a
Botsford, Keith. *The Yale Poetry Review*, I (Spring 1946), 34–37.

L 8.b
Dillon, George. *Poetry*, LXVIII (May 1946), 97–100.

L 8.c
Koch, Vivienne. *Briarcliff Quarterly*, III (April 1946), 7–9.

L 8.d
Meyer, Gerard P. *Saturday Review of Literature*, XXIX (March 23, 1946), 7–8.

L 8.e
Schwartz, Selwyn S. *Voices*, no. 126 (Summer 1946), 55–57.

L 9 TRANSPORT TO SUMMER
New York: Alfred A. Knopf, 1947

L 9.a
Anonymous. *Christian Science Monitor,* May 24, 1947, p. 17.

L 9.b
Anonymous. *Kirkus Reviews,* XV (March 15, 1947), 187.

L 9.c
Anonymous. *U.S. Quarterly Book List,* III (December 1947), 345–346.

L 9.d
Blackmur, Richard P. *Poetry,* LXXI (February 1948), 271–276.

L 9.e
Bogan, Louise. *The New Yorker,* XXIII (May 3, 1947), 116.

L 9.f
Deutsch, Babette. *New York Herald Tribune Weekly Book Review,* August 31, 1947, p. 4.

L 9.g
Eberhart, Richard. *Accent,* VII (Summer 1947), 251–253.

L 9.h
Flint, R. W. *Voices,* no. 131 (Fall 1947), 50–52.

L 9.i
Ingalls, Jeremy. *Saturday Review of Literature,* XXX (April 12, 1947), 48.

L 9.j
Lowell, Robert. *The Nation,* CLXIV (April 5, 1947), 400–402.

L 9.k
Martz, Louis L. *The Yale Review,* n.s. XXXVII (December 1947), 339–341.

L 9.l
Matthiessen, Francis O. *New York Times Book Review,* April 20, 1947, pp. 4, 26.

L 9.m
Schwartz, Delmore. *Partisan Review*, XIV (September–October 1947), 531–532.

L 9.n
Swallow, Alan. *New Mexico Quarterly Review*, XVIII (Winter 1948), 460–461.

L 9.o
Tejera, Victor. *Journal of Philosophy*, XLV (February 26, 1948), 137–139.

L 9.p
Viereck, Peter. *Contemporary Poetry*, VII (Winter 1948), 14–15.

Reprinted in *Trinity Review*, VIII (May 1954), 45–46.

L 9.q
Viereck, Peter. *The Kenyon Review*, X (Winter 1948), 154–157.

L 10 THREE ACADEMIC PIECES
Cummington, Mass.: The Cummington Press, 1947

L 10.a
Rosenthal, M. L. *New York Herald Tribune Weekly Book Review*, May 9, 1948, p. 21, cols. 1 and 2.

L 11 THE AURORAS OF AUTUMN
New York: Alfred A. Knopf, 1950

L 11.a
Anonymous. *Booklist*, XLVII (October 1, 1950), 58.

L 11.b
Anonymous. *Cleveland Open Shelf*, (October 1950), 19.

L 11.c
Anonymous. *Kirkus Reviews*, XVIII (July 15, 1950), 411.

L 11.d
Anonymous. *Time*, LVI (September 25, 1950), 106, 108, 110.

L 11.e
Anonymous. *U.S. Quarterly Book Review*, VI (December 1950), 418–419.

L 11.f
Bennett, Joseph. *The Hudson Review*, IV (Spring 1951), 134–137.

L 11.g
Bennett, Joseph. *Nine*, III (April 1952), 261–264.

L 11.h
Bogan, Louise. *The New Yorker*, XXVI (October 28, 1950), 129–130.

L 11.i
Daiches, David. *The Yale Review*, n.s. XL (December 1950), 355–356.

L 11.j
Deutsch, Babette. *New York Herald Tribune Book Review*, October 29, 1950, p. 6.

L 11.k
Flint, F. Cudworth. *Virginia Quarterly Review*, XXVII (Summer 1951), 477–478.

L 11.l
Frankenberg, Lloyd. *New York Times Book Review*, September 10, 1950, p. 20

L 11.m
Garrigue, Jean. *Saturday Review of Literature*, XXXIV (February 10, 1951), 17–18.

L 11.n
Humphries, Rolfe. *The Nation*, CLXXI (September 30, 1950), 293.

L 11.o
Jackinson, Alex. *Voices*, no. 144 (January–April 1951), 52–53.

L 11.p
Koch, Vivienne. *The Sewanee Review*, LIX (Autumn 1951), 644–667.

L 11.q

McDonald, Gerald. *Library Journal,* LXXV (October 1, 1950), 1669.

L 11.r

Moore, Marianne. *Poetry–New York,* no. 4 (1951), 7–9.

L 11.s

O'Connor, William Van. *Poetry,* LXXVII (November 1950), 109–112.

L 11.t

Rainer, Dachine. *Retort,* V (December 1951), 47.

L 11.u

Rosenthal, M. L. *The New Republic,* CXXIV (May 7, 1951), 26–28.

L 11.v

Thompson, James R. *Beloit Poetry Journal,* I (Spring 1951), 31.

L 12 THE NECESSARY ANGEL
New York: Alfred A. Knopf, 1951
London: Faber and Faber, 1960

L 12.a

Anonymous. *Booklist,* XLVIII (February 1, 1952), 183.

L 12.b

Anonymous. Cincinnati *Enquirer,* December 2, 1951, sec. 4, p. 19.

L 12.c

Anonymous. *Kirkus Reviews,* XIX (September 1, 1951), 524.

L 12.d

Anonymous. *The New Yorker,* XXVIII (February 23, 1952), 111.

L 12.e

Anonymous. *Perspectives USA,* no. 2 (Winter 1953), 190.

L 12.f

Anonymous. London *Times,* January 28, 1960, p. 15.

L 12.g
Anonymous. *Times Literary Supplement*, March 18, 1960, p. 179.

L 12.h
Anonymous. London *Times Weekly Review*, February 4, 1960, p. 10.

L 12.i
Anonymous. Tulsa *Daily World*, July 8, 1951, sec. V, p. 9.

L 12.j
Anonymous. *U.S. Quarterly Book Review*, VIII (June 1952), 134–135.

L 12.k
Alvarez, A. London *Observer*, February 14, 1960, p. 21.

L 12.l
L.B. *The Harvard Advocate*, CXXXV (March 1952), 23–24.

L 12.m
Bollinger, Evangeline. *The Hartford Courant*, January 27, 1952, magazine section, p. 18.

L 12.n
Bradbury, Malcolm. *Manchester Guardian*, March 18, 1960, p. 8, cols. 5 and 6.

L 12.o
E.C. Bridgeport *Post*, December 2, 1951, sec. B, p. 4.

L 12.p
Carruth, Hayden. *The Nation*, CLXXIV (June 14, 1952), 584–585.

L 12.q
Chapin, Ruth. *Christian Science Monitor*, December 27, 1951, p. 7.

L 12.r
Clarke, Austin. Dublin *Irish Times*, March 5, 1960, p. 7.

L 12.s
Deutsch, Babette. *New York Herald Tribune Book Review*, December 9, 1951, p. 4.

L 12.t
Dinkins, Paul. Dallas *Morning News*, March 2, 1952, part 6, p. 6.

L 12.u
E.E. Oxford *Times*, February 19, 1960, p. 22.

L 12.v
Eberhart, Richard. *Accent*, XII (Spring 1952), 122–125.

L 12.w
Edwards, John H. San Francisco *Chronicle*, January 27, 1952, *This World*, p. 11.

L 12.x
Fjelde, Rolf. *The New Republic*, CXXVI (February 4, 1952), 19–20.

L 12.y
Heringman, Bernard. *The Kenyon Review*, XIV (Summer 1952), 520–523.

L 12.z
Holden, Theodore L. Hartford *Times*, November 17, 1951, p. 16.

L 12.aa
Holley, Fred. Norfolk *Virginian Pilot*, December 9, 1951, sec. V, p. 3.

L 12.bb
Honig, Edwin. *Voices*, no. 148 (May–August 1952), 34-35.

L 12.cc
Hynes, Sam. *Time and Tide*, XLI (March 26, 1960), 357.

L 12.dd
Kermode, Frank. *Spectator*, CCI (October 3, 1958), 454–455.

L 12.ee
Kermode, Frank. *Spectator*, CCIV (February 26, 1960), 295.

L 12.ff
LeBrun, P. *Essays in Criticism*, XI (April 1961), 226–232.

L 12.gg
Levin, Harry. *The Yale Review*, n.s. XLI (Summer 1952), 615–616.

L 12.hh
Mason, Franklin. Baltimore *Evening Sun*, November 28, 1951, p. 40.

L 12.ii
Meyer, Gerard P. *Saturday Review of Literature*, XXXIV (December 29, 1951), 11-12.

L 12.jj
O'Connor, William Van. *New York Times Book Review*, December 2, 1951, pp. 7, 22.

L 12.kk
Reed, Henry. *The Listener*, LXIII (April 14, 1960), 675-676.

L 12.ll
Rockwell, Kenneth. Dallas *Times Herald*, December 30, 1951, sec. 3, p. 5.

L 12.mm
Scott, Winfield Townley. Providence *Journal*, December 2, 1951, sec. 6, p. 8.

L 12.nn
Spencer, Martha L. Hartford *Times*, December 11, 1951, p. 22.

L 12.oo
Taylor, Dan. *Shenandoah*, III (Spring 1952), 22-24.

L 12.pp
Unterecker, John. *The New Leader*, XXXIV (December 17, 1951), 25.

L 12.qq
Vazakas, Byron. *New Mexico Quarterly Review*, XXII (Winter 1952), 434-439.

L 12.rr
R.F.W. Boston *Herald*, December 30, 1951, new book section, p. 11.

L 12.ss
Wagner, C. Roland. *The Hudson Review*, V (Spring 1952), 144-148.

L 12.tt
Wharton, Will. St. Louis *Post-Dispatch*, January 3, 1952, p. 2B.

L 12.uu
K.Y. London *Daily Telegraph*, April 8, 1960, p. 17.

L 12.vv
Young, Margaret. Houston *Post*, June 3, 1951, sec. V, p. 5.

L 13 SELECTED POEMS
London: The Fortune Press, 1952

L 13.a
Clarke, Austin. Dublin *Irish Times*, February 14, 1953, p. 6, cols. 3–4.

L 13.b
Davie, Donald. *Twentieth Century*, CLIII (June 1953), 455–462.

L 13.c
Hanshell, H. *Tablet*, CCI (April 25, 1953), 341–342.

L 14 SELECTED POEMS
London: Faber and Faber, 1953

L 14.a
Anonymous. *British Book News*, no. 152 (April 1953), 246.

L 14.b
Anonymous. *Times Literary Supplement*, June 19, 1953, p. 396.

L 14.c
Bergonzi, Bernard. *Nine*, IV (Winter 1953–1954), 48–51.

L 14.d
Davie, Donald. *Twentieth Century*, CLIII (June 1953), 455–462.

L 14.e
Empson, William. *The Listener*, XLIX (March 26, 1953), 521.

Reprinted in *Trinity Review*, VIII (May 1954), 25.

L 14.f
Fraser, G. S. *New Statesman and Nation*, n.s. XLV (February 14, 1953), 181.

L 14.g
Murphy, Richard. *Spectator*, CXC (February 13, 1953), 191–192.

L 14.h
Reeves, James. *Time and Tide*, XXXIV (April 4, 1953), 456.

L 14.i
Spender, Stephen. *Encounter*, I (October 1953), 61–65.

L 15 COLLECTED POEMS
New York: Alfred A. Knopf, 1954
London: Faber and Faber, 1955

L 15.a
Anonymous. *Booklist*, LI (January 1, 1955), 197.

L 15.b
Anonymous. *Bookmark*, XIV (February 1955), 110.

L 15.c
Anonymous. *Kirkus Reviews*, XXII (August 15, 1954), 557.

L 15.d
Anonymous. Pasadena *Star-News*, February 20, 1955, p. 27.

L 15.e
Anonymous. *U.S. Quarterly Book Review*, XI (March 1955), 69.

L 15.f
Bogan, Louise. *The New Yorker*, XXX (December 11, 1954), 198–202.

L 15.g
Carruth, Hayden. *Poetry*, LXXXV (February 1955), 288–293.

L 15.h
Ciardi, John. *The Nation*, CLXXIX (October 16, 1954), 346–347.

L 15.i
Cole, Thomas. *Imagi*, VI, no. 4 (1955), unpaged.

L 15.j
Cunliffe, Marcus. *Manchester Guardian*, October 25, 1955, p. 6.

L 15.k
Davie, Donald. *Shenandoah*, VI (Spring 1955), 62–64.

L 15.l
Deutsch, Babette. *New York Herald Tribune Book Review*, October 3, 1954, p. 3.

L 15.m
Engle, Paul. *Chicago Sunday Tribune*, October 24, 1954, *Magazine of Books*, p. 2.

L 15.n
Ferling, Lawrence. San Francisco *Chronicle*, November 28, 1954, p. 22.

L 15.o
Fraser, G. S. *Partisan Review*, XXII (Spring 1955), 270–272.

L 15.p
Frumkin, Gene. *Coastlines*, I (Summer 1955), 37–38.

L 15.q
Holloway, John. *Spectator*, CXCII (November 18, 1955), 682–683.

L 15.r
Honig, Edwin. *Voices*, no. 157 (May–August 1955), 27–30.

L 15.s
Jacobsen, Josephine. Baltimore *Evening Sun*, December 14, 1954, p. 30.

L 15.t
Jarrell, Randall. *Harper's Magazine*, CCIX (November 1954), 100.

L 15.u
McDonald, Gerald. *Library Journal*, LXXX (January 1, 1955), 80.

L 15.v
Meyer, Gerard P. *Saturday Review,* XXXVII (December 4, 1954), 26–27.

L 15.w
Minard, Ralph. Hartford *Times,* October 2, 1954, p. 22.

L 15.x
Morse, Samuel French. *New York Times Book Review*, October 3, 1954, pp. 3, 21.

L 15.y
O'Neill, Lois D. Louisville (Ky.) *Courier-Journal,* October 10, 1954, sec. 3, p. 11.

L 15.z
Perrine, Laurence N. Dallas *Times Herald,* November 28, 1954, sec. 7, p. 3.

L 15.aa
Philbrick, Charles H. Providence *Journal,* October 10, 1954, sec. 6, p. 8.

L 15.bb
Poore, Charles. *New York Times,* February 3, 1955, p. 21.

L 15.cc
Reynolds, Horace. *Christian Science Monitor,* February 12, 1955, p. 13.

L 15.dd
Schwartz, Delmore. *The New Republic,* CXXXI (November 1, 1954), 16–18.

L 15.ee
Shapiro, Karl. Chicago *Sun-Times,* November 28, 1954, sec. 2, p. 4.

L 15.ff
Simpson, Louis. *American Scholar,* XXIV (Spring 1955), 240.

L 15.gg
Webster, Harvey C. *The New Leader,* XXXVIII (May 2, 1955), 25–26.

L 16 OPUS POSTHUMOUS
New York: Alfred A. Knopf, 1957
London: Faber and Faber, 1959

L 16.a
Anonymous. *Booklist,* LIV (September 15, 1957), 41.

L 16.b
Anonymous. Bridgeport *Post,* August 11, 1957, sec. B, p. 4.

L 16.c
Anonymous. *Kirkus Reviews,* XXV (June 1, 1957), 408.

L 16.d
Anonymous. Los Angeles *Mirror-News,* September 23, 1957, sec. II, p. 5.

L 16.e
Anonymous. *The New Yorker,* XXXIII (December 7, 1957), 245–246.

L 16.f
Anonymous. London *Times,* January 28, 1960, p. 15.

L 16.g
Anonymous. *Times Literary Supplement,* March 18, 1960, p. 179.

L 16.h
Anonymous. London *Times Weekly Review,* February 4, 1960, p. 10.

L 16.i
Beatty, Richmond C. Nashville *Tennessean,* September 15, 1957, p. 7E.

L 16.j
Brady, Charles A. Buffalo *Evening News,* August 17, 1957, p. 8.

L 16.k
Campbell, Gary, Jr. Indianapolis *News,* September 7, 1957, sec. I, p. 2.

L 16.l
Clarke, Austin. Dublin *Irish Times,* March 5, 1960, p. 7.

L 16.m
Coldwell, David. Dallas *Times Herald,* September 29, 1957,
book section, p. 22.

L 16.n
Cooley, Franklin D. Richmond *Times-Dispatch,* September 1,
1957, p. L–5.

L 16.o
Deen, Rosemary F. *Commonweal,* LXVI (September 20, 1957),
620–621.

L 16.p
Derleth, August. Madison (Wis.) *Capital Times,* August 8, 1957,
p. 12.

L 16.q
Deutsch, Babette. *New York Herald Tribune Book Review,*
September 1, 1957, p. 8.

L 16.r
Dodsworth, Martin. Oxford (England) *Isis,* January 27, 1960,
p. 32.

L 16.s
Evans, Sir Ifor. Birmingham (England) *Post,* January 19, 1960,
p. 3.

L 16.t
Fraser, G. S. *New Statesman and Nation,* n.s. LIX (January 9,
1960), 43–44.

L 16.u
Gibbs, Barbara. *Poetry,* XCII (April 1958), 52–57.

L 16.v
Grieg, Michael. San Francisco *Examiner,* October 27, 1957,
modern living section, p. 8.

L 16.w
Hecht, Anthony. *The Hudson Review,* X (Winter 1957–1958),
606–608.

L 16.x
Hoffman, Frederick J. *Progressive,* XXI (December 1957), 37.

L 16.y
Howe, Irving. *The New Republic,* CXXXVII (November 4, 1957), 16–19.

L 16.z
Jennings, Elizabeth. *London Magazine,* VII (May 1960), 85–87.

L 16.aa
Kermode, Frank. *Spectator,* CCI (October 3, 1958), 454–455.

L 16.bb
Kermode, Frank. *Spectator,* CCIV (January 1, 1960), 21.

L 16.cc
Keyser, Janet. Fort Wayne *News-Sentinel,* October 24, 1957, p. 9.

L 16.dd
Kirsch, Robert R. Los Angeles *Times,* September 13, 1957, sec. III, p. 5.

L 16.ee
Lampton, Ludlow. *Time and Tide,* XLI (February 27, 1960), 230.

L 16.ff
McDonald, Gerald. *Library Journal,* LXXXII (October 1, 1957), 2460.

L 16.gg
Meacham, Harry M. Richmond *News-Leader,* August 23, 1957, p. 13.

L 16.hh
Nims, John Frederick. *Chicago Sunday Tribune,* August 25, 1957, *Magazine of Books,* p. 4.

L 16.ii
O'Neill, Frank. Cleveland *News,* August 21, 1957, p. 13.

L 16.jj
Page, Margaret. Houston *Post,* August 4, 1957, magazine section, p. 19.

L 16.kk
Peel, Robert. *Christian Science Monitor*, August 22, 1957, p. 11.

L 16.ll
Pitchford, Kenneth. *Poetry Broadsides*, I (Winter 1957–1958), 15.

L 16.mm
Poore, Charles. *New York Times*, August 22, 1957, p. 25.

L 16.nn
Reed, Henry. *The Listener*, LXIII (April 14, 1960), 675–676.

L 16.oo
Rexroth, Kenneth. *The Nation*, CLXXXV (October 19, 1957), 268–269.

L 16.pp
Seymour, William Kean. *Poetry Review*, LI (London, April–June 1960), 104–105.

L 16.qq
Shapiro, Karl. *Prairie Schooner*, XXXII (Fall 1958), 245–247.

L 16.rr
Stallman, R. W. Hartford *Times*, August 17, 1957, p. 20; magazine section, p. 13.

L 16.ss
Stewart, John L. *Dartmouth Alumni Magazine*, L (January 1958), 6–7.

L 16.tt
Stowe, George W. Hartford *Times*, August 17, 1957, p. 20.

L 16.uu
Vader, Anthony J. *Critic*, XVI (October 1957), 36.

L 16.vv
Walsh, John. Louisville (Ky.) *Courier-Journal*, September 15, 1957, sec. 4, p. 6.

L 16.ww
Williams, William Carlos. *New York Times Book Review*, August 18, 1957, p. 6.

L 17 LETTERS OF WALLACE STEVENS
New York: Alfred A. Knopf, 1966
London: Faber and Faber, 1967

L 17.a
Anonymous. *Times Literary Supplement*, March 30, 1967,
p. 266.

Although "anonymous," this would seem to be an early or
abridged version of K 153.

L 17.b
Bankert, Marianne. *Critic*, XXVI (October 1967), 86.

L 17.c
Bogan, Louise. *The New Yorker*, XLIII (March 4, 1967), 162.

L 17.d
Bogan, Louise. *Virginia Quarterly Review*, XLIII (Spring 1967),
lxv.

L 17.e
Booth, Philip. *Christian Science Monitor*, December 15, 1966,
p. 11.

L 17.f
Borkland, Elmer. *Book Week*, IV (February 12, 1967), 15–16.

L 17.g
Borkland, Elmer. *Choice*, IV (April 1967), 164–165.

L 17.h
Borroff, Marie. *The Yale Review*, LVI (Spring 1967), 446–448.

L 17.i
Corman, Cid. *Caterpillar*, I (October 1967), 103–130.

L 17.j
Donoghue, Denis. *New York Review of Books*, VII (December 1,
1966), 6.

L 17.k
Hamilton, Ian. *Listener*, LXXVII (February 16, 1967), 235.

L 17.l
Howard, Richard. *Poetry*, CXI (October 1967), 39–40.

L 17.m
Kermode, Frank. *Encounter*, XXVIII (May 1967), 65-70.

L 17.n
Kramer, Hilton. *The New Leader*, XLIX (December 5, 1966), 18.

L 17.o
Kroll, Jack. *Newsweek*, LXVIII (November 28, 1966), 114.

L 17.p
Kunitz, Stanley. *The New Republic*, CLV (November 12, 1966), 23-26.

L 17.q
Litz, A. Walton. *The Nation*, CCIV (January 16, 1967), 85-87.

L 17.r
McNeil, Helen. *Partisan Review*, XXXIV (Fall 1967), 635-638.

L 17.s
Pearson, Norman Holmes. *New York Times Book Review*, November 6, 1966, p. 4.

L 17.t
Pritchett, V. S. *New Statesman and Nation*, LXXIII (March 31, 1967), 439-440.

L 17.u
Riddel, Joseph N. *American Literature*, XXXIX (November 1967), 421.

L 17.v
Rosenthal, M. L. *Spectator*, CCXVIII (March 24, 1967), 340.

L 17.w
Stanford, Donald E. *The Southern Review*, III (Summer 1967), 757-763.

L 17.x
Tanner, Tony. *London Magazine*, VII (April 1967), 105-111.

L 17.y
Tindall, William York. *Saturday Review*, XLIX (November 19, 1966), 42-43.

L 17.z
Willingham, John R. *Library Journal,* XCI (December 1, 1966),
5972.

L 18 PLAY REVIEWS

L 18.a
Carlos Among the Candles (presented at the Neighborhood
Playhouse, New York City, October 20, 1917; see C 52).

Anonymous. *New York Times,* October 22, 1917, p. 13.

Block, Ralph. *New York Tribune,* October 22, 1917, p. 9.

L 18.b
Three Travelers Watch a Sunrise (presented at the Province-
town Playhouse, New York City, February 13, 1920; see C 49).

Monroe, Harriet. *Poetry,* XVI (April 1920), 33–35.

L 18.c
General review

Cambon, Glauco. "Teatro di Wallace Stevens." *Verri,* no. 2
(Winter 1957), 25–34.

M. Dissertations

Dissertation Abstracts is abbreviated DA.

M 1

Bertholf, Robert J. "The Vast Ventriloquism." Ph.D. dissertation, University of Oregon, 1968. *DA*, XXIX (1969).

M 2

Betar, George V. "Imagination and Reality in Wallace Stevens' Prose and Early Poetry." Ph.D. dissertation, University of Southern California, 1962. *DA*, XXIII (1963).

M 3

Bevis, William W. "The Poetry of *Harmonium*: The Development of Wallace Stevens, 1915–1923." Ph.D. dissertation, University of California at Berkeley, 1969. *DA*, XXX (1969).

M 4

Blessing, Richard A. "The Dynamic Rock: A Study of *The Collected Poems of Wallace Stevens*." Ph.D. dissertation, Tulane University, 1967. *DA*, XXVIII (1968).

M 5

Burney, William A. "Wallace Stevens and George Santayana." Ph.D. dissertation, State University of Iowa, 1962. *DA*, XXIX (1963).

M 6

Buttel, Robert W. "Prelude to *Harmonium*: The Development of Style and Technique in Wallace Stevens' Early Poetry." Ph.D. dissertation, Columbia University, 1962. *DA*, XXVII (1967).

M 7

Eder, Doris L. "Wallace Stevens: The Major Poems." Ph.D. dissertation, CUNY, 1969.

M 8

Fields, Kenneth W. "The Rhetoric of Artifice: Ezra Pound, Wallace Stevens, Walter Conrad Arensberg, Donald Evans, Mina

Loy, and Yvor Winters." Ph.D. dissertation, Stanford University, 1967. *DA*, XXVIII (1968).

M 9
Forslund, David E. "The Function of Allusions in the Poetry of Wallace Stevens." Ph.D. dissertation, University of Arizona, 1965. *DA*, XXVI (1965).

M 10
Fuchs, Daniel. "The Comic Spirit of Wallace Stevens: An Aspect of the Poet's Mind." Ph.D. dissertation, Columbia University, 1960. *DA*, XXI (1960).

M 11
Gangewere, Robert J. "The Aesthetic Theory of Wallace Stevens." Ph.D. dissertation, University of Connecticut, 1966. *DA*, XXVII (1967).

M 12
Gaughan, Gerald C. "Wallace Stevens and Stéphane Mallarmé: A Comparative Study in Poetic Theory." Ph.D. dissertation, Northwestern University, 1966. *DA*, XXVII (1967).

M 13
Gilbertson, Mary J. "Wallace Stevens' Meditative Poems." Ph.D. dissertation, Cornell University, 1964. *DA*, XXV (1965).

M 14
Girlinghouse, Mary J. "The New Romantic of Wallace Stevens." Ph.D. dissertation, The Catholic University of America, 1970. *DA*, XXXI (1970).

M 15
Guereschi, Edward F. "The Inventive Imagination: Wallace Stevens' Dialectic of Secular Grace." Ph.D. dissertation, Syracuse University, 1969. *DA*, XXXI (1970).

M 16
Hamlin, William C. "A Thematic Study of Reality, Death, Order and Imagination in the Poetry of Wallace Stevens." Ph.D. dissertation, University of Missouri, 1963. *DA*, XXIV (1963).

M 17
Hammond, Mac S. "Sound and Grammar in Wallace Stevens'

'The Man with the Blue Guitar.' " Ph.D. dissertation, Harvard University, 1962.

M 18
Heringman, Bernard. "Wallace Stevens: The Reality of Poetry." Ph.D. dissertation, Columbia University, 1955. *DA*, XVI (1956).

M 19
Hines, Thomas J. " 'The Outlines of Being and Its Expressings': Husserl, Heidegger, and the Later Poetry of Wallace Stevens." Ph.D. dissertation, University of Oregon, 1969. *DA*, XXXI (1970).

M 20
Kessler, Edward L. "Controlling Images of Wallace Stevens." Ph.D. dissertation, Rutgers University, 1967. *DA*, XXVIII (1967).

M 21
Lana, Jean H. "Wallace Stevens' *Notes toward a Supreme Fiction:* A Critique." Ph.D. dissertation, Cornell University, 1968. *DA*, XXIX (1968).

M 22
Lauter, Estella L. " 'The World Must Be Measured by Eye': The Presentation Poetry of Wallace Stevens." Ph.D. dissertation, University of Rochester, 1966. *DA*, XXVII (1966).

M 23
Lawless, Sister Mary K. "The Ceramics of Wallace Stevens: Aspects of Imagery and Theme." Ph.D. dissertation, University of Notre Dame, 1963. *DA*, XXIV (1963).

M 24
Lensing, George S. "The Aspiring Clown of Wallace Stevens: A Study of 'The Comedian as the Letter C' as Preliminary Statement." Ph.D. dissertation, Louisiana State University, 1966. *DA*, XXVII (1966).

M 25
Lentricchia, Frank R., Jr. "The Poetics of Will: Wallace Stevens, W. B. Yeats, and the Theoretic Inheritance." Ph.D. dissertation, Duke University, 1966. *DA*, XXVII (1966).

M 26
Logan, John F. "The Blue Guitar: A Semantic Study of Poetry." Ph.D. dissertation, University of Texas, 1962. *DA*, XXIII (1962).

M 27
Lord, Georgianna W. "The Annihilation of Art in the Poetry of Wallace Stevens." Ph.D. dissertation, Ohio State University, 1962. *DA,* XXIV (1963).

M 28
Lovell, James H., Jr. "Form and Structure in the Poetry of Wallace Stevens." Ph.D. dissertation, Vanderbilt University, 1963. *DA,* XXIV (1963).

M 29
Middlebrook, Diane W. "The Mythology of Imagination: A Study of the Poetry of Walt Whitman and Wallace Stevens." Ph.D. dissertation, Yale University, 1968. *DA,* XXIX (1969).

M 30
Morrison, J. M. "Wallace Stevens and the Forms of Lyric Poetry." Ph.D. dissertation, Harvard University, 1969. See *WSN,* I (April 1970), 14–15.

M 31
Morse, Samuel French. "An Examination of the Practice and Theory of Wallace Stevens." Ph.D. dissertation, Boston University, 1952.

M 32
Mulqueen, James E. "Emerson and Stevens: Transcendentalism and Radical Transcendentalism." Ph.D. dissertation, Purdue University, 1970. *DA,* XXXI (1971).

M 33
Murphy, Francis E. "The Concept of Nature in the Poetry of Wallace Stevens." Ph.D. dissertation, Harvard University, 1960.

M 34
Nassar, Eugene P. "Wallace Stevens: An Anatomy of Figuration." Ph.D. dissertation, Cornell University, 1962. *DA,* XXIII (1962).

M 35
O'Neal, Charles R. "Wallace Stevens and the Arts." Ph.D. dissertation, Indiana University, 1964. *DA,* XXV (1965).

M 36
Peterson, Margaret L. W. "Wallace Stevens and the Idealist Tradition: A Study of the Philosophical Background of Stevens'

Poetry." Ph.D. dissertation, Stanford University, 1965. *DA,* XXVI (1965).

M 37
Pinkerton, Jan. "Wallace Stevens: Politics and the Tropics." Ph.D. dissertation, Harvard University, 1968.

M 38
Powell, Grosvenor E. "Romantic Mysticism and the Poetry of Wallace Stevens." Ph.D. dissertation, Stanford University, 1965. *DA,* XXVI (1966).

M 39
Ransom, James C. "The Anecdotal Imagination: A Study of Wallace Stevens' *Harmonium.*" Ph.D. dissertation, Yale University, 1969. *DA,* XXXI (1970).

M 40
Rice, Oliver L. "The Dilemma of Reality in Stevens' *Harmonium.*" Ph.D. dissertation, University of Illinois, 1966. *DA,* XXVII (1966).

M 41
Riddel, Joseph N. "The Never-Ending Meditation: A Study of Myth, Metaphor and the Poetry of Order in the Works of Wallace Stevens." Ph.D. dissertation, University of Wisconsin, 1960. *DA,* XXI (1960).

M 42
Robillard, Richard H. "The Rhetoric of Wallace Stevens: He That of Repetition Is Most Master." Ph.D. dissertation, Brown University, 1963. *DA,* XXIV (1964).

M 43
Rosenfeld, Norman. "Definitions of Poetry in the Essays and Poems of Wallace Stevens." Ph.D. dissertation, University of Pittsburgh, 1965. *DA,* XXVI (1965).

M 44
Savage, Muriel S. "Wallace Stevens: Poetry as Religion." Ph.D. dissertation, Northwestern University, 1968. *DA,* XXIX (1969).

M 45
Schneider, Daniel J. "Wallace Stevens: The Application of His Theory of Poetry to His Poems." Ph.D. dissertation, Northwestern University, 1957. *DA,* XVII (1957).

M 46
Semel, Jay M. "Structure of Belief in the Poetry of Wallace Stevens." Ph.D. dissertation, University of South Carolina, 1970. *DA*, XXXI (1971).

M 47
Steele, Leighton G. "The Winter World of Wallace Stevens." Ph.D. dissertation, University of California at Santa Barbara, 1966. *DA*, XXVIII (1967).

M 48
Stephenson, William C. "The Meditative Poetry of Wordsworth and Wallace Stevens." Ph.D. dissertation, University of Minnesota, 1969. *DA*, XXX (1969).

M 49
Stein, Herbert J. "Art of Uncertainty: Studies in the Early Career of Wallace Stevens." Ph.D. dissertation, Indiana University, 1965. *DA*, XXVI (1965).

M 50
Stratman, David G. "Matthew Arnold and Wallace Stevens: Imagination as Value." Ph.D. dissertation, University of North Carolina, 1970. *DA*, XXXI (1071).

M 51
Sukenick, Ronald. "A Wallace Stevens Handbook: A Reading of His Major Poems and an Exposition of His Theory and Practice." Ph.D. dissertation, Brandeis University, 1962. *DA*, XXIV (1963).

M 52
Swetman, Glenn R. "The Poetics of Wallace Stevens: An Examination of the Basic Structure of His Poetry." Ph.D. dissertation, Tulane University, 1966. *DA*, XXVII (1967).

M 53
Swigger, Ronald T. "The Life of the World: A Comparison of Stevens and Rilke." Ph.D. dissertation, Indiana University, 1967. *DA*, XXIX (1968).

M 54
Tisdale, Robert G. "The Major Style of Wallace Stevens: The Idiom of the Hero." Ph.D. dissertation, Yale University, 1968. *DA*, XXIX (1968).

M 55
Wagner, C. Roland. "The Savage Transparence—Examples of Morality and Spirit in Philosophy, Religion and Literature." Ph.D. dissertation, Yale University, 1952.

M 56
Whitbread, Thomas B. "The Late Poems of Wallace Stevens." Ph.D. dissertation, Harvard University, 1959.

M 57
Wilbur, Robert H. H. "George Santayana and Three Modern Philosophical Poets: T. S. Eliot, Conrad Aiken, and Wallace Stevens." Ph.D. dissertation, Columbia University, 1964. *DA*, XXVI (1965).

M 58
Woodman, Leonora B. "Wallace Stevens and the Poetry of Rebirth." Ph.D. dissertation, University of Missouri, 1970. *DA*, XXXI (1971).

M 59
Yeargers, Marilyn M. "Poesis: The Theme of Poetry-Making in the Poetry of Wallace Stevens and Paul Valéry." Ph.D. dissertation, Michigan State University, 1969. *DA*, XXXI (1970).

Appendix / Index

Appendix

An Unauthorized Printing

1.1 TEA
A separate edition printed for Frederic Prokosch

TEA | * | WALLACE | STEVENS | VENICE | 1939

Collation: [1]⁶. Pp. [1–12].

Typography and paper: Set in 8D and 6D Aster. Three (numbered 1 to 3): white laid Arches paper; three (lettered a to c): cream laid Ingres paper; three (lettered A to C): ochre laid Canson paper; one (numbered X): Italian vellum paper.

Pagination: pp. 1–4: blank (frontispiece signed 'F. Prokosch' pasted on p. 4); p. 5: title page; p. 6: blank; p. 7: text; p. 8: colophon; pp. 9–12: blank.

Contents: "Tea" ('when the elephant's-ear in the park').

Colophon: p. 8: Ten hand-illustrated copies of this poem were printed: three on Arches, numbered 1–3; three on Ingres, numbered a–c; three on Canson, numbered A–C; and one on Italian vellum, numbered X.

Binding: Wrapper, marbled in green and silver on pale cream laid paper, folded round the first and last blank leaves; on the front a gold label lettered across in black: 'TEA | * | WALLACE STEVENS'.

The poem "Tea" was first printed in *Rogue*, I, 1 (March 15, 1915), 12 (see C 44), and reprinted in *H-1923;* it was later collected in *CP* and *Palm.*

Locations: Nicolas J. Barker; King's College, Cambridge.

Note: The Sotheby & Co. catalogue of the book sale held on May 1 and 2, 1972, contained Lot 263, previously unrecorded: "Stevens (Wallace) TEA Limited to 10 copies, of which this is No A of 3 on Canson, frontispiece. 32 mo. Venice, 1939."
    Research by Nicolas Barker, editor of *The Book Collector* and distinguished typophile, to whom I am indebted for this infor-

399

mation and permission to publish it, has apparently shown that
the Aster type in which this pamphlet was printed was introduced
by Simoncini S.p.A. in 1957 and generally available in 1958. It
is Mr. Barker's opinion that "'Tea' belongs to a group which can
be fairly firmly dated as having been printed in 1969." The de-
tailed results of Mr. Barker's investigations of this and other
printings by Mr. Frederic Prokosch are to be published shortly
in a book provisionally titled *The Butterfly Books*.

Index

When a poem in a publication in Section A appeared in every edition and printing of that work, this index gives only the general publication identification, e.g., A 1. If, however, the poem did not appear in each edition, the specific identification is given, e.g., A 1.b–A 1.c.3.

Parentheses are used around titles of long poems that include the indexed title.